Laos satisfies all the ro[...] trees, saffron-robed m[...] temples, all set amongst a rich tapestry of tropical river islands, ethnic minority villages, cascading waterfalls and vivid, green rice paddies, and bound together by the mighty Mekong River, the country's lifeline.

The vernacular architecture that other countries have swept away in a maelstrom of redevelopment survives in Laos. Simple wooden village homes, colonial-era brick-and-stucco shophouses and gently mouldering monasteries mark Laos out as different.

Traditional customs are also firmly intact: incense wafts out of streetside wats, monks collect alms at daybreak and the clickety-clack of looms weaving richly coloured silk can be heard in most villages.

As compelling as these sights and sounds are, the lasting impression for most visitors is of the people and their overwhelming friendliness.

Many believe the best thing about Laos is the constant call of *sabaidee* its people. This is a land that endures the terrible legacy of being the most bombed country per capita in the world, yet its people transform bomb casings into flower pots and bomb craters into fish ponds. Regardless of their history and their poverty, people here radiate a sunny, happy disposition.

Life is simple in Laos but the people radiate an infectious joie de vivre that ensures that good food and great company are the pinnacle of enjoyment. If you're seeking a relaxed pace of life and a warm welcome, you've come to the right place.

David W Lloyd

# Best of
## Laos

### ❶ Vientiane

Possibly the world's most laid-back capital city. Spend a couple of quiet days here enjoying the fantastic food from both Laos and around the world, in a slew of excellent restaurants. Wine and coffee lovers will also feel right at home. Alongside this there are magnificent temples and monuments to discover. Page 31.

### ❷ Vang Vieng

With one of the most beguiling settings in all of Laos, this town has put its tubing craze days behind it and is now once again a great place for exploring the magical limestone mountain scenery that surrounds it. Page 66.

### ❸ Luang Prabang

One of Asia's most captivating and classically stylish cities. Protected by its UNESCO status, the town is a pure joy to wander around, with dozens of temples, lovely cafés and riverside bars. Local life here still plays out to the sound of chanting monks and the rhythmic boom of temple drums. Page 79.

**Footprint** Handbook

# Laos

DAVID W LLOYD

# This is
## Laos

## ❹ Muang Ngoi Neua

A tranquil riverside village set among towering peaks. Trek to waterfalls and caves, visit ethnic minority villages, kayak along the river, or simply swing in a hammock and marvel at the vista from your very own bungalow balcony. Page 116.

## ❺ Luang Namtha

In the far north of the country, this far-flung town is a good base for trekking to tiny villages to get a taste of authentic rural Laos among stunning mountain scenery. Page 129.

## ❻ Bokeo Nature Reserve

The Bokeo jungle offers the chance to see gibbons in their natural habitat and sleep deep in the forest. Page 140.

## ❼ Plain of Jars

Just outside the remote city of Phonsavanh, these bizarre stone urns lie scattered across rolling grasslands in an area that saw some of the most intensive US bombing. Page 153.

## ❽ Vieng Xai

These caves, where the Pathet Lao formed its headquarters while sheltering from intense US bombing, provide a vivid insight into the country's troubled past. The town itself is home to numerous small lakes and visitors will often be invited to join the locals in a game of pétanque. Page 167.

## ❾ Nam Et-Phou Louey National Protected Area

Home to numerous endangered species and a huge variety of birds. Book onto the award-winning Nam Nern Night Safari for your best chance of spotting nocturnal mammals such as slow loris and civet cats. Page 174.

## ⑩ Kong Lor Cave

A river cuts through the mountain for some 7.5 km and the spellbinding cave, 90 m wide and 100 m high, can be explored by boat. This is best done as part of the classic motorcycle road trip known as the 'Loop'. Pages 182 and 195.

## ⑪ Wat Phou

The atmospheric 12th-century ruins of Wat Phou are an enchanting place to wander at sunrise or in the late afternoon light. Nearby Champasak is a charming town on the banks of the river. Page 225.

## ⑫ 4000 Islands

In the far south of the country in the broad sweep of the mighty Mekong, the pace of life on these river islands is super relaxed, even by Lao standards, and there's little else to do but sink in and enjoy it. Page 249.

CHINA

*Gulf of Tonkin*

ng

peu

# Route planner
## Laos

putting it all together

Laos may not be in the brochures of many tour companies, but it is a beautiful country with a great deal to offer including elegant towns, excellent cuisine, a leisurely pace of life and a population which is probably the most welcoming and relaxed in Asia. The former royal capital of **Luang Prabang** – designated a World Heritage Site by UNESCO – is a solid contender for Southeast Asia's most beautiful city with a spellbinding array of gilded temples, weathered colonial façades and art deco shophouses packed onto a small peninsula. Today's sleepy capital, **Vientiane**, along with the other Mekong towns of **Pakse**, **Savannakhet** and **Thakhek**, is also elegant with its French architectural heritage largely intact. In the south of the country, **Wat Phou** – an outlier of the Cambodian kingdom of Angkor – is beguiling, and the Mekong islands of **Siphandon** are a great place to relax, swing in a hammock and even spot dolphins. The country has a number of utterly fascinating historical sites, from the enigmatic stone urns that litter the **Plain of Jars** to the caves at **Vieng Xai**, which were used by the Communist Pathet Lao as their headquarters. Laos has also firmly established itself as one of the region's premier outdoor tourism destinations, with a wide range of activities from trekking to rock climbing and kayaking. However, what visitors tend to remember best of all is the warmth of the people and the pleasure that comes from visiting a country where there is still no Burger King, KFC or McDonald's in sight.

## Itineraries

Because travelling in Laos can be a bit of a lottery, it is strongly recommended that you allow some leeway in your schedule. Roads are subject to landslides and bus schedules can be rather hit and miss in more remote areas. Those on organized tours have distinct advantages in this regard as they will have a local guide who can apply pressure and secure seats on overbooked planes. Local guides are also much more aware of when problems are likely to arise. A lone traveller, who doesn't speak Lao, may be left floundering on the tarmac.

Nonetheless, a three- to four-week visit to Laos is sufficient to see much of the country – or at least that fraction of the country that it is possible to see. The main issue, perhaps, is how to combine a visit to the north with a trip to the south where Pakse, Champasak, Wat Phou and the Mekong islands are to be found. Vientiane to Pakse is a journey of around 750 km and many people (because they have booked a flight into and out of Vientiane) then have to retrace those 750 km to catch their plane out. The alternative is to enter and exit at different ends of the country. There are now plenty of hassle-free borders to choose from along the whole length of Laos. For example, it's possible to enter at Chiang Khong/Houei Xai in the far north, travel south, and then exit at Pakse/Chongmek. Alternatively, you can enter from Cambodia through the

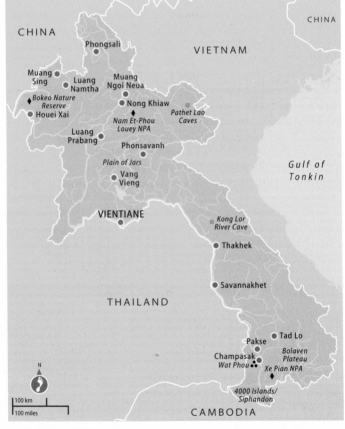

Siphandon area at Don Kralor (where Lao visas are now available at the border) and exit to Vietnam via Vieng Xai at Na Maew or at Sop Hun for Dien Bien Phu (though Vietnam visas will be required in advance). See page 332.

## One to two weeks

A one-week trip will require careful planning and prioritizing. If you fly into **Vientiane**, you could head north to wonderfully preserved **Luang Prabang** via the stunning scenery of **Vang Vieng**. Or fly from Vientiane to **Luang Namtha** for some fantastic trekking before overlanding back to Luang Prabang. Alternatively, after flying to Luang Prabang, fly on to **Pakse** for a trip south to the beguiling **Wat Phou**.

With an extra week, you could venture to remote **Vieng Xai** and see the caves where the Pathet Lao formed the new government and then head across to the **Nam Et-Phou Louey National Protected Area**. Or, from Pakse in the south, you could visit **Siphandon (4000 Islands)** and **Wat Phou**.

## Three to four weeks

With one month it is better to start at the extreme north or the south of Laos. You could travel overland to **Siphandon** in southern Laos via Don Kralor from Cambodia. Before heading north, take a side trip to the **Bolaven Plateau** and stay in the pretty village of **Tad Lo** and visit the many captivating waterfalls and the area's coffee plantations. Next, head upriver to charming **Champasak** for the UNESCO World Heritage Site of **Wat Phou**. Alternatively, visit the **Xe Pian** wetlands or the historic crumbling core of **Savannakhet** and nearby national protected areas (NPAs) for their trekking opportunities. Overland to **Thakhek** and do the motorcycle loop around the limestone scenery of central Laos, visiting the mind-blowing **Kong Lor River Cave** en route. Or fly direct to **Vientiane** in order to catch a flight to **Phonsavanh** and explore the mysterious **Plain of Jars**, then continue to **Xam Neua** and the Pathet Lao caves at **Vieng Xai**. From here, work your way toward **Luang Prabang** via the exciting Nam Nern Night Safari in the **Nam Et-Phou Louey National Protected Area**. Following this, take the wonderful, winding road to picturesque **Nong Khiaw** (with its boat access to the nearby riverside village of **Muang Ngoi Neua**) then cross over to Luang Prabang, from where you can head north to the trekking areas of **Luang Namtha**, **Muang Sing** and **Phongsali**. From Luang Prabang you could also catch a boat up the Mekong towards the Thai border and stop at **Houei Xai** for the unbeatable Gibbon Experience in the forest of **Bokeo Nature Reserve**. Deciding what to do is a difficult conundrum, but one thing is for sure: Laos is a country that should not be rushed, so don't try and build too much in.

# When to go to Laos

... and when not to

The best time to travel is during the relatively cool and dry winter months from October/November to March when the temperature averages around 20°C. Not only is the weather more pleasant at this time of year but the roads are also in better shape. However, temperatures in upland areas, like the Plain of Jars and the Bolaven Plateau, can be surprisingly cold during these months, dropping as low as 8°C at night. In mountainous Xieng Khoung Province, temperatures can drop to freezing point in December and January.

The second half of the dry season, from April through to the first rains in May or June, sees temperatures soar to up to 40°C in many lowland areas. It the north, it can be very hazy as smoke from burning off the secondary forest hangs in the air. This can cause itchiness of the eyes. What's more, it means that views are restricted and sometimes flights are cancelled.

During the rainy season, from June through to September/October, the tropical lowlands receive an annual average rainfall of 1250 mm a year. Temperatures during these months are 30-40°C. Average rainfall in Vientiane is 1700 mm, although in Northern Laos and the highlands it is much wetter, with more than 3000 mm each year. From June or July, as the wet season wears on, unsurfaced roads begin to deteriorate and overland transport in some areas becomes difficult.

## Weather Vientiane

| January | February | March | April | May | June |
|---|---|---|---|---|---|
| 28°C 17°C 15mm | 30°C 16°C 18mm | 31°C 18°C 35mm | 33°C 21°C 90mm | 32°C 23°C 191mm | 31°C 23°C 259mm |

| July | August | September | October | November | December |
|---|---|---|---|---|---|
| 30°C 23°C 295mm | 30°C 23°C 344mm | 30°C 22°C 253mm | 29°C 20°C 119mm | 28°C 18°C 52mm | 27°C 14°C 20mm |

## Festivals

Being of festive inclination, the Lao celebrate New Year four times a year: the international New Year in January, Chinese New Year in January/February, Lao New Year (Pi Mai) in April and Hmong New Year in December. The Lao Buddhist year follows the lunar calendar, so many of the festivals are movable. The first month begins around the time of the full moon in December. There are also local festivals (see under individual regions). **Note** The list below is not exhaustive, but does include the most important festivals. Many Chinese, Vietnamese and ethnic minority festivals are also celebrated in Laos.

### January

1 Jan **New Year's Day**. Public holiday celebrated by *baci* throughout the country.

6 Jan **Pathet Lao Day**. Public holiday, parades in main towns.

20 Jan **Army Day**. Public holiday.

Movable **Boun Pha Vet**. To celebrate King Vessanthara's reincarnation as a Buddha. Sermons, processions, dance, theatre. This is a popular occasion for the ordination of young monks.

### February

Movable **Magha Puja**. This celebrates the end of Buddha's time in the monastery and the prediction of his death. It is principally celebrated in Vientiane and at Wat Phou, near Champasak.

Movable, Jan/Feb **Chinese New Year**. Celebrated by Chinese and Vietnamese communities in Laos. Many Chinese and Vietnamese businesses shut for 3 days.

### March

8 Mar **Women's Day**. Public holiday.

22 Mar **People's Party Day**. Public holiday.

Movable **Boun Khoun Khao**. Harvest festival centred on the wats.

### April

13-15 Apr **Pi Mai**. Public holiday to celebrate Lao New Year. The 1st month of the Lao New Year is actually Dec but festivities are delayed until Apr when days are longer than nights. By Apr it's also heating up, so having hose pipes levelled at you and buckets of water dumped on you is more pleasurable. The festival also serves to invite the rains. Pi Mai is one of the most important annual festivals, particularly in Luang Prabang (see page 109). Statues of the Buddha (in the 'calling for rain' posture) are ceremonially doused in water, which is poured along an intricately decorated trench (*hang song nam pha*). The small stupas of sand, decorated with streamers, in wat compounds are symbolic requests for health and happiness over the next year. It is celebrated with traditional Lao folk singing (*mor lam*) and the circle dance (*ramwong*). There is usually a 3-day holiday to celebrate Lao New Year. Similar festivals are held in Thailand,

## ON THE ROAD

### Baci

The *baci* ceremony is a uniquely Lao *boun* (festival) and celebrates any auspicious occasion – marriage, birth, achievement or the end of an arduous journey, for instance. It dates from pre-Buddhist times and is animist in origin. It is centred on the *phakhouan*, a designer tree made from banana leaves and flowers (or, today, some artificial concoction of plastic) and surrounded by symbolic foods. The most common symbolic foods are eggs and rice – symbolizing fertility. The *mophone* hosts the ceremony and recites memorized prayers, usually in Pali, and ties cotton threads (*sai sin*) around the wrists of guests symbolizing good health, prosperity and happiness. For maximum effect, these strings must have three knots in them. It is unlucky to take them off until at least three days have elapsed, and custom dictates that they never be cut. Many people wear them until, frayed and worn, they fall off through sheer decrepitude. All this is accompanied by a *ramvong* (traditional circle dance), in turn accompanied by traditional instruments – flutes, clarinets, xylophones with bamboo crosspieces, drums, cymbals and the *kaen*, a hand-held pipe organ that is to Laos what the bagpipes are to Scotland.

Cambodia and Myanmar (Burma). If you attend the festival, keep your money, cameras, etc, in plastic to save them from getting wet. 'Sok Dee Pi Mai' – good luck for the New Year – is usually said to one another during this period.

### May

**1 May  Labour Day**. Public holiday with parades in Vientiane.
**Movable  Visakha Puja**. To celebrate the birth, enlightenment and death of the Buddha, celebrated in local wats.
**Movable  Boun Bang Fai**. The rocket festival, is a Buddhist rain-making festival. Large bamboo rockets are built and by monks and carried in procession before being blasted skywards. The higher a rocket goes, the bigger its builder's ego gets. Designers of failed

rockets are thrown in the mud. The festival lasts 2 days.

### June/July

**1 Jun  Children's Day**. Public holiday.
**Movable  Khao Phansa**. The start of Buddhist Lent and a time of retreat and fasting for monks. The festival starts with the full moon in Jun/Jul and continues until the full moon in Oct. It all ends with the **Kathin** ceremony in Oct when monks receive gifts.

### August

**13 Aug  Lao Issara**. Public holiday, Free Lao Day.
**23 Aug  Liberation Day**. Public holiday.
**Movable  Ho Khao Padap Dinh**. The celebration of the dead.

## September/October

Movable **Boun Ok Phansa**. This is the end of Buddhist Lent when the faithful take offerings to the temple. It is held in the '9th month' in Luang Prabang and the '11th month' in Vientiane, and marks the end of the rainy season. Boat races take place on the Mekong River, with crews of 50 or more men and women participating. On the night before the race small rafts are set afloat on the river.

## October

12 Oct **Freedom from the French Day**. Public holiday which is only really celebrated in Vientiane.

**Lai Heua Fai (Fireboat Festival)** See Luang Prabang, page 110.

## November

Movable **Boun That Luang**. Celebrated in all Laos' *thats*, most enthusiastically in Vientiane (see page 50). Includes religious rituals, local fairs, processions, beauty pageants and other festivities.

## December

Movable **Hmong New Year**.
2 Dec **Independence Day**. Public holiday, military parades, dancing and music.

# What to do
# in Laos

**activities from trekking to traditional massage**

Laos is starting to garner a reputation as one of the prime adventure and ecotourism destinations in the region. The pleasure of floating lazily down the Nam Song on an inner tube – once ruined by thumping speakers at every bar – is once again returning to a more peaceful experience. Kayaking is also an option: most trips are pleasant, rather tame, days out but there are also some rapids to ride if you choose the right time of year. There are wonderful trekking opportunities through stunning mountainous landscapes, home to a variety of ethnic groups. Other activities, such as rafting, rock climbing, ziplining and cycling, are emerging but they are still not as developed as they are in Thailand. Elephant-related activities are also possible and there is the excellent Gibbon Experience in Bokeo plus the Nam Nern Night Safari in Nam Et-Phou Louey National Protected Area. Safety is always an issue when participating in adventurous sports in Laos: make sure you are fully covered by your travel insurance; check the credentials of operators offering adventure activities; and make sure that vehicles and safety equipment are in a good condition. Note that medical care in Laos is still very limited, see page 338.

## Caving

Laos has some of the most extensive caves in the region. Some of the best are around Vang Vieng, where caving tourism has been developed. Another highlight is the amazing Kong Lor River Cave in the centre of the country. There are hundreds of caves around Vieng Xai, once a secret hideout for more than 20,000 people, but only a few are open to tourists; for those interested in history, these caves should be a first stop. Contact **Green Discovery**, www.greendiscoverylaos.com. Also see www.visit-viengxay.com.

## Cycling and mountain biking

Laos has to be one of the toughest but most rewarding countries in the world for cycle-tourists. The north is particularly challenging and at times it feels like no road is either straight or flat for more than a few feet. Many cyclists bring their own wheels but it's possible to rent them from tour operators all over Laos. Guesthouses in most towns also rent bicycles, though most aren't

## The best wildlife experiences

- Look out for wild elephants while trekking through the stunning wilderness of **Phou Khao Khouay National Protected Area**, www.trekkingcentrallaos.com, page 62.
- Visit a camp, 15 km out of Luang Prabang, for the rehabilitation of elephants previously employed in the logging trade, www.elephantvillage-laos.com, page 112. Or take an elephant trek through the wetlands of **Xe Pian**, page 229, and be sure not to miss the annual elephant festival in February.
- Catch a glimpse of the rare, black-cheeked crested gibbons chortling out soprano tunes from the jungle's canopy, with the **Gibbon Experience**, T084-212021, www.gibbonexperience.org, page 140.
- Venture out into the darkness to spot wildlife by boat on the Nam Nern Night Safari in the protected jungle of **Nam Et-Phou Louey National Protected Area**, page 174.
- Ask locally about opportunities to explore **Nakai Nam Theun National Protected Area**, one of the most important eco regions in Laos, with rare and endangered wildlife. Sustainable ecotourism and wildlife viewing options are under development. See page 196.
- Keep your fingers crossed and you might just spot the beautiful, rare, freshwater dolphins in **Siphandon**, page 249.

suitable for riding around the country. Mountain bikes can be found for hire in various outdoor hotspots including Nong Khiaw and Vang Vieng. Traffic is quite light but often speeds along the highways, particularly the southern roads. Most major roads are sealed and for the most part traverse quite hilly areas. Cycling is offered by several tour agencies; Luang Namtha is a popular place to start, and **Green Discovery**, www.greendiscoverylaos.com, runs excellent cycling tours. Also contact **NK Adventure** in Nong Khiaw (page 119) and tour operators in Phonsavanh (page 152).

### Kayaking and rafting

Laos is crisscrossed by rivers which carve their way through stunning scenery. Kayaking and rafting are offered in a number of locations around the country. Before undertaking a trip ensure that the boats are in good condition and that you are supplied with safety equipment, such as helmets and life-jackets. Most kayaking and rafting trips must be organized from a provincial capital or Vientiane. The Nam Song which flows through Vang Vieng offers water-borne tours for most tastes. Luang Prabang, Luang Namtha, Nong Khiaw and Muang Ngoi Neua all have opportunities for river-based activities. There is also good kayaking around the Bolaven Plateau (see pages 220 and 235). Contact **Green Discovery**, www.greendiscoverylaos.com or **Xplore-Asia**, www.xplore-asia.com.

## Rock climbing

Laos has stunning karst rock formations, caves and cliffs and is an ideal destination for rock climbers. However, rock climbing is still relatively new to Laos and only a few areas have been developed. Vang Vieng offers upwards of 200 routes for beginners through to advanced level climbers. Contact either **Adam's Climbing School** (see page 74) or **Green Discovery** (see page 74). A newer place that has fast become extremely popular is the **Green Climbers Home** (see page 191)

## Shopping tips

Popular souvenirs from Laos include **handicrafts and textiles**, which are sold pretty much everywhere. The market is usually a good starting point as are some of the minority villages. Boutique shops are now available predominantly in Luang Prabang, with a handful in Vientiane. The smaller, less touristy towns sell silk at the cheapest price. Xam Neua (see page 162) and around is where some of the best naturally dyed silk is weaved, but it is not the easiest place to purchase it. Much of this high-quality silk makes its way to Luang Prabang and Vientiane, where it is sold at much higher prices. There are a number of ethical places to buy, however, including the **TAEC** boutique (see page 93) in Luang Prabang, and **Sao Ban** (see page 52) in Vientiane. Vientiane's markets are also worth a browse, but it is best to take local guide if possible.

If you wish to have something made, most tailors can whip up a simple *sinh* (Lao sarong) in a day but you might want to allow longer for adjustments or other items. **Ock Pop Tok** (see page 110) in Luang Prabang also has a fantastic reputation for producing top-shelf, naturally dyed silk. Vientiane and Luang Prabang offer the most sophisticated line in boutiques, where you can get all sorts of clothes from the utterly exquisite to the frankly bizarre. Those on a more frugal budget will find some tailors who can churn out a decent pair of trousers on Sisavangvong in Luang Prabang and around Nam Phou in Vientiane. It is a good idea to bring a pattern/picture of what you want.

**Silverware**, most of it in the form of jewellery and small pots (though some of the ones you see may not be made of real silver), is traditional in Laos. The finest silversmiths have always worked out of Vientiane and Luang Prabang. Chunky antique ethnic-minority jewellery, including bangles, pendants, belts and earrings, is usually found in markets in the main towns, or antique shops in Vientiane, particularly around Nam Phou. Look for traditional necklaces that consist of wide silver bands, held together with a spirit lock (a padlock to lock in your scores of souls). Though silver is common, gold jewellery is the preference of the Lao Loum (lowland Laos) and its bright yellow colour is associated with Buddhist luck (often it is further dyed to enhance its orange goldness); the best quality gold is to be found in Vientiane.

Craftsmen in Laos are still producing **wood carvings** for temples and coffins. Designs are usually traditional, with a religious theme.

If you are looking for evenings out at cultural events, or are keen to dance the night away, Laos is not the place for you. The all-night party scene in Vang Vieng has withered, although it still provides a reasonable bar scene. In Pakse, Luang Prabang and Vientiane those who want to keep drinking after midnight head to the local bowling alleys which turn into stand-in clubs in the absence of anywhere else and make for a good night out mixing with locals, expats and other tourists.

Live music is popular in Laos and in most towns it is possible to find a bar or beer garden with a live band playing. Karaoke is hugely popular too, but whether that counts as entertainment is a matter of personal taste...

which offers a great variety of routes all within easy reach of a beautiful set of bungalows in the middle of a valley outside Thakek. Lastly, there is a limited amount of climbing up in Nong Khiaw – contact **Jewel Travel** for details (see page 118).

### Spas

Luang Prabang is the place to go for a range of wonderful spas. For extreme indulgence try the spa at **La Résidence Phou Vao** (see page 105). For a cheaper luxury alternative try the **Spa Garden** (see page 112), which offers a wide selection of massage and beauty treatments.

### Trekking

Treks are offered in abundance and the most northerly parts of the country are especially geared up for this sort of activity. Many treks are now based out of Vieng Phouka and Muang Long, Nong Khiaw and Muang Ngoi Neua. In other parts of the country, treks have been launched in Savannakhet (to the sacred forest of the Dong Phou Vieng National Protected Area, see page 207),

Phongsali (to remote ethnic minority areas, see page 122), and Champasak provinces (in and around the Xe Pian National Protected Area, see page 229) and a more responsible trek has been launched in the Akha-sensitive area of Muang Sing (see page 136). The Bolaven Plateau also offers great trekking from 1 to 5 days. Other destinations include Vang Vieng (see page 66); Luang Prabang (see page 79); Luang Namtha (see page 129); Bokeo Nature Reserve (see page 140); Vieng Phouka (see page 131); Savannakhet (see page 198); and Tad Lo (see page 236).

When trekking in Laos, it is imperative to abide by local customs in order to support efforts to keep tourism sustainable and low impact. For a different perspective on the landscape, try elephant trekking around Luang Prabang, Xe Pian Wetlands and Tad Lo.

For more information, contact the **National Tourism Administration of Lao PDR**, www.trekkingcentrallaos.com. Details of local trekking operators are also given in each chapter.

# Where to stay
## in Laos

from colonial villas and eco-lodges to homestays

Rooms in Laos are rarely luxurious and standards vary enormously. You can pay double what you would in Bangkok for similar facilities. At higher end hotels, rates are subject to 10% government tax and 10% service charge.

However, the hotel industry is expanding rapidly. There is a reasonable choice of hotels in Vientiane, Luang Prabang and Pakse and an expanding number of budget options in towns on the tourist trail. First-class and boutique hotels exist in Vientiane and Luang Prabang and there are other high-quality properties all over the country. More and more guesthouses are providing air conditioning, and en suite bathrooms are becoming the norm. Smaller provincial towns, having previously had only a handful of hotels and guesthouses (some of them French colonial villas) now have a growing number of rival concerns as tourism takes off. In rural villages, local homes are transformed into B&Bs on demand. Many towns have a large choice of very cheap, and in some cases good accommodation, including dorm beds. In the southern provinces, upmarket and boutique accommodation has cropped up in Champasak Province. There are several good eco-lodges in the country, most notably the **Boat Landing** at Luang Namtha (see page 133) and the **Kingfisher Ecolodge** at Ban Kiet Ngong (see page 230). Many tour companies offer homestay in ethnic minority villages and camping as part of a package tour.

General camping is not available but may form part of an organized tour. A luxury boat with overnight accommodation sails between Pakse and Wat Phou.

## Price codes

**Where to stay**

$$$$ over US$100
$$$ US$46-100
$$ US$30-45
$ under US$30

Prices refer to the cost of a standard double/twin room in high season.

**Restaurants**

$$$ over US$12
$$ US$6-12
$ under US$6

Prices refer to the cost of a two-course meal not including drinks.

# Food & drink
## in Laos

sticky rice, aromatic spices and French cuisine

## Food

Lao food is similar to that of Thailand, although the Chinese influence is slightly less noticeable. Lao dishes are distinguished by the use of aromatic herbs and spices such as lemongrass, chillies, ginger and tamarind. The best place to try Lao food is often from roadside stalls or in the markets. The staple Lao foods are *kao niao* (glutinous rice), which is eaten with your hands, and or *pa dek* (fermented fish, distinguishable by its distinctive smell), often laced with liberal spoons of *nam pa* (fish sauce). Being a landlocked country, most of the fish is fresh from the Mekong. One of the delicacies that shouldn't be missed is *mok pa* (steamed fish in banana leaf).

Dishes on most menus are variations of two themes: fish and bird. *Laap*, also meaning 'luck' in Lao, is a traditional ceremonial dish made from raw fish or meat crushed into a paste, marinated in lemon juice and then mixed with chopped mint. It is called *laap sin* if it has a meat base and *laap paa* if it's fish based. Beware of *laap* in cheap street restaurants, however: it is sometimes concocted from raw offal and served cold and should be consumed with extreme caution. Overall though, *laap* is cooked well for the *falang* palate.

*Phanaeng kai* is stuffed chicken with pork, peanuts and coconut milk with a dash of cinnamon. *Kai ping* is grilled chicken eaten with sticky rice. Another popular Lao dish is *tam som* – often called *som tam* – a spicy green shredded papaya salad served with chilli peppers, spices and fish sauce. This dish can be fiery hot at times, so you should stipulate how hot (*phet*) you want it!

The most commonly used **vegetables** are aubergines, tomatoes, cabbage, corn, cucumbers and lettuce, often cooked together, pureed and eaten with sticky rice. **Soups** usually accompany meals – there are many different types and they are invariably a mixture of fish and meat infused with aromatic herbs. These include *keng no mai* (bamboo shoot), *keng khi lek* (vegetable and buffalo skin), *ken chut* (without pimentos), *keng kalami* (cabbage with fish or pork), *kenghet bot* (mushroom) and *tom khaa kai* (chicken with coconut milk).

## FOOD

### Nam pa

No meal would be complete without a small dish of *nam pa* to spoon onto almost any savoury dish. Like *nam plaa* in Thailand, *nuoc mam* in Vietnam and *ngan-pyaye* in Myanmar (Burma), *nam pa* is an essential element of Laotian gastronomic life. To make the sauce, freshwater fish is packed into containers and steeped in brine. (Elsewhere in the region, it is made from saltwater fish, but because Laos is landlocked, freshwater fish is used instead.) The resulting brown liquid – essentially the by-products of slowly putrifying fish – is drained off and bottled. A variation is *pa dek*, *nam pa* with small chunks of fermented fish added, often with rice husks too. This variation tends to be used in cooking and is kept in an earthenware pot – often outside as the aroma is so strong.

The Lao are partial to **sweets**: sticky rice with coconut milk and black beans (which can be bought in bamboo tubes in the markets) and grilled bananas are favourites. **Fruit** is available but not as widely available as you might expect.

There is a well-ingrained **Vietnamese** culinary tradition and **Chinese** food is never hard to find. *Feu (or pho)*, Vietnamese noodle soup is everywhere and usually comes served with a huge pile of fresh herbs. Most restaurants outside the main towns do not have menus but will nearly always serve *feu* and *laap* or local specialities. Indeed, their generic name is *raan khai feu* 'restaurants that sell *feu*'. Vietnamese spring rolls are also common – you can either have *yaw jeun* (deep-fried spring rolls) or *yaw dip* (fresh spring rolls) and both are usually served with fresh herbs and rice noodles.

The French left a legacy of sophisticated cuisine in Laos. **French** food is widely available in restaurants, and street cafés usually serve delectable fresh croissants, crusty baguettes, *pain au chocolat* and a selection of sticky pastries, which can be washed down with a powerful cup of Lao coffee. Bread or *khao jii* is baked daily and often served with vegetables, pâté, fried eggs or an omelette. The Lao however have a habit of eating baguette sandwiches with fish sauce sprinkled on top (these are widely available in Vientiane, Savannakhet and Pakse). Menus in many of Vientiane's restaurants still have a distinctly French flavour to them. Vintage Bordeaux and Burgundies occasionally emerge from the cellars of restaurants too – although most of the fine vintages have now been consumed. Hotels in the larger towns often provide international menus and continental breakfasts. Even in small towns it is easy enough to create a continental breakfast: baguettes are widely available, wild honey can usually be tracked down, and fresh Bolaven coffee is abundant.

## Drink

Urban areas have access to safe water, but all water should be boiled or sterilized before drinking. Bottled water is widely available, however, and produced locally, so it is cheap. Soft drinks are now sold almost everywhere and Pepsi and Coke are ubiquitous. *Nam saa*, weak Chinese tea, is also served. There is now local milk production, so milk and yoghurt can be found, but fresh milk is not widely available and coffee with milk (*cafe nam hawn*) is more often served with condensed milk.

The local brew is rice wine. The white variety is called *lau-lao* (Lao alcohol) and is made from fermented sticky rice; *fanthong*, or red *lao-lao* is fermented with herbs. Bottled *lao-lao* is also widely available. Imported beers, wines and spirits can be found in hotels, restaurants, bars and nightclubs but are not particularly cheap. Beerlao is available as a light lager, a dark lager and there is also a new variant, the 'premium' Beerlao Gold. The legacy of adding ice to beer lives on in most beer gardens even in these days of 24-hour electricity. Beerlao also has the advantage of being reasonably priced – about 10,000 kip for a bottle in a basic bar or eatery. In Vientiane there are quite a few excellent wine bars and the range of wine on offer in other cities is also now reasonably good.

## Eating out

Restaurant food is, on the whole, hygienically prepared, and as long as street stall snacks have been well cooked, they are usually safe. Such stalls are a great place to sample regional specialities. Expect to pay between US$2-8 per head for a meal in main towns and less outside. By ordering only Lao food in local restaurants it is still possible to pay US$2 or less for a meal.

Really upscale restaurants are only to be found in Vientiane and Luang Prabang. Good French cuisine is available in both cities. Salads, steaks, pizzas and more are all on offer. Expect to pay anywhere over US$10 for a good meal. Lao restaurants are better value for money. Indian restaurants have found their way around the country meaning it is now possible to get some excellent Indian cuisine in such obscure places as Vieng Xai.

Far more prevalent are lower-end Lao, Chinese-Lao and Vietnamese restaurants which can be found in every town. Food in these places is usually good and excellent value for money. You'll find a cold beer and a good range of vegetarian and meat-based dishes for between US$3 and US$5. In towns on the tourist trail these local restaurants are complemented by places geared to the demands of tourists. Here you'll find fruit smoothies, Indian food, burgers

## ON THE ROAD
### The universal stimulant – the betel nut

Throughout the countryside in Southeast Asia, and in more remote towns, it is common to meet men and women whose teeth are stained black, and gums red, by continuous chewing of the 'betel nut'. This, though, is a misnomer. The betel 'nut' is not chewed at all: the three crucial ingredients that make up a betel 'wad' are the nut of the areca palm (*Areca catechu*), the leaf or catkin of the betel vine (*Piper betel*), and lime. When these three ingredients are combined with saliva they act as a mild stimulant. Other ingredients (people have their own recipes) are tobacco, gambier, various spices and the gum of *Acacia catechu*. The habit, though also common in South Asia and parts of China, seems to have evolved in Southeast Asia and it is mentioned in the very earliest chronicles. The lacquer betel boxes of Myanmar (Burma) and Thailand, and the brass and silver ones of Indonesia, illustrate the importance of chewing betel in social intercourse. Galvao in his journal of 1544 noted: "They use it so continuously that they never take it from their mouths; therefore these people can be said to go around always ruminating."

Among Westernized Southeast Asians the habit is frowned upon: the disfigurement and ageing that it causes, and the stained walls and floors that result from the constant spitting, are regarded as distasteful products of a more primitive lifestyle. But beyond the elite it is still widely practised.

and pizza very cheaply. Finally, right at the bottom end – in terms of price if not necessarily in terms of quality – are stalls that charge around US$2 for filled baguettes or simple single-dish meals.

# Vientiane
# & around

In 1563, King Setthathirat made the riverine city of Vientiane the capital of Laos. Or, to be more historically accurate, Wiang Chan, the 'City of the Moon', became the capital of Lane Xang.

In those days it was a small fortified city with a palace and two wats, which had grown prosperous from the surrounding fertile plains and the taxes levied from trade going upriver.

Today Vientiane is the sleepiest of all Southeast Asia's capital cities. Snuggled into a curve of the Mekong and cut off from the outside world for much of the modern period, its colonial heritage remains largely intact. While the last few years have brought greater activity, it is still a quiet city of golden temples, crumbling mansions and tree-lined boulevards, but with the benefits of excellent restaurants, wine bars and a £31 million riverfront development.

Around Vientiane are several places of interest. Ban Pako and Nam Ngum make worthwhile weekend retreats, while Vang Vieng is a popular stopover for the adventure crowd on the way to Luang Prabang.

**Best** for
Museums ▪ Restaurants ▪ Riverfront walks

# Footprint
## picks

### ★ That Luang, page 31
This gleaming gold wat is the
national symbol of Laos and
the country's holiest site.

### ★ Wat Phra Kaeo, page 40
Formerly home to the Emerald Buddha, Wat Phra Kaeo has some
of the finest sculpture in Laos.

### ★ Lao National Museum, page 41
The place to swat up on some history before visiting the rest of
the country.

### ★ Phou Khao Khouay Protected Area, page 62
Accessible yet seldom visited park, with jungle-covered mountains,
waterfalls and wild elephants.

### ★ Vang Vieng caves, page 68
Former party town reinventing itself as a centre for outdoor and
adrenalin activities.

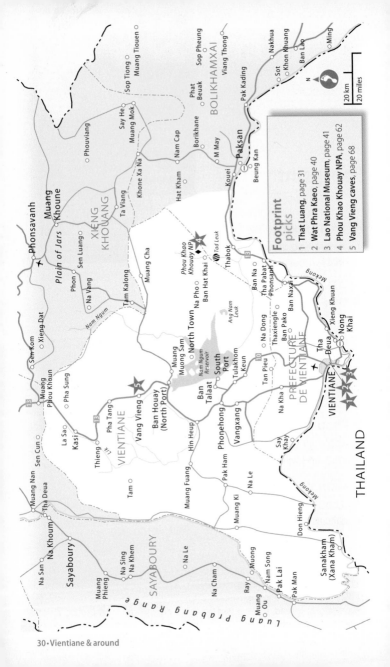

Footprint
picks

1 That Luang, page 31
2 Wat Phra Kaeo, page 40
3 Lao National Museum, page 41
4 Phou Khao Khouay NPA, page 62
5 Vang Vieng caves, page 68

# Vientiane

Vientiane's appeal lies in its largely preserved fusion of Southeast Asian and French colonial culture. Baguettes, filter coffee and Bordeaux wines coexist with spring rolls, noodle soup and papaya salad. Colourful tuk-tuks scuttle along tree-lined boulevards, past old Buddhist temples and cosmopolitan cafés. Hammer-and-sickle flags hang at 10-pin bowling discos and chickens wander the streets. But, as in the rest of Laos, the best thing about Vientiane, is its people. Take the opportunity to stroll around some of the outlying *bans* (villages) and meet the wonderful characters who make this city what it is. *Phone code: 021 for landlines, 020 for mobiles. Colour map 2, B2.*

## Sights
*wide boulevards, crumbling French buildings and a handful of wats*

Most of the interesting buildings in Vientiane are of religious significance. All tour companies and many hotels and guesthouses will arrange city tours and excursions to surrounding sights but it is just as easy to arrange a tour independently with a local tuk-tuk driver; the best English speakers (and thus the most expensive tuk-tuks) can be found in the parking lot beside Nam Phou and also beside Wat Mixay. Those at the Morning Market (Talaat Sao) are cheaper. Most tuk-tuk drivers pretend not to carry small change, so make sure you have the exact fare with you before taking a ride.

### ★That Luang
*That Luang Rd, 3.5 km northeast of the centre; daily 0800-1200 and 1300-1600 (except 'special' holidays); small entry charge. A booklet about the wat is on sale at the entrance.*

That Luang is Vientiane's most important site and the holiest Buddhist monument in the country. The golden spire looks impressive at the top of the hill and dominates the skyline in the northeast of the city.

According to legend, a stupa was first built here in the third century AD by emissaries of the Moghul Emperor Asoka; it is supposed to have contained the breast

# Essential Vientiane

## Finding your feet

Vientiane is small and manageable. The core of the city is negotiable on foot, while outlying hotels and places of interest are accessible by bicycle. Although traffic has increased, cycling remains the best and most flexible way to tour the city, with tuk-tuks, scooters, motorbikes and taxis available for longer trips.

The city is divided into *bans* or **villages**, mainly centred on their local wats, and larger *muang* or **districts**: Muang Sikhottabong lies to the west, Muang Chanthabouli to the north, Muang Xaisettha to the east and Muang Sisattanak to the south. There are few street signs, but because the city is so small and compact it doesn't take long to get to grips with the layout. The names of major **streets** or *thanon* usually correspond to the nearest wat, while traffic lights, wats, monuments and large hotels serve as directional landmarks. When giving directions to a tuk-tuk it is better to use a map with Lao script or say the name of a nearby landmark, as street names still leave locals a little bewildered. A good quality free city map can be picked up in almost every hotel and tourist-friendly restaurant.

## Best restaurants
**Côte d'Azur**, page 46
**Le Silapa**, page 46
**Pimenton**, page 46

## When to go

November to February is the most comfortable time with warm sunny days. From March to May it can be debilitatingly hot, with some very humid days as the southwest monsoon hits in May/June. Rains continue until October when the northeast monsoon brings drier cooler weather. Average annual rainfall in Vientiane is 1700 m.

## Time required

Two to three days would allow a leisurely visit of the capital but those pressed for time often pass through in 24 hours, preferring to head straight up to Vang Vieng or Luang Prabang.

## Best places to stay
**Green Park Boutique Hotel**, page 43
**Lao Orchid Hotel**, page 43
**Settha Palace Hotel**, page 43
**Hotel Day Inn**, page 44

## Weather Vientiane

| January | February | March | April | May | June |
|---|---|---|---|---|---|
| 28°C | 30°C | 31°C | 33°C | 32°C | 31°C |
| 17°C | 16°C | 18°C | 21°C | 23°C | 23°C |
| 15mm | 18mm | 35mm | 90mm | 191mm | 259mm |

| July | August | September | October | November | December |
|---|---|---|---|---|---|
| 30°C | 30°C | 30°C | 29°C | 28°C | 27°C |
| 23°C | 23°C | 22°C | 20°C | 18°C | 14°C |
| 295mm | 344mm | 253mm | 119mm | 52mm | 20mm |

bone of the Buddha. Excavations on the site, however, have located only the remains of an 11th- to 13th-century Khmer temple, making the earlier provenance doubtful in the extreme. The present monument, encompassing the previous buildings, was built in 1566 by King Setthathirat, whose statue stands outside. Plundered by the Thais and the Chinese Haw in the 18th century, it was restored by King (Chao) Anou at the beginning of the 19th century. He added the cloister and the Burmese-style pavilion containing the That Sithamma Hay Sok. The stupa was restored by l'École Française d'Extrême-Orient (whose conservators were also responsible for the restoration of parts of Angkor Wat at the start of the 20th century) but was rebuilt in 1930 because many Lao disapproved of the French restoration.

The reliquary is surrounded by a square cloister, with an entrance on each side, the most famous on the east. There is a small collection of statues in the cloisters, including one of the Khmer king Jayavarman VII. The cloisters are used as lodgings by monks who travel to Vientiane for religious reasons and especially for the annual **Buon That Luang festival** (see page 50). The base of the stupa is a mixture of styles, Khmer, Indian and Lao – and each side has a *hor vay* (small offering temple). This lowest level represents the material world, while the second tier is surrounded by a lotus wall and 30 smaller stupas, representing the 30 Buddhist perfections. Each of these originally contained smaller golden stupas but they were stolen by Chinese raiders in the 19th century. The 30-m-high spire dominates the skyline and resembles an elongated lotus bud, crowned by a banana flower and parasol. It was designed so that pilgrims could climb up to the stupa via the walkways around each level. It is believed that originally over 450 kg of gold leaf was used on the spire.

There used to be a wat on each side of the stupa but only two remain: Wat Luang Nua to the north and Wat Luang Tai to the south. The large new wat-like structure is the headquarters of a Buddhist organization. The outer walls are used to stage art exhibitions.

Although That Luang is considered to be the most important historical site in Vientiane, most visitors will feel that it is not the most interesting, impressive or beautiful, largely because it seems to have been constructed out of concrete. Wat Sisaket and Wat Phra Kaeo (see pages 37 and 40) are certainly more memorable buildings. Nonetheless, it is important to appreciate the reverence in which That Luang is held by most Lao, including the many millions of Lao who live across the border in Thailand. The *that* is the prototype for the distinctive Lao-style angular *chedi*, which can be seen in northeast Thailand, as well as across Laos.

### Revolutionary Monument

Also known as the Unknown Soldier's Memorial, this hilltop landmark is just off Phon Kheng Road and visible from the parade ground (which resembles a disused parking lot) in front of That Luang. Echoing a *that* in design, it is a spectacularly dull monument, built in memory of those who died during the revolution in 1975. The **Pathet Lao Museum**, to the northwest of That Luang, is only open to VIPs and never to the public but there are a few tanks, trucks, guns and aircraft used in the war lying in the grounds: these can be seen from the other side of the fence.

**Patuxai**
*Junction of That Luang Rd and Lane Xang Av. Daily 0800-1200 and 1300-1630, small charge.*

# 1 Vientiane

➡ **Vientiane maps**
1 Vientiane, page 34
2 Vientiane centre, page 38

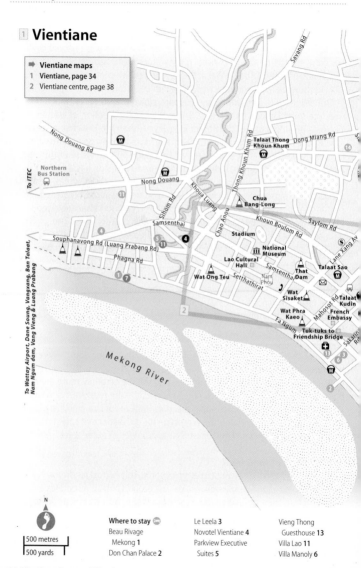

**Where to stay** 🛏
Beau Rivage
  Mekong **1**
Don Chan Palace **2**

Le Leela **3**
Novotel Vientiane **4**
Parkview Executive
  Suites **5**

Vieng Thong
  Guesthouse **13**
Villa Lao **11**
Villa Manoly **6**

At the end of That Luang is the Oriental answer to Paris's Arc de Triomphe and Vientiane's best-known landmark, the monstrous Victory Monument or Patuxai. It was originally called Anou Savali, officially renamed the Patuxai or Victory Monument, but is affectionately known by locals as 'the vertical runway'. It was

# BACKGROUND

## Vientiane

Vientiane is an ancient city. There was probably a settlement here, on a bend on the left bank of the Mekong, in the 10th century but knowledge of the city before the 16th century is thin and dubious. Scholars do know, from the chronicles, that King Setthathirat decided to relocate his capital here in the early 1560s. It seems that it took him four years to build the city, constructing a defensive wall (hence 'Wiang', meaning a walled or fortified city), along with Wat Phra Kaeo and a much-enlarged That Luang.

Vieng Chan, as it was called, remained intact until 1827 when it was ransacked by the Siamese; this is why many of its wats are of recent construction. Francis Garnier in 1860 wrote of "a heap of ruins" and having surveyed the "relics of antiquity" decided that the "absolute silence reigning within the precincts of a city formerly so rich and populous, was … much more impressive than any of its monuments". A few years later, Louis de Carné wrote of the vegetation that it was like "a veil drawn by nature over the weakness of man and the vanity of his works".

The city was abandoned for decades and erased from the maps of the region. It was only conjured back into existence by the French, who commenced reconstruction at the end of the 19th century. They built rambling colonial villas and wide tree-lined boulevards, befitting their new administrative capital, Vientiane. At the height of American influence in the 1960s, it was renowned for its opium dens and sex shows.

built by the former regime in memory of those who died in the wars before the Communist takeover, but the cement ran out before its completion. Refusing to be beaten, the regime diverted hundreds of tonnes of cement, part of a US aid package to help with the construction of runways at Wattay Airport, to finish off the monument in 1969. In 2004, the Chinese funded a big concrete park area surrounding the site, including a musical fountain; it's a pity they didn't stretch the budget to finance the beautification of the park's centrepiece.

A small sign explains that, although Patuxai might look grand from a distance, on closer inspection "it appears like a monster of concrete". The top affords a bird's eye view of the leafy capital, including the distant glittering, golden dome of the old Russian circus, now the rarely used National Circus. The interior of the monument is reminiscent of a multi-storey car park (presumably as a counterpoint to the parade ground next to the Revolutionary Monument), with graffiti sporadically daubed on top of unfinished Buddhist bas-reliefs in reinforced concrete. The frescoes under the arches at the bottom represent mythological stories from the Lao version of the *Ramayana*, the *Phra Lak Pralam*. Until 1990 there was a bar on the bottom floor; today Vientiane's youth hang out on the parapet.

Today Vientiane is a quiet capital with an urban population of around 460,000 (up from 70,000 in 1960). There are around 695,500 inhabitants (about 10% of the population of Laos) in the Vientiane municipality but this extends far beyond the physical limits of the city. Before 1970 there was only one set of traffic lights in the whole city and, even with the arrival of cars and motorbikes from Thailand in recent years, the streets are a far cry from the congestion of Bangkok. Unlike Phnom Penh and Ho Chi Minh City, there are only scattered traces of French town planning; architecture is a mixture of east and west, with French colonial villas and traditional wooden Lao buildings intermingled with Chinese shophouses and more contemporary buildings. Some locals worry that foreign investment and redevelopment will ruin the city – already some remarkably grotesque buildings are going up – but officials seem to be aware that there is little to be gained from creating Bangkok in microcosm.

Vientiane's citizens are proud of their cultural heritage and are usually very supportive of the government's attempts to promote it. The government has tried, by and large, to maintain the national identity and protect its citizens from harmful outside influences. This is already starting to change; with the government reshuffle in 2006 came a gradual loosening of the cultural stranglehold. Elections in 2011 saw just one independent (non-party) candidate elected as well as 33 women. President Sayasone, born 1936, was re-elected.

In 2013, Vientiane saw the completion of a US$31-million redevelopment project, which has transformed the riverfront from a dirt road lined with basic restaurants to a dual-lane road and concrete river bank including public gardens and recreation area, especially popular at dawn and dusk.

## Wat Sisaket

*Junction of Lane Xang Av and Setthathirat Rd. Daily 0800-1200 and 1300-1600, small charge. No photographs in the sim.*

Further down Lane Xang is the Morning Market or Talaat Sao (see page 53). A major waterpark has been constructed in the park just behind Talaat Sao. Beyond the market, where Setthathirat meets Lane Xang, is one of Vientiane's two national museums, Wat Sisaket. Home of the head of the Buddhist community in Laos, Phra Sangka Nagnok, it is one of the most important buildings in the capital and houses over 7000 Buddha images. Wat Sisaket was built in 1818 during the reign of King Anou. A traditional Lao monastery, it was the only temple that survived the Thai sacking of the town in 1827-1828 (possibly out of respect for the fact that it had been completed only 10 years before the invasion), which now makes it the oldest building in Vientiane. Sadly, it is seriously in need of restoration.

The main sanctuary, or *sim*, with its sweeping roof, shares many stylistic similarities with Wat Phra Kaeo (see below): window surrounds, lotus-shaped pillars and carvings of deities held up by giants on the rear door. The *sim* contains 2052 Buddha statues (mainly terracotta, bronze and wood) in small niches in the top half of the wall. There is little left of the Thai-style *jataka* murals on the lower walls but the depth and colour of the originals can be seen from the few remaining pieces. The ceiling was copied from temples King Anou had seen on a visit to Bangkok. The standing image to the left of the altar is believed to have been cast in the same proportions as King Anou. Around the *sim*, set into the ground, are small *bai sema* or boundary stones. The *sim* is surrounded by a large courtyard, which originally had four entrance gates (three are now blocked). Behind the *sim* is a large trough, in the shape of a *naga*, used for washing the Buddha images during the water festival (see page 50).

## ② Vientiane centre

**Where to stay** 🛏
Auberge Sala Inpeng 1 *B1*
Beau Rivage Mekong 3 *C1*
Best Western 5 *C2*
Chanta Guesthouse 7 *B2*
Chanthapanya 40 *B2*
Day Inn 4 *B4*
Green Park Boutique 38 *C6*
Lani Guesthouse 9 *B2*

Lao Orchid 37 *B1*
LV City Riverine 11 *C2*
Mali Namphu Guesthouse
  29 *B3*
Phornthip Guesthouse
  16 *B1*
Settha Palace 23 *A4*
Soukchaleun Guesthouse
  24 *B2*

Vayakorn Guesthouse
  28 *B2*
Villa Manoly 9 *C5*
Youth Inn 10 *C2*

**Restaurants** 🍴
Amphone 22 *B2*
Aria 5 *B2*
Bistro 22 2 *C5*

N

| 200 metres |
| 200 yards |

The cloisters were built during the 1800s and were the first of their kind in Vientiane. They shelter 120 large Buddhas in the attitude of subduing Mara (see page 316), plus a number of other images in assorted *mudras*, and thousands of small figures in niches, although many of the most interesting Buddha figures are now in Wat Phra Kaeo. Most of the statues date from the 16th to 19th centuries but there are some earlier images. Quite a number were taken from local monasteries during the French period.

➡ **Vientiane maps**
1  Vientiane, page 34
2  Vientiane centre, page 38

Chinese Llao-Ning
 Dumpling Restaurant **4** *C1*
Côte d'Azur **23** *C2*
Full Moon Café **6** *C2*
Joma **11** *C3*
La Terrasse **28** *B2*
Lao Kitchen **1** *B2*
Le Banneton **8** *C2*
Le Croissant d'Or **12** *B2*

Le Silapa **3** *B1*
Le Trio Coffee **10** *C3*
Makphet **39** *B1*
Nazim **16** *C2*
Noy's Fruit Heaven **15** *B2*
Pimenton **16** *C2*
PVO Vietnamese
 Food **14** *C3*
Seendat **24** *A6*

Sputnik Burger **17** *C3*
Sticky Fingers **19** *C2*
Vieng Savanh **7** *A1*
Xang Khoo **18** *B3*

**Bars & clubs** 🍸
Baravin **20** *B4*
Chokdee **21** *C2*
I-Beam **9** *B2*

Jazzy Brick **38** *C3*
Khop Chai Deu **26** *C3*
Spirit House **42** *B1*
Wine 95 **13** *C3*

The whole ensemble of *sim* plus cloisters is washed in a rather attractive shade of caramel, and combined with the terracotta floor tiles and weathered roof presents a most satisfying sight. An attractive Burmese-style library, or *hau tai*, stands on Lane Xang outside the courtyard. The large casket inside used to contain important Buddhist manuscripts.

Just behind Wat Sisaket is a complex of colonial houses in a well-maintained garden.

### ★ Wat Phra Kaeo
*Setthathirat Rd, daily 0800-1200 and 1300-1600 (closed public holidays), small entry charge. No photographs in the* sim.

Almost opposite Wat Sisaket is the other national museum, Wat Phra Kaeo, also known as Hor Phra Kaeo. It was built by King Setthathirat in 1565 to house the Emerald Buddha (or Phra Kaeo), now in Bangkok, which he had brought from his royal residence in Chiang Mai. It was never a monastery but was kept instead for royal worship. The Emerald Buddha was removed by the Thais in 1779 and Wat Phra Kaeo was destroyed by them in the sacking of Vientiane in 1827. (The Thais now claim the Emerald Buddha as the most important icon in their country.) The whole building was in a bad state of repair after the sackings, with only the floor remaining fully intact. Francis Garnier, the French explorer who wandered through the ruins of Vieng Chan in 1860, describes Wat Phra Kaeo "shin[ing] forth in the midst of the forest, gracefully framed with blooming lianas, and profusely garlanded with foliage". Louis de Carné in his journal, *Travels in Indochina and the Chinese Empire* (1872), was also enchanted, writing when he came upon the vegetation-choked ruin that it "made one feel something of that awe which filled men of old at the threshold of a sacred wood".

The building was expertly reconstructed in the 1940s and 1950s and is now surrounded by a garden. During renovations, the interior walls were restored using a plaster made of sugar, sand, buffalo skin and tree oil.

The *sim* stands on three tiers of galleries, the top one surrounded by majestic lotus-shaped columns. The tiers are joined by several flights of steps and guarded by *nagas*. The main, central (southern) door is an exquisite example of Lao wood sculpture with carved angels surrounded by flowers and birds; it is the only notable remnant of the original wat. (The central door at the northern end, with the larger carved angels, is new.)

The *sim* now houses a superb assortment of Lao and Khmer art and some pieces of Burmese and Khmer influence, mostly collected from other wats in Vientiane.

### That Dam
Travelling north on Chanta Khoummane, look out for the distinctive brick That Dam, or Black Stupa. It is renowned for the legend of the seven-headed *naga*, which is supposed to have helped protect the Vientiane from Thai invaders (conveniently forgetting that the city was comprehensively sacked by the Thais in 1827). The *naga* now lies dormant inside the stupa, waiting to seize upon another chance. The stupa was renovated in 1995 but still has an air of neglect.

## ★ Lao National Museum

*Samsenthai Rd, opposite the National Culture Hall. Daily 0800-1200 and 1300-1600, small entry charge. No photographs allowed.*

This place was formerly called the Revolutionary Museum but in these post-revolutionary days it has been redesignated the National Museum. The museum's collection has grown over the last few years and now includes a selection of historical artefacts from dinosaur bones and pre-Angkorian sculptures to a comprehensive photographic collection on Laos' modern history. The rhetoric of these modern collections has been somewhat toned down from the old days, when photographic descriptions would refer to the 'running dog imperialists' (Americans).

One of the highlights of the museum is a dazzling array of personal effects from the revolutionary leader Kaysone including his exercise machine, a spoon he used and even the coconut he once had a sip from. Downstairs there is a collection of ancient artefacts, including stone tools and quite poignant burial jars. Upstairs the museum features a range of artefacts and busts as well as a small exhibition on ethnic minorities. The final section of the museum comprises mostly photographs tracing the country's struggle against the 'brutal' French colonialists and American 'imperialists'.

## Wat Ong Teu

Wat Ong Teu (identified by its bright orange monks' quarters) is located on Setthathirat, which runs parallel to Samsenthai. It was constructed by King Setthathirat in the 16th century, was ransacked by the Siamese in 1827 and then rebuilt during the late 19th and 20th centuries. The wat houses one of the biggest Buddhas in Vientiane, weighing several tonnes, which sits at the back of the *sim* and gives the monastery its name: Temple of the Heavy Buddha. The wat is also noted for its magnificent sofa and its ornately carved wooden doors and windows, with motifs from the *Phra Lak Pralam* (the *Ramayana*, see box, page 312). The monastery runs one of the larger Buddhist schools in Laos and is home to the Deputy Patriarch of the Lao monastic order, Hawng Sangkharat. The wat comes alive every year for the **That Luang festival** (see page 50).

## Wat Chan

A short walk away, on the banks of the Mekong (junction of Chao Anou and Fa Ngum), is Wat Chan, or Wat Chanthabuli. It was wrecked by the marauding Thais in 1827 and now only the base of a single stupa remains in front of the *sim*. The stupa originally had Buddha images in the 'Calling for Rain' attitude on each side (see page 316) but only one remains. Inside the reconstructed *sim* is a remarkable bronze Buddha from the original temple on this site. The wat is also renowned for its panels of sculpted wood on the doors and windows.

## Chua Bang-Long

For those who have had their fill of Theravada Buddhist wats, there is a fine Mahayana Buddhist *chua* (pagoda) tucked away down a narrow lane off Khoun

### The Story of Quan Am

Turned onto the streets by her husband for some unspecified wrong doing, Quan Am dressed as a monk and took refuge in a monastery. There, a woman accused her of fathering and then abandoning her child. Accepting the blame (why, no one knows), she was again turned out onto the streets, only to return to the monastery much later when, on the point of death, she confessed her true identity. When the Emperor of China heard the tale, he made Quan Am the Guardian Spirit of Mother and Child, and couples without a son now pray to her. Quan Am's husband is sometimes depicted as a parakeet, with the goddess holding her adopted son in one arm and standing on a lotus leaf, the symbol of purity.

Boulom, near Chao Anou. The Chua Bang-Long was established by Vientiane's large and active Vietnamese population, who are said to have outnumbered Lao in the city before the outbreak of the Second World War. A statue of the Chinese goddess Quan Am (see box, above) stands in front of a Lao-style *that* which, in turn, fronts a large pagoda, almost Cao Dai in style. The pagoda has been extensively renovated and embellished over the last few years. Not far away, at the intersection of Samsenthai and Khoun Boulom is another, much smaller and more intimate pagoda.

### Wat Simuang
*Setthathirat Rd, east of town; daily 0600-2000; during celebrations the temple stays open until 2200.*

Wat Simuang contains the town foundation pillar (*lak muang*), which was erected in 1563 when King Setthathirat established Vientiane as the capital of the kingdom of Lane Xang. It is believed to be an ancient Khmer boundary stone, which marked the edge of the old Lao capital. Although the temple means 'Holy City Monastery', many locals vouch that it's named after pregnant Madame Simuang, who sacrificed herself, her baby and her horse by jumping in the hole dug for the foundation pillar before the consecrated stone was erected. The *sim* was reconstructed in 1915 around the foundation pillar, which forms the centre of the altar. In front of the altar is a stone Buddha thought to have magical powers because it survived the temple's razing. It is believed that if you lift the Buddha off the pillow three times and make a wish then you are indebted to return an offering of fruit and flowers. Wat Simuang may not be charming, refined or architecturally significant but for many locals it is the most important monastery in the capital and is considered the luckiest. Hawkers selling offerings of fruit, flowers, candles and incense line the surrounding streets, supplying the scores of people who come here hoping for good fortune. In the grounds of the wat are the ruins of what appears to be a Khmer laterite *chedi*.

## Statue of King Sisavangvong

Just beyond Wat Simaung, where Setthathirat and Samsenthai meet, is the statue of King Sisavangvong. The original statue, carved by a Lao sculptor, apparently made the king look like a dwarf so it was destroyed. The present statue (there's a copy of it in Luang Prabang) was, peculiarly, donated by the Russians and, just as strangely, it survived the revolution.

## Listings Vientiane maps p34 and p38

### Tourist information

**Lao National Tourism Authority**
*Lane Xang (towards Patuxai), T021-212251, www.tourismlaos.org.
Mon-Fri 0830-1200 and 1300-1600.*
Provides information on ecotourism operators and trekking opportunities in provincial areas. This is a good starting point if you want to organize a trip to Phou Khao Khouay NPA. The English-language *Vientiane Times* runs items of Lao news, plus snippets translated from the local newspapers and listings.

### Where to stay

**$$$$ Green Park Boutique Hotel**
*248 Khouvieng Rd, T021-264097, www.greenparkvientiane.com.*
Designed in a modern East-meets-West style, this hotel is set alongside Vientiane's primary park. Beautiful rooms with all the mod cons, Wi-Fi and super-duper bathtubs. Beautiful garden and excellent pool. The only drawback is that it's further out from the city centre and river, but still within walking distance and makes a fantastic luxury option. Recommended.

**$$$$ Settha Palace Hotel**
*6 Pang Kham Rd, T021-217581, www.setthapalace.com.*
The stunning **Settha Palace** was built in 1936 and opened as a hotel in 1999. Its French architecture, period furniture, plush rooms complete with black marble sinks and bathtubs and tropical gardens and pool sit more easily with the essence of Vientiane than the other top-level hotels. It is considered by those in search of a little old world charm to be the best hotel in town. Recommended.

**$$$$-$$$ Best Western Vientiane**
*2-12 François Ngin Rd, T021-216906, www.bestwesternvientiane.com.*
The service here is hard to fault and facilities are good: restaurant, bar, basic gym, small pool and free airport pick-up. Now far better equipped than when it was the **Tai Pan** hotel, the rooms offer the level one would expect from **Best Western**, but there are more charming places to stay.

**$$$ Lao Orchid Hotel**
*Chao Anou, T021-264134, www.lao-orchid.com.*
Beautiful spacious rooms with stunning modern furnishings, polished floorboards and large showers. Outstanding value (4½-star accommodation for a 3-star price) and popular with business travellers. Advanced bookings imperative in peak season. Includes breakfast and Wi-Fi. Recommended.

## $$ Auberge Sala Inpeng
*063 Unit 06, Inpeng St, T021-242021, www.salalao.com.*
An absolute gem for a capital city. 9 very attractive bungalows set in a small garden in a quiet street. Breakfast included.

## $$ Beau Rivage Mekong
*Fa Ngum Rd, T021-243350, www.hbrm.com.*
One of the first Western-style boutique hotels in Vientiane has somewhat quirky, dated decoration in shades of pink. Nonetheless it has a great riverside location: outside of the centre but just a 5-min walk to the hustle and bustle. Some rooms have river views; garden view rooms are cheaper. Includes breakfast which is served at the popular **Spirit House** next door.

## $$ Chanthapanya
*Nokeo Khoummane Rd, T021-244284, www.chanthapanyahotel.com.*
A well-located hotel that offers good value for money and interesting (if quirky) interiors. Furnished with modern Lao wooden furniture, comfy beds, fridge, TV, hot water, phone, a/c. Includes breakfast.

## $$ Hotel Day Inn
*059/3 Pang Kham Rd, T021-222985, dayinn@laopdr.com.*
Run by a friendly Cambodian, Ms Ly, this renovated villa (the former Indian embassy) is in a good position in a quiet part of town, just to the north of the main concentration of bars and restaurants. Attractive rooms are large, airy and clean with a/c and excellent bathrooms; good breakfast and complimentary airport transfer included. Wi-Fi available. Recommended.

## $$ Lani Guesthouse
*281 Setthathirath Rd, T021-214919, www.lanigh.laotel.com.*
This lovely old-style Vientiane building is in a charming location and is run by pleasant staff. Rooms are tad more expensive in the main house.

## $$ LV City Riverine Hotel
*48 Fa Ngum Rd, Mixay, T021-214643, www.lvcitylaos.com.*
A good central choice. The suite has a 4-poster bed, textile decor and a good-sized bathroom. The deluxe rooms have beds raised on small platforms but with smaller bathrooms; standard rooms are very good with thoughtful extras like a clothes stand. Very helpful staff. Wi-Fi and breakfast included.

## $$ Villa Manoly
*Ban Phyavat, T021-218907, manoly20@hotmail.com.*
A wonderful ramshackle French colonial villa crowded with objets d'art, curios, books and ancient TV sets. It's like a rambling private house. There's a pool in the garden. 12 rooms are in the main building and 8 rooms in a new block with small patios out front overlooking the pool. Recommended.

## $$-$ Vayakorn Guesthouse
*91 Nokeo Khoummane Rd, T021-241911, www.vayakorn@yahoo.com.*
Central and clean, with friendly staff. Wonderful airy rooms, tastefully decorated with polished floors and modern furniture. Hot water, a/c and TV. Breakfast isn't included but is excellent value. Recommended. The **Vayakorn Inn** is also good and can be found just around the corner. Wi-Fi available.

## $ Chanta Guesthouse
*Setthathirat Rd (opposite Mixay Temple), T021-243204.*

The shabby foyer doesn't do this place justice. Rooms are homely, with polished floorboards, TV, good bathrooms, wooden furniture and great cotton bedclothes. Cheaper rooms have shared facilities; more expensive ones are en suite with a/c.

### $ Mali Namphu Guesthouse
*114 Pang Kham Rd, T021-215093, www. malinamphu.com.*
Difficult to spot as it looks like a small shopfront but the façade is deceiving, as the foyer opens onto a beautifully manicured courtyard surrounded by quaint terraced rooms. Some of the rooms are way better than others so if possible ask to see a few.

### $ Phornthip Guesthouse
*72 Inpeng Rd, T021-217239.*
A quiet, family-run and very friendly guesthouse, but perhaps a little overpriced. Rooms are large with en suite bathrooms, some have a/c. There's a courtyard at the back of the guesthouse, but no garden. Bicycle hire available. Some room deals include breakfast.

### $ Soukchaleun Guesthouse
*121 Setthathirat Rd (opposite Mixay temple), T021-218723, soukchaleun_gh@ yahoo.com.*
Quaint guesthouse with a range of rooms, from fan-cooled with shared bathroom through to a/c en suite. Comfortable and homely. Clean, friendly and good value.

### $ Vieng Thong Guesthouse
*Ban Phiawat, opposite Wat Phiavat in a side street, T021-212095.*
Family-style house, plus modern extension, in a nice garden with a café. Super-friendly staff. Large rooms with thick duvets, rattan furniture, TV, china tea-sets and hot water showers. Pleasant

but a little expensive, especially for the older rooms. The newer rooms are much more attractive.

### $ Youth Inn
*29 Fa Ngum Rd; also on François Ngin Rd; T021-217130, youthinn@hotmail.com.*
A Vietnamese-run operation with 2 locations in the heart of town. The standard-sized rooms are spotlessly clean and are compact with a/c. The owners are sometimes friendly and sometimes not.

## Serviced apartments

### $$$$ Parkview Executive Suites
*Av Souphanouvong (near the **Novotel**), T021-250888, www.parkviewexecutive. com.*
Serviced residence complex of 116 units, catering for both long- and short-term stays. Fitness centre, pool, sauna, jacuzzi, tennis court, office space and secretarial support. A bit off the beaten track.

## Restaurants

Lao food stalls can be found at the **Dong Palane Night Market**, on Dong Palane, and the night markets near the corner of Chao Anou and Khoun Boulom Rd. There are various other congregations of stalls and vendors around town, most of which set up shop around 1730 and close by 2100. Be sure to sample Lao ice cream with coconut sticky rice.

The Chinese quarter is around Chao Anou, Heng Boun and Khoun Boulom and is now home to ever more Korean, Vietnamese and Japanese restaurants, though some of the smaller, old Chinese noodle and tea houses remain. This is a lively spot in the evenings. There are a number of noodle shops here, all of which serve a palatable array of vermicelli, *muu daeng* (red pork), duck and chicken.

The Korean-style barbeque, *sindat*, is extremely popular, especially among the younger Lao, as it is a very social event and very cheap.

In terms of Western dining, there are some very fine options in town.

### $$$-$$ Bistro 22
*22 Samsenthai Rd, T055-527286.*
Thoroughly French and thoroughly good. The lamb shank is supremely good. A place to treat yourself.

### $$$-$$ Côte d'Azur
*62/63 Fa Ngum Rd, T021-217252, jmdazur@laotel.com. Daily 1100-1400, 1800-2230. Closed Sun lunch.*
A fine selection of dishes from the south of France, plus excellent wood-fired pizzas and delicious seafood dishes. Recommended.

### $$$-$$ Le Silapa
*17/1 Sihom Rd, T021-219689. Daily 1130-1400, 1800-2200; closes for a month during the rainy season and for a week over Lao New Year.*
Anthony and Frederick provide a fantastic French-inspired menu and intimate atmosphere for fine dining without blowing the budget. The innovative modern meals (such as tilapia with a vegetable marmalade, lime and black olives sauce) would be as at home in the fine dining establishments of New York and London as they are here. Great-value set lunch menu. Part of the profits are donated to disadvantaged families, usually for expensive life-saving surgical procedures. Wine degustation evenings are occasionally held. Highly recommended.

### $$$-$$ Pimenton
*6 Nokeo Khoummane, T021-215506, www.pimentonrestaurant-vte.com.*
This is a truly excellent addition to the culinary scene. A cool, minimalist industrial interior and a mouthwatering menu of steaks with various cuts from various continents all cooked to perfection. Also has some fantastic salads to complement the meat alongside a well-curated wine list and delectable cocktails. Well worth your money.

### $$ Xang Khoo
*68 Pangkham Rd, T021-219314.*
A very charming little restaurant with tiled floor, beamed ceiling and a casually refined air. Offers a fantastic value lunch deal with excellent savoury crêpe and good pasta dishes. The French owner is a great person to ask for other food and drink suggestions. Good value Prosecco and superb coffee from the local **Le Trio** roasters.

### $$-$ Amphone
*Off Setthathirat Rd on Soi Wat Xieng Gneun, T020-7771 1138.*
Offers Lao and international food in a lovely alfresco garden setting just off the main drag.

### $$-$ Aria
*8 Rue François Ngin, T021-222589.*
Divine ice cream, a 16-page wine list, and a long mouthwatering menu of home-made pastas, ravioli, risottos and pizzas with real buffalo mozarella. The best place in town for pizza. The very welcoming owner is an Italian expat.

### $$-$ Chinese Liao-ning Dumpling Restaurant
*Fa Ngum Rd, T021-240811.*
*Daily 1100-2230.*
No-frills Chinese joint that's all about the food. Fabulous steamed or fried

dumplings and a wide range of vegetarian dishes. Not somewhere to linger, but great a good place to get your dumpling hit.

### $$-$ La Terrasse
*55/4 Nokeo Khoummane Rd, T021-218550. Mon-Sat 1100-1400 and 1800-2200.*
Large fail-safe menu offering French, European, Lao and some Moroccan food. Great 1970s-style comfort food, including an excellent 'plat du jour' each day. Good desserts, especially the chocolate mousse, and a wide selection of French wine. Fantastic service. Recommended.

### $$-$ Lao Kitchen
*Heng Boun, T021-254332, www.lao-kitchen.com.*
A must visit, **Lao Kitchen** serves up the best of Lao food in a funky environment. It's best to dine in a group and share dishes including the grilled fish, Lao sausage, and the Luang Prabang stew. Delicious.

### $$-$ Nazim
*39 Fa Ngum Rd, T021-223480. Daily 1000-2230.*
Authentic Indian (north and south) and Halal food, very popular, with indoor and outdoor seating. They have another restaurant in Vang Vieng as well as a branch in Luang Prabang.

### $$-$ Seendat
*Sihom Rd, T021-213855. Daily 1730-2200.*
This restaurant has been going for well over 20 years and is a favourite amongst the older Lao for its good food (*sindat*) and atmosphere. Recommended.

### $ Full Moon Café
*François Ngin Rd, T021-243373. Daily 1000-2300.*

Huge pillows, good lighting and great music make this place very relaxing. Asian fusion cuisine and Western favourites. Fantastic chicken wrap and good Asian tapas. The Ladybug shake is a winner. Also offers a book exchange and free Wi-Fi.

### $ Makphet
*In a new location behind Wat Ong Teu, T021-260587, www.friends-international.org.*
Fantastic Lao non-profit restaurant that helps raise money for street kids and is run by former street kids. Modern Lao cuisine with a twist. Selection of delectable drinks such as the iced hibiscus with lime juice. Beautifully decorated with modern furniture and painting by the kids. Also sells handicrafts and toys produced by the parents from vulnerable communities.

### $ PVO Vietnamese Food
*San Phiavat, T021-214444.*
A firm favourite that's been going strong for years. Full menu of freshly prepared Vietnamese food and also superb baguettes stuffed with your choice of pâté, salad, cheese, coleslaw, vegetables and meats.

### $ Sputnik Burger
*Setthathirath Rd, T030-937 6504.*
It's hard to miss this place thanks to the sawn in half VW Beetle out front. Each half contains a table for two making this a fun place to dine. The interior is cool too and the chefs do a very good line in American burgers and great fries on the side.

### $ Sticky Fingers
*François Ngin Rd, T021-215972. Tue-Sun 1000-2300.*
Not as popular as it once was, this is still a solid choice for a laid-back meal. The

Lao and international menu includes everything from Middle Eastern through to modern Asian. Comfort food, including pasta and burgers, fantastic salads and filling breakfasts. Deliveries available.

### $ Vieng Savanh
*Heng Boun, T021-213990.*
*Open 1000-1000.*
Always busy with long queues forming in the early evening for takeaways, this simple restaurant is not a place to come for the decor – red plastic chairs and kitsch pictures are the order of the day here. The roll-your-own fresh rolls are great fun and delicious. A local institution, but don't expect service with a smile…

## Cafés, patisseries and juice bars

### Joma
*Setthathirat Rd, T021-215265. Mon-Sat 0700-2100.*
Hugely popular. A modern, café with other branches in Hanoi and Luang Prabang. A good selection of tasty pastries, bagels, sandwiches, pastas, salads, pizzas, yoghurts and coffee.

### Le Banneton
*Nokeo Khoumanne Rd, T021-217321, bpricco@laopdr.com.*
Sister café to the Luang Prabang outlet, this classy French café-cum-boulangerie serves a range of excellent cakes, breads and quiches. Very cool a/c interior with cream walls and old black and white prints. A great place to escape the heat.

### Le Croissant d'Or
*Top of Nokeo Khoummane Rd, T021-223741. Daily 0700-2100.*
French bakery with a small selection of pastries including good cheap croissants.

### Le Trio Coffee
*Setthathirat Rd, near Nam Phou, T020-2339 4020, letriocoffee@gmail.com.*
Beautiful, tiny coffee shop. Much of the space is taken up by the **Le Trio** roasting machine which is used by Micka to produce a variety of excellent roasts. Also sells a range of quality coffee paraphernalia. A place for serious coffee drinkers.

### Noy's Fruit Heaven
*Heng Boun, T030-526 2369.*
Fresh fruit is piled high at the entrance to this friendly, relaxed juice bar that can create just about any shake you can think of. Noy is lovely and will go out of her way to make her customers happy. She also serves good breakfasts and lunches. A great spot.

## Bars and clubs

One of the highlights of Vientiane is to stroll along the Mekong watching the sunset, followed by a *Beerlao* at one of the bars on the waterfront.

## Bars

### Baravin
*265 Samsenethai Rd, T021-217700.*
A 'very, very French' wine bar for real wine lovers, it has the air of an undiscovered gem. The decor is wine-heavy, with racks lining the walls. Recommended.

### Chokdee Belgian Beer Bar
*Fa Ngum, T027-263847.*
A huge selection of Belgian brews in this small, cosy bar. Also does good food. Grab a seat at the bar or on the small balcony on the 1st floor. A great addition to the capital's drinking scene

### I-Beam
*Setthathirath Rd, opposite Ong Tue temple, T021-254528. Open 1800-1200.*
A sleek bar with a solid range of cocktails and some good tapas. Live music events on weekends sees the place packed out with a friendly buzz. A nice option after dinner is to go to **I-Beam** for a glass of wine and order a dessert from **Le Silapa** above it (see Restaurants).

### Jazzy Brick
*Setthathirat Rd, next to Le Trio Coffee (see above).*
Very sophisticated, modern den, serving delectable cocktails, with jazz cooing in the background. Decorated with an eclectic range of quirky and kitsch artefacts. Very upmarket and perhaps a bit pretentious.

### Khop Chai Deu
*Setthathirat Rd (near the corner with Nam Phou).*
Probably the most popular bar for tourists in Vientiane. Casual setting and nightly band. Also serves food, but it is better to eat elsewhere.

### Paris Cocktail
*Th Tha Deua, T021-353919.*
This intimate drinking den is so named because the owner and head mixologist, Tony, spent years pouring well-executed cocktails in the French capital. A little bit of a wander from the action, it's worth the stroll, especially for the happy hour from 1700-2000.

### Spirit House
*Follow Fa Ngum Rd past the Mekong River Commission, T021-243795, www.thespirithouselaos.com.*
Happy hour 1700-2000 every night, so it's perfect for a sundowner. Beautiful wooden bar in perfect river location for sunsets. Good range of snacks including burgers and a delicious Cumberland sausage. Some of the best cocktails in the city. Popular with expats. Wi-Fi.

### Wind West
*By traffic lights, Luang Prabang Rd.*
The place to join a fun bunch of locals for drinks and live music. It has an unfortunate name and looks pretty dim from the outside, but it's actually quite fun.

### Wine 95
*Setthathirat Rd (next to Jazzy Brick), T020-5550 2957, wine95vientiane@gmail.com.*
**Wine 95**'s long bar is a great place to pull up a bar stool, sample some excellent wine and chat with fellow patrons; however, it is an extremely pricey place to do so. Upstairs is a refined lounge area with comfortable high-backed chairs. Upmarket.

## Entertainment

### Cinema
**French Cultural Centre**, *Lang Xang Rd, T021-215764, www.if-laos.org.* Shows exhibitions, screens French films and also hosts the **Southeast Asian Film Festival**. Check the *Vientiane Times* for up-to-date details or pick up its quarterly programme.
**Lao-International Trade Exhibition & Convention Center (ITECC)**, *T4 Rd – Ban Phonethane Neua, T021-416002, www.laoitecc.info.* Shows international films.

### Exhibitions
Keep an eye on the *Vientiane Times* for upcoming international performances at the **Lao Cultural Centre** (the building that looks like a big cake opposite the museum).

COPE Visitors' Centre, *National Rehabilitation Centre, Khou Vieng Rd (signposted), www.copelaos.org. Open 0900-1800, free.* **COPE (Cooperative Orthotic and Prosthetic Enterprise)** has set up an interesting exhibition on UXO (unexploded ordnance) and its effects on the people of Laos. It includes a small movie room, photography, UXO and a range of prosthetic limbs (some, which are crafted out of UXO). The exhibition helps raise money for the work of COPE, which includes the production of prosthetic limbs and the rehabilitation of patients.

T'Shop Lai, *Vat Inpeng St (behind Wat Inpeng), T021-223178, www.artisanslao. com. Mon-Sat 0800-2000, Sun 0800-1500.* Exhibitions of crafts made by disadvantaged people, as well as a great shop.

## Karaoke

This could almost be the Lao national sport, and there's nothing like bonding with the locals over a heavy-duty karaoke session. Karaoke places are everywhere – just keep your ears out for the off-key bellowing. Good spots include the **Blue Note** in the Lao Plaza Hotel, www.laoplazahotel.com, or the more expensive, upmarket **Don Chan Palace**, www.donchanpalacelaopdr.com.

## Live music

Bands will perform almost every night at **Khop Chai Deu** and at the **Music House**, on Fa Ngum, T021-212123. The **French Cultural Centre**, on Lang Xang, hosts a variety of musical performances, from local bands through to hip-hop ensembles.

Occasionally, music concerts and beauty pageants are held at the **Lao National Culture Hall**, opposite the National Museum. No official notice is given of forthcoming events but announcements sometimes appear in the *Vientiane Times* and large banners will flank the building.

## Traditional dance

**Lao National Theatre**, *Manthathurath Rd, T020-550 1773.* Daily shows of traditional Lao dancing. Tickets available at the theatre. Performances are less regular in low season.

Festivals

**1st weekend in Apr  Pi Mai** (Lao New Year) is celebrated with a 3-day festival and a huge water fight. It is advisable to put your wallet in a plastic bag and invest in a turbo water pistol. There are numerous *bacis* (good luck celebrations) and the traditional greeting at this time of year is 'Sok Dee Pi Mai' (good luck for the New Year).

**Sep/Oct  Boun Ok Phansa** is a beautiful event on the night of the full moon at the end of Buddhist Lent. Candles are lit in all homes and candlelit processions take place around the city's wats and through the streets. Then, thousands of banana-leaf boats holding flowers, tapers and candles are floated out onto the river. The boats represent your bad luck floating away.

**Sep/Oct  Boun Souang Heua**, the boat-racing festival, is held towards the end of the rainy season. Boat races (*souang heua*) take place with 50 or so men in each boat; they power up the river in perfect unison. An exuberant event, with plenty of merrymaking.

**12 Oct  Freedom of the French Day** is a public holiday.

**Nov (date varies each year)  Boun That Luang** is celebrated in all of Vientiane's

## Living in sinh

A lovely experience is to wear the *sinh*, the Lao traditional banded sarong. It isn't at all necessary to wear one but the Lao love the fact that you are taking an interest in their culture and are likely to shower you with compliments. If you are attending a wedding, funeral or plan to visit a government office, it is a sign of respect to wear one. Depending on the fabric, a *sinh* can be whipped up in most markets in a day but if you are travelling to an area famed for its weaving such as Xam Neua all the better.

*thats* but most notably at That Luang (the national shrine). Originally a ceremony in which nobles swore allegiance to the king and constitution, it amazingly survived the Communist era. On the festival's most important day, **Thak Baat**, thousands of Lao people pour into the temple at 0600 and again at 1700 to pay homage. Monks travel from across the country to collect offerings and alms from the pilgrims. It is a really beautiful ceremony, with monks chanting and thousands of people praying. Women who attend should invest in a traditional *sinh* (traditional skirt). A week-long carnival surrounds the festival with fireworks, music and dancing. Recommended.

## Shopping

### Books

**Book Café**, *53/2 Heng Boun Rd, T020-689 3741*. Owned and operated by the expat author of *Laos, the Lao... and you* (a recommended read), this small shop has a good range of fiction and books on SEA. Operates a book swap scheme.
**Monument Books**, *124/1 Nokeo Khoummane Rd, T021-243708, www.monument-books.com*. The largest selection of new books in Vientiane, including Southeast Asian speciality books as well as coffee-table books.

A good place to pick up Lao-language children's books to distribute to villages on your travels.
**Vientiane Book Center**, *32/05 Fa Ngum Rd, T021-212031, vientianebookcenter@yahoo.com*. A limited but interesting selection of used books in a multitude of languages.

### Clothing, fashion, and textiles

Every hue and design is available in the **Talaat Sao** (Morning Market). For cheaper (but still good quality) fabric, pop across the road to **Talaat Kudin**; the fabric section is in the covered area at the back of the market. A *sinh*, the traditional Lao skirt, can be made within the day – just pick the length of fabric and the patterned band for the bottom of the skirt.
**Cama Craft**, *Mixay Rd, T021-501271*. Handmade clothes in Hmong styles.
**Couleur d'Asie Concept Store**, *Nokeo Khoummane Rd, T020-2815 7690*. Sells clothes, jewellery, accessories, furniture and decorations designed by the owner, Viviane Althey Inthavong. Also has a space for exhibitions and a good café-cum-restaurant.
**Lao Cotton**, *Luang Prabang Rd, out towards Wattay Airport, approximately 400 m on right from Novotel, T021-215840*. Good range of material, shirts and

## The art of ikat

In the handicraft shops in Vientiane, it is possible to buy distinctively patterned cotton and silk *ikat*. A technique of patterning cloth characteristic of Southeast Asia, *ikat* is produced all over the region, from the hills of Myanmar (Burma) to the islands of Eastern Indonesia. The word comes from the Malay word *mengikat*, which means to bind or tie. Very simply, bundles of warp or weft fibres (or, in one Balinese case, both) are tied with material or fibre (or more often plastic string these days), so that they resist the action of the dye. Hence the technique's name: resist dyeing. By dyeing, re-tying and dyeing again through a number of cycles it is possible to build up complex patterns.

This initial pre-weaving process can take anything from two to 10 days, depending on the complexity of the design. *Ikat* is distinguishable by the bleeding of the dye which inevitably occurs no matter how carefully the threads are tied; this gives the finished cloth a blurred finish. The earliest *ikats* date from the 14th-15th centuries.

To prepare the cloth for dyeing, the warp or weft is strung tight on a frame. Individual threads, or groups of threads, are then tied together with fibre and leaves. In some areas wax is then smeared on top to help in the resist process. The main colour is usually dyed first, secondary colours later. With complex patterns (which are done from memory; plans are only required for new designs) and using natural dyes, it may take up to six months to produce a piece of cloth. Today, the pressures of the marketplace mean that it is more likely that cloth is produced using chemical dyes (which need only one short soaking, not multiple long ones – six hours or so – that some natural dyes require), and motifs have generally become larger and less complex. Traditionally, warp *ikat* used cotton while weft *ikat* used silk. Silk in many areas has given way to cotton, and cotton sometimes to synthetic yarns.

handbags; ask to have a look at the looms. Another branch on Samsenthai.
**Lao Textiles by Carol Cassidy,** *Nokeo Khoummane Rd, T021-212123, www.laotextiles.com. Mon-Fri 0800-1200 and 1400-1700, Sat 0800-1200.* Exquisite silk fabrics, including ikat and traditional Lao designs, made by an American in a beautifully renovated colonial property. Dyeing, spinning, designing and weaving all done on site. It's pricey, but many of the weavings are real works of art; custom-made pieces available on request.

**Laoderm,** *Sasmenthai Rd, T021-254769. Mon-Sat 0800-1800.* Boutique selling original designs. Shirts, blouses and dresses weaved from linen, cotton and silk in muted tones
**Sao Ban,** *Chao Anou Rd, T025-5100034, www.saobancrafts.com.* A wonderful range of well-designed good-quality cotton and silk products as well as bags, bamboo ware and recycled bomb products. This is a very easy place to spend money, not only because of the excellent stock, but because it is a member of PADETC, a Lao NGO that

integrates socially sustainable programs in education, agriculture, micro-finance, handcrafts and community leadership. Highly recommended.

**Satri Laos**, *Setthathirat, T021-244387, www.satrilao.laopdr.com*. If Vientiane had a Harrods this would be it. Upmarket boutique retailing everything from jewellery, shoes, clothes, furnishings and homeware. Beautiful stuff, though most is from China, Vietnam and Thailand.

## Galleries

The main shops are along Setthathirat, Samsenthai and Pang Kham. The **Morning Market (Talaat Sao)** is also worth a browse, with artefacts, such as appliquéd panels, decorated hats and sashes, basketwork both old and new, small and large wooden tobacco boxes, sticky-rice lidded baskets, axe pillows, embroidered cushions and a wide range of silverwork. The likelihood of finding authentic antiques is pretty low. **Talaat Kudin** offers cheaper artefacts and silks but not as great a selection as Talaat Sao.

**Camacraft**, *Nokeo Khoummane, T020-556 1660*. NGO which retails handicrafts produced by the Hmong people. Embroidery, mulberry tea, Lao silk.

**Indochine Handicrafts**, *Samsenthai Rd next to the big wine barrel, T021-263619, maiphone@hotmail.com*. Larger size collectibles, not really suitable for the suitcase shopper.

**MaiChan Fine Arts & Handicrafts**, *Samsenthai Rd, T021-263619, www. maichanhandicraft.wordpress.com*. This is a neat little shop with lots of treasures including a wide range of scarves and hangings.

**Oot-Ni Art Gallery**, *Samsenthai Rd, T021-214359, www.ootni-yenkham.laopdr. com*. This is an Aladdin's Cave of serious objets d'art.

**T'Shop Lai**, *Wat Inpeng Soi, www. laococo.com*. As well as very high quality handicrafts, this fantastic and delightfully scented shop sells wonderful furniture as well as shampoos, face creams and the like, all of which are 100% natural and organic.

## Jewellery and silverware

Many of the stones sold in Vientiane are of dubious quality, but silver and gold are more reliable. Gold can be good value. Silver is cheap but not necessarily pure silver; nevertheless, the selection is interesting, with amusing animals, decorated boxes, old coins, earrings and silver belts. There's a wide selection in the **Morning Market (Talaat Sao)**. Silver, gold and gem shops on Samsenthai are concentrated along the stretch opposite the **Asian Pavilion Hotel**; there are also gold shops further west towards the Chinese quarter. There are also a couple of shops around the fountain selling interesting designs and also wallet-friendly costume jewellery.

**Sao Ban**, *Chao Anou Rd, T025-510 0034, www.saobancrafts.com*. Sells a great range of silver jewellery and is a member of PADETC, a Lao NGO that integrates socially sustainable programs in education, agriculture, micro-finance, handcrafts and community leadership.

## Markets and shopping malls

Vientiane has several excellent markets. **Morning Market (Talaat Sao)**, *off Lane Xang Av*. Busiest in the mornings (from around 1000), but operates all day. There are money exchanges here (quite a good rate), and a good selection of foodstalls selling Western food, soft drinks and ice-cream sundaes. It sells imported Thai goods, electrical appliances, watches, DVDs and CDs,

stationery, cosmetics, a selection of handicrafts (see above), an enormous choice of Lao fabrics, and upstairs there is a large clothing section, silverware, gems and gold and a few handicraft stalls. There is also a modern shopping-centre addition to the Morning Market. It is pricier and less popular, and stocked with mostly Thai products sold in baht. On the 2nd floor, there is a reasonable food court. Next to it, the most enormous shopping mall should be open by the time you read this.
**Talaat Kudin**, *on the other side of the bus stop*. This is a ramshackle market with an interesting produce section. It offers many of the same handicrafts and silks as the Morning Market but is a lot cheaper.
**Talaat Thong Khoun Khum**, *on the corner of Khoun Khum and Dong Miang roads*. The largest produce market. It is sometimes known as the **Evening Market** but it's busiest in the mornings.
**Talat Sao Mall**, *www.talatsaomall.com*. 8 storeys of shops, restaurants, cinema, gym, disco and hotel.

Other markets include **Talaat That Luang**, south of the parade ground; **Talaat Dong Palane**, Dong Palane Rd (there's a sign near the temple, pointing down a lane, as the bulk of the market has been moved away from the main road); and **Talaat Chin**, which is good for electrical goods, CDs, DVDs, toys, clothes, furniture and cheap imported tat.

## What to do

### Aerobics
Open-air aerobics kicks off every morning in the park along the Mekong.

### Cooking
**Villa Lao**, *see Where to stay, T021-242292*. Cooking classes, covering all aspects of meal preparation, from purchasing the ingredients to eating the meal.

### Cycling
Bicycles can be hired from several places in town, see Transport, page 57. A good outing is to cycle downstream along the banks of the Mekong. Cycle south on Tha Deua Rd until Km 5 (watch the traffic) and then turn right down one of the tracks towards the river. A path, suitable for bicycles, follows the river from Km 4.5. There are monasteries and drink sellers en route.

### Football
Regular national league matches are held at the National Stadium in the centre of town.

### Kickboxing
Held intermittently at the Soxai Boxing Stadium and more regularly about 200 m past the old circus in Baan Dong Paleb.

### Language courses
**Vientiane College**, *Singha Rd, T021-414873, www.vientianecollege.com*.

### Massage, saunas and spas
The best massage in town is given by the blind masseuses in a street off Samsenthai Rd, 2 blocks down from **Simuang Minimart** (across from Wat Simuang). There are 2 blind masseuse businesses side-by-side and both are fantastic: **Traditional Clinic**, T020-5565 9177, and **Porm Clinic**, T020-562 7633 (no English spoken). They are indicated by blue signs off both Khou Vieng and Samsenthai roads. Recommended.

Mandarina, *74 Pang Kham, T021-218703.* A range of upmarket treatments costing US$5-30. Massages, facials, body scrubs, mini-saunas, oils and a jacuzzi.

Oasis Spa Massage & Beauty, *18/01 François Ngin Rd, T021-243579.* Provides very good, strong massages (*keng –* means strong in Lao).

Papaya Spa, *opposite Wat Xieng Veh, T020-561 0565, www.papayaspa.com.* **Papaya** is a favourite with locals looking to spoil themselves. You feel more relaxed the minute you walk through the gates. Offers massage, sauna, facials. Lovely gardens. Recommended.

Wat Sok Paluang, *Sok Paluang.* Peaceful leafy setting in the compound of Wat Sok Paluang. Herbal sauna, followed by herb tea (2000 kip) and massage by 2 young male masseurs (4000 kip); very relaxing but some women have reported groping. Vipassana meditation is held every Sat 1600-1730, free, T021-216214. To get there, walk through the small stupas to the left of the wat; the sauna is a rickety building on stilts on the right-hand side, recognizable by the blackened store underneath.

## Rugby

Lao Rugby, *www.laorugby.com.* Teaches rugby in schools and also works with street children and a drugs rehabilitation centre. Details of games and training sessions can be found on their website.

## Sports clubs and fitness centres

Several hotels in town permit non-residents to use their fitness facilities for a small fee, including the **Tai Pan** (rather basic), **Lao Plaza**, **Lane Xang**, **Don Chan** and **Novotel**. See Where to stay.

Australia Club Recreation Centre, *Km 3, Tha Deua Rd, T021-314921.* A beautiful setting, with one of the nicest pools in Vientiane. It's a lovely place for a swim followed by a glass of wine as the sun sets. Also has a small restaurant and a squash court. Short-term membership available but cheaper if you get a member to sign you in; loiter around some of the expat drinking holes and you might find someone willing. A tuk-tuk to the centre is 20,000-30,000 kip.

Sengdara, *77/5 Phonthan Rd, T021-414058. Daily 0500-2200.* Modern fitness centre with gym, pool and sauna. US$5 for use of all the facilities for a day, massage extra.

## Swimming

The Australia Club Recreation Centre *(see Sports clubs, above).* Has a fantastic saltwater pool with superb Mekong views. Several hotels in town permit non-residents to use their fitness facilities for a small fee.

Lane Xang Hotel, *Pangkham Rd.* Not the loveliest of settings but secluded and conveniently located. 30,000 kip.

Lao Plaza Hotel, *63 Samsenthai Rd.* A very clean pool on the 3rd floor, with a great view of the city, open to non-guests for US$5.

Nongchan Water Park, *Khou Vieng St T021-219386. Open 1000-1800.* 30,000 kip, children 20,000 kip.

Settha Palace Hotel, *6 Pang Kham Rd (see Where to stay).* Lovely royal blue pool with matching sun loungers in landscaped gardens. The most luxurious (with a hefty US$7.50 entrance fee).

Sokpaluang Swimming Pool, *Sok Paluang Rd, south of centre. Daily 0800-2000.* Good-sized pool for serious swimmers, paddling pool for children, costumes for hire, restaurant and bar.

Tai-Pan Hotel , *2-12 François Ngin Rd.* Open to non-guests. Rather basic.

**Vientiane Swimming Pool**, *close to the* **Settha Palace Hotel**. *Daily 0800-2000. 10,000 kip.* This is the 1950s retro trip with communist-red decor.

### Tennis

**Vientiane Parkview**, *Luang Prabang Rd, T021-250888.* Expensive but easily the best court in town. Book in advance. **Vientiane Tennis Club**, *National Stadium.* Equipment for hire. Floodlit courts stay open until 2100. Bar.

### Ten-pin bowling

Bowling is very popular, particularly as the bars in the bowling centres are often the only ones open after curfew. The **Lao Bowling Center**, behind the Lao Plaza Hotel, T021-218661, is good value and offers food and Beerlao late into the night.

### Thak Baat

Every morning at daybreak (0530-0600) monks flood out of the city's temples, creating a swirl of orange on the streets, as they collect alms. It is truly beautiful to see the misty, grey streets come alive with the robe-clad monks. Foreigners are more than welcome to participate and it feels much less intrusive doing so here than in Luang Prabang. Just buy some sticky rice or other food from the vendors and kneel beside others.

### Tour operators

For general travel information on getting to Phou Khao Khouay, visit the **National Tourism Authority** (see page 43). Most tour operators will include 'eco' somewhere in their name but this doesn't necessarily mean very much. **Asian Trails Laos**, *Unit 10, Ban Khounta Thong, Sikhottabong District, T021-263936,* *www.asiantrails.travel.* A Southeast Asian specialist and very professional outfit. **Exotissimo**, *6/44 Pang Kham Rd, T021-241861, www.exotissimo.com.* Various tours and travel services. Excellent but pricey. **Green Discovery**, *Setthathirat Rd, next to Kop Chai Deu, T021-223022, www.green discoverylaos.com.* Specializes in ecotours and adventure travel. Recommended.

### Yoga

**Vientiane Yoga Studio**, *Sokpaluang Rd, Soi 1 (1st soi on the right after you turn onto Sokpaluang from Kuvieng Rd), www. vientianeyoga.weebly.com.* Various style of yoga and pilates classes, plus dance.

## Transport

### Air

See Getting there, page 329.
**Wattay International Airport**, T021-512012, is 6 km west of town and has international connections with **Cambodia**, **Vietnam** and **Thailand**. It is also the hub of Laos' domestic airline system, and to travel from the north to the south or vice versa it is often necessary to change planes here. Both international and domestic terminals have restaurants, telephone, taxi service and information booth. The international terminal also has ATMs, a post office, hotel desk and internet (upstairs).

**Airline offices** **Lao Airlines**, 2 Pang Kham Rd, T021-212054, www.laoairlines. com, also at Wattay Airport; T021-212051. Mon-Fri 0800-1200 and 1300-1600, Sat 0800-1200. **Thai Airways**, Head Office, M and N Building Luang Prabang Rd, not far past the Novotel, T021-222527, www.thaiairways.com, Mon-Fri 0830-1200, 1300-1500, Sat 0830-1200; and at Wattay Airport, T021-512024. **Vietnam**

**Airlines**, Lao Plaza Hotel, T021-217562, www.vietnamairlines.com.vn, Mon-Fri 0800-1200, 1330-1630.

## Bicycle and motorbike

For those energetic enough in the hot season, bikes are the best way to get around town. Many hotels and guesthouses have bikes available; there are also bike hire shops dotted around town. Expect to pay about 20,000 kip per day. Markets, post offices and government offices usually have 'bike parks' where it is advisable to leave your bike. A small minding fee is charged.

**First One Motorbikes**, Rue François Ngin, T020-555 2899, k.naphaivong@ gmail.com. For choice and experience, this place is hard to beat. Run since 2000 by avid biker, Mr Joy, here you can rent small automatic or semi-automatic bikes, 400cc choppers and 250cc off road machines. Prices range from about 80,000 kip up to US$50 or more.

## Bus

Buses service outlying areas, but not the city itself. These buses run from the station next to the Talaat Sao/Central bus station, next to the Morning Market (see below).

Almost every guesthouse in town can sell you private bus tickets to the most of the following destinations and they clearly display times and prices on boards outside. Many will also offer a pick-up service direct from your hotel. However, if you want to go your own way, you'll need to venture out to one of the 3 main public bus terminals: Southern, Northern and Central bus station (next to the Morning Market).

VIP buses are very comfortable allowing you to sleep during the trip.

For night journeys, book a double if you don't want to be stuck sleeping next to a stranger. Robberies have been reported on the night buses so keep valuables secure.

**Southern bus station** Route 13, 9 km north of the city centre (T021-740521). Public buses depart daily for destinations in southern Laos. Prices change fairly regularly, but they are clearly posted on official boards in the stations. The southern bus station has a range of stores and a pharmacy. To **Paksan** (150 km), 5 per day throughout the morning, 1½ hrs. To **Lak Sao** (for the Vietnamese border, 335 km), 8 hrs, 3 morning services. To **Thakhek** (360 km), 3 daily, 5-6 hrs plus a VIP bus in the early afternoon. To **Savannakhet** (483 km), 8 daily in the early morning, 8 hrs. To **Pakse** (736 km), 8 daily, 13 hrs; there are also overnight express buses to Pakse, 11 hrs. Buses to **Hanoi** also run from here, but it is far easier to book these from a guesthouse.

**Northern bus station** Route 2, towards the airport 3.5 km from the centre of town, T021-261905. Northbound buses leave regularly and have a/c. For the more popular routes, there are also VIP buses. To **Luang Prabang** (400 km), standard buses, 8 daily, 10 hrs; VIP buses 2 daily in the early morning, 8 hrs. To **Udomxai** (550 km), standard buses 2 daily, 13 hrs; 1 VIP bus in the afternoon. To **Luang Namtha** (648 km), daily, 19 hrs. To **Phongsali** (815 km), daily, 26 hrs. To **Houei Xai** (895 km), daily, 25-30 hrs. To **Sayaboury** (485 km), 2 daily, 12-15 hrs. To **Xam Neua** (850 km), 3 per day, 30 hrs. To **Phonsavanh** (365 km), 4-5 per day, 12+ hrs.

### Central (Talaat Sao) bus station

Across the road from Talaat Sao (Morning Market), in front of Talaat Kudin, on the eastern edge of the city centre, T021-216507. Destinations, distances and fares are listed on a board in English and Lao. Most departures are in the morning and can leave as early as 0400, so travellers on a tight schedule should check departure times the night before. There is a useful map at the station, and bus times and fares are listed in Lao and English. Staff at the ticket office speak only a little English so ask in the planning office if you need help. The times listed below depend on the weather and number of stops.

To the **Southern bus station**, 0600-1800 every 30 mins. To the **Northern bus station**, catch the Nongping bus (5 daily) and ask to get off at '*Thay Song*'. To **Wattay Airport**, every 30 mins 0640-1800. To **Vang Vieng**, 5 daily, 3½ hrs.

Numerous buses criss-cross the province; most aren't very useful for tourists. To **Barksarp**, 6 daily. To **Ban Keun** (via Ban Thabok for Phou Khao Khouay), 9 daily. To **Xieng Khuan**, bus No 14 every 15 mins, 1 hr. To **Nam Ngum**, daily, 3 hrs. To **Vang Vieng**, 3 daily, but the VIP buses and minivans are preferable – this is for those who are flat broke only. To **Thakek**, 3 daily. To **Savannakhet**, 3 daily. To the **Friendship Bridge** (Lao side), every 15 mins. To **Nong Khai** (Thai side of the Friendship Bridge), 6 daily 0730-1800, about 1 hr including immigration. To **Udon Thani**, 6 daily 0800-1800.

### Car

**Avis**, Settathirath Rd, opposite Rue François Ngin, T021-223867, www.avis.la. Everything from a compact to a 4WD. Drivers can be hired and airport pick-up/drop-off is available. Operates in all areas of Laos PDR and cross border into Thailand, Vietnam and China.

### Train

Trains cross the Friendship Bridge into Thailand and run to **Bangkok**, thus avoiding the need to change trains to cross the border (though you will still need to change trains in Nong Khai). See box on the Friendship Bridge border, page 61.

### Tuk-tuks

Tuk-tuks usually congregate around tourist destinations: **Nam Phou**, **Talaat Sao** and **Talaat Kudin**. Tuk-tuks can be chartered for longer out-of-town trips or for short journeys of 2-3 km within the city. There are now fares to the most popular destinations posted clearly at the main pick-up points so there is no need to haggle.

There are also shared tuk-tuks, on regular routes on main streets. For shared tuk-tuks to the **Friendship Bridge**, see border crossing box, page 61, although if you buy your ticket from an agent, a pick-up is invariably included and takes the hassle out of the journey.

# Around
## Vientiane

There are plenty of short trips from Vientiane, ranging from the popular backpacker hotspot of Vang Vieng, through to the stunning Phou Khao Khouay National Protected Area. Vang Vieng has become very popular with action sports enthusiasts, with kayaking, caving and rock climbing all on offer. For years the Nam Ngum dam has been a popular weekend escape for Vientiane residents and is starting to gain appeal with the tourist set.

## South of the city
*beer factory, a 'white' elephant and a whimsical sculpture park*

### Along Thanon Tha Deua (Route 2)
*Bus No 14 from the Talaat Sao bus station follows Route 2 southeast towards Tha Deua, the Friendship Bridge, to Thailand and Xieng Khuan (Garden of the Buddhas). For immigration formalities at the bridge, see border crossings box, page 61.*

Although it isn't officially recognized as a tourist sight, the **Beerlao factory** ① *Km 12, Thanon Tha Deua (Route 2), T021-812000, www.beer-lao.com, free tours 0900-1130, 1300-1600,* is surprisingly interesting and worth the trip. Visitors are warmly welcomed then taken on a mini tour and plied with the award-winning ale. Beerlao has become something of a national symbol and the locals swell with pride if you share their enthusiasm for their amber liquid.

Two kilometres further on is **555 Park (Saam Haa Yai)**. These extensive but rather uninspiring gardens encompass Chinese pavilions, a lake and a small zoo. In the 1980s, a white elephant was captured in southern Laos. Revered for its religious significance, it had to be painted to ensure it was not stolen on the way to the capital. It was originally kept in the Saam Haa gardens but has since been moved to the zoo, where it is paraded in front of the crowds during the **That Luang** festival. White elephants are not really white, but pink.

### Xieng Khuan (Garden of the Buddhas)
*Route 2 (25 km south of Vientiane); daily 0800-1630; admission 5000 kip, plus 5000 kip for cameras. Food vendors sell drinks and snacks. Getting there: 1 hr by bus No 14 from the Central (Talaat Sao) bus station. Alternatively, charter a tuk-tuk; hire a private*

*vehicle; or, better yet, take a motorbike or cycle (the road follows the river and is reasonably flat).*

Otherwise known as the Garden of the Buddhas or Buddha Park, Xieng Khuan is a few kilometres beyond Tha Deua on Route 2, close to the border with Thailand. It has been described as a Laotian Tiger Balm Gardens, with reinforced concrete Buddhist and Hindu sculptures of Vishnu, Buddha, Siva and other assorted deities and near-deities. There's also a bulbous-style building with three levels containing smaller sculptures of the same gods.

The garden was built in the late 1950s by a priest/monk/guru/sage/artist called Luang Pu Bunleua Sulihat, who studied under a Hindu *rishi* in Vietnam and then combined the Buddhist and Hindu philosophies in his own view of the world. He left Laos because his anti-Communist views were incompatible with the ideology of the Pathet Lao (or perhaps because he was just too weird) and settled across the Mekong near the Thai town of Nong Khai, where he built a bizarre concrete theme park for religious schizophrenics, called Wat Khaek. With Luang Pu's forced departure from Laos, his garden came under state control and it is now a public park. Luang Pu died in 1996 at the age of 72 but remains popular in Laos and northeastern Thailand.

## East of the city
*history museum, nature retreat and a reclining Buddha*

### Kaysone Phomvihane Museum
*Km 6, Route 13 south, T021-911215. Take a bus from Vientiane's Central (Talaat Sao) bus station or cycle. 5000 kip. Camera 10,000 kip. Daily 0800-1600.*

This museum, mostly visited by schoolchildren, commemorates the exploits and leadership of the Lao PDR equivalent of Vietnam's Ho Chi Minh. Kaysone was the critical character in Laos' recent history: revolutionary fighter, inspired leader and statesman (see page 286).

### Ban Pako → *Colour map 2, B3.*
*Take the Paksan bus from Vientiane's Central (Talaat Sao) bus station and get off at Som Sa Mai (1 hr). From here, take a boat to Lao Pako (25 mins). Alternatively, the route makes a great trail bike ride; the last 20 km are on dirt and can get quite wild, especially in the wet season.*

Ban Pako lies 50 km northeast of Vientiane, on the banks of the Nam Ngum River (off Route 13). There is a quiet and secluded 'nature lodge' here, established by an Austrian couple a few years back. It's a lovely place to retreat to, for swimming, boating, trekking, rafting, walks to local Lao villages and relaxing in the herbal sauna.

### Tha Pabat Phonsanh
About 80 km down the Paksan road, is Pabat Phonsanh, built on a plug of volcanic rock in the middle of a coconut plantation. It is known for its footprint of the Buddha and has a statue of a reclining Buddha (*mudra*) rarely seen in Laos.

# BORDER CROSSING

## Friendship Bridge (Thailand)

The bridge is 20 km southeast of Vientiane; catch the Thai–Lao International bus from the Talaat Sao terminal, 90 minutes at 0730, 0930, 1240, 1430, 1530 and 1800 to Nong Khai bus station. Or take one of the Friendship Bridge tuk-tuks from town. The border is open daily 0730-1800. Shuttle minibuses cross the bridge every 20 minutes, stopping at the Thai and Lao immigration posts, where an overtime fee is charged at weekends and on public holidays.

There are good facilities at the Lao border, including a telephone box, a couple of duty-free shops, snack stalls and a post office. Allow up to 1½ hours to get to the bridge and through formalities on the Lao side. The paperwork is pretty swift, unless you are arriving in Lao and require a visa or are leaving the country and have overstayed your visa.

Coming into Laos, you will require a passport-sized photograph and the name of your guesthouse or hotel. There is a sign indicating the price of transport into Vientiane.

The Thai side is über-efficient but not nearly as friendly. Tuk-tuks wait to take people to Nong Khai (10 minutes); Udon Thani is another hour further on.

If you get stuck in Nong Khai, **Mut Mee Guesthouse** (www.mutmee.com) is recommended. From Udon Thani you can get to Bangkok easily by budget airline; AirAsia and Nok Air fly several times daily.

The alternative to all this is to take a train from the Thanaleng Station on the Lao side into Thailand. The station has its own visa control point.

## Listings East of the city

### Where to stay

#### Ban Pako

**$$ Ban Lao Pako Eco Lodge**
*On the banks of Nam Ngum River, 50 km east of Vientiane, T030-965 8150, www. banpako.net.*

Accommodation is in a Lao-style longhouse or in single bungalows in a beautiful spot overlooking the river. There is also a wooden herbal sauna and treks are on offer. The restaurant serves good Lao and European food. Breakfast included for the bungalow rooms. A great little weekend getaway.

## Phou Khao Khouay National Protected Area
### one of Laos' most beautiful and accessible nature reserves

★Phou Khao Khouay (pronounced *poo cow kway*) National Protected Area is one of Laos' premier national protected areas. The area extends across 2000 sq km and incorporates an attractive sandstone mountain range. It is crossed by three large rivers, smaller tributaries and two waterfalls at Tad Leuk and Tad Sae, which weave their way into the Ang Nam Leuk reservoir, a stunning man-made dam and lake on the outskirts of the park. Within the protected area is an array of wildlife, including wild elephants, gibbons, tigers, clouded leopards and Asiatic black bears.

### Visiting the park

The park is a two-hour drive northeast from Vientiane, along Route 13 South; a good vehicle is recommended. To get to Ban Na you need to stop at Tha Pabat Phonsanh, 80 km northeast of Vientiane (see above); the village is a further 2 km from here. For Ban Hat Khai, 100 km northeast of Vientiane, continue on Route 13 to Ban Thabok, where a *songthaew* can usually take you the extra 7 km to the village. Buses to Paksan from the Central (Talaat Sao) bus station and That Luang market in Vientiane stop at Thabok. Most people, however, take a tour.

Although treks can be organized through local guide offices in **Ban Na** ⓘ *T020-2220 8286/62*, and **Ban Hat Khai** ⓘ *T020-2224 0303*, advance notice is required so it's advisable to go with a tour operator from Vientiane instead. Visit www.trekkingcentrallaos.com and contact the **National Tourism Authority** in Vientiane (see page 43) for advice or **Green Discovery Laos** (see page 74).

It costs 2000 kip per person to enter the park and 5000 kip per vehicle.

### Tad Leuk

Accessed by dirt track (one hour) or boat from Ban Thabok (the waterfall sign is easily seen on the left), these are the most visited falls in the park and contain several large undulating tiers. It is a good picnic spot, with swimming possible in the lake behind the waterfall although it is sometimes too rough. Tad Leuk has a visitor information centre which has toilets and washing facilities and also rents camping equipment. There's also a good little snack stand on a platform, offering a view of the falls. Mr Khamsavay Kingmanolath, the supervisor at Tad Leuk, organizes good-value treks from Tad Leuk (US$7-10 per group).

### Tad Sae

These are the most stunning falls in the park but don't boast the facilities of Tad Leuk. The falls tumble down seven tiers, flowing for about 800 m before plummeting 40 m into a magnificent river gorge. There is a small, clear pool that's perfect for swimming. To get to the waterfall, take the road from Ban Thabok and turn right at the fork (it's signposted).

## Ban Na

These days the principal draw-cards for Phou Khao Khouay are the organized treks and the elephant observation tower, both of which are based on the small farming village of Ban Na (meaning 'rice field'). The village's sugar cane plantations and river salt deposits attract a herd of wild elephants (around 30), which have, in the past, destroyed the villagers' homes and even killed a resident. This has limited the villagers' ability to undertake normal tasks, such as collecting bamboo. To help compensate, the village, in conjunction with some NGOs, has constructed an **Elephant Observation Tower** 4 km from Ban Na and has started running trekking tours to see the elephants in their natural habitat.

It is possible to stay overnight at the elephant tower, to try and catch a glimpse of the giant pachyderms lapping up salt from the nearby salt lick in the early evening. One- to three-day treks through the national park cross waterfalls, pass through pristine jungle and, with luck, offer the opportunity to hear or spot the odd wild elephant. This is an important ecotour that contributes to the livelihood of the Ban Na villagers and helps conserve the elephant population.

Advance notice is required, so it's advisable to book with a tour operator in Vientiane (see page 56). If you are travelling independently you will need to organize permits, trekking and accommodation with the village directly. To do this, visit www.trekkingcentrallaos.com and contact the **National Tourism Authority** in Vientiane (see page 43) or **Green Discovery Laos** (see page 74). Visitors will need to bring drinking water and basic snacks. Do not try to feed the elephants, they are very dangerous.

## Ban Hatkhai

This village is home to 90 families from the Lao Loum and Lao Soung ethnic groups and is a starting point for organized treks crossing the Nam Mang River and the Phay Xay cliffs. Most treks take in the **Tad Sae falls**. Homestay accommodation is available in the village.

## Listings Phou Khao Khouay National Protected Area

### Where to stay

The visitor centre at Tad Leuk rents out tents, mattresses, mosquito nets and sleeping bags. Toilets and washing facilities are on site. It is also possible to organize a homestay in one of the surrounding villages or stay overnight in the **Elephant Observation Tower** near Ban Na. Ban Hatkai and Ban Na also offer homestay accommodation.

### What to do

Trips are organized by the **National Tourism Administration** in Vientiane, opposite the French Language Centre, near the Morning Market, T021-212251, www.trekkingcentrallaos.com. This centre also has an exhibition about Phou Khaou Khouay.

a couple of stop-offs on the way to Vang Vieng

### Dane Soung

*Route 13 North, turn left at the 22 km mark towards Ban Houa Khoua. Dane Soung is 6 km down the track and is only accessible in the dry season.*

About 30 km from Vientiane, on the Luang Prabang road, is Dane Soung, an area where large fallen rocks have formed a cave. There are Buddhist sculptures inside and a footprint of the Buddha on the left of the entrance. Too steep for tuk-tuks, it tends to be only private cars and motorbikes that make it here.

### Vangxang

*80 km north of Vientiane on Route 13.*

Vangxang, which means elephant drinking hole, is a lovely place to stop on the way to Vang Vieng. Worth a look are the amazing Buddha sculptures carved into a cliff face 2 km from the **Vang Xang Resort**. The 10 Angkorian relief sculptures are believed to be more than 500 years old, with two of them hovering at about 4 m. Aside from the carvings, walks through the jungle are the only diversion.

### Nam Lik Forest

Near Phonehong, 17 km from Hin-Heup and 10 km from Route 13 is **Green Discovery's Jungle Fly**, a new series of ziplines up to 180 m long and 37 m high in the Nam Lik Forest. Contact www.greendiscoverylaos.com for more information and to find out about their kayak and camping combination tours.

## Listings North of the city

### Where to stay

**Vangxang**

**$ Vang Xang Resort**
*13 Neau Rd, Ban Phonengerun, T023-21526, T020-545 4076 (mob).*

The resort has cute basic cottage-style bungalows, with hot water. Lao restaurant and man-made lake. A popular stop for cycle tourists, but not somewhere to go out of your way for.

## Nam Ngum dam and reservoir

a popular weekend escape with boating and a local market

The Nam Ngum dam, 90 km from Vientiane, is the pride of Laos. It provides electricity for much of the country and its energy exports to Thailand are Laos' second biggest foreign exchange earner. Dotted with hundreds of small islands, the lake is very picturesque.

# BACKGROUND
## Nam Ngum dam and reservoir

Many people believe that the dam was built with Soviet aid following the victory of the Communists in 1975. In fact, construction began in the 1960s under the auspices of the Mekong Development Committee and was funded by the World Bank and Western nations. Indeed a large slice of the country's aid budget went into the construction of the dam, which was officially opened in the early 1970s. After the Communist victory, two of the lake's islands became open prisons for the most 'culturally polluted' of Vientiane's population. Two thousand drug addicts, prostitutes and other 'low lifers' were rounded up and shipped out here. One island was allocated for men and the other for women. Semi-submerged tree-trunks pose a navigational hazard, as no one had the foresight to log the area before it was flooded. The underwater cache of timber has now been spotted by the Thais; sub-aqua chainsaws are used to take out the 'treasure'.

### Exploring the lake

Access to the Nam Ngum reservoir is via Phonhong on Route 13: turn right at the strategically placed concrete post in the middle of the road, then head left to the village of Ban Talaat on the southwest shores of the reservoir. The market here is worth a browse (the word 'talaat' means market), as minority groups from the surrounding area come to the village to sell their wares and produce. From Ban Talaat, turn right across the narrow bridge to reach the dam, about 4 km up the road. An alternative route to the dam is via Route 10 out of Vientiane, which passes through much prettier countryside and traverses the Nam Ngum by ferry. Turn right at the end of the road for the dam. Hourly buses leave from the Central (Talaat Sao) bus station by the Morning Market in Vientiane daily for Ban Talaat and from there take a bus or organize a *songthaew* to Nam Ngum. There are boats from the dam to Ban Pao Mo on the other side of the reservoir. The trip should take around two hours and cost about US$10 per hour but it will be necessary to bargain hard with the boatmen before crossing the lake. Boats can also be hired out; again, barter hard to get a good hourly rate. Vang Vieng is two hours' ride from the dam.

### Listings Nam Ngum dam and reservoir

#### Where to stay

**$$$-$$ Vansana Nam Ngum Resort**
*On the riverfront, T023-241162, www. vansanahotel-group.com.*
20 tasteful rooms overlooking the water, and a freshwater swimming pool. One of the more pleasant options on the water, but a little tired.

**$$ Dansavanh Nam Ngum Resort**
*Southern end of Nam Ngum, T021-217595, www.dansavanh.com.*
This place caters heavily to Chinese and local clientele and is paired up with the

golf course. Live music in the evenings that may require earplugs. 209 rooms.

**$$ Long Ngum View Resort**
*Southern end of Nam Ngum, T021-214872, www.longngumview-resort.com.*
A wide range of accommodation from hotel rooms to simple bamboo and thatched roof bungalows with views across the water. There is a pretty open-air restaurant and a wide variety of water sports are on offer.

### Restaurants

There are several floating restaurants lining the shore which are atmospheric.

## Vang Vieng and around

**spectacular setting for adventure activities, surrounded by towering karst mountains**

The drive to Vang Vieng, on the much improved Route 13, follows the valley of the Nam Ngum River north to Phonhong and then climbs steeply onto the plateau where Vang Vieng is located, 160 km north of Vientiane. The surrounding area is inhabited by the Hmong and Yao hill peoples and is particularly picturesque: craggy karst limestone scenery, riddled with caves, crystal-clear pools and waterfalls. In the early morning the views are reminiscent of a Chinese Sung Dynasty painting.

The town itself is nestled in a valley on the bank of the Nam Song River. It enjoys cooler weather and offers breathtaking views of the mountains of Pha Tang and Phatto Nokham. There are a number of 16th- and 17th-century monasteries in town; the most notable are Wat That at the northern edge of the settlement and Wat Kang, 100 m or so to the south.

The town's laid-back feel and the tubing craze that kicked off here in the early 2000s made it a haunt for backpackers and it became a must-visit stop on the party banana pancake trail for many years. The late-night river bars and 'happy pizzas' have since been clamped down on and while it continues to pull in a good flow of backpackers, it is, thankfully, a far calmer place than it once was.

While the drop in 'happy pizza' eating backpacker numbers may have hurt some businesses in the short term, it has left the town a more pleasant place and the surrounding landscape has helped to establish Vang Vieng as a centre for those seeking to get into the great outdoors, with excellent cycling, walking, rock climbing, caving, and kayaking on offer. This is one of the most stunning and easily accessible parts of Laos. It is hoped that with the passing of the tubing scene and all that came with it, Vang Vieng will go from strength to strength by capitalizing on its abundance of beautiful spots.

### Tip...
Hobo Maps produces a remarkably detailed map of the town and surrounding area with caves, paths and walks all marked. It sells for 25,000 kip from most guesthouses. It is well worth the purchase, especially if you want to explore much of the surrounding area that is not marketed by tour operators.

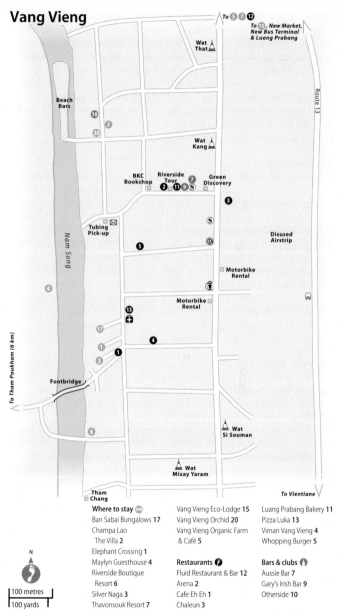

# Vang Vieng

To ⑤ ⑦ ⑫
To ⑮, New Market,
New Bus Terminal
& Luang Prabang

Wat That

Route 13

Beach Bars

⑩
②
⑳

Wat Kang

BKC Bookshop
Riverside Tour
②⑪⑨Ⓢ ⑦
Green Discovery

③

Nam Song

✉ Tubing Pick-up
⑤
Ⓢ
@

Disused Airstrip

☐ Motorbike Rental

④

ⓘ

⑬
✚
Motorbike Rental

⑰

④

① 
③ 
❶

Footbridge

To Tham Poukham (6 km)

⑥

Wat Si Souman

Wat Mixay Yaram

☐ Tham Chang

To Vientiane

N

100 metres
100 yards

**Safety** Laos is a very safe country for tourists but a disproportionate number of accidents and crimes seem to happen in Vang Vieng. Theft is routinely reported here, ranging from robberies on the river to the opportunist theft of items from guests' rooms. It is usually advisable to hand in any valuables to the management of your guesthouse or to padlock your bag and leave cash stashed in a very good hiding spot. Another major problem in the past was the sale of illegal drugs, but this is being clamped down on to some extent. **Vang Vieng Hospital** is on the road parallel to the river; in most cases it is much better to go to Vientiane or Thailand, see page 338. ▸▸ *For details of the significant safety risks involved in adventure activities, see Tour operators, page 74.*

## Nam Song River

Vang Vieng has become synonymous with tubing down the Nam Song and today, now that many of the bars are shut, it is a very pleasant experience. There are still enough bars to have a good time, but not so many as to destroy the piece and create the feeling of an invasion that one hung over the town. Tubes can be picked up from the Old Market area where the tubing company has formed a cartel. Without stops the 3-km tubing from the Organic Farm back to town can take one to two hours if done quickly, but most people do it in three to four hours or take all day, choosing to stop along the way to drink, play volleyball or use the flying fox swings at the many bars dotted along the river on the way into town.

Many tour operators offer kayaking trips as well. Popular routes include kayaking down the Nam Song to the caves, especially Tham Nam (Water Cave), see below. ▸▸ *See What to do, page 73.*

## ★Caves

Vang Vieng is known for its limestone caves, sheltered in the mountains flanking the town. Pretty much every guesthouse and tour operator offers tours to the caves (the best of these is **Green Discovery**) and, although some caves can be accessed independently, it is advisable to take a guide to a few as they are dark and difficult to navigate. Often children from surrounding villages will take tourists through the caves for a small fee. Don't forget to bring a torch, or even better a headlamp, which can be picked up cheaply at the market both in Vang Vieng and Vientiane. Many of the larger caves have an entrance fee of around 10,000 kip and many have stalls where you can buy drinks and snacks. You can buy the **Hobo** map from the town which clearly gives the location of the best sites.

In addition to those listed below, there are many more caves in the vicinity of Vang Vieng, most to the west and north. It is possible to hire a bicycle or motorcycle in Vang Vieng, take it across the river and cycle to the caves and villages on the other side of the Nam Song as all the sites are between 2 km and 15 km from Vang Vieng. ▸▸ *See What to do, page 74.*

**Tham Chang** ⓘ *Access via the Vang Vieng Resort south of town (see Where to stay).* Of Vang Vieng's myriad caves, this is the most renowned. It passes right under a mountain and is fed by a natural spring, perfect for an early morning dip. From the spring, it is possible to swim into the cave for quite a distance (bring a waterproof torch, if possible). The cave is said to have been used as a refuge from Chinese Haw bandits during the 19th century and this explains its name: *chang* meaning 'loyal'. The entrance fee includes electric illumination of the cave. Although the cave is not the most magnificent of Vieng Vang's caves, it serves as a superb lookout point.

**Tham Poukham** ⓘ *7 km from Vang Vieng, 10,000 kip.* Another popular cavern, Tham Poukham is often referred to as the 'Cave of the Golden Crab' while the extremely pretty swimming hole outside it is called the Blue Lagoon. It's believed that if you catch a golden crab you will have a lifetime of fortune. To get there, cross the footbridge near the Villa Nam Song, and then follow the road for a further 6 km until you reach the village of Ban Nathong. From the village, the cave is a short climb up a steep hill. Mossy rocks lead the way into the main cavern where a large bronze reclining Buddha is housed. Here there is an idyllic lagoon with glassy green-blue waters, perfect for a dip.

**Tham None** ⓘ *4 km north of Vang Vieng, 10,000 kip*, is known locally known as the 'Sleeping Cave' because 2000 villagers took refuge there during the war. The large cave is dotted with stalagmites and stalactites, including the 'magic stone of Vang Vieng', which reflects light. There are also lots of bats residing in the grotto. This cave is very popular with tour groups and rock climbers.

**Tham Xang** ⓘ *14 km north of Vang Vieng on the banks of the Nam Song, 10,000 kip*, also known as the 'Elephant Cave', is named after the stalagmites and stalactites that have created an elephant formation on a ledge. The cave also contains some Buddha images, including the footprint of Buddha. Although the cave itself is relatively nondescript the bell used by monks is made of a former bomb.

**Tham Nam (Water Cave)** ⓘ *15 km from town, follow the signposted path from Tham Xang, 10,000 kip*, a long spindly cave that is believed to stretch for at least 7 km. It takes about two hours to explore the cavern and at the entrance there is a crystal-clear pool, perfect for a dip. This is one of Vang Vieng's most interesting caves and in the wet season needs to be explored with an inner tube or by wading, while pulling yourself along a rope, although tour operators will take you beyond the roped area too. It's not easy and should not be attempted alone. At times the cavern is an extremely tight fit and commando-type crawling is required; a hard helmet with lamp attached is necessary. In spite of the difficulties, it is an incredible caving experience. To get to these two caves follow Route 13 north and turn left at Km 14, then follow this dirt road for 1 km until you reach the river. Boats charge 10,000 kip to cross the river to see Tham Xang, from which you can walk to Tham Nam.

## Kasi → *Colour map 2, A2.*

Kasi sits on a road connecting Kasi with Nan district in Luang Prabang Province. This road provides an alternative way of getting to the World Heritage town of

Luang Prabang for travellers coming from Vientiane or Vang Vieng, bypassing the Phoukhoun mountain pass and shortening the journey. This is a good option for those heading to Sayabouly or those who want to visit the massive Khoun Lang Cave. There is a narrow entrance but it opens to a single large passageway of 250 m in length which is full of stalactites, stalagmites and flowstone. The Khoun Lang Nature Park is also home to waterfalls and dense forest.

## Listings Vang Vieng and around

### Tourist information

There is now an official tourist information office on the main road.

### Where to stay

The town's popularity has ensured a uniformity among almost all places catering to budget tourists. However, there are now also a few good mid-range options and some very good upmarket resorts. Accommodation in the centre of town is usually cheaper, but try to get a room with a view of the river, as it is stunning. The bamboo bridge leads across the river bungalow on the far shore, but note that in the rainy season the only bridges in operation are the Namsong bridge (small charges apply) and the high bridge leading past the **Vang Vieng Orchid** to the island bars.

**$$$$-$$$ Riverside Boutique Resort**
*On the river, T023-511729, www. riversidevangvieng.com.*
By far and away the best lodgings in town. Swish rooms are well furnished with tasteful decorations and drawings. The suites come with gigantic balconies and sunloungers; the ultimate – the Tai Deng – has the best views in Vang Vieng. Worth every penny. Good-sized pool and a spa due to open. Mediocre restaurant.

**$$$ Silver Naga**
*On the river bank, T023-511822, www. silvernaga.com.*
Very tasteful rooms with wooden floors and large comfortable beds. Rooms facing the river have fantastic views – those from the higher floors are truly exceptional. Breakfast is served on a lovely deck right on the river. There is a great pool, also with knockout views. Recommended.

**$$$-$$ Ban Sabai Bungalows**
*On the banks of the river, T023-511088, www.xayohgroup.com.*
A lovely complex of bungalows with balconies in a spectacular location, with all the modern fittings. However, the rooms are not well lit, the water is not very hot, the bathroom is badly designed with the sink in the shower compartment and the breakfast service is very unpolished. Rooms 1-4 are near the laundry room and although not too noisy, light sleepers will be disturbed. Bungalows closer to the river are a bit more expensive. Those happy with the less glamorous side of rustic will love it here, but luxury lovers will not. The views from the balconies are top drawer and the staff are extremely friendly.

**$$$-$$ Thavonsouk Resort**
*On the river, T023-511096, www. thavonsouk.com.*

Offers 5 different styles of accommodation across a sprawling riverfront premises. Rooms are much more attractive on the outside than they are inside. Standard rooms come with tacky wood-imitation tiles. Some mid-range bungalows are great value with massive balconies fitted with sunbeds. There is a traditional Lao house, decorated with Lao furnishings, suitable for a family or big group, plus suites (TV, fridge, bath, a/c) and standard accommodation. Fantastic restaurant. Keep your eye out for local home-grown pop star, Aluna and her father, Alom, who run this family business.

**$$ Elephant Crossing**
*On the Nam Song River, T023-511232, www.theelephantcrossinghotel.com.*
Looking a little tired, this is nonetheless a good mid-range option with great views. Australian-run riverfront hotel classically decorated with modern wooden furnishings.

**$ Champa Lao the Villa**
*Khemsong St, northern end of town, T020-5501 8501, www.champa-lao.com.*
What this place lacks in views it more than makes up for in character. An 80-year-old Lao stilt house with plenty of comfy, ethnic fabric covered seating and bamboo hammocks to kick back in. Run by a super-friendly husband and wife team who offer good service and sound advice. Alongside the main house a couple of small bungalows are set in the lush, dense garden. If this is full try **Champa Lao Bungalow** run by the same people.

**$ Maylyn Guesthouse**
*On the opposite side of the river to town, T020-5560 4095.*

Easily the best place to stay on the 'other side', these simple bungalows are set in a well-kept garden and the owners help make it a great place to unwind for a few days. A good base from which to explore the caves.

**$ Vang Vieng Orchid**
*On the river road, T023-511172.*
Very comfortable rooms with fan or a/c, hot water in the bathrooms and clean tiled floors. The rooms with private balconies are well worth the few extra dollars because you will have a phenomenal view. The proximity to the infamous **Bucket Bar** makes this place quiet noisy.

**Out of town**
The places on the outskirts of town are great for those who wish to escape into a more natural landscape. The lack of facilities and transport in the area ensures tranquillity but also makes it quite difficult to get to town.

**$$-$ Vang Vieng Eco-Lodge**
*7 km north of town, T021-413370, www. vangvieng-eco-lodge.com.*
Although this isn't an eco-lodge it is still a beautiful place to stay and ideal for those who want to enjoy the scenery around Vang Vieng and not venture into the town itself. Set on the banks of the river with stunning gardens and beautiful rock formations, it is a perfect place to get away from it all. The bungalows are naturally ventilated but also come with fans. The rooms are special, with wood-beamed ceilings, Lao fabrics and 4-poster beds. Bathrooms are all unique and some have sunken tubs. Good Lao restaurant. Activities arranged.

### $ Vang Vieng Organic Farm
*3 km north of town in Ban Sisavang,*
*T023-511174, www.laofarm.org.*
Now that the noise from the tubing bars has subsided, the farm's tranquillity has been restored. Run by Mr T (who inadvertently started the tubing craze) who does great community work, promotes organic growing raises money for school buses. This is a very worthwhile place to lay your head. The accommodation is quite basic, but it is clean and the location is good. Also runs volunteering projects. Well worth a visit even if you don't stay here. Hugely popular restaurant, serving great starfruit wine and famous mulberry pancakes.

### Kasi
Rooms are available at several guesthouses in town.

### $ Somchith
*Route 13, Main Rd.*
The most popular place is this small guesthouse above a restaurant in the centre of town.

### Restaurants

There is a string of eating places on the main road through town, with the same menu in almost every establishment – generally hamburgers, pasta, sandwiches and basic Asian.

### $$-$ Arena
*A couple of doors down from the Luang Prabang bakery, T020-7818 1171. Open all day.*
Glass walls enclose this restaurant-cum-cafe that, in typical Vang Vieng style, serves a bit of everything. It's clean and has fast Wi-Fi and is a decent option for a light lunch and to escape the heat. Popular with backpackers.

### $$-$ Luang Prabang Bakery Restaurant
*Just off the main road.*
One of the more expensive places in town serving a wide range of cakes and ice creams in the daytime and popular for cocktails in the evening. The standards aren't as high as the prices, but this remains a popular spot and is often busy when everywhere else is dead. Good Wi-Fi.

### $ Cafe Eh Eh
*Right next to the Elephant Crossing alley.*
This newcomer to the scene is a funky little space knocking out excellent shakes, good sandwiches and some delicious cakes – the cheesecake is a highlight. Also sells a nice range of gifts and cards. Recommended.

### $ Chaleun
*Opposite Green Discovery on the main road, T023-254335.*
The decor is basic in the extreme, but this is probably the best of the restaurants clustered around this part of town, particularly for the quality of the Lao dishes.

### $ Fluid
*2 km outside town, www.vangvieng.biz.*
Fantastic views, laid-back vibe, good staff and good food. Well worth the trip outside town. Highly recommended.

### $ Organic Farm Café
*Further down the main road from Fluid (see above).*
Small café offering over 15 fruit shakes and a fantastic variety of food. Mulberry shakes and pancakes are a must and the harvest curry stew is delicious. Try the fresh spring rolls, with pineapple dipping sauce as a starter.

## $ Pizza Luka
*Signposted near the hospital.*
*Open from 1800.*
Freshly made Italian-style pizza with a range of quality toppings, this is the best pizza joint in town, hands-down. Friendly service and a relaxed vibe. The house red isn't bad either. Recommended.

## $ Viman Vang Vieng
*Near the Silver Naga, T020-5892 6695.*
Great restaurant run by Kaz, a German-Thai gentleman who came to Vang Vieng as a tourist years ago and returned to set up shop here. He prides himself on making the best schnitzel this side of Bavaria; it's excellent and comes served with great fried potatoes. Kaz also does some quality Lao dishes and some Thai classics. His own artwork hangs on the walls. He is very passionate about the area and full of information. Well worth a visit.

## $ Whopping Burger
*1 block south of Arena (see above),*
*whoppingburger@hotmail.co.jp.*
This place does exactly what it says on the tin. Huge buns, huge patties and a decent portion of hand-cut fried on the side. Nice wooden seating, friendly owners and normally bustling.

## Bars and clubs

Now that the party scene has died down, nightlife is a little lacklustre for those who come here expecting a wild night. However, there are a few bars on the road toward the tubing pick-up point that still get busy later on in the evenings, notably **Gary's Irish Bar** and the **Aussie Bar**.

For something a little more local, it's worth taking a look at some of the Lao joints that line the road on which the buses travel. These are open-air beer terraces with Beerlao flags string around them. Find a busy one and you'll likely have a good night. Down by the bamboo bridge there are a couple of bars with low tables and cushions on the ground that make great places for sundowners. The **Otherside** (on the main street by the river) is also a good spot for sunset beers and does a reasonable range of food. The most notable place is **Fluid Bar** (www.vangvieng.biz) which is 2 km outside town on the river. Here the lovely owners care a lot about the local area and are keen to promote longer stays here following the decline in visitors post-tubing craze days. This is a lovely spot to go and swing in a hammock, enjoy some good drinks and maybe a shisha.

## Shopping

**BKC Bookshop**, *T023-5118694.*
A reasonable range of second-hand books and guides to buy and exchange. **New Market**, *2 km north of town.* Has the greatest selection of goods.

## What to do

### Ballooning
Ballooning above the beautiful karst landscape of Vang Vieng is simply awe-inspiring. Flights (US$70, child US$40) operate twice a day and can be booked via most agents including **Green Discovery**.

### Kayaking and rafting
See also Tour operators, below. Kayaking is very popular around Vang Vieng and competition between operators has become fierce. Options range from day

trips on calm waters to a trip to the Nam Lik River to kayak its rapids and see more far flung villages such as the Thai Dam village of Ban Vang Mon.

## Rock climbing

Vang Vieng is the best established rock-climbing area in the country, and there are now 200 routes ranging from 4a to 8b. Many of the climbs were bolted by **Adam's Climbing School** or people associated with it. Adam's is the longest running outfit in town. Both **Adam's** and **Green Discovery** (see Tour operators, below) offer climbing courses almost every day in high season. The best climbing sites include: **Sleeping Cave**, which offers 14 separate routes; **Sleeping Wall**, a tough 20-m crag, which features 19 separate climbs, including a few ascents requiring some tricky manoeuvring and steep overhangs.

## Tour operators

Tour guides are available for hiking, rafting, and visiting the caves and minority villages, from most travel agents and guesthouses. Safety issues need to be considered when taking part in any adventure activity. There have been fatalities in Vang Vieng from boating, trekking and caving accidents. The Nam Xong River can flow very quickly during the wet season (Jul and Aug) and tourists have drowned here. Make sure you wear a life-jacket and ensure you are not on the river after dark. Make sure all equipment is in a good state of repair. A price war between operators has led to cost cutting, resulting in equipment that is not well maintained or non-existent. The more expensive, companies are usually the best (see also Tour operators, page 56).

**Adam's Climbing School**, *near the Silver Naga hotel, T020-5010832, www. laos-climbing.com.* The friendly owner, Adam, believes himself to be the first Lao rock climber – he's been climbing since 1997. He began in the rock climbing Mecca of Krabi, Thailand, before a stint in Germany and setting up in Laos in 2005. He and his team are super-encouraging so this is a great place for novices to learn. The huge variety of rock on offer also means it's a good place for more experienced climbers. Half-day to 3-day courses. Also rents motorbikes and can arrange ballooning trips. Highly recommended.
**Green Discovery**, *main road, T023-511440, www.greendiscoverylaos.com.* Caving, kayaking, hiking and rock climbing plus motorbike tours and mountain bike tours. Very professional and helpful. Recommended.
**VLT Natural Tours**, *near* **Ban Sabai** *(see Where to stay), T023-511369, T020-5520 8283, www.vangviengtour.com.* A long-running outfit, this company offers a huge variety of options including cooking tours, fishing and camping trips. Also runs combined trekking, caving, tubing and kayaking tours.

## Tubing

Floating slowly along the Nam Song is an ideal way to take in the stunning surroundings of misty limestone karsts, jungle and rice paddies. The drop-off point is 3 km from Vang Vieng, near the Organic Farm. The tubing rental company in town still charges 55,000 kip. A deposit of 60,000 kip must also be paid. Rental begins at 0800 and it is best to start early to make the most of your trip down-river.

## Transport

Vang Vieng is on Route 13 between Vientiane and Luang Prabang so a bus between Vientiane and anywhere up north (or vice versa) will pass through even if it is not on the itinerary. The journey to/from the capital takes about 3 to 4 hrs and from Luang Prabang around 5 to 7 hrs. See also Vientiane Transport, page 56.

### Bicycle and motorbike hire

There are many bicycles for rent in town. There are also a few motorbike rental places, one of the best is opposite the **Silver Naga** hotel where a friendly young family rent out everything from automatic scooters to fully manual 250cc off-road bikes. Prices from around 60,000 kip, but it gets cheaper the longer you rent for.

### Bus

Buses leave from the bus terminal at the New Market, 2 km north of town. There are toilets, shops and cafés. Almost every guesthouse and tour agency in Vang Vieng sells bus tickets. The minivan service is great because it includes a pick-up at your guesthouse.

**Private minivan transport and VIP buses** To **Vientiane**: minivans leave at 0900 and there are 3 VIP buses per morning, 3 hrs. To **Luang Prabang**: minivans leave at 0900 and sometimes again at 1400, up to 9 hrs depending on the state of the road. VIP buses at 0900. To **Phonsavanh**: 1 per morning, 7 hrs.

### Tuk-tuk

Tuk-tuks are available for hire for trips to the cave. It is best to ask at your guesthouse for the standard going rate and ideally ask them to arrange a tuk-tuk for you – this is much easier than trying to negotiate yourself.

## Kasi

### Bus/truck

There are connections south to **Vang Vieng** (2 hrs) and north to **Luang Prabang** (4 hrs).

# Northern Laos

dense forests, hilltribes and river adventures

Much of Laos' northern region is rugged and mountainous, a remote borderland with a significant minority population of hill peoples.

Until recently, in some areas at least, the only way to travel was by boat, along one of the rivers – many fast-flowing – which have cut their way through this impressive landscape. Today road travel is much improved, though still not easy in some more remote parts.

The key centre of the north is the old royal capital of Luang Prabang, one of the world's most beautiful cities and a World Heritage Site. To the east is the Plain of Jars, the Nam Et-Phou Louey National Protected Area and Vieng Xai, a former stronghold of the Pathet Lao, while to the north is a string of small towns that are becoming increasingly popular places to visit. Eco-resorts in peaceful forest settings, treks to upland villages, night river safaris and graphic insights into the country's recent history are among the highlights of this region.

**Best** for
Caves ▪ Homestays ▪ Temples ▪ Trekking

# Footprint
## picks

★ **Luang Prabang**, page 79

Golden temples, charming cafés and boutique hotels.

★ **Tad Kuang Si**, page 101

Spectacular waterfalls, best appreciated in the wet season.

★ **Nam Ou River and Muang Ngoi Neua**, page 116

An ideal spot to laze in a hammock and soak up the scenery.

★ **Vieng Phouka**, page 131

A great base for trekking and exploring local caves.

★ **The Gibbon Experience**, page 140

Explore the jungle canopy of Bokeo Nature Reserve by zipline.

★ **Phonsavanh and Plain of Jars**, pages 148 and 153

Mysterious stone jars in a landscape scarred by war.

★ **Pathet Lao caves at Vieng Xai**, page 167

Fascinating cave city used as a revolutionary base during the war.

★ **Nam Nern Night Safari**, page 174

Venture up the river on a long-tail boat to spot rare animals.

CHINA

VIETNAM

MYANMAR (BURMA)

Lan Toui

Muang Uthai
Ngay Neua

Hat Xa

Phongsali

PHONGSALI

Muang Sing
Mohan
Boten
Nateui
Muang Khua

Muang La

Muang Ngoi Neua

Muang Et
Sop Bao
Sop Hao

Luang Namtha

Xieng Kok

LUANG NAMTHA

Udomxai

Muang Saphoun

Xam Xai

Pathet Lao Caves

Na Maew

Vieng Phouka

BOKEO

Muang Moeng

Pakmong

Nong Khiaw & Ban Saphoun

Nam Bak

HUA PHAN

Vieng Xai

Houei Xai

UDOMXAI

Nam Et-Phou Louey NPA

Muang Muoi

Sao Hintang

Nam Nouan

Xam Tai

Chiang Khong

Muang Houn

Pak Ou Caves

LUANG PRABANG

Vieng Thong

Muang Na

Pung Thac

Pak Beng

Tha Suang

Luang Prabang

Tham Phiu

Muang Kham

Nam Khan

Muang Ngeun

Hongsa

Tad Kuang Si

Nong Tang

Muang Khoune

Nong Het

Mep

SAYABOURY

Phonsavanh

Kasi

Na Vang

Muang Mok

VIETNAM

Sayaboury

Na Sing

VIENTIANE

Plain of Jars

XIENG KHOUANG

Vang Vieng

Tam Kalong

THAILAND

Na Le

BOLIKHAMXAI

Na Cham

Keun

Paksan

Viang Thong

Pak Kading

Khamkeut

Pak Lai

Tha Pabat Phonsanh

Ban Lao

Lak Sao

Nakok

VIENTIANE

Muang Hin Boun

Kene Thao

THAILAND

Pak Hin Boun

Botene

Thakhek

Nong Bok

N

50 km
50 miles

# Luang Prabang
## & around

★In terms of size, Luang Prabang hardly deserves the title 'city' (the population is around 40,000) but in terms of grandeur the appellation is more than deserved. Luang Prabang is the town that visitors often remember with the greatest affection. Its rich history, incomparable architecture, easygoing atmosphere, good choice of restaurants, friendly population and stunning position, surrounded by a crown of mountains, mark it out as exceptional.

Anchored at the junction of the Mekong and Nam Khan rivers, the former royal capital was founded on Mount Phousi – a small rocky hill with leafy slopes – and has been a mountain kingdom for over 1000 years. Despite a few welcome concessions to modern life, including great food, and electricity, Luang Prabang still oozes the magic of bygone days. In the 18th century there were more than 65 wats in the city; many have been destroyed over the years but over 30 remain intact. UNESCO have not only designated the city as a World Heritage Site, but also the best-preserved traditional city in Southeast Asia.

Yet for all its magnificent temples, this royal 'city' feels more like a provincial town: in the early evening children play in the streets, while women cook; old men lounge in wicker chairs and young boys play *takraw*. The town's timelessness can be observed by simply walking the ancient streets. *Phone code: 071. Colour map 2, A2.*

# Essentials Luang Prabang

## Finding your feet

Luang Prabang is a small town and the best way to explore is either on foot or by bicycle. Bicycles can be hired from most guesthouses for 20,000 kip per day. For longer journeys, such as out to the waterfalls, tuk-tuks and *saamlors* are available for hire. Motorbikes here are more expensive than elsewhere in Laos, costing up to 16,000 kip per day. Expect to leave your passport as deposit.

## Best restaurants

**3 Nagas**, page 106
**Café Toui**, page 107
**Dyen Sabai**, page 107
**Khai Phaen**, page 107
**L'Éléphant**, page 107

## When to go

Luang Prabang lies 300 m above sea level on the upper Mekong, at its confluence with the Nam Khan. The most popular time to visit the town is during the comparatively cool months of November and December but the best time to visit is from December to February. After this the weather is hotting up and the views are often shrouded in a haze, produced by shifting cultivators using fire to clear the forest

### Tip...

Many of the excellent restaurants in Luang Prabang offer cookery courses where you learn how to prepare local staples such as *jaew bawng* (chilli salsa) or *mok pa* (fish steamed in banana leaves). **Tamarind** restaurant (see page 107) is highly recommended for its enchanting jungle garden school.

for agriculture. This does not really clear until May or, sometimes, June. During the months of March and April, when visibility is at its worst, smoke can cause soreness of the eyes, as well as preventing planes from landing.

In terms of festivals, on the October full moon, the delightful **Lai Heua Fai** (Fireboat Festival) takes place (see page 110).

### Tip...

The two-day journey along the Mekong between Luang Prabang and Houei Xai/Pakbeng remains hugely popular and is considered a rite of passage in Southeast Asia. See page 113 for details.

## Time required

The main sights in Luang Prabang could be seen in a couple of days but you could easily spend four or five. It's a beautiful place to hang out, eat well and wander the streets.

### Tip...

Luang Prabang is a great place to pick up textiles made in nearby ethnic communities-- try **Ock Pop Tok** (see page 110) or **TAEC Boutique** (see page 110). Also well worth a visit is the **Traditional Arts and Ethnology Centre** (see page 93).

Luang Prabang is a small town and the sights are conveniently close together, the majority dotted along the main Sakkaline, Sisavangvong and Souvanna Khampong roads. Most are walkable – the important ones can be covered within two leisurely days – but a bike is the best way to get around. To begin with it may be worth climbing Mount Phousi or taking a stroll along the Mekong and Nam Khan river roads to get a better idea of the layout of the town. Most of Luang Prabang's important wats are dotted along the main road, Phothisarath. When visiting the wats it is helpful to take a guide to obtain entry to all the buildings, which are often locked for security reasons. Without a guide, your best chance of finding them open is early in the morning. For a walking tour of the town, see page 93.

## Royal Palace

*Sisavangvong Rd, daily 0800-1100 and 1330-1600 (closed Tue), small admission charge. Shorts, short-sleeved shirts and strappy dresses prohibited; shoes should be removed and bags must be put in lockers. No photography.*

Also called the **National Museum**, the Royal Palace is right in the centre of the city on the main road, Sisavangvong, which runs along the promontory and allowed royal guests ready access from the Mekong. Unlike its former occupants, the palace survived the 1975 revolution and was converted into a museum the following year. It replaced a smaller wooden palace on the same site.

Construction of the palace started in 1904, during the reign of Sisavang Vong, and took 20 years. It was built by the French for the Lao king, in an attempt to bind him and his family more tightly to the colonial system of government. Although most of the construction was completed by 1909, the two front wings were extended in the 1920s and a new, more Lao-style roof was added. These later changes were accompanied by the planting of the avenue of palms and the filling in of one of two fish ponds. Local residents regarded the ponds as the 'eyes' of the capital, so the blinding of one eye was taken as inviting bad fortune by leaving the city unprotected.

The subsequent civil war seemed to vindicate these fears. The palace is Khmer in style, cruciform in plan and mounted on a small platform of four tiers. The only indication of French involvement can be seen in the two French lilies represented in stucco on the entrance, beneath the symbols of Lao royalty. There are a few Lao motifs but, in many respects, the palace is more foreign than Lao: it was designed by a French architect, with steps made from Italian marble; built by masons from Vietnam; embellished by carpenters from Bangkok; and funded by the largesse of the colonial authorities. While the palace itself is modest, its contents are spectacular.

The museum now contains a collection of 15th- to 17th-century Buddha statues and artefacts from wats in Luang Prabang such as the ancient bronze drums from Wat Visoun. Notable pieces include an ancient Buddha head, an offering from Indian dignitaries, and a reclining Buddha with the unusual addition of mourners. The most important piece is the **Golden Buddha**, from which the city derives its name. Some believe that the original is kept in a bank vault in Vientiane or Moscow, although most dispel this as rumour. It is 90% solid gold, stands 83 cm high and weighs around 53 kg. Reputed to have come from Ceylon, and to date from between the first and ninth centuries, the statue was brought to Cambodia in the 11th century, given to King Phaya Sirichanta, and then taken to Lane Xang by King Fa Ngum, who had spent time in the courts of Angkor and married into Khmer royalty.

**Entrance Hall** The main entrance hall of the palace was used for royal religious ceremonies, when the Supreme Patriarch of Lao Buddhism would oversee proceedings from his gold-painted lotus throne.

# 1 Luang Prabang

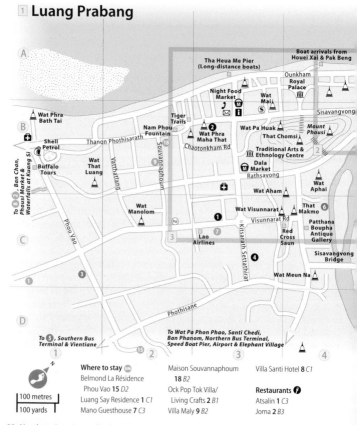

**Where to stay** 🛏
Belmond La Résidence
Phou Vao **15** D2
Luang Say Residence **1** C1
Mano Guesthouse **7** C3

Maison Souvannaphoum
**18** B2
Ock Pop Tok Villa/
Living Crafts **2** B1
Villa Maly **9** B2

Villa Santi Hotel **8** C1

**Restaurants** 🍴
Atsalin **1** C3
Joma **2** B3

**King's Reception Room** The room to the immediate right of the entrance was the King's Reception Room, also called the **Ambassadors' Room**. It contains French-made busts of the last three Lao monarchs, a model of the royal hearse (which is kept in Wat Xieng Thong) and a mural by French artist Alex de Fontereau, depicting a day in the life of Luang Prabang in the 1930s.

**Coronation Room (Throne Room)** To the rear of the entrance hall, the Coronation Room was decorated between 1960 and 1970 for Sisavang Vatthana's coronation, an event which was interrupted because of the war. The walls are a brilliant red with Japanese glass mosaics embedded in a red lacquer base with gilded woodwork. They depict scenes from Lao festivals, such as boat racing. The carved throne has a gold three-headed elephant insignia; on one side is a tall pot to hold the crown. To the right of the throne, as you face it, are the ceremonial coronation swords and a glass case containing 15th- and 16th-century crystal and gold Buddhas, many from inside the 'melon stupa' of Wat Visoun. Because Luang Prabang was constantly raided, many of these religious artefacts were presented to the king for safekeeping. At the back, to the right of the entrance, is the royal *howdah*, a portable throne was used during battle. The throne is covered with shields to protect it.

**Private Apartments** In comparison to the state rooms, the royal family's private apartments are modestly decorated. They have been left virtually untouched since Sisavang Vatthana and family left for exile in Xam Neua Province. The **King's Library** backs onto the Coronation Room: Sisavang Vatthana was a well-read monarch, having studied at the École de Science Politique in Paris. Behind the library, built around a small inner courtyard are the queen's modest bedroom, the king's bedchamber and the royal yellow bathroom, with its two regal porcelain thrones standing side by side. These rooms are cordoned off but you can still see them. The king's bed is a marvellous construction with a three-headed elephant insignia. The remaining rooms

Mekong River

Tourist Boats to Pak Ou

Souvanna Khampong

Sakkaline

Nam Khan

Nam Khan

Wat Tao Hai

To Pak Ou, Northern Bus Terminal & Xang Hai

To Airport, & Ban Hat Hien

➡ **Luang Prabang maps**
1 Luang Prabang, page 82
2 Luang Prabang detail, page 88
3 Luang Prabang walking tour, page 96

# BACKGROUND

## Luang Prabang

According to legend, the site of Luang Prabang was chosen by two resident hermits. Buddha was believed to have glanced in Luang Prabang's direction, saying a great city would be built there. Details are sketchy regarding the earliest inhabitants of Luang Prabang but historians imply the ethnic Khmu and Lao Theung groups were the initial settlers. They named Luang Prabang, 'Muang Sawa', which literally translates as Java, hinting at some kind of cross-border support. By the end of the 13th century, Muang Sawa had developed into a regional hub.

A major turning point in the city's history came about in 1353, when the mighty Fa Ngum travelled up the Mekong, backed by a feisty Khmer army, and captured Muang Sawa. Fa Ngum imported Khmer traditions including Theravada Buddhism and great architecture, but his constituents and army, wary of his warmongering ways, exiled him in 1373, and his son, Oun Heuan, then assumed the throne.

In 1478 the city was invaded by Vietnamese. After several years occupying and ransacking the place, they were driven out and the kingdom embarked upon a massive reconstruction campaign. During this period some of Luang Prabang's finest monuments were built, including Wat Xieng Thong. Luang Prabang's importance diminished in the 18th century, following the death of King Souligna Vongsa and the break-up of Lane Xang, but it remained a royal centre until the Communist takeover in 1975. During the low point of Laos' fortunes in the mid-19th century, when virtually the whole country had become tributary to Bangkok (Siam), only Luang Prabang retained a semblance of independence. Luang Prabang didn't suffer as much as other provincial capitals during the Indochina wars, narrowly escaping a Viet Minh capture in 1953. During the Second Indochina War, however, the Pathet Lao cut short the royal lineage, forcing King Sisavang Vatthana to abdicate and sending him to a re-education camp in northeastern Laos where he, his wife and his son died from starvation.

Fortunately, UNESCO's designation of Luang Prabang as a World Heritage Site has restricted redevelopment. The old town – essentially the promontory – is protected while elsewhere only limited building is permitted (no building, can be higher than three storeys). Although the new road went ahead, the authorities built a bypass to ensure that the town wasn't disrupted.

include a small portrait gallery, dining room and the children's bedroom, which is decorated with musical instruments and headdresses for *Ramayana* actors. In the hallway linking the rooms is a miscellany of interesting objects, including an intricately patterned *sinh*, worn by the queen, and a royal palanquin, which would have been tied to an elephant. Domestic rooms, offices and library are located on the ground floor beneath the state apartments.

**Other reception rooms**  To the left of the entrance hall is the reception room of the **King's Secretary**, and beyond it, the **Queen's Reception Room**, which together house an eccentric miscellany of state gifts from just about every country except the UK. Of particular note is the moon rock presented to Laos by the USA following the Apollo 11 and 17 lunar missions. Also in this room are portraits of the last King Sisavang Vatthana, Queen Kham Phouy and Crown Prince Vongsavang, painted by a Soviet artist in 1967.

**King's Chapel**  On the right wing of the palace, next to the King's Reception Room, is the king's private chapel, which houses the Pra Bang. It also contains four Khmer Buddhas, ivories mounted in gold, bronze drums used in religious ceremonies and about 30 smaller Buddha images from temples all over the city.

**Haw Prabang**  This small ornate pavilion is located in the northeast corner of the palace compound, to the right of the entrance to the Royal Palace. It was designed by the Royal Architect of the time to house the Pra Bang and was paid for by small donations sent in from across the country. The Pra Bang should move here sometime in the future.

**Other buildings**  In the left-hand corner (south) of the compound, is the **Luang Prabang Conference Hall**, built for the official coronation of Savang Vatthana, which was terminally interrupted by the 1975 revolution. The southwestern corner of the compound is now used as the **Royal Theatre**, where traditional performances are held.

## Wat Mai
*Sisavangvong Rd, daily 0800-1700, admission 20,000 kip.*

Next to the Royal Palace is Wat Mai. This royal temple, inaugurated in 1788, has a five-tiered roof and is one of the jewels of Luang Prabang. It took more than 70 years to complete. It was officially called Wat Mai Souvanna Phommaram and was the home of the Buddhist leader in Laos, Phra Sangkharath, until he moved to That Luang in Vientiane. Auguste Pavie and his crew took up residence here while trying to win Luang Prabang over from the Siamese who controlled the Lao court at the time. The Siamese thought that detaining Pavie in the compound would keep him out of their way but the Frenchman struck up a friendship with a local abbot, who acted as a runner between the king and Pavie. The temple housed the Pra Bang from 1894 until 1947 and, during Pi Mai (New Year), the Pra Bang is taken from the Royal Palace and installed at Wat Mai for its annual ritual cleansing, before being returned to the palace on the third day.

Today, Wat Mai is probably the most popular temple after Wat Xieng Thong. The façade is particularly interesting: a large golden bas-relief tells the story of Phravet (one of the last reincarnations of the Gautama or historic Buddha), with village scenes, including wild animals, women pounding rice, and people at play. The interior is an exquisite amalgam of red and gold, with pillars similar to those in Wat Xieng Thong and Wat Visoun. The temple is indicative of Luang Prabang architecture, aside from the roofed veranda, whose gables face the sides rather than the front. The central beam at Wat Mai is carved with figures from the Hindu story of the birth of Ravanna and Hanuman. Behind the temple is a new construction where two classical racing boats are kept, ready to be brought out for Pi Mai (Lao New Year) and the August boat-racing festival. ▸▸ *See Festivals, page 109.*

## Mount Phousi
*The western steps lead up from Sisavangvong Rd, daily 0700-1800. If you want to watch the sun go down, get there early, but expect to have to jostle for position. Arrive at dawn and you are likely to be one of a handful there.*

Directly opposite the Royal Palace is the start of the climb up Mount Phousi, the spiritual and geographical heart of the city and a popular place to watch the sunset over the Mekong. Luang Prabang was probably sited at this point on the Mekong, in part at least, because of the presence of Phousi. Many capitals in the region are founded near sacred hills or mountains, which could become local symbols of the Hindu Mount Mahameru or Mount Meru, the abode of the gods and also the abode of local tutelary spirits.

As you start the ascent, to the right is **Wat Pa Huak** ⓘ *daily 0800-1800*. It is worth visiting because the monastery has some fine 19th-century murals, depicting classic scenes along the Mekong. There are a few Buddha images here that date from the same period and a fine carved wooden mosaic on the temple's exterior, depicting Buddha riding Airavata, the three-headed elephant from Hindu mythology.

From Wat Pa Huak, 328 steps wind up Phousi, a gigantic rock with sheer forested sides, surmounted by a 25-m-tall *chedi*, **That Chomsi**. The *chedi* was constructed in 1804, restored in 1914 and is the starting point for the colourful Pi Mai (New Year) celebrations in April (see Festivals, page 109). Its shimmering gold-spired stupa rests on a rectangular base, ornamented by small metal Bodhi trees. Next to the stupa is a little sanctuary, from which the candlelit procession descends at New Year, accompanied by effigies of Nang Sang Khan, the guardian of the New Year, and naga, protector of the city. The drum, kept in the small *haw kong* on the east side of the hill, is used on ceremonial occasions. The summit of Phousi affords a panoramic view of Luang Prabang and the mountains. The Mekong lies to the north and west, with the city laid out to the southeast.

A path next to the *ack-ack* cannon leads down to **Wat Tham Phousi**, which is more like a car port than a temple, but which is home to a rotund Buddha, Kaccayana (also called Phra Ka Tiay). At the top of the steps leading out of the wat are two tall cacti, planted defiantly in the empty shell casings of two large US bombs – the monks' answer to decades of war.

## Mekong monsters, real and imagined

It is said that the *pa beuk*, the giant catfish of the Mekong, was only described by Western science in 1930.

That may be so, but the English explorer and surveyor, James McCarthy, goes into considerable detail about the fish in his book *Surveying and exploring in Siam*, which was first published in 1900 and draws upon his travels in Siam and Laos between 1881 and 1893. He writes: "The month of June in Luang Prabang is a very busy one for fishermen. Nearly all the boats are employed on fishing, each paying a large fish for the privilege. Two kinds of large fish, *pa beuk* and *pa lerm*, are principally sought after... A *pa beuk* that I helped to take weighed 130 lbs; it was 7 ft long and 4 ft 2 in round the body; the tail measured 1ft 9 in. The fish had neither scales nor teeth, and was sold for 10 rupees. The roe of this fish is considered a great delicacy. The fish is taken in June, July and August, when on its upward journey. Returning in November, it keeps low in the river, and a few stray ones only are caught."

McCarthy also recounts a story he had heard of a mythical river serpent of the Mekong: "It lives only at the rapids, and my informant said he had seen it. It is 53 ft long and 20 in thick. When a man is drowned it snaps off the tuft of hair on the head [men wore their hair in this manner], extracts the teeth, and sucks the blood; and when a body is found thus disfigured, it is known that the man has fallen victim to the *ngeuak*, or river serpent, at Luang Prabang."

### Wat Siphouttabath (Wat Pha Phoutthabat)

Located down a path to the north of Wat Tham Phousi, just off the central road running along the promontory, is a compound containing three monasteries. Of them, **Wat Pa Khe** is most notable, predominantly for its carvings of 17th-century Dutch and Italian traders. Why these traders are depicted in a Buddhist temple in Luang Prabang remains a mystery, although many suspect it may have been influenced by trading merchants from the East India Company, who travelled through the area in the late 16th century. Behind the *sim* is a shrine housing a 3-m-long footprint of the Buddha. The shrine is normally only open during festive occasions, so you will need to ask someone for a key. Flanking the shrine is a small pavilion where Cambodia's former King Sihanouk entertained the press (in his usual publicity-centric fashion) during King Sisavang Vong's cremation ceremony.

### Wat Xieng Mouan and Wat Pa Phai

A block back from Sisavangvong Road is the old monastery site of **Wat Xieng Mouan**. The *sim* here was constructed in 1879, although work is believed to have started decades earlier. The temple features a few impressive sculptures and an imposing fresco of *nagas* on the ceiling. UNESCO has funded an artistic training centre for monks here to ensure that skills are available to continue restoration work in the future. The novices are being taught the crafts of woodcarving, painting and Buddha-making.

Also in the same block is **Wat Pa Phai**, called the Bamboo Monastery, although there isn't an overwhelming amount of bamboo in evidence. The *sim*, however, is decorated with colourful serpents and peacocks.

### Wat Sene (Wat Saen)

Further up the promontory, Wat Sene was built in 1718 and was the first *sim* in Luang Prabang to be constructed in Thai style, with a yellow and red roof. The exterior may lack subtlety, but the interior is delicate and refined, painted red, with gold patterning on every conceivable surface. *Sene* means 100,000 and the wat was built with a local donation of 100,000 kip from someone who discovered 'treasure' in the Nam Khan river. At the far end of the wat compound is a building containing a large, gold, albeit rather crudely modelled, image of the Buddha in the 'calling for rain' *mudra* (standing, arms held stiffly down). Note the torments of hell depicted on the façade of the building (top, left). The temple was restored in 1932, with further renovations in 1957. One of Laos' most sacrosanct abbots, the recently deceased Ajahn Khamchan, was ordained at the temple in 1940.

## 2 Luang Prabang detail

**Where to stay**
3 Nagas **4** *B3*
Ammata Guesthouse **20** *A3*
Apsara **1** *B4*
Apsara Rive Droite **15** *B4*
Mekong Riverview **2** *A5*
Oui's Guesthouse **21** *B5*

Nam Khan Riverside **3** *B2*
Pa Phai **8** *A2*
Pack Luck **7** *A3*
Sokdee Residence **5** *A2*
Villa Ban Lakkham **10** *B5*

**Restaurants**
3 Nagas **3** *B3*
Big Tree Café & Gallery **4** *A2*
Café Ban Vat Sene **1** *B2*
Café Toui **9** *A2*
Couleur Café **6** *B2*
Dyen Sabai **12** *B2*

100 metres
100 yards

## Wat Xieng Thong

*Xiengthong Rd, daily 0800-1700, 20,000 kip.*

Wat Xieng Thong Ratsavoraviharn, usually known as just Wat Xieng Thong, is set back from the road, at the top of a flight of steps leading down to the Mekong. It is arguably the finest example of a Lao monastery, with graceful, low-sweeping eaves, beautiful stone mosaics and intricate carvings. The wat has several striking chapels, including one that houses a rare bronze reclining Buddha and another sheltering a gilded wooden funeral chariot. The back of the temple is encrusted with a stunning glass mosaic depicting a Bodhi tree, while inside, resplendent gold-stencilled pillars support a ceiling with *dharma* wheels. The temple's tranquility is further enhanced by beautiful gardens of bougainvillea, frangipani and hibiscus, shaded by banyan and palm trees.

This monastery was a key element in Luang Prabang's successful submission to UNESCO for recognition as a World Heritage Site. The striking buildings in the tranquil compound are decorated in gold and post-box red, with imposing tiled roofs, intricate carvings, paintings and mosaics, making this the most important and finest royal wat in Luang Prabang. It was built by King Setthathirat in 1559, and is one of the few buildings to have survived the successive Chinese raids that marked the end of the 19th century. It retained its royal patronage until 1975 and has been embellished and well cared for over the years: even the crown princess of Thailand, Mahachakri Sirindhorn, has donated funds for its upkeep.

➡ **Luang Prabang maps**
1 Luang Prabang, page 82
2 **Luang Prabang detail, page 88**
3 Luang Prabang walking tour, page 96

**The sim** The *sim* is a perfect example of the Luang Prabang style, with its low, sweeping roof in complex overlapping sections. The roof is one of the temple's most outstanding features and is best viewed at a distance. Locals believe that the roof has been styled to resemble a bird, with its wings stretched out to protect her young. The eight central wooden pillars have stencilled motifs in gold and the façade is finely decorated. The beautiful gold-leaf inlay is predominantly floral in design but a few of the images illustrate *Ramayana*-type themes and the interior stencils depict *dharma* wheels and the enigmatic King Chantaphanit.

In an ancient form of the modern-day Mousetrap game, a serpent-like aqueduct sits above the right-hand side of the main entrance. During Lao New

Year water is poured into the serpent's tail, causing it to gush along to its mouth and tip onto the Buddha image below. The water then filters down a drain, flowing under the floor and eventually spouting out of the mouth of the mirrored elephant on the exterior wall.

At the rear of the *sim* is a mosaic representation of the thong copper 'Tree of Life' in glass inlay. This traditional technique can also be seen on the 17th-century doors of That Inheng, near Savannakhet in central Laos (see page 205).

**Side chapels** Behind the *sim* are two red *haw song phra* (side chapels): the one on the left is referred to as **La Chapelle Rouge** (the Red Chapel) and houses a rare Lao reclining Buddha in bronze, dating from the 16th century, which was shown at the 1931 Paris Exhibition. The image was kept in Vientiane and only returned to Luang Prabang in 1964. Several other Buddha images, of varying styles, dates, and materials, surround the altar. The exterior mosaics on the *haw song phra*, which relate local tales, were added in 1957 to honour the 2500th anniversary of the Buddha's birth, death and enlightenment. Somewhat unusually, the fresco features a heroic character from local Lao folklore, Siaw Sawat. The other *haw song phra*, to the right of the *sim*, houses a standing image of the Buddha which is paraded through the streets of the city each New Year and doused in water. A small stone chapel with an ornate roof stands to the left of the *sim*.

**Chapel of the Funeral Chariot** The **haw latsalot** (chapel of the funeral chariot) is diagonally across from the *sim* and was built in 1962. The centrepiece is the grand 12-m-high gilded wooden hearse, with its seven-headed serpent, which was built for King Sisavang Vong, father of the last sovereign, and used to carry his urn to the stadium next to Wat That Luang (see below) where he was cremated in 1959. It was built on the chassis of a six-wheel truck by the sculptor Thid Tan. On top of the carriage sit several sandalwood urns, none of which contain royal ashes. Originally the urns would have held the bodies of the deceased in a foetal position until cremation. The mosaics inside the chapel were never finished but the exterior is decorated with some almost erotic scenes from the *Ramayana* (or local *Phalak Phalam*), sculpted in enormous panels of teak wood and covered with gold leaf. Glass cabinets feature several puppets that were once used in royal performances.

**Other structures** The **Tripitaka Library**, near the boat shelter, was added in 1828. The **haw kong** at the back of the garden was constructed in the 1960s and near it is the site of the copper tree, from which Wat Xieng Thong took its name.

### Wat Pak Khan

At the far northeast end of Phothisarath Road is Wat Pak Khan, which is not particularly noteworthy other than for its scenic location overlooking the confluence of the two rivers.

## Wat Visounnarat (Wat Wisunarat)
*Daily 0800-1700, 20,000 kip.*

This is better known as Wat Visoun and is on the south side of Mount Phousi. It is a replica of the original wooden building, constructed in 1513, which had been the oldest building in Luang Prabang, until it was destroyed by marauding Chinese tribes. Louis Delaporte's sketches from the 1860s show the original temple as boat- or coffin-shaped. The wat was rebuilt in 1898 and, in keeping with the original style, renovators tried to ensure that the brick and stucco construction resembled the original medieval shapes of the lathed wood. The arch on the northwest side of the *sim* is original and the only remaining piece of the 16th-century building.

The *sim* is virtually a museum of religious art, with numerous 'Calling to the Rain' Buddha statues: most are more than 400 years old and have been donated by locals. One of the biggest philanthropists was Prince Phetsarat who donated them in order to redeem the temple after the Haw invasion. Wat Visoun also contains the largest Buddha in the city and old stelae engraved with Pali scriptures (called *hin chaleuk*).

The big stupa, commonly known as **That Makmo** ('melon stupa'), was built by Queen Visunarat in 1504. It is of Sinhalese influence with a smaller stupa at each corner, representing the four elements. The stupa originally contained hundreds of small Buddha images, many of which were pilfered by the Haw. The remaining images were relocated to the Royal Museum for safe-keeping.

## Wat Aham
*Next door to Wat Visoun, daily 0800-1700, 20,000 kip.*

Wat Aham was built by a relative of the king in 1823 and, before Wat Mai took over the function, was the residence of the Supreme Patriach of Lao Buddhism, Sangkharat. The interior has beautiful pillars and roof and overbearing modern murals of the torments of hell, and has a panoramic view of Luang Prabang. The two banyan trees outside are important spirit shrines.

## Wat Phra Maha That
Close to the **Hotel Phousi** on Phothisarath Road, this is a typical Luang Prabang wat, built in the 1500s and restored at the beginning of this century. The ornamentation of the doors and windows of the *sim* merit attention, with their graceful golden figures from the *Phalak Phalam* (the *Ramayana*). The pillars, ornamented with massive *nagas*, are also in traditional Luang Prabang style and reminiscent of certain styles adopted in Thailand. The front of the *sim* was renovated in 1991. The monastery contains a stupa, holding the ashes of Prince Phetsarath and his younger brother Prince Souvanna Phouma.

## Wat Phra Bath
Behind the market at the far northwest end of Phothisarath Road is Wat Phra Bath (or Phraphoutthabat Tha Phralak). The original wooden temple on this site dated back to the 17th century but most of the present structure was built in 1959 by the local Chinese and Vietnamese community. It doesn't evoke the grandeur of other

temples in town but is worth a visit for its picturesque position above the Mekong. It is renowned for its huge Buddha footprint – 'bath' is the Pali word for footprint.

## Wat That Luang

Behind the sports field on Phou Vao Road is Wat That Luang. Rumour suggests that the original structure was built by Indian missionaries, although evidence suggests that the royal wat was built in 1818 by King Manthaturat. Note the bars on the windows of the *sim* in wood and gold leaf, typical of Luang Prabang. The gold stupa, in front of the compound, was built in 1910 and contains the ashes of King Sisavang Vong and his brother. King Sisavang Vong is remembered fondly in the city and many offerings are left here. The stone stupa contains relics of the Buddha and is the site of the **Vien Thien** (candlelit) festival in May (see Festivals, page 110). There are also some traditional *kuti*, or monks' quarters, with carved windows and low roofs.

When James McCarthy visited Wat That Luang at the end of the 19th century, he was told of the ceremonies that were performed here on the accession of a new 'chief'. In his book *Surveying and exploring in Siam* (1900) he writes that the "Kamus assembled and took the oath of allegiance, swearing to die before their chief; shot arrows over the throne to show how they would fight any of its enemies, and holding a lighted candle, prayed that their bodies might be run through with hot iron and that the sky might fall and crush them if they proved unfaithful to their oaths".

## Wat Manolom

South of Wat That Luang (between Phou Vao and Kisarath Settathirat), Wat Manolom was built by the nobles of Luang Prabang to entomb the ashes of King Samsenthai (1373-1416) and is notable for its large armless bronze Buddha statue, one of the oldest Lao images of the Buddha, which dates back to 1372 and weighs two tonnes. Locals maintain that the arm was removed during a skirmish between Siamese and French forces during the latter part of the 19th century. The Lao have replaced the missing appendage with an unsuccessful concrete prosthetic. The monastery has an attractive weathered look and the usual carved doors and painted ceilings. While it is not artistically significant, the temple – or at least the site – is thought to be the oldest in the city, dating back, it is said, to 1375 and the reign of Fa Ngum. Close by are the ruins of an even older temple, **Wat Xieng Kang**, dating from 1363.

## Wat Pa Phon Phao and Santi Chedi

*3 km northeast of town, near Ban Phanom, daily 0800-1000 and 1300-1630, entry by donation.*

Outside town, **Wat Pa Phon Phao** is a forest meditation centre renowned for the teachings of its famous abbot, Ajahn Saisamut, one of the most popular monks in Lao history. Better known to tourists, though, is **Santi Chedi**, known as the Peace Pagoda. It looks as though it is made of pure gold from a distance and it occupies a fantastic position. The wat's construction, funded by donations from

Lao living abroad and from overseas Buddhist federations, was started in 1959 but was only completed in 1988; the names of donors are inscribed on pillars inside. It is modelled on the octagonal Shwedagon Pagoda in Yangon (Rangoon) and its inner walls are festooned with gaily painted frescoes of macabre allegories. The lurid illustrations depict the fate awaiting murderers, adulterers, thieves, drunks and liars who break the five golden rules of Buddhism. Less grotesque paintings, extending up to the fifth floor, document the life of the Buddha. On the second level, it is possible to duck through a tiny opening to admire the Blue Indra statues and the view of Luang Prabang.

### Traditional Arts and Ethnology Centre
*Ban Khamyong, T071-253364, www.taeclaos.org, Tue-Sun 0900-1800, 25,000 kip.*

This fantastic museum is dedicated to the various ethnic groups that inhabit Laos. It is a non-profit centre with a permanent exhibition featuring interesting photographs, religious artefacts, clothing, traditional household objects and the various handicrafts practised by the different groups. Within the exhibition there is a focus on the Hmong and their New Year celebrations; the Khmu, their baskets and the art of backstrap looms; the Mien Yao embroidery and Lanten Taoist religious ceremonies; the Tai Dam bedding and Tai Lue culture. This museum is well worth a visit – particularly for anyone who is planning to venture further north to go trekking.

Attached to the centre is a handicraft shop selling beautiful silks with a large proportion of the profits directly supporting ethnic artisan communities. There's also a café and a small library.

## Architectural tour → Numbers in the text relate to the map on page 96.
### the city's history reflected in its buildings

In a town as small as Luang Prabang, it is easy enough just to set out and find your own route. However, the following walking tour takes in Luang Prabang's architectural highlights (secular as well as religious) and concentrates on the peninsula and the streets that form the original core of the city. The route and the most interesting buildings are shown on the map on page 96. For a guide to the secular architectural styles described in this tour, see page 94.

The start of the tour is on Thanon Phothisarath in front of the **Royal Palace** (**1**; see page 81). Historically, the area to the west of the palace was considered the noble quarter of town, the east was inhabited by the middle classes, while the working class lived around the foot of Phousi. Walking from the Royal Palace along Phothisarath Road southwest towards the post office, look out for the **traditional Lao house** (**2**) in front of Wat Mai. This is a construction on stilts with a closed veranda. Continuing along Phothisarath Road, the former French colonial **Gendarmerie** (**3**) – now the Children's Cultural Centre – is on your left, with gables on the façade. There's another example of a French colonial building, the **Central Bank of Laos** (**4**), on your right.

## A guide to Luang Prabang's secular buildings

**Traditional Lao** The traditional Lao house is rectangular, supported on timber stilts, with a two-sided steep roof and built of bamboo, wood or daub. The stilts help to protect the occupants against wild animals at night and also help to keep the living area dry, especially during the rainy season. The underside also provides a shaded spot for working during the day, as well as area for storage. Living above ground is said to be a characteristic of the Lao and a 16th-century Lao text, the *Nithan Khun Borom*, records that the Lao and Vietnamese Kingdoms of Lane Xang and Dai Viet agreed to demarcate their respective zones of influence according to house style: people living in houses raised on stilts would owe allegiance to Lane Xang, those on the ground, to Dai Viet.

The traditional Lao house is divided into three principal sections, recognizable from the exterior: the sleeping room, the veranda, and the kitchen. Under the main roof is the sleeping area and the very characteristic veranda is contiguous to it. The kitchen is linked to the main building by an open deck commonly used for bathing and washing. Roof, gables, rafters and balustrade are ornamented with lots of savoir-faire. All aspects of the building process of traditional Lao houses were governed by strict rules: the orientation of the building, the date when building could commence, the setting of the wooden piles, and so on, all had to conform to spiritual guidelines.

**French colonial** The French introduced new technologies and materials into house construction, in particular the fired brick and the ceramic roof tile. Traditionally, these materials were reserved for wat construction – explaining why almost all buildings of pre-colonial vintage that you see in Laos today are religious. The main characteristics of French colonial architecture are: extensive roof area to protect against the onslaught of sun and rain; large window openings, paned and shuttered; verandas; arcades; a monumental entrance; a fireplace and chimney breast; brick and wooden decorative details expressing different construction systems (for instance, columns, capitals, rafters and lintels) and ceramic roof tiles.

Turn right onto Kittsarath Setthathirat Road and walk down towards the Mekong. Just past the post office, on the right, is a **Lao house showing French colonial influences** (5). Take the first road on your right to see more examples of traditional Lao houses. In some cases the ground level area, which was once open, has been enclosed to increase the habitable space, using a variety of materials, such as bricks, wood and bamboo (this practice is also very common in Thailand). Traditionally, the under-house area was used for weaving and lounging during the hottest hours of the day. At night, animals were corralled under the house to keep them safe. Fires were also lit here at night during the coldest months of the year.

At the very end of this street, just beside the Royal Palace, are two opulent **Lao-French colonial-style houses** (6), one of which is now a hotel. Turn left to reach the Mekong River road and then right to walk along the riverbank. The **Royal Taxes**

**Lao-French colonial**  As French influences gathered momentum through Lao society, so Laos' indigenous builders began to incorporate some aspects of French architectural design into their constructions. For example, some houses which in most other respects conform to the traditional Lao house style, have French openings and a grandiose doorway leading to an impressive staircase.

**Lao-French colonial-Lao**  In the same way as Lao builders adopted some French elements, so French architects and builders embraced Lao stylistic features. This is particularly evident in the use of temple-style ornamentation, on the roof for example.

**International-modern**  Many houses are now built of concrete and the bungalow has become common throughout the country. In many cases, traditional Lao architectural motifs and designs are merely made from concrete rather than the traditional wood. But concrete has also allowed some innovations in design: cantilevers, flat roofing, pre-fabricated elements and geometric ornamentation are all linked in part to this change in building medium from wood and bamboo to concrete. 'International modern' is used for both domestic buildings and compartments (shophouses).

**Lao contemporary**  Modern homes fall into two categories. Either they are very much in keeping with traditional Lao style, or they embrace modern design and construction materials wholesale. Houses in the first category are part of an evolution of the traditional Lao house: the main entrance has shifted to the gable side, the veranda is smaller, while the open area between the piles below the main house is enclosed with brick or concrete walls and has become part of the house. Wood is still used for exterior facing for the first floor, but the walls of the ground floor are now made from stone and bricks. This is the most common form of house built in Laos today.

The second category of Lao contemporary house is built entirely of brick and concrete and most Lao consider it to be more luxurious.

office (7), now operating as a tourism company, lies behind the Royal Palace. It is decorated with the classic three-headed elephant insignia. To see some truly beautiful examples of traditional Lao architecture, enter **Wat Xieng Mouan** (8; see page 87) and take the exit into the alley running behind the temple. Opposite the wat is a **traditional Lao house** (9).

Continue up to Phothisarath Road, turn left and take a look at the **compartment buildings** (10) on both sides of the street. These skilfully combine commercial and residential functions under the same roof, much like the Chinese 'shophouse' found throughout Southeast Asia, in which the ground floor serves as a business, shop or workshop. The Lao traditionally never lived and worked in the same building; they always ran their businesses from some other location, even if it was a street-side stall just a few yards away from their home. It is therefore safe to assume that these 'compartments' were used by Chinese and Vietnamese immigrants. They are built in a variety of styles, mainly French colonial and Lao-French colonial.

Walking on towards the tip of the peninsula, there are several other notable buildings, including the **French colonial school (11)** and the **Villa Santi Hotel (12)**, on the left-hand side of the road, and **Villa Savanh (13)**, a traditional Lao compartment building on the right. At **Wat Xieng Thong (14;** see page 89) take the exit from the monastery on the east side to look at the modest **bamboo house (15)** down the alley.

At the tip of the peninsula, turn back along the Mekong River road. On the left is the **Calao Inn (16)**, an example of a renovated colonial building and the only Portuguese building on the peninsula. Immediately after the inn, take the first road on your left and then turn right. Along this road, at the first intersection, are two very fine **Lao houses** showing **French colonial influences (17)**. Past the intersection further along the same street, the **School of Fine Arts (18)** is one of few Lao traditional-style buildings in Luang Prabang, with two adjoining roofs. Return to the Mekong River road along which are a number of buildings showing various degrees of international influence.

Cross the peninsula to the Nam Khan river road and then follow the road south around Phousi. Along the road are a number of examples of Lao traditional and Lao-French colonial buildings. On Rathsavong Street is the **French colonial hospital (19)**, now the most expensive hotel in Laos, the **Amantaka**, www.amanresorts.com/amantaka. Further along, turn right towards Nam Phou. This

**3 Luang Prabang walking tour**

| Royal Palace **1** | Wat Xieng Mouan **8** | Calao Inn **16** |
| Traditional Lao house **2** | Traditional Lao house **9** | Lao houses with French |
| Gendarmerie **3** | Compartment buildings **10** | colonial influence **17** |
| Central Bank of Laos **4** | French colonial | School of Fine Arts **18** |
| Lao-French colonial | school **11** | French colonial |
| house **5** | Villa Santi Hotel **12** | hospital (Amantaka) **19** |
| Lao-French colonial | Villa Savanh **13** | Lao-French colonial |
| house **6** | Wat Xieng Thong **14** | buildings **20** |
| Royal Taxes office **7** | Bamboo house **15** | Maison Souvannaphoum **21** |

→ **Luang Prabang maps**
1 Luang Prabang, page 82
2 Luang Prabang detail, page 88
3 Luang Prabang walking tour, page 96

street has a number of **Lao-French colonial buildings** (**20**), showing French influences on Lao architecture. Follow the road until it reaches the **Maison Souvannaphoum** (**21**) on the left. Take a minute to have a look at the main building (not the new annexes), which was built in 1962 in a modern French-colonial style. The tour ends north of here at the post office.

## West bank of the Mekong

*an alternative day trip to Pak Ou caves*

The monasteries and villages on the right bank of the Mekong are accessible by boat from Luang Prabang. For anyone who does not fancy spending three hours on a boat travelling to and from the Pak Ou caves, this makes for an enchanting alternative excursion. Also on the right bank are two hills, **Phou Thao** and **Phou Nang**, named after Luang Prabang's very own Romeo and Juliet: Thao Phouthasene and Nang Kang Hi were lovers who died in tragic but romantic circumstances only to find themselves transformed into rock and incorporated in the local landscape. The hills are said to look like a man and woman sleeping next to each other.

### Wat Long Khoun
*Daily 0800-1700, small entry charge for foreigners. Boats run from the boat pier downstream from the Royal Palace to the other side of the river, near Wat Long Khoun or Ban Xiang Men. Public ferries also run regularly across the river for 5000 kip.*

The first stop is usually Wat Long Khoun at the top of a flight of steps leading up from the riverbank, almost opposite Wat Xieng Thong. This wat was built in two stages and was renovated by the École Française de l'Extrême-Orient in 1994 at a cost of FF400,000. The oldest section of the wat is at the back and dates from the 18th century. The beautifully sculpted door was made in 1937. The *sim* on the river side of the compound is a delightful building, small, well-proportioned and intimate. It has some vibrant but fading Jataka murals. On the exterior, either side of the main doorway, are two bearded warriors with swords slung over their backs, which appear to be representations of Chinese Haw soldiers. The kings of Lane Xang are said to have come on three-day retreats to this spot, to prepare for their coronation.

### Wat Tham
*100 m upstream from Wat Long Khoun, daily 0800-1700, small charge.*

A well-trodden path leads upstream to Wat Tham, literally 'cave monastery', nestled in Sakkarin Savannakuha Cave, above a dilapidated *sala*. The wat is a limestone cave temple with stairs and balustrades cut out of the stone. The interior is very dark but is worth exploring, as it is stacked with

> **Tip...**
> It is easier to explore sights outside the city with a tour operator, as roads are unmarked and rural communities are less used to tourists. Many hotels organize trips.

ancient, rotting Buddha images. During **Pi Mai** celebrations the cave temple comes alive with pilgrims and candles. Resident children, with the aid of dim torches, will lead visitors down into the airless cavern, pointing out notable rock formations and the Buddha images. Fearful that the torches may not be powered by long-life batteries, visitors may emerge into the light with a degree of relief. This is not an experience for the claustrophobic. If the cave is locked ask someone at Wat Long Khoun to let you in.

## Wat Chom Phet and Wat Xiang Men

Leading from Wat Long Khoun downstream is another well-trodden track. Before reaching the small community of Ban Xiang Men, a stairway leads up to **Wat Chom Phet** ⓘ *small entry charge*, a hilltop *sim* offering fine views over the Mekong River and Luang Prabang. The site has been apparently abandoned as a religious site, although the mouldering *sim*, kiltering *chedis* and profusion of apricot-coloured lilies give the place a rather attractive 'lost wat in the forest' feel. It is worth coming up for the view of Luang Prabang alone – a perfect panorama of the city.

Continuing downstream, the track passes through **Ban Xiang Men**, a peaceful village where households cultivate the exposed riverbanks during the dry season, taking advantage of the annual deposition of silt, which is especially fertile. **Wat Xiang Men** was originally built in 1592 by Chau Naw Kaewkumman, son of Setthathirat, and has undergone extensive renovations since. The doors date from the original construction, as do several artefacts within the wat. This temple is particularly sacred to local residents because the Pra Bang was located here for a week when it returned to Luang Prabang from Vientiane in 1867. About 1 km downstream, in a clearing in the middle of the forest, is the **royal cemetery**. There are sculptures depicting those members of the royal family who could not be cremated for religious reasons, such as children who died as infants and victims of contagious diseases. It is hard to find a local guide willing to take you there as most are terrified of ghosts.

## Ban Chan

Ban Chan is on the northern bank of the Mekong, 5 km downstream from Luang Prabang (about 15 minutes by boat) or 4 km on the road beyond the evening market to Ban Sangkhalok and a short crossing by boat (villagers will paddle you across). The village is known for its local pottery industry and mostly produces thongs (large water storage jars) and salt pots. Boats regularly cross the river – although the fare varies depending on the number of passengers. You can charter a boat from the main pier on the Mekong for a couple of hours. It is possible to cross over to Wat Long Khoun, walk downstream and catch another boat back to the Luang Prabang bank of the river either at Ban Xiang Men or Ban Chan. Or the circuit can be completed in the reverse direction. There are a couple of foodstalls in Ban Xiang Men.

### Ban Phanom and around

Ban Phanom is 6 km east of Luang Prabang. This is a 300-year-old weaving village, where shawls (*pha biang*) and sarongs (*pha sin*) are made from silk and cotton. Although best known for its weaving, the village's main economic activity is rice cultivation. The 100 or so families in Ban Phanom are members of the Lue minority, who originated from Yunnan in southern China. They were traditionally the king's weavers, soldiers and palace servants. King Sisavang Vong's dancers were traditionally handpicked from this village at the age of six or seven and were required to undergo intensive training aimed at increasing their flexibility.

Some of the larger producers have turned their houses into small shops and it is now possible to buy lengths of cloth at any time. Tourists are more than welcome to wander around and look at the process of silk manufacture, from the silk worm's inception to finish, with the weavers clacking away at their looms.

The French explorer Henri Mouhot stumbled across Angkor Wat in 1860 but succumbed to a malarial attack in Luang Prabang on 10 November the following year: his last journal entry read, "Have pity on me, O my God". Resident foreign aid workers spent months searching for his grave before rediscovering it in 1990, 2 km beyond Ban Phanom, at the top of a bank looking down into the Nam Khan, a tributary of the Mekong. **Henri Mouhot's tomb**, 3 km from Ban Phanom, was constructed six years after his death, in 1867, and was designed by another French explorer, Doudart de Lagrée. It is also possible to get a boatman to take you the extra kilometres. If you are unsure ask villagers in Ban Phanom for directions; children will sometimes show visitors the way.

### Ban Hat Hien

This village is on the airport road; fork right before the terminal and at the end of the road is Luang Prabang's knife-making village. Residents beat scrap metal over hot stoves to make blades and tools. The flames are fanned by bellows, originally made from teak tubes and operated with plungers. The results of their labours can be seen in the markets in town. From the nearby Nam Khan, villagers harvest 'seaweed', which is dried, fried and eaten with sesame in a dish known as *khai pehn*; it is sold all over the country.

The Pak Ou caves are perhaps the most popular excursion from Luang Prabang and are located 25 km upstream from the city, set in a limestone cliff opposite the mouth of the Nam Ou tributary (Pak Ou means 'Mouth of the Ou'). For many, it is the boat ride, rather than the caves themselves that make this a worthwhile day out. The two caves are studded with thousands of wood-and-gold Buddha

## BACKGROUND

### Pak Ou caves

The two sacred caves were supposedly discovered by King Setthathirat in the 16th century but it is likely that the caverns were associated with spirit (*phi*) worship before the arrival of Buddhism in Laos. For years the caves, which locals still believe to be the home of guardian spirits, were inhabited by monks. The king visited them every New Year, staying at Ban Pak Ou on the opposite bank of the Mekong, where there is a royal wat with beautiful old murals on the front gable. The famous French traveller, Francis Garnier, also visited the caves on his travels in the 1860s.

Some of the Buddha images in the caves are thought to be more than 300 years old, although most date from the 18th and 19th centuries. In the past, gold and silver images were in abundance but these have all been stolen; now the Buddha images are crafted from wood, copper or stone.

images – 2500 in the lower cave and 1500 in the upper – and are one of the main venues for Pi Mai in April, when hundreds make the pilgrimage upriver from Luang Prabang. During the dry season the river shrinks, exposing huge sandbanks, which are improbable gold fields. Families camp out on the banks of the Mekong and pan for gold, most of which is sold to Thailand.

### Exploring the caves

Many restaurants, hotels, guesthouses and tour companies in Luang Prabang will arrange this boat trip, which is the best way to reach the caves. Otherwise, boats can be chartered from Tha Heua Me or from one of the stairways leading down to the river along Manthatourath, where boatmen wait for business. Boats will often stop at Xang Hai (see below) and Ban Pak Ou, across the water from the caves, where enterprising villages have set up thatched stalls serving sticky rice, barbecued Mekong fish and t*am maak houng* (spicy green papaya salad), plus cold drinks and snacks. It is also possible to take a tuk-tuk to the caves, but that option is far less fun.

Torches are available but candles make it possible to see reasonably well after your eyes have become accustomed to the dark. The lower cave, really a deep overhang, is named **Tham Ting**, while the upper, an enervating climb up 100 or so slippery steps, is called **Tham Phum**. A carved wooden frieze, supporting two massive wooden doors flanks the entrance of the cave. Aside from the numerous Buddha images, the cave features a statue of one of Buddha's disciples and a carved wooden water channel for the ceremonial washing of the sculptures. The cave is around 54 m long and the sculptures range from 10 cm to 1.5 m in height. Many of the images are in the distinctive attitude of the Buddha calling for rain (the arms held by the side, with palms turned inwards).

### Xang Hai

Xang Hai is 20 km upstream from Luang Prabang, on the way to Pak Ou caves and a standard stop-off on a Pak Ou tour. In the rainy season the villages grow glutinous or 'sticky' rice and in the dry season they ferment it in water and yeast to brew *lao-lao*, a moonshine whisky. The village has now become rather touristy, with scores of stalls selling textiles, ceramics, souvenirs from Thailand and China, opium pipes and weights, ethnic clothes, and some *lao-lao* too. Villagers are delighted to give visitors a tasting session.

## South of the city

spectacular waterfalls but lots of visitors

### Tad Sae

*Head south along Route 13 for 17 km and turn off for Ban En (signposted); follow this track for 2 km. From the village you can buy a cheap boat ticket to take you to the falls, 10,000 kip. Foodstalls and a restaurant on site. A tuk-tuk from Luang Prabang will cost about US$22.*

Seventeen kilometres (30 minutes) south of Luang Prabang are the beautiful multi-tiered, limestone cascades of Tad Sae, which make for a great half-day trip during the rainy season. (In the dry season, the waterfall is reduced to a mere trickle.) The falls sit at the confluence of the Huay Say and Nam Khan rivers and feature a multitude of crystal-clear swimming holes, similar to Kuang Si but on a smaller scale. With the addition of kayak trips, elephant rides and a zipline course run by **Flight of the Nature** ⓘ *www.flightofthenature.com*, these falls are no longer a peaceful haven but the area remains a beautiful spot and is a big hit with adrenalin junkies.

### ★ Tad Kuang Si

*30 km south Luang Prabang; admission 20,000 kip. Travel agents run tours or you can charter a tuk-tuk for about US$22 (make sure you agree how long you want to spend at the falls). Slow boats take 1 hr downriver and 2 hrs back, via Ban Ou (a pretty little village), where it is necessary to take a tuk-tuk (or walk) the last 6 km to the waterfalls. A 3rd possibility is to take a speedboat from either Tha Heua Xieng Keo (3 km downstream from Luang Prabang) or Ban Don, a few kilometres upstream.*

These waterfalls are 30 km south of Luang Prabang on a tributary of the Mekong. The trip to the falls is almost as scenic as the cascades themselves, passing through small Hmong and Khmu villages and vivid green, terraced rice paddies.

The falls are stunningly beautiful, misty cascades flowing over limestone formations, which eventually collect in several tiered, turquoise pools. Originally the waterfall's surroundings were inhabited by numerous animals, including the deer that give the falls their name, Kuang Si. However, the only wildlife you're likely to see today are some Asiatic black bears, rescued from poachers, in enclosures halfway between the entrance and the falls. The United Nations Development

Programme (UNDP) has cleared a path to the falls which winds right up to the top. The bottom level of the falls has been turned into a park and viewing area, with a small platform that affords good photo opportunities. The local village's economy seems increasingly to depend on the tourist business, so you'll find a large number of vendors selling snacks and drinks and some souvenirs. The site also has public toilets and changing rooms.

Although the waterfall is impressive year round, in the summer, the water cascades so gently over the various tiers of the falls that it's possible to scramble behind the curtains of water without getting wet. In the rainy season, the gallons of water roaring down the mountain catch the imagination and could form the backdrop for any Indiana Jones or James Bond adventure. Best of all, and despite appearances, it's still possible to take the left-hand path halfway up the falls and strike out through the pouring torrents and dripping caves to the heart of the waterfall. The pools above the falls are sheltered and comparatively private and make a wonderful spot for a swim; the second tier is best for a dip. If you follow the water either upstream or downstream there are plenty of other shady swimming spots. Note that swimming is only permitted in designated pools and, as the Lao swim fully clothed, you should wear modest swimwear and bring a sarong (this is a very popular area for Lao people to come and picnic).

## Hmong villages
traditional mountain villages with opportunities for trekking

There are numerous Hmong villages within a shortish distance of Luang Prabang and on the way to Kuang Si falls. For more information about the Hmong, see page 304.

**Ban Long Lan** is east of town. To get there, take the main road upstream. At Ban Pak Xuang, just before the bridge over the river Xuang, turn right to follow this tributary of the Mekong. Just before reaching Ban Kokvan turn right onto a track to Ban Natan. From here an even smaller track leads off to the left. It follows the Houei Hia, a small stream, between two mountains and works its way upwards to the mountain village of Ban Longlan. Allow about two hours to get there; in the rainy season you will need a trail bike or 4WD. Few tourists visit this village so dress modestly and be especially sensitive to local sensibilities. This village is populated by people who were resettled in efforts to stop poppy growing and now their main form of income is farming vegetables.

Another Hmong village downstream from Luang Prabang is **Ban Long Lao**. Again this is a village rarely visited by tourists and it is best to go with a guide. Contact **Fair Trek** (www.trekking-in-laos.com) which can arrange visits and has also opened a community-based tourism project with a bungalow lodge in the pretty village of **Long Lao Mai**.

## Tourist information

### Luang Prabang Tourist Information Centre
*Sisavangvong Rd, T071-212487.*
Aside from provincial information, it offers a couple of good ecotourism treks (which support local communities). The office also has informative displays on Lao culture and its ethnic groups.

## Where to stay

Accommodation in Luang Prabang is generally high quality, with some extremely tasteful converted houses featuring dark woods and crisp white linens. The restored colonial villas on the peninsula and along Phou Vao Rd tend to get booked up, particularly during national holidays. For the more upmarket options, advance bookings are recommended at all times except in the wet season.

Around Lao New Year, hotels and guesthouses can almost charge what they like but during the wet season prices tend to be a lot lower, with smaller establishments dropping prices by around a 3rd and more expensive hotels knocking off about 20%. Internet rates are considerably cheaper than rack rates for hotels in the upper price range.

Some of the best-value accommodation can be found toward the tip of the peninsula around Wat Xieng Thong, and also among the quiet streets around Phou Vao. Another option is to stay slightly out of the old town where your money will go a lot further.

### $$$$ 3 Nagas Alila
*Sakkaline Rd, T071-253888, www. alilahotels.com/3nagas.*
Housed in a beautifully restored building, this boutique hotel is a beauty. Attention to detail is what sets it apart from the rest: from the 4-poster bed covered with local fabrics to the large deep-set bathtub with natural handmade beauty products. There's a lovely sitting area in each room, plus traditional *torchis* walls and teak floors. The **3 Nagas** restaurant opposite the hotel is also excellent.

### $$$$ Maison Souvannaphoum
*Phothisarath, T071-212200, www. angsana.com.*
Formerly Prince Souvannaphouma's residence, this place really is fit for royalty. There are 4 spacious suites and 23 rooms. Great location close to the night market. The service is top notch.

### $$$$ Mekong Riverview
*At the very tip of the peninsula, T071-254900, www.mekongriverview.com.*
This relative newcomer is an excellent addition to the town. Rooms with polished wood floors are individually decorated and come with gorgeous wooden furniture including writing bureaux in the suites. Riverview rooms have huge, very private balconies complete with wicker chairs, perfect for an afternoon snooze. Breakfast is served al fresco. Refined.

### $$$$ Xieng Thong Palace
*Next to Wat Xieng Thong, T071-213200, www.xiengthongpalace.com.*
Housed in the last residence of the royal family, this is a true luxury property. The 2-storey suites are the highlight,

with their private indoor plunge pools.
A fantastic buffet breakfast is served
overlooking the river. Superb service
and a top-end spa.

### $$$$-$$$ The Belle Rive
*Souvannakhamphong Rd, T071-260733,
www.thebellerive.com.*
Sumptuous well-equipped rooms
occupy elegant colonial-style buildings
facing the Mekong on a quiet part
of the peninsula. Watch boats drifting
past from the garden patio of the
hotel's restaurant. The attraction of
this hotel lies in its nostalgic charm;
you almost expect to find Graham
Greene or Noel Coward staying here.
A Luang Prabang classic.

### $$$$-$$$ Villa Maly
*Souvannaphoum Rd, T071-253903,
www.villa-maly.com.*
This is a gorgeous boutique hotel set
around a beautiful pool with ivory-
coloured umbrellas in a leafy garden.
A former royal residence, it is stylish and
petite, and the rooms are suitably plush.
The bathrooms, however, are a little on
the small side. The service here remains
impeccable and polished.

### $$$$-$$$ Villa Santi Hotel
*Sisavangvong Rd, T071-252157, www.
villasantihotel.com.*
Almost an institution in Luang
Prabang, this is a restored house from
the early 20th century that served as
the private residence of the first King
Sisavangvong's wife and then Princess
Manilai. It's a charming place, full of
character and efficiently run, and it has
recently received a facelift. There are
6 heavenly suites in the old building,
and 14 newer rooms, with baths and
showers, in a stylish annexe.

### $$$ The Apsara
*Kingkitsarath, T071-254670, www.
theapsara.com.*
Ivan Scholte, wine connoisseur and
antique collector, has done a perfect job
on this establishment. It oozes style. The
stunningly beautiful rooms are themed
by colour, with 4-poster beds, changing
screen, big bathtub and lovely balcony.
Very romantic with a modern twist.
The rooms in the 2nd building are also
magnificent with *terrazzo* showers you
could fit an elephant in. The foyer and
lovely restaurant (see Restaurants, below)
are decorated with Vietnamese lanterns,
Burmese offering boxes and modern art.
Its sister hotel, **Apsara Rive Droite**, across
the river, is also a gorgeous place to stay.

### $$$-$$ Villa Ban Lakkham
*Souksasuem Rd, T085-7125 2677, www.
villabanlakkham.com.*
Dark woods, deep reds, black-and-white
photography and river-view rooms
with pretty panelled French doors lend
this hotel an old world charm. Low
season 'hot deals' are great value. Lao,
Vietnamese and Western breakfasts.
Free bikes. Very welcoming.

### $$ Ammata Guesthouse
*37 Khunsua Rd, T071-212175,
phetmanyp@yahoo.com.au.*
Very popular guesthouse with
largish rooms decorated simply and
stylishly with wooden furniture
and polished floorboards. Hot
water and en suite bathroom.

### $$ Nam Khan Riverside
*Kingkitsarath Rd, T020-9721 8789,
namkhanriverside@gmail.com.*
Not as plush as some of the options along
the Nam Khan, this hotel nonetheless
wins out thanks to the lower prices and
the balconies overlooking the water on

which breakfast can be served. Managed by the friendly Mr Minh Duc, aka Ben, who is happy to give advice on what to see and do. Prices drop substantially in low season.

## $$ Oui's Guesthouse
*At the end of the peninsula in Ban Khili on Sukkaserm, T071-252374, ouisguesthouse@gmail.com.*
Run by 3 sisters, this is a charming little guesthouse with sparkling new rooms and polished floorboards, hot water, TV and fridge. Nicely decorated with local artefacts.

## $$ Pack Luck
*Ban Vat Nong, opposite* L'Éléphant, *T071-253373, packluck@hotmail.com.*
This boutique hotel has 5 rooms that you couldn't swing a cat in but are very tastefully decorated with beautiful fabrics. The luxurious bathrooms have deep slate bathtubs. Lots of character.

## $$ Sokdee Residence
*Just off Ounkham Rd, T071-252555, www.sokdeeresidence.com.*
Down a quiet, pleasant sidestreet, this small hotel offers clean rooms with wooden floors and comfortable beds plus individual outdoor seating areas. Good value in a great location.

## $ Mano Guesthouse
*Phamahapasaman Rd, T071-253112.*
A clean guesthouse, with a tiled ground floor and wood upstairs, this is a charming, family-run option, with some a/c. A large chess board is carved into a stone table outside. The owners speak English and some French.

## $ Pa Phai
*Opposite Wat Pa Phai.*
For those looking for a very cheap option with plenty of authenticity, this is a good choice. The old traditional house has seen very little in the way of renovation – think bamboo walls, no a/c and rock hard beds. Still, it's clean, well located and the price is right. Also offers a laundry service and bike hire.

### Outside of town

## $$$$ Belmond La Résidence Phou Vao
*4 km east of the airport, T071-212 5303, www.residencephouvao.com.*
A stunning location with expansive views over the green hills. Every detail in this hotel is perfect, from the fragrance of frangipani that wafts through the foyer to the carefully lit infinity pool. Rooms are huge with beautiful décor, lounge area and simply divine bathrooms. This is a luxury hotel through and through. In the low season rates drop substantially. A real treat.

## $$$$ Grand Luang Prabang Hotel & Resort
*Ban Xiengkeo, 4 km from town, T071-253851, www.grandluangprabang.com.*
Beautifully restored hotel in the former Prince Phetsarath's residence. Simple, classically decorated rooms set in lovely gardens. Try to get a room with a view of the river. An extremely relaxing place to hole-up for a few days.

## $$$$ Kiridara
*Ban Naviengkham, 5-min tuk-tuk ride from town, T0871-261888, www. snhcollection.com.*
Set on a hill, the **Kiridara** offers breathtaking views over Luang Prabang, a beautiful pool and a range of tasteful rooms and suites making this a wonderful choice for those seeking out-of-town lodgings. The pick-up/drop-off service is very handy and the service and buffet breakfasts are first-rate.

#### $$$$ Luang Say Residence
*Just off the Phou Vao Rd, a few mins from town, T071-260891, www. luangsayresidence.com.*
Stunning, all-suite property with the air of a sprawling colonial country club and a future classic. 4-poster beds, huge, well-appointed bathrooms, deep arm chairs and private verandas with mountain views all combine to make these rooms rather special. Also has a fantastic restaurant, bar serving tapas and the best pool in town.

#### $$$ Ock Pop Tok Villa
*125/10 Ban Saylom, Living Craft Centre, T071-212597, www.ockpoptok.com/stay.*
4 individually designed rooms are on offer in a fabulous villa overlooking the Mekong. Breakfast is served in the beautiful café on the river. This is a very tranquil and special option. Guests are eligible for a discount on the weaving classes in the **Living Craft Centre**.

---

### Restaurants

Note that Luang Prabang has a curfew; most places won't stay open past 2400.
Luang Prabang produces a number of culinary specialities that make interesting souvenirs. The market is a good starting point for buying these, although restaurants have also latched onto their popularity. The most famous is *khai pehn*, dried river weed from the Nam Khan, mixed with sesame and fried. *Cheo bong*, a spicy, smoky purée made with buffalo hide, is also popular. Other delicacies include: *phak nam* (a watercress that grows around waterfalls and used in soups and salads), *mak kham kuan* (tamarind jam) and *mak nat kuan* (pineapple jam).
One of the best local culinary experiences is to eat at the Lao food stalls that run on a lane off the night market on Sisavangvon Rd, 1600-2200. Here you can pick up fresh spring rolls (*nem dip*) papaya salad (*tam som*), sticky rice (*khao niao*), the local delicacy Luang Prabang sausage (*sai oua*), barbecue chicken on a stick (*gai*) or fish (*pa*), dried buffalo (*sin savanh*) and dried seaweed. For meat and fish, we recommend one of the stalls closest to the river end run by the rather rotund and serious looking Lao grill master and his smiling wife. There are also a number of cheap buffets where you can get a selection of local curries and dishes. If you don't want your food too spicy ask for '*bo pet*'.

#### $$$ Tangor
*63 Sisavangvong Rd, T071-260761, www. letangor.com.*
Justly popular French-run restaurant that's a hit not only with tourists, but with Luang Prabang's expat set. Creative and well-executed fusion cuisine and classics. Superb presentation and attentive service. An all-round winner. Don't miss the *ceviche* or the pork skewers and try the excellent tarte tatin for pudding. Delectable.

#### $$$-$$ 3 Nagas
*Opposite the hotel of the same name, Sakkaline Rd, T071-253888.*
The food here is both Lao and Western and highly recommended. The restaurant also has an exemplary wine list and its own unique concoctions of cocktails.

#### $$$-$$ The Apsara
*See Where to stay.*
Lao/Thai/Western fusion restaurant offering dishes such as braised pork belly and pumpkin, and great fish cakes. Try their delicious red curry cream soup with lentils and smoked duck or braised beef shin Chinese style. Good value.

### $$$-$$ Couleur Café/Restaurant
*Ban Vat Nong, T020-55621064.*
The French expats in town still have nothing but praise for this place with its French and Lao meals and chic setting. Good wine list and great steaks.

### $$$-$$ L'Éléphant
*Ban Vat Nong, T071-252482, contact@elephant-restau.com.*
Upmarket and utterly delectable cuisine in a fantastic ambiance. The French dishes are excellent (try the lamb shank) and so are the faithful renditions of Lao classics. A good place to treat yourself. Highly recommended.

### $$ Café Toui
*Sisavangatthana Rd, T020-5657 6763, www.cafetoui.com.*
Run by the lovely Toui, this small, intimate café-cum-restaurant is perhaps the best place to enjoy Lao food in a comfortable setting. Recommended dishes include the red fish curry, sublime Luang Prabang sausage and the buffalo steak. If you can't decide, the tasting platter is also a solid choice. Those who eat here once are highly likely to return. A gem.

### $$ Khai Phaen
*Sisavang Vatana Rd, T030-515 5221, www.tree-alliance.org.*
Opened in 2014, this is a sister restaurant to the other Friends International NGO establishments, including the excellent **Makphet** in Vientiane. As such, it runs as a training restaurant for former street youth. Managed by Anousin aka 'Noy'; this latest addition to the chain is every inch as good as the others. Don't miss the Sandan's cashew nut crusted banana fritter with kaffir lime and coconut ice cream, nor the crispy cinnamon pork belly. Delectable dining with a feel-good factor. Highly recommended.

### $$ Ock Pok Tock Silk Road Café
*2 km out of town at the Living Crafts Centre, T071-212597, www.ockpoptok. com/eat. Closed for dinner.*
A free tuk-tuk service whisks guests out to this café right on the banks of the Mekong in a wonderfully peaceful spot. The brunches with granola and fresh yoghurt make for a healthy late start to the day. For lunch, try the lemongrass chicken or the fried river weed – a local speciality.

### $$ Pizza Phan Luang
*Phan Luang, across the Nam Khan, T020-5692 2529.*
Best visited in the dry season when it's possible to wander across the bamboo bridge, **Pizza Phan Luang** serves good quality, wood-fired pizzas in a romantic candlelit atmosphere.

### $$ Tamarind
*Facing Wat Nong, T020-7777 0484, www. tamarindlaos.com. Mon-Sat 1100-1800.*
Pretty restaurant offering brilliant modern Lao cuisine. The sampling platter is a fantastic way to try a few different Lao classics. On Fri nights the fish BBQ dinner is a lively affair with a large selection of Lao dips and information about Lao food and eating customs. The owners, Joy and Caroline, have received many accolades and can give you lots of information on the area. Their cooking classes are also a hit.

### $$-$ Dyen Sabai
*Ban Phan Luang, T020-5510 4817.*
Depending on the season, guests reach this cosy restaurant with pretty lighting via a bamboo bridge or a short paddle boat ride across the river. The unusual cocktails and Lao food are not to be missed, nor the amazing sunset views. This is a highly recommended spot.

### $$-$ Tum Tum Cheng
*Just off Sakkaline Rd, T071-252019.*
Lao food prepared by a Hungarian expat.
Tasty fusion-style meals. Very comfortable
outdoor seating. Also offers classes in
Lao cooking and classical Lao dancing.

### $ Atsalin Restaurant
*Visunnarat Rd, T020-999 9933.*
For those looking for a quick hit of Lao
food on a budget, this no-frills joint is
hard to beat. Absolutely delicious slow-
cooked pork topped rice and a range of
other Lao staples. Not a place to linger,
but a fine place to eat well, very cheaply.

### $ Thai Food Restaurant
*Opposite the school.*
This pavement restaurant has no name
or phone number, just a simple sign
advertising 'Thai Food'. Serves a very
good *pad ka prao* and a superb *pad
thai*. Tasty and cheap and very friendly
owners, although limited English is
spoken. Good option for a quick lunch.

## Cafés and bakeries

Big Tree Café and Gallery
*46 Ban Vat Nong, T020-7777 6748, www.
bigtreecafe.com. Open 0730-2100.*
Small, cosy café serving excellent, bitter
espresso. Large photography prints of
Laos line the walls. Beautiful views from
the seats across the road on the river.
Also serves some good Korean food
thanks to the Korean owner.

Café Ban Vat Sene
*Sakkhaline Rd, opposite Wat Sene.*
A very pleasant option, with a breezy,
colonial atmosphere, the white walls
contrasting with the polished dark
wooden floors, tables and chairs.
Great for breakfast. The French food
is a treat. Good place for coffee or tea.
Outside tables offer excellent views

of the school opposite and the noise
of the kids playing at lunch add to the
excellent atmosphere. An easy place to
lose an afternoon.

Joma
*Sisavangvong Rd near Nam Phou
fountain, T071-252292.*
With several other branches in Hanoi,
**Joma** serves an array of comfort foods
including sandwiches, quiche and
bagels alongside Western coffees
and a big range of shakes. Now has a
2nd branch along the Nam Khong River.

La Banneton
*Sakkhaline Rd, T020-5973 2608,
dricker@yahoo.fr. Open 0730-2000.*
Beautiful open-fronted French café
with views of Wat Sop Sickharam.
Superb pastries and a simple menu
of classics including *feuillete*, croque
monsieur and salads.

L'Étranger
*Kingkitsarath Rd, near Hive Bar, T020-
5547 1736.*
Great little bookshop-cum-café. The
upstairs is exceptionally comfortable
with cushions and low tables. This is
the perfect place to wind down, grab
a book and have a cuppa. Outstanding
breakfasts. A movie is shown daily at 1900.

## Bars and clubs

A sunset beer at one of the many
restaurants overlooking the river is
divine – just take a wander along the
Mekong and see which one takes your
fancy. After everything closes most
locals head to **Dao Fa** or **Yensabai** and
finish the night with noodles on Phou
Vao Rd. The other popular late-night
drinking option is the bowling alley;
ask any tuk-tuk driver and they'll be
able to get you there.

### Chez Matt
*Opposite Icon Klub, T020-7777 9497.*
The French owner, Matthieu, takes his wine very seriously, ensuring this is one of the best (if not *the* best), places in town to order by the glass or bottle. Established late 2013, this chic, open-fronted space boasts attentive staff and a fine selection of charcuterie and cheese boards.

### Dao Fa nightclub
*On the way to the Southern bus station.*
Extremely popular with locals and plays Asian dance music at deafening volumes. Standing room only. Fun to try once.

### Hive Bar
*Kingkitsarath Rd, next to L'Étranger, T020-5999 5370.*
One of the first bars to open on what has become something of a strip, **Hive** is still going strong and draws in crowds with its fashion shows and dance performances. Also a decent spot for some Western fodder, such as pizzas.

### Icon Klub
*Just off of Sisavangvong Rd near the Khan River, T071-254905, www.iconklub. com. Open 1730-2400.*
Run by the lovely Elizabeth since 2009, **Icon** is a tiny bar that's perfect for well-made cocktails and interesting conversation with your fellow patrons and the owner herself. Good music. Don't miss the *Old Fashioned*.

### Lao Lao Garden
*Kingkitsarath Rd.*
A tiered landscaped terrace, with low lighting and cheap cocktails many featuring *lao lao*), that's become a favourite backpacker haunt. A bonfire keeps you cosy in the winter months. The Lao-style barbecue is great.

### Red Bul Bar
*In the bar area opposite Hive, www. redbulbarluangprabang.com.*
Popular with locals, expats and backpackers alike, this bar has a pool table, table football and a party atmosphere when it fills up. A good place to meet new people.

### Utopia
*On the Khan River in Ban Aphay.*
Landscaped gardens, a sand volleyball court popular with locals as well as tourists, and a long wooden deck overlooking the Khan. Great for a drink at sunset.

### Yensabai
*Phou Vao Rd. Open 2100-late.*
Normally the last bar standing, this is the place to head to when **Dao Fa** has closed its doors. Popular with locals and the odd backpacker. The late-night noodle shop opposite is an institution.

## Entertainment

### Theatre and dance
Traditional dance performances, influenced by the *Ramayana*, are held at the **Theatre Phalak Phalam** in the Royal Palace compound, T071-253705, Mon, Wed and Sat at 1800, 75,000-180,000 kip. The traditional dance of Luang Prabang, which is incorporated into most shows, is more than 600 years old.

An ethnic fashion show is held at **Hive** bar most nights in conjunction with Kop Noi.

## Festivals

**Apr  Pi Mai** (Lao New Year; movable) is the time when the tutelary spirits of the old year are replaced by those of the new. It has special significance in Luang Prabang, with some traditions that are no longer observed in Vientiane. In the past, the king and queen would clean the principal Buddha images in the city's main wats, while masked dancers pranced through the streets re-enacting the founding of the city by 2 mythical beasts. People from all over the province descend on the city. The newly crowned Miss New Year (Nang Sang Khan) is paraded through town, riding on the back of the auspicious animal of the year.

**May** **Vien Thien** (movable), the candlelit festival.

**Aug** **Boat races** (movable). Boats are raced by the people living in the vicinity of each wat.

**Oct** **Lai Heua Fai** (**Fireboat Festival**). Each village creates a large boat made of bamboo and paper and decorated with candles and offerings. These are paraded down the main street to Wat Xieng Thong where they are judged and sent down into the Mekong River to bring atonement for sins. Temples and houses are decorated with paper lanterns and candles. People also make their own small floats to release in the Mekong.

**Dec** **Luang Prabang Film Festival**, www.lpfilmfest.org, showcases Southeast Asian cinema. The project also produces educational activities for young Lao.

## Shopping

### Books

**L'Étranger**, *see Cafés, above.* Perhaps the best bookshop in the country.
**Monument Books**, *Thou Gnai Thai Rd (near the Mekong), T071-254954, www.monument-books.com.* Part of a small chain that began in Cambodia back in 1993, **Monument** stocks most books written on Laos in both English and French.

**Yensabai Books & Art**, *Ratsavong Rd (opposite the Phousi steps), T020-2299 9917.* A charming little bookstore that also sells a range of cards and offers art classes.

### Fashion and textiles

**Kin Thong Lao Silk**, *48/3 Sakkaline Rd (opposite the school), T020-5554 6184.* Run by the informative Mrs Kin Thong who hails from Sam Tay village near Sam Neua – an area well known for its silk weaving and from where she sources all her stock. Prices range from 150,000 kip right up to 5,000,000 kip for a large hanging. A huge range of beautiful designs.

**Ock Pop Tok**, *near L'Éléphant restaurant, T071-253219.* Specializes in naturally dyed silk. Clothes, furnishings and hangings made mostly made at the dedicated **Living Crafts Centre** just outside of town. Alongside traditional designs, a popular range of **Ock Pop Tok** originals are created. A new outlet, the **Ock Pop Tok Boutique**, is located on Sisavanvong opposite Vat Sene. Recommended.

**Satri Lao Silk**, *Sisavangvong Rd, T071-219295.* Beautiful silks and handicrafts. The quality is reflected in high prices.

**Ma Te Sai**, *42 Ban Aphai, T071-260654.* A lovely place to buy gifts for those back home, with everything from scarves and bags to photo frames and cosmetics on offer. **Ma Te Sai** means 'where is it from' in Lao, reflecting the fact that the owner sources everything from within Laos and works directly with many local artisans.

**TAEC Boutique**, *Sisavangvong Rd, near Vat Sene, T071-253364, www.taeclaos. org.* Run by the **Traditional Arts & Ethnology Centre**, this is a fantastic little shop with items ranging from table runners and scarves to hangings in both

100% silk and natural-dye cottons. A large percentage of the profits goes directly to the rural ethnic minority villages where the products are made. Very helpful and knowledgeable staff. Highly recommended.

### Galleries

**Fibre2Fabric**, *71 Ban Vat Nong (next door to Ock Pop Tok), T071-254761, www. fibre2fabric.org*. A fantastic gallery exhibiting textiles of different ethnic groups. Local weavers are often on hand to explain the weaving processes.
**Friends Visitor Centre**, *Kitsalat Rd, www.fwab.org/laos*. A fantastic photography gallery is housed on the 3rd floor of this building which also acts as the training centre for the new **Lao Friends Hospital For Children**. Photography has been donated from a raft of respected artists including Paul Wager and Kenro Izu. Well worth a visit.
**Kinnaly Gallery**, *Sakkaline Rd, T020-55557737*. Opened in 2006, this French-run gallery specializes in black-and-white photography.
**Kop Noi**, *Ban Aphay, www.kopnoi.com*. This little shop has a rotating exhibition on the 2nd floor. It also exhibits work by renowned Lao photographer SamSisombat.

### Handicrafts

The night market is a great place for handicrafts, as are **Ma Ta Sei**, **Ock Pop Tok** and **TAEC Boutique**.

### Jewellery

**Naga Creations**, *Sisavangvong Rd, T071-212775*. Lao silver with semi-precious stones. Contemporary and classic pieces available, including innovative work by the jeweller **Fabrice**.

### Markets

**Night market**, *sprawling across several blocks of Sisavangvong Rd. Daily 1700-2230*. Hundreds of villagers flock to the market to sell their handicrafts, ranging from silk scarves to embroidered quilt covers and paper albums. It shouldn't be missed.
**Phousi market**, *1.5 km from the centre of town*. This is now the place to head for cheap goods rather than quality.
**Talat Dala**, *housed in market building in the middle of town on the corner of Setthathirat Rd and Chao Sisophon Rd*. Alongside sports clothes and mobile phone shops a few artisans and jewellers remain, but be prepared to haggle.

### Silver

One of Luang Prabang's traditional crafts is silversmithing. Most tourists buy silver from either the **night market** or **Talat Dala**; however, many of these pieces are made elsewhere. A few expert silversmiths still ply their trade in the lanes that run toward the river from the Nam Phou Fountain.

## What to do

### Cookery classes

**Bamboo Tree**, *Soukhaserm Rd, T020-2242 5499*. A relative newcomer to the cookery class scene, **Bamboo Tree** has a great setting by the river with plenty of outdoor space. After an optional visit to the local market to buy fresh ingredients learners can choose which dishes to cook before enjoying a feast together. Popular options are the stuffed lemongrass, the river fish and the paw paw salad.
**Tamarind**, *facing Wat Nong, T020-7777 0484, www.tamarindlaos.com*. This successful restaurant runs specialized

classes for groups in their enchanting jungle garden school outside of town. Recommended.

### Elephant tours and activities
**Elephant Village**, *15 km from Luang Prabang (visits and activities can be organized through their office on Sisavangvong Rd), T071-252417, www.elephantvillage-laos.com.* Established in conjunction with **Tiger Trails** in Luang Prabang, old working elephants are given a home here. To keep the elephants active, the operators run activities for tourists, including experiencing life as a *mahout* (elephant keeper).

### Sauna and massage
**L'Hibiscus Spa**, *45 Sakkaline, no phone.* Housed in an atmospheric old building with gorgeous floor tiles and filled with a wonderful scent. **L'Hibiscus** offers a good range of treatments including hot stone massage and traditional Lao massage in a supremely relaxing setting.
**Maison Souvannaphoum**, *see Where to stay.* A spa with a range of luxurious and expensive treatments. For sheer indulgence.
**Red Cross Sauna**, *opposite Wat Visunnarat, reservations T071-212303. Daily 0900-2100 (1700-2100 for sauna).* This is a no-frills massage outfit that's very popular with locals. Visitors can opt for an hour of massage and follow it up with a Lao herbal sauna. Profits go to the Lao Red Cross.
**The Spa** *at La Résidence Phou (see Where to stay), T071-212530, www.residencephouvao.com.* Offers very expensive 3-hr massage courses. This includes a 1-hr massage for each person, the class, a handbook and oils.
**Spa Garden**, *Ban Phonheauang, T071-212325, spagardenlpb@hotmail.com.*

Tucked away in a very quiet and peaceful location, the mid-range **Spa Garden** offers many massage and beauty treatments including Lao massage, aromatherapy massage and facials.

### Tour operators
**Buffalo Tours**, *8/40 Ban Nongkham, T071-254395, www.buffalotours.com.* Very well-regarded operator with offices throughout Southeast Asia. Managed by Mr Touy, this office can arrange local tours around Luang Prabang, cooking classes in local villages and also travel throughout the whole of Laos. Very helpful.
**Green Discovery**, *Sisavangvong Rd, T071-212093, www.greendiscoverylaos.com.* Rafting and kayaking trips that pass through grade I and II rapids. Also cycling tours around Luang Prabang, homestays and trips to Pak Ou caves. Great staff.
**Tiger Trail**, *Sisavangvong Rd, T071-252655, www.laos-adventures.com.* Adventure specialists: elephant treks, biking, rafting and much more.

### Weaving classes
**Ock Pop Tock Weaving Centre**, *2 km out of town on the river, bookings at Ock Pop Tock shop.* A variety of 1- to 3-day weaving classes are offered with learners being taught one-on-one by master weavers. Also has a great on-site café and peaceful accommodation.

### Air
**Luang Prabang International Airport** (LPQ), 4 km northeast of town, T071-212172/3, is a small airport but has a couple of places to eat, handicraft shops, ATMs and a foreign exchange desk. You

can get a tuk-tuk into town, but many guesthouses will arrange to pick you up if you ask in advance. **Lao Airlines**, Phamahapasaman Rd, T071-212172, has daily connections with **Vientiane** and **Pakse**. International services to **Siem Reap**, **Phnom Penh**, **Hanoi**, **Singapore**, **Chiang Mai**, **Bangkok**, and **Jinghong**.

### Bicycle hire
Bikes can be rented for 20,000 kip per day from most guesthouses.

### Boat
Most boats leave from the 2 docks behind the Royal Palace. For boat times and destinations, either consult the board at the main pier on the Mekong or ask at one of the many travel agents in town.

**To Houei Xai/Pakbeng** The 2-day boat trip down the Mekong between Houei Xai and Pakbeng has become a rite of passage for travellers in Southeast Asia. There are options to suit everyone, from speedboats (not recommended as they are noisy and can be dangerous, and remove the charm of the voyage) and slow boats, to the most luxurious way to make the trip which is on the **Luangsay Cruise** (office on Sisavangvong Rd, T071-252553, www. luangsay.com) which makes the trip in 2 days and 1 night, stopping over at Pak Ou caves en route and staying overnight at their lodge in Pakbeng (see page 142).

**To Nong Khiaw and Muang Khoua** Due to the new Chinese-built dam, this once hugely popular journey is no longer possible in one hit. It is possible to arrange a van and boat combination, but it is very expensive and not simple. It's now much better to take the bus, which follows much of the same course and is also spectacular.

### Bus/truck
There are 2 main bus stations, the northern and the southern, each generally serving destinations in the respective direction. Tuk-tuks are readily available to take passengers into town. Check which terminal your bus is using, as unscheduled changes are possible. Buses can be booked at many of the travel agents in town.

Local buses head to **Nong Khiaw**, **Xam Neua**, **Phongsali** and **Houy Say**. Large, comfortable buses depart for **Vang Vieng**, 6 hrs, and **Vientiane**, 9 hrs. The road south to Vang Vieng is extremely twisty and rarely flat, making for a spectacular journey, but a difficult one for those suffering from motion sickness. The stop-off point halfway is one of the most dramatic in the world, let alone Laos.

Minivans are a good option as they include pick-up at your accommodation and can often also be booked there. Vans depart for **Nong Khiaw**, 0830, 4 hrs; **Vang Vieng**, 0800 and 1400, 5 hrs; **Phonsavanh**, 0830, 7 hrs; **Luang Namtha**, 0800, 7 hrs; and **Udomxai**, 0800, 5 hrs.

International buses can be booked to **Vietnam** (Vinh, Hanoi, Danang and Hué), **Thailand** (Chiang Mai and Chiang Rai) and various destinations in **China**.

# North of
# Luang Prabang

The stunning settlements of Nong Khiaw and Neua in
the north of Luang Prabang Province have become firm
favourites with the backpacker set. Both places have an
idyllic setting and have thankfully avoided becoming
Vang Vieng-like party towns, their serenity still intact
despite the influx of tourists. The gently undulating
journey to this part of Laos follows the beautiful route
of the Nam Ou past mountains, teak plantations and
dry rice fields. There is plenty to do, including trekking
to waterfalls, kayaking, rock climbing, village visits and
cycling. However, this is also a great part of the country
in which to enjoy a good book, swing in a hammock and
sink into the wonderfully slow pace of life.

## Nong Khiaw, Ban Saphoun and around → *Colour map 1, B4.*
**scenic and laid-back riverside villages, well set-up for adventure tourism**

Nong Khiaw lies 22 km to the northeast of Nam Bak and is a delightful little
village on the banks of the Nam Ou, surrounded by limestone peaks and flanked
by misty mountains – the largest of which is the aptly named Princess Mountain.
The remote little town is one of Laos' prettiest destinations. There are, in fact, two
settlements here: Ban Saphoun on the east bank of the Nam Ou, and Nong Khiaw
on the west. Of the two, Ban Saphoun (the old village) offers the best views and
has the best riverside accommodation. Confusingly, the combined village is known
by both names and sometimes Muang Ngoi which is actually another town to the
north and also the name of the district.

The road trip between Udomxai and Xam Neua is one of the most spectacular in
Laos, moving through stunning scenery dotted with remote villages. Nong Khiaw
sits by the bridge where Route 1 crosses the river. It is a beautiful spot – the sort of
place where time stands still, journals are written, books read and stress is a deeply
foreign concept.

It is possible to swim in the river (women should wear sarongs) or walk around the town or up the cliffs. The bridge across the Nam Ou offers fine views and photo opportunities.

A new trail has been created by the local community to the top of Pa Daeng Mountain – it's a tough hike, but it affords absolutely wonderful views across the town and the river valley. More strenuous sections of the path have ropes to help you haul your way up. Be sure to take plenty of water. A small fee is payable at the entrance to the trail to help maintain it.

### Around Nong Khiaw

The most obvious attractions in the area are the caves used by locals when the US bombed the area. **Tham Pha Thok** ⓘ *2.5 km southeast of the bridge, 30-min trek to Tham Pha Thok: ask at any tour company or restaurant for directions, or better yet, take a guide who can give you some background information and history as no information displayed*, was a Pathet Lao regional base during the civil war. It was divided into sections – a hospital section, a police section and a military section. Old remnants exist, including campfires and ruined beds, but other than that there is little evidence of it being the PT headquarters until you see the bomb crater at the front. To get there you walk through beautiful rice paddies. There is also a second cave, **Tham Pha Kwong**, but this was closed at the time of writing.

A further 2 km along the road, at Ban Nokien, is the **Than Mok waterfall**. To get there, you can either walk or charter a boat (negotiate the price with the boatman at the pier); remember to agree a return time. There's a small fee

# Essential North of Luang Prabang

## Best places to stay

**Mandala Ou**, Nong Khiaw, page 116
**Nong Kiau Riverside Resort**, Ban Saphoun, page 117
**Manotham Guesthouse**, Muang Khua, page 121

### Finding your feet

There is an airport at Phongsali though no flights were scheduled at the time of writing. Boat services have become irregular following road improvements. Nong Khiaw and Muang Khua can be reached from Luang Prabang by a combination of van and boat, but it's better (and just as scenic) to take the bus. You may find a boat service between Muang Khua and Nong Khiaw, along the beautiful Nam Ou River, surrounded by mountainous scenery. Buses and *songthaew* run to most towns and villages, but timetables are not always accurate. It is often a matter of asking at the bus station or waiting by the main road for hours and flagging down a bus on its way through. For shorter distances *songthaew* are more regular. The journey to Phongsali passes through some superb scenery.

### Tip ...

To help you feel even more relaxed while you're in Nong Khiaw, the massage place attached to **Sabai Sabai** restaurant is excellent.

to see the waterfall. It's difficult to find on your own, so consider a guide. The best time to go is in the morning, so as not to have to rush the climb up to the falls or cut short your time there before dark.

If you go to the boat landing it is sometimes possible to organize a fishing trip with one of the local fishermen, for very little money. You might need someone to translate for you.

## ★Muang Ngoi Neua → *Colour map 1, B4.*

The town of Muang Ngoi Neua lies 40 km north of Nong Khiaw, along the Nam Ou River. This small town now has electricity and many of the dirt paths have been paved, but it remains surrounded by ethnic villages and retains its charm. Its increased popularity means that backpackers seem to outnumber tourists in peak times, nevertheless, Muang Ngoi Neua is a small slice of utopia, set on a peninsula at the foot of Mount Phaboom, shaded by coconut trees, with the languid river breeze wafting through the town's small paths. Most commonly known as **Muang Ngoi**, the settlement has had to embellish its name to distinguish it from Nong Khiaw, which is also often referred to as Muang Ngoi (see above). It's the perfect place to go for a trek to surrounding villages, or bask the day away swinging in your hammock.

### Around Muang Ngoi Neua

**Tham Kang**, a large limestone cave, with a glassy river running through it, is a pleasant 30-minute walk south of town. Follow the road out of town, turn left where the morning market is held and head through the school grounds and along a narrow path through vegetation. Follow the path on the left to avoid wading through very deep and very cold water. Just past the school, villagers will collect the small entrance fee. The cave is over 30 m high and exceptionally dark inside, so bring a torch. There's a swimming hole at ground level.

**Tham Pa Kaew** is a further five minutes' walk along the trail. Inside the cave is a small Buddha image and there's also a crystal-clear pool that's great for a dip. On the other side of the path are sticky rice paddies, where you can catch a glimpse of locals planting or harvesting the rice by hand. Another 30 minutes' walk along the same path leads to some friendly Khmu and Lao villages.

## Listings Nong Khiaw, Ban Saphoun and around

### Where to stay

Most places offer Wi-Fi internet access.

#### Nong Khiaw

**$$$ Mandala Ou**
*Near the bus station, T030-537 7332, www.mandala-ou.com.*

A newcomer to the seen, this special resort is full of personal touches thanks to the lovely German/Thai couple who run it. Gorgeous setting with many wonderfully decorated rooms offering river and mountain views from a large veranda. Excellent food including fantastic home-baked bread. There is also a small swimming pool with a bar with knock-out views. An ultra-relaxing spot. Highly recommended.

## Ban Saphoun

**$$$ Nong Kiau Riverside Resort**
*Turn off right beside the bridge, T020-5570 5000, www.nongkiau.com.*
Stunning bungalows and restaurant. The upscale rooms are beautifully decorated in modern Asian East-meets-West style, with 4-poster beds, mosquito nets and tiled hot-water bathrooms. For those looking for something a little more upmarket than the average guesthouse, this exquisite place fits the bill perfectly. The restaurant has a great selection of wines, and internet is available. Book in advance as it is a favourite of the tour groups. Recommended.

**$$ Sunset Guesthouse**
*Down a lane about 100 m past the bridge, T071-810033, sunsetgh2@hotmail.com.*
Definitely trading on the views, given the prices and rather basic rooms, but the fact is you couldn't ask for a better setting from which to watch the sunset. The charming, sprawling bamboo structure looks out onto various levels of decking that serve as a popular restaurant in the evenings, although service can be a little slack. The rooms vary in quality, so ask to see a few.

**$ Nam Noun Guesthouse**
*Just back from the river, T020-5577 4462.*
At the lower end of the price range in town, these bungalows are nonetheless some of the best as they are set back from the river. Clean and complete with small verandas and hammocks. A top choice if the purse strings are tight.

## Muang Ngoi Neua

**$ Lattanavongsa Guesthouse**
*Northern side of the main road, T030-514 0770.*
2 cluster bombs line the steps leading up to these attractive bungalows, which face onto garden. There are polished floorboards, large beds and reasonably lit rooms with bathroom.

**$ Ning Ning Guesthouse**
*Behind the boat landing, T030-514 0863.*
This place has a restaurant with a great view for sunset. Double and twin bungalows, with separate Western-style toilet and hot shower; the smarter rooms have large comfy double beds with super-white linen andmosquito nets; breakfast included. The food in the adjoining restaurant is great and the owner speaks good English. A popular spot.

## Restaurants

Most of the guesthouses have cafés attached. For more expensive options head for either the **Riverside** which has a good wine list, or **Mandala Ou** which offers well-thought-out meals and fine views. For a cheap local fix try the noodle stall next to the bridge on the Ban Saphoun side of town. For something more local, opt for one of the simple places on the road toward the lookout climb.

## Nong Khiaw

**$ Chennai**
*Main road on the Nong Khiaw side, T020-9559 9786.*
One of 2 Indian restaurants right next to each other. There is little to choose between them as it seems the close proximity keeps the standard very high

in both. Fantastic food and smooth service. Recommended.

## Ban Saphoun

### $ Alex Restaurant
*100 m before the bridge.*
A family-run place, this restaurant does some decent Lao food and also some reasonable Western dishes. Very warm and welcoming, there is always a good atmosphere which keeps people coming back night after night.

### $ Sabai Sabai
*Near the turn off for Sunrise and Alex, T020-5858 6068.*
Run by Mr Ken, this garden restaurant serves traditional Lao food. Try the pumpkin soup with coconut milk and egg served with fresh bread or in the evening opt for the Lao barbecue featuring chicken, pork and beef. The massage place attached is the best in town by a country mile.

## Muang Ngoi Neua
Aside from the many guesthouse restaurants, which serve good-quality Lao food, there are also a number of places to eat along the main road. Most have exactly the same food on offer; in fact, many of them just copy their competitors' menus. The fruitshake stands in the centre of town are good value.

### $$-$ Sainamgoi Restaurant & Bar
*In the centre of the village.*
Tasty Lao food in a pleasant atmosphere, with good background music. There's a bar – the only one in town – in the next room.

### $ Nang Phone Keo Restaurant
*On the main road.*
All the usual Lao food plus some extras: try the 'falang roll' for breakfast (a combination of peanut butter, sticky rice and vegetables).

### $ Sengdala Restaurant & Bakery
*Along the main road.*
Very good, cheap Lao food, terrific pancakes and freshly baked baguettes.

### $ Sky Bar & Restaurant
*See Where to stay, above.*
Ambient in the evening although the food is not great.

## What to do

Good-quality bicycles can be rented from **NK Adventure**. There's a movie house on the main road marked 'Cinema' but it was closed at the time of writing.

**Nong Khiaw and Ban Saphoun**
**Green Discovery**, *on the Ban Saphoun side, T071-819 0081, www. greendiscoverylaos.com.* Managed by the affable Tom, this branch of the nationwide tour operator offers everything from half-day ambles to multi-day treks including cycling, hiking and long-tail boat rides.
**Jewel Travel Laos,** *T071-253910, www.jeweltravellaos.com.* This is the agent to contact for rock climbing, with 1- to 3-day packages on offer and training available for complete novices. The climbing is on Deer Wall which offers routes from grades 5a-6b (French system).
**Motorbike Rental Donkham,** *T020-5888 8995.* Rents automatic and semi-automatic bikes and can advise on routes for you to explore solo.

**NK Adventure**, *main road, Nong Khiaw side, T020-5868 6068, bounhome68@hotmail.com*. Run by the very helpful Mr Boun Home and his friend Mang, both of whom were born in the town, this small tour company offers a one-day boat trip to Khmu villages or a trek to Tad Mok waterfall through rice paddies followed by a 2-hr kayak trip back. 2-day trips include a trek through forest to a Hmong/Khmu homestay followed by a trek to the river to kayak back to town. Active travellers should check out the new bicycle/kayak tour option, cycling out to a waterfall trek and returning via the river.

### Muang Ngoi Neua

Trekking, hiking, fishing, kayaking, trips to the waterfalls and boat trips can be organized through most guesthouses.

## Transport

### Nong Khiaw and Ban Saphoun
**Boat**

Boat services have become irregular following road improvements, although you may find a service to **Muang Ngoi Neua**, 1 hr, from the boat landing. Otherwise, most local agents run day trip boats and it is often possible to jump on one of those. There are no regular boats to **Luang Prabang** following the construction of the dam; however, if enough people wish to make the trip it is possible to arrange a boat to the dam and then a van from there to Luang Prabang. Speak to **NK Travel** (see Tour operators, above).

**Bus/truck**

Buses en route from surrounding destinations stop in Nong Khiaw briefly.

Basic timetables are offered but buses can be hours early or late, so check details on the day. It is often a matter of waiting at the bus station for hours and hoping to catch the bus on its way through. Plonking yourself in a restaurant on the main road usually suffices but you will need to flag down the bus as it passes through town. To **Luang Prabang**, 3-4 hrs. Also several departures daily to **Nam Bak**, 30 mins, and on to **Udomxai**, 4 hrs.

Alternatively, you could take one of the more regular *songthaew* to **Pak Mong**, 1 hr, where there is a small noodle shop-cum-bus station on the west side of the bridge, and then catch another vehicle on to **Udomxai/Vientiane**.

Travelling east on Route 1, there are buses to **Vieng Kham**, 0900, 2 hrs, and a village 10 km from **Nam Nouan**, where you can change and head south on Route 6 to **Phonsavanh** and the **Plain of Jars**. There are direct buses north to **Xam Neua** and the village near Nam Nouan (useful if you are heading for the Nam Nern Night Safari, see box, page 174), which can be caught from the toll gate on the Ban Saphoun side of the river when it comes through from Vientiane, but it's usually quite crowded.

### Muang Ngoi Neua
**Boat**

From the landing at the northern end of town, slow boats travel north along the beautiful Nam Ou River, surrounded by mountainous scenery, to **Muang Khua**, 5 hrs. Slow boats also go south (irregularly) to **Nong Khiaw**, 1 hr. Departure times vary and depend on there being sufficient passengers.

Muang Khua is nestled into the banks of the Nam Ou, close to the mouth of the Nam Phak, in the south of Phongsali Province. Hardly a destination in itself, it's usually just a stopover between Nong Khiaw and Phongsali although it is increasingly used as an overnight stop by travellers heading to Dien Bien Phu in Vietnam. Muang Khua is a great place to kick back for a few days if you want to take a break from the well-worn travellers' path. Rather scruffy around the edges, the town nonetheless has a certain charm and has a bank, post office and Telecom office. Take a wander across the rickety old bridge and walk along the river past small villages or sit in the market and enjoy some local food.

Located at the junction of two rivers and on Route 4 to Vietnam, Muang Khua has long been a crossroads between Vietnam and Laos. A French garrison was based in Muang Khua until 1954, when it was ousted by Vietnamese troops in the aftermath of the battle at Dien Bien Phu. For a brief period from 1958, Polish and Canadian officials of the Comité International de Contrôle were quartered in the town to monitor the ceasefire between the Pathet Lao and the Royal Lao government. Nowadays, Muang Khua is home to a burgeoning market in Vietnamese goods, trucked in from Dien Bien Phu. The border with Vietnam has now opened to tourists but the road is still under construction on the Lao side; a steady and increasing trickle of tourists seem to be making their way through on this route.

### Around Muang Khua

Trekking can be arranged here either via the small tourist office or via the **Nam Ou Guesthouse** (see Where to stay, below). The Akha, Khmu and Tai Dam are the main hilltribes in the area. There are some villages along the river just outside town, but for the larger settlements you will need a guide to visit. Trekking around Muang Khua is fantastic and still a very authentic experience, as this region remains largely unexplored by backpackers. The friendly villagers are very welcoming to foreigners, as they don't see as many here as somewhere like Muang Sing.

### Towards Phongsali

You can travel from Muang Khua to Phongsali either by road or river. The road journey is a long one, made more difficult when the pickup is full. However, it's a great experience and the hilltribes you come across along the way are very interesting and the scenery toward the Phongsali end of the trip is utterly breathtaking. Alternatively, catch a boat direct from Muang Khua. It's also a beautiful trip, especially for birdwatching, with kingfishers everywhere. The river is quite shallow in places and there is a fair amount of white water, so take a blanket. Boats stop at Hat Xa, 20 km or so to the northeast of Phongsali, where you may find yourselves stuck, as there are no buses to Phongsali after mid-afternoon. See Transport, below.

## BORDER CROSSING
### Sop Hun–Tay Trang (Vietnam)

The border linking Vietnam's Dien Bien Phu with this part of Laos is now open daily 0800-1700. A Laos visa can be obtained on arrival, but Vietnamese visas cannot. There is limited transport on the Laos side to Muang Khua. There is a direct bus from Muang Khua to Dien Bien Phu, which lets you off for border formalities. It leaves from the opposite side of the river bank to Muang Khua at 0600, so it is necessary to get to the river bank in good time to make the crossing – take a torch as it may be quite dark this early. Most guesthouses in Muang Khua can help with information.

## Listings Muang Khua

### Where to stay

**$ Manotham Guesthouse**
*Across the old bridge, T020-5588 0058.*
The owner makes this place one to seek out. A cheery elderly man, he'll likely invite you to a communal dinner and gently encourage the drinking of *lao lao* after feeding you massive portions of home-cooked food. He will also help guests arrange transport on to Vietnam. Clean, very simple rooms. Recommended.

**$ Nam Ou Guesthouse & Restaurant**
*Follow the signs at the top of the hill, T020-2283 3789.*
Looking out across the river, this guesthouse is a good ultra-budget option and very popular with backpackers. Singles, twins and doubles, some with hot water en suites, and 3 rooms with river views.

### Restaurants

This is a small town with very few eateries, although what it lacks in restaurants, it makes up for in pool tables; very small children show a frightening aptitude and you should be prepared to have an instant audience if you try your hand. Noodles and baguettes are available in the market and most guesthouses serve food.

**$ Nam Ou Guesthouse & Restaurant**
*See Where to stay.*
An incomparable location for a morning coffee overlooking the river; it has an English menu and friendly staff. This is the most reliable place to eat in town.

**$ Saifon**
*By the river.*
A basic restaurant with a small selection of dishes translated into English on the menu. Service can be a little haphazard.

### Transport

**Boat**
Road travel is now more popular but irregular boats still sometimes travel south on the Nam Ou River to **Muang Ngoi Neua**, 3 hrs, and **Nong Khiaw**, 4 hrs. Boats also run north to **Phongsali**, via the river port of **Hat Xa**, 20 km northeast of Phongsali, 3-5 hrs, 90,000-100,000 kip per person, minimum 10 people. From Hat Xa, it is a 1-hr pickup ride to Phongsali, but there are

no services after mid-afternoon so you may have to stay the night.

Boats from Muang Khua are scheduled to leave at 0900-1000 but won't leave without enough passengers; it's best to get to the dock early and wait. In the low season, there may not be any scheduled boats but you could gather up a few more interested tourists and charter a boat – ask at the **Nam Ou Guesthouse**.

**Bus/truck/pickup**
You can also travel to **Phongsali** by road; the buses can get crowded but the scenery is superb. Buses run 3 times per day and take approximately 3½ hrs.

## Phongsali → *Colour map 1, A3. Phone code: 088.*
**out-of-the-way Chinese-influenced town with good trekking**

High up in the mountains at an altitude of 1628 m, this northern provincial capital provides beautiful views and an invigorating climate. It is especially stunning from January to March, when wildflowers bloom in the surrounding hills. The town can be cold at any time of the year, so take some warm clothes. Mornings tend to be foggy and it can also be very wet. There is an end-of-the-earth feel in the areas surrounding the main centre, with dense pristine jungle surrounded by misty mountains.

Phongsali was one of the first areas to be liberated by the Pathet Lao in the late 1940s. The town's architecture is a strange mix of Chinese post-revolutionary concrete blocks, Lao wood-and-brick houses with tin roofs, and bamboo or mud huts with straw roofs. The most attractive part of town is a series of shophouses that wind away from the **Phongsaly Hotel** towards Hat Xa. The town itself is home to about 20,000 people, mostly Lao, Phou Noi and Chinese, while the wider district is a potpourri of ethnicities, with around 25 different minorities inhabiting the area.

### Towards Udomxai
The road from Phongsali to Udomxai has been upgraded, but it remains rather bumpy and one of the tougher journeys in Laos, a fact that further ensures few international visitors make it this far. This is rather a pity, as the surroundings and scenery are incredible. Break the journey at **Pak Nam Noi**, which lies at the intersection of the two roads going either to Muang Khua or Udomxai.

## Tourist information

**Provincial Tourism Office**
*Signposted as 60 m off the main road, T088-210098.*
Can arrange a variety of guided eco-treks, including village homestays, for up to 5 nights.

## Where to stay

**$ Ban Homsawan**
*Near the tourist office, T020-2239 5018.*
In a town severely short of quality digs, this is one of the better options. Renovated in 2013, it has good beds, large rooms and hot water.

**$ Phongsaly Hotel**
*Around the corner from the Kaysone Monument, T088-210042.*
A wide variety of rooms are on offer in this rather uninspiring hotel. A 4-storey monstrosity, it has large double and twin rooms with hot-water bathrooms. Good views from the roof. More expensive rooms have a/c, although that is often not needed in these parts.

**$ Yu Houa Guesthouse**
*Across the road from the market, T088-210186.*
A 3-storey building with 6 clean twin and double rooms with hard beds, bathrooms and Western toilets. It's a little scruffy around the edges, but there are sweeping views of the valley from the rooms at the back. Restaurant downstairs.

## Restaurants

There are a number of places to grab a bowl of noodles, meat on a stick or some sticky rice around the market.

**$ Phongsaly Hotel**
*See Where to stay.*
A good bet, with a variety of dishes including Thai, Chinese and Lao.

**$ Yu Houa Guesthouse**
*See Where to stay.*
A short Lao and Chinese section on an English menu. Cheap and good.

## What to do

**Trekking**
The tourism office can arrange guided treks around Boun Neua and Phongsali with homestays for 400,000 kip for 1 day for 2 people or 800,000 kip for 2 days. It will also arrange visits to 400-year-old tea trees at a plantation at Ban Komaen, where a homestay is also possible. Most of the tour agencies in Luang Prabang and Luang Namtha also run group treks around Phongsali.
**Northern Traveling and Information Service Center,** *on the main road, not far from Yu Houa restaurant, T088-210594, northerntraveletr@yahoo.com.*
Offers 15 treks ranging from 1-5 days with prices starting at 300,000 kip for 1 person. Also offers internet and telephone services; motorbike rental is available for 150,000-180,000 kip per day.

## Transport

**Air**
There is an airport at Phongsali but at the time of writing no flights were scheduled.

## Bus/truck and boat

Buses to **Hat Xa** leave at around 0700 and midday from the bus station, 500 m from the centre of Phongsali on the road to Hat Xa (if walking, allow 30 mins to get there). Buses also depart for **Udomxai**, **Pak Nam Noi**, **Luang Prabang** and **Boun Neua** in the early morning. Check at the station or ask at your guesthouse for current times and arrive early to try and bag a seat.

If you want to charter a minivan to **Udomxai**, this is possible through the tourist office.

For boat information see under **Muang Khua**, Transport, page 121. For motorbike hire see What to do, above. For information on getting to the Vietnamese border, see box, page 121.

# Northwest
## Laos

Northwestern Laos comprises dramatic, misty mountainous scenery, clad with thick forests and peppered with small villages. This area is home to a variety of ethnic minority groups including the Akha, Hmong, Khmu and Yao and is a firm favourite with trekkers. The mighty Mekong forges its way through picturesque towns, such as Pakbeng and Houei Xai, affording visitors a wonderful glimpse of riverine life.

## Udomxai (Oudom Xai) and around → *Colour map 1, B3. Phone code: 081.*
### major travel hub somewhat lacking in charm

Udomxai, the capital of Udomxai Province, is a hot and dusty town that is used as a pit-stop but the local tourist board, with the help of a German NGO, have done a lot promote the area's other attractions, see below. Udomxai was razed during the war and the inhabitants fled to live in the surrounding hills; what is here now has been built since 1975, which explains why it is such an unattractive settlement. Since the early 1990s, the town has been experiencing an economic boom – as a result of its position at the intersection of roads linking China, Vietnam, Luang Prabang and Pakbeng – and commerce and construction are thriving. It also means that Udomxai has a large Chinese and Vietnamese population, a fact that appears to rile the locals.

The town's truck-stop atmosphere doesn't enamour it to tourists. However, the town does make a decent stop-off point at a convenient junction; it's one of the biggest settlements in northern Laos and has excellent facilities, including banks, internet, post office and Telecom office.

# Essential Northwest Laos

## Finding your feet

There are airports at Udomxai and Luang Namtha with connections to Vientiane for those short on time. With the development of overland links, river transport has languished, but the route upstream from Luang Prabang to Houei Xai via Pakbeng, on the border with Thailand, remains hugely popular and is well worth doing (see page 113). Note that the boats can get very busy in peak season. There are good bus connections to most towns, the main transport hubs being Udomxai, Luang Namtha's and Houei Xai. Allow plenty of time if travelling to Sayaboury.

## Best places to stay

Muang La Resort, page 127
Boat Landing Guesthouse and Restaurant, page 133
Luangsay Lodge, page 142

## When to go

December to February.

## Time required

Allow at least a week to take in the main sights of Northwest Laos, longer if you want to take the boat or do the Gibbon Experience.

## Best places to eat

Boat Landing Guesthouse and Restaurant, page 134
Forest Retreat's Bamboo Lounge, page 134
Taileu Guesthouse and Restaurant, page 138

## Around Udomxai

Udomxai Province is populated by 23 different ethnic minority groups, with strong contingents of Hmong, Akha and Khmu. The village of **Ban Ting**, behind Udomxai is interesting to wander through. Its wat includes a Buddhist high school for monks and offers a good view of the town and surrounding mountains. Treks to other villages can also be arranged. ▸▸ *See What to do, page 128.*

## Muang La

Muang La is located 28 km north of Udomxai, off Route 4 to Phongsali, and makes a lovely stop en route or a great day out from Udomxai. **Wat Ban Pakkla** is considered one of the most sacred temples in the area, due to the presence of a 400-year-old, gold-plated Buddha image, known as the Pra Xaek Kham. Steeped in superstition and highly auspicious, the temple is the place to go if you want to make your dreams come true.

Muang La has gained popularity with travellers for its **hot springs**. Set in beautiful surroundings, the springs are a favourite spot for locals, who come for a dip in the very hot waters. If you bathe here, wear a sarong or something discreet. The other section of the springs has been cordoned off and is part of the **Muang La Resort**, see Where to stay.

### Tip...

A more luxurious option for travelling by boat between Luang Prabang and Houei Xai is to take the two-day **Luangsay Cruise**, www.luangsay.com, which stops en route to visit riverside villages. See page 144.

## Tourist information

**Provincial Tourism Office**
*Near the river on the main road in the centre of town, T081-212482, www. oudomxay.info. Oct-Mar Mon-Fri 0800-1200 and 1330-1600, Apr-Sep Mon-Fri 0730-1200 and 1330-1600.*
Offers helpful advice.

## Where to stay

**$$$$-$$$ Kamu Lodge**
*Ban Nyong Hay, Udomxai Province; book via the office in Luang Prabang at 44/3 Ban Wat Nong, Kham Kong Rd, T071-260319, T020-5603 2365 (mob), www. kamulodge.com. On the banks of the Mekong, 2½ hrs upstream from Luang Prabang and accessible only by boat.*
Accommodation is in modern canvas tents, decorated with local furnishings. The Lao restaurant is set amongst the paddy fields. Also runs treks and activities, such as gold panning, rice planting and archery. This is a place to truly get away from it all as there is no internet. The price includes boat transfer.

**$ Litthavixay Guesthouse**
*About 100 m before the turning onto the airport road, T081-212175, litthavixay@ yahoo.com.*
Large clean single, double and triple rooms with hot-water shower attached. Opt for the nicer upstairs rooms if possible; fan rooms are cheaper. Wi-Fi available. The restaurant serves a selection of foreign breakfast dishes. Car hire is also possible.

**$ Surinphone**
*150 m into town from the station, T081-212789.*
29 comfortable and clean a/c rooms with TV and decent beds, and hot-water shower rooms. All in all, this is a reasonable a choice, though the furnishings are starting to look a little dated now.

**$ Villa Keoseumsack**
*2 doors down from the Sinphet Restaurant, T081-312170, seumsack@ hotmail.com.*
'Villa' is perhaps a little overstated, but this is still perhaps the best option in town with its polished floors, large double beds, desks, wardrobes and hot-water showers. Fan rooms are cheaper.

### Muang La

**$$$$ Muang La Resort**
*By the river on the edge of the village, www.muangla.com.*
This small resort with 8 rooms is set amid well-tended gardens and receives consistently rave reviews thanks to the great service, fantastic location and relaxing atmosphere. Just 5 wooden villas, offering 10 bedrooms, give guests the feeling that they have found something very special. The fine rooms feature French fans, silk lanterns and rain showers in the bathroom. The resort faces the river and hot springs, and opposite is an active salt mine which is accessible via a bridge. The spa is first rate and features a deep pool filled with natural hot spring water with a captivating mountain view. Superb restaurant. A true slice of heaven.

## Restaurants

As well as those listed below, **Litthavixay Guesthouse** (see Where to stay) can whip up some good dishes, including Western-style pancakes and breakfasts. There are a number of restaurants on the 1st left turn after the bridge; all do good Lao and Chinese food. Noodle soup shops are scattered throughout town and stalls in front of the market sell beer and tasty snacks from nightfall.

### $ Kanya Restaurant
*Just off the main street not far from the tourist office.*
This is popular with Lao tour guides and has a menu in English offering the usual staples. The pork vermicelli is tasty and the iced coffees are served long.

### $ Sinphet Restaurant
*On the main road, opposite Linda Guesthouse.*
One of the best options in town. English menu, delicious iced coffee with Ovaltine, great Chinese and Lao food. Try the curry chicken, *kua-mii* or yellow noodles with chicken. Also does sandwiches, fruit shakes and pancakes.

### Muang Houn
There are 2 eating places facing each other next to the market. Both serve noodles, eggs and sticky rice, no menu. Fresh baguettes are available from the market in the morning.

## What to do

### Massage
Traditional Lao herbal sauna and massage is offered by the **Red Cross Centre**, behind the main stupa past the Phuxay Hotel, T022-211477, daily 1330-1930. Look out for the signs on the main road.

### Paper making
*Po Saa* paper-making courses (Feb-Apr) can be arranged in a nearby village as can a half-day cooking course. Contact the tourism office for more information.

### Trekking
The **Provincial Tourism Office** has teamed up with the **German Development Service** and **UNIDO** to run a series of treks from 1-3 days visiting villages rarely seen by tourists. These treks can also take you to the Chom Ong Cave and the Nam Kat Waterfall.

## Transport

### Air
The airport is close to town and has flights to **Vientiane**. **Lao Airlines** has an office at the airport, T081-312047.

### Boat
One of the nicest ways to get to **Luang Prabang** or **Houei Xai** is to take a bus from Udomxai to **Pakbeng** (see page 141) and catch a boat from there.

### Bus/truck/songthaew
Udomxai is the epicentre of northern travel. If arriving in Udomxai to catch a connecting bus, it's better to leave earlier in the day as transport tends to peter out in the afternoon.

The bus station is 1 km east of the town centre from where buses leave for **Nong Khiaw**, 3 hrs; **Pak Mong**, 2 hrs; **Luang Prabang**, 5 hrs; **Vientiane**, 15 hrs; **Luang Namtha**, 4 hrs; and **Boten** (the Chinese border) 82 km. You will need to check if you are eligible for a visa at the Boten border as this is subject to change.

There are services north on Route 4 to **Phongsali**, 9-12 hrs. This trip is long so bring something soft to sit on and try to get a seat with a view.

There are plenty of *songthaew* on standby waiting to make smaller trips to destinations like **Pak Mong** and **Nong Khiaw**; if you miss one of the earlier buses, it may be worthwhile bargaining with the drivers; if they can get enough money, or can round up enough passengers, they will make the extra trip.

### Muang Houn

Regular buses south to **Pakbeng**, 2 hrs; and north to **Udomxai**, 4-5 hrs.

## Luang Namtha and around → *Colour map 1, B2. Phone code: 086.*

**sleepy, remote town that serves as a good base for exploring**

The provincial capital was obliterated during the war and the concrete structures erected since 1975 have little charm. As in other towns in the north of Laos, the improvement in transport links with China and Thailand has led to burgeoning trade. The area has established itself as a major player in Laos' ecotourism industry, primarily due to the Nam Ha National Protected Area (see page 131) and the environmentally friendly Boat Landing Guesthouse (see page 133). Facilities such as banks, ATMs and Wi-Fi are widely available in town.

**Luang Namtha**

To 1 3, Muang Sing & Udomxai
Luang Namtha Museum
Kaysone Monument
Luang Namtha Provincial Tourism Office & Eco Guide Unit
NIT
Lao Telecom
Bike Rental
Night Market
Green Discovery
KNT
To 1
Intra-Provincial Bus Station
To 12, Boat Landing, Airport, Lao Airlines, That Poum Park, Inter-Provincial Bus Station & Houei Xai


**Where to stay**
Boat Landing Guesthouse & Restaurant **12**
Manychan Guesthouse **4**
Phou Lu III **1**
Thoulasith Guesthouse **3**

**Restaurants**
Baw Pen Yang **1**
Forest Retreat's Bamboo Lounge **2**
Lai's Place **3**
Yamuna **4**

N
100 metres
100 yards


### Sights

The **Luang Namtha Museum** ⓘ *near the Kaysone Monument, Mon-Fri 0800-1130, 1300-1600, 10,000 kip*, is worth a visit. The museum houses a collection of indigenous clothing and artefacts, agricultural tools, weapons, textiles and a collection of Buddha images, drums and gongs.

In the centre of town is a good **night market** with a range of food stalls and some handicrafts – this can be a good place to meet others in the evening.

The old **That Poum Pouk** ⓘ*3 km west of the airfield, 5000 kip, take a tuk-tuk from the market*, sits in a ruinous state on a hill. Local sources suggest that the stupa was built as part of a competition between the Lanna Kingdom (in northern Thailand) and the Lane Xang Kingdom

## Visiting an Akha village

Many people have complained that visiting tribal villages is similar to visiting a human zoo. Here are some tips on how to avoid this experience:

- Always visit an Akha village with an Akha or locally endorsed guide rather than on your own.
- Never touch the spirit symbol, spirit gate, spirit house or swing and do not walk through the Akha entrance gate. Touching any of these things is believed to bring bad luck to the village.
- If you wish to give gifts, such as money, to the Akha people, these should be offered only to the village chief.
- Accept food and drink if it is offered to you. The Akha may also offer you a massage; it's OK to accept.
- Rather than watching people go about their work, ask if you can help them.

to prove which of the two kingdoms had the most merit. Severe damage due to bombing in 1964 led local villagers and monks to reconstruct the stupa but this proved a fruitless exercise as further bombing in 1966 dislodged the stupa, parts of which can still be seen lying on the ground. Incredibly, much of the original stucco and an encrypted stelae survived the attacks. A new stupa has been built behind the ruined one. The trip to That Poum Pouk is most pleasant in the afternoon.

### Villages around Luang Namtha

Luang Namtha Province has witnessed the rise and decline of various Tai kingdoms and now over 30 ethnic groups reside in the province, making it the most ethnically diverse province in the country. Principal minorities residing here include Tai Lue, Tai Dam, Lanten, Hmong and Khamu. There are a number of friendly villages around the town of Luang Namtha. As with all other minority areas, you should only visit the villages with a local guide or endorsed tourism organization.

**Ban Nam Chang** is a Lanten village 3 km along a footpath outside Luang Namtha; just ask the way. **Ban Lak Khamay** is quite a large Akha village 27 km from Luang Namtha on the road to Muang Sing. It was resettled from a nearby location higher in the hills in 1994 as part of a government programme to protect upland forests. The community now grows teak and rubber trees. The village chief speaks Lao. The settlement features a traditional Akha entrance; if you pass through this entrance you must visit a house in the village, or you will be considered an enemy. Otherwise you can simply pass to one side of the gate, but be careful not to touch it. Other features of interest in Akha villages are the swing, which is located at the highest point in the village and used in the annual swing festival (you must not touch the swing), and the meeting house, where unmarried couples go to court and where newly married couples live until they have their own house. There is another, smaller Akha village a few kilometres on towards Muang Sing.

**Ban Nam Dee** is a small bamboo paper-making Lanten village located about 6 km northeast of Luang Namtha. The name of the village means 'good water' and, not surprisingly, if you continue on from Ban Nam Dee for 1 km, you will come to a waterfall. The trip to the village is particularly scenic, passing through verdant green rice paddies dotted with huts. A motorbike rather than a bicycle will be necessary to navigate these villages and sights as the road is very rocky in places and unsuitable for cyclists. Villagers usually charge for access to the waterfall.

The small Tai Lue village of **Ban Khone Kam** is also worth a visit. The settlement is based on the banks of the Nam Tha, halfway between Luang Namtha and Houei Xai, and is only accessible by boat or by foot. The friendly villagers offer **homestays** here, for one or two nights, providing an interesting cultural insight into the daily lives of the region's boatmen and rice farmers.

**Ban Vieng Nua**, 3 km from the centre of town, is a Tai Kolom village famous for its traditional house where groups can experience local dancing and a good luck *baci* ceremony. Contact the tourism office (see page 133) for further information and to make bookings.

## ★ Vieng Phouka and around

Before the roads in the region were upgraded, Vieng Phouka was the place to stay overnight when travelling between Luang Namtha or Muang Sing and the Mekong. Located south of Luang Namtha (and 125 km north of Houei Xai), the town is surrounded by a variety of minority villages – Akha, Hmong, Lahu and Khmu, with the Khmu comprising about 90% of the population.

The local tourism authority, **Vieng Phouka Eco Guide Service** ⓘ *T081-212400 (T020-5598 5289 mob), www.luangnamtha-tourism.org*, organizes treks in the surrounding area, which is not as busy as Luang Namtha and recommended by trekkers. ▸▸ *See What to do, page 135.*

The 5-km-long **Nam Aeng Cave**, 12 km north of Vieng Phouka, is famous locally for an annual ceremony held on 13 January, when elders call up the large fish that inhabit part of the cave. The **Nom Cave**, a four-hour walk from the town, was once home to a famous sacred Buddha, but this has now been pilfered. During the revolution the Nom Cave served as a hideout. Around the area are a few scattered remains of the wall from the ancient city of Kuvieng, much of which has been dismantled by local villagers at the government's insistence.

Both Luang Namtha and Vieng Phouka make great bases from which to venture into the **Nam Ha National Protected Area**, one of a few remaining places on earth where the rare black-cheeked crested gibbon can be found (see below). If you're lucky, you can hear the wonderful singing of the gibbons in the morning.

### Nam Ha National Protected Area (NPA)

This area has firmly established itself as a major player in Laos' ecotourism industry, primarily due to the **Nam Ha Ecotourism Project**, which was established in 1993 by NTA Lao and UNESCO to help preserve Luang Namtha's cultural and environmental heritage in the Nam Ha National Protected Area. The Nam Ha NPA is one of the largest protected areas in Laos and consists of mountainous areas

## BORDER CROSSING
### Boten–Mohan (China)

The border between Boten (Laos) and Mohan (China) is open to international traffic daily 0800-1600. There have been reports of some citizens getting Chinese visas here but it depends on your nationality, so if you plan to do this be sure to check in advance (it is less risky to organize a visa in advance in Vientiane).

After crossing into China, the first town you come to is Mengla (two hours from Boten). But Mengla is a nasty introduction to China, reverberating with the tiresome sounds of karaoke and prostitutes until the early hours. It is better to try to get to the much better town of Jinghong or Chieng Houng (five hours from Mengla).

Coming into Laos from China, you can pick up a 30-day Lao visa at the border. You can change remaining yuan into Lao kip at the border. The bus station is a walk down the hill. Boten is a strange place which briefly boomed into a casino town (see below). Today the casinos and upmarket hotels are empty and the town has a very strange atmosphere.

If you want to make it to Luang Namtha, you should aim to cross the border in the morning when there are a lot of buses, rather than in the afternoon when there are fewer and you could find yourself stranded. If there isn't a direct bus, take the first bus to Udomxai and change at Natuei. If you want to go to Vientiane and there isn't a direct bus, your best bet is to catch a bus to Udomxai and transfer there to Vientiane/Luang Prabang.

dissected by several rivers. It is home to at least 38 species of large mammal, including the black-cheeked crested gibbon, tiger and clouded leopard, and over 300 bird species, including the Blythe's kingfisher. The Nam Ha project has won a UN development award for its outstanding achievements in the area.

The organization currently leads one- to five-day treks in the area and can arrange extended treks on special request. The treks offer the chance to visit traditional villages, explore various forest habitats, take river trips, stay in a jungle camp and support local conservation efforts. Check with the **Luang Namtha Eco Guide Unit** (see page 134) or **Green Discovery** (see Tour operators, page 134) for departures; an information session about the trek is given at the guide's office. Prices cover the cost of food, water, transportation, guides, lodging and the trekking permit. All the treks utilize local guides who have been trained to help generate income for their villages. Income for conservation purposes is also garnered from the fees for trekking permits into the area.

### Boten → Colour map 1, B2.

Boten lies on the border with China and, until the construction of the massive Chinese-funded 'Golden Boten City' project, it was nothing but a truck stop. The Boten City project saw large-scale casino development and thousands of Chinese flood the town including businessmen, prostitutes and gamblers. However, the boom didn't last and it soon gained a reputation as a Sin City. Press reports of gamblers being held hostage until they could pay their debts surfaced and locals told tales of bodies being found in rivers. Things came to a head in 2011 when the main casino and those around it were shut down. The population, which had swollen to an estimated 10,000 quickly shrank back down to under 2000 and the grand buildings now stand empty. The Lao authorities have suggested a vague new goal could be an international conference centre or an ecotourism destination. All in all, this is a very sad case of a Special Economic Zone gone very, very wrong.

## Listings Luang Namtha and around *map p145*

### Tourist information

**Luang Namtha Provincial Tourism Office**
*T086-211534, luangnamtha-tourism-laos.org.*
Better than it once was, but for the best information it is still best to head for **Green Discovery** (see page 134).

### Where to stay

There has been a sudden rush of guesthouses popping up here over the last few years but the Boat Landing, the best ecotourism venture in the country is still the stand-out choice in the area.

**$$ Boat Landing Guesthouse & Restaurant**
*Ban Kone, T086-312398, www. theboatlanding.laopdr.com.*
Further out of town than most other guesthouses, this place is located right on the river. Time stands still here. It's an eco-resort that has got everything just right: pristine surroundings, environmentally friendly rooms, helpful service and a brilliant restaurant serving northern Lao cuisine. The rooms combine modern design with traditional materials and decoration;

breakfast included. The gardens brim with butterflies and birds; the best time, weather-wise, is Oct/Nov. Recommended.

**$ Phou Lu III**
*A 5-min walk from the main strip on the river, T020-004400.*
Pretty, spacious rattan bungalows line the river and provide the prettiest place to stay on a tight budget.

**$ Thoulasith Guesthouse**
*Off the main road, T086-212166, thoulasithguesthouse@gmail.com.*
Beautiful wooden building with a wrap-around balcony set in a compound with a garden, tables and chairs, making it a good spot to meet fellow travellers. Rooms come with TV, desk, hot-water bathroom (3 rooms have bathtubs) and free Wi-Fi. Friendly management. There's a decent restaurant and it's very close to the night market for your evening meal. A top choice in this budget range.

**Vieng Phouka**
There are a few basic guesthouses in the southern part of town and there is little to choose between them. **Bo Kung ($)** is a decent option with very simple rooms.

## Restaurants

**$$-$ Boat Landing Guesthouse & Restaurant**
*See Where to stay, T086-312398.*
*Open 0700-2100.*
The best place to eat in town, with a beautiful dining area and exceptionally innovative cuisine: a range of northern Lao dishes made from local produce that supports local villages. Highly recommended.

**$$-$ Forest Retreat's Bamboo Lounge**
*Main road, T020-6668 0031, www.*
*bambooloungelaos.com.*
A small 'gourmet café' run by a super-friendly Kiwi couple who serve up good pizza and a solid range of drinks in a warm and welcoming environment. This is an excellent place to eat and to get up-to-date information on what to do in the local area. They can also arrange treks and various tours. Recommended.

**$ Baw Pen Yang Restaurant and Art Gallery**
*Down the sidestreet by Lai's.*
Opened in 2014, this is a very welcome addition to the town, providing comfortable seating, a good range of hearty breakfasts and also artwork by a local artist which is available for purchase.

**$ Lai's Place**
*On the main road.*
A fantastic little spot with great owners serving very tasty Lao food. A place you're likely to return to.

### Bakeries, cafés and street stalls

There is a bakery and cake shop near the market that sells mouthwatering treats; try the green tea cake. There are a few *feu* stalls by the main market. At night, food vendors gather at the night market, selling meat on a stick and waffles from pretty, candlelit stalls.

## Shopping

The night market sells textiles woven by the women of Luang Namtha and warm clothes for travellers who've forgotten that it's cold in the mountains. There is an ever-growing range of other handicrafts on offer making this quite a pleasant place to do some gift shopping.

## What to do

### Massage and sauna
There are a few herbal saunas in town; bring your own towels.

### Tour operators
If you want to trek from Luang Namtha and you're travelling solo or as a couple, it's expensive. Try to hook up with people before you get there or at your guesthouse. Agencies also put up boards requesting more takers. The larger the group, the cheaper the price.
**Forest Retreat Laos,** *see Restaurants.*
Kiwi-owned, this company has an ethical focus and looks to plough profits back into local communities and promote responsible trekking. Offers kayaking, cycling, trekking or a mix of all 3. These folk are wonderfully passionate about the National Protected Area and Luang Namtha itself.
**Green Discovery,** *main road, T086-211484, www.greendiscoverylaos.com. Office open daily 0730-2100.* Offers 1- to 7-day kayaking/rafting, cycling and trekking excursions into the Nam Ha NPA. Excellent guides.
**Luang Namtha Eco Guide Unit,** *T086-211534, www.luangnamtha-tourism.org.* Information on 1- to 4-day treks into the

Nam Ha NPA. Biking tours, boat trips and tuk-tuk tours also possible. The tourism office has also set up an **Eco Guide** unit at Muang Nalea.

## Vieng Phouka

The local tourism office runs 4 different treks of 1 to 3 days around the local villages, the Nam Ha National Park and caves, including food, camping and accommodation with a host family. The guides (trained by the LNTA and the EU) are usually Khmu and Akha from the surrounding villages. Contact the **Vieng Phouka Eco Guide Service Unit**, T084-212400. Daily 0800-1200, 1330-1700.

## Transport

### Air

Luang Namtha's airport is 6 km south of the city centre. Shared tuk-tuks wait outside the terminal for arriving flights and run to anywhere in town. There are 3 flights a week direct to **Vientiane** with **Lao Airlines**, T086-212072, which has an office south of town on the main road.

### Bicycle/motorbike

Bicycles and motorcycle are available for hire from various places around town, but the place in front of **Zuela Guesthouse** has the best choice and very helpful staff. Motorbike tours of up to 5 days can also be arranged here.

### Boat

Slow boats are the best and most scenic travel option but their reliability will depend on the tide and, in the dry season (Jan-May) they often won't run at all as the water level is too low. There isn't really a regular boat service from **Luang Namtha**, so you will have to charter a whole boat or hitch a ride on a boat making the trip already. The **Boat Landing Guesthouse** is a good source of information about boats; if arrangements are made for you, a courtesy tip is appreciated.

### Bus/truck/songthaew

The inter-provincial bus station and its ticket office are 10 km south of town. A newer intra-provincial bus station is on the main road, 100 m south of the town strip. From the intra-provincial bus station: to **Muang Sing**, 3 daily, 1½ hrs, additional pickups may depart throughout the rest of the day, depending on demand. To **Boten** (Chinese border), service is variable, 2 hrs.

From the inter-provincial bus station: to **Udomxai**, several daily, 4 hrs; to **Houei Xai**, 0900 and 1330, 4 hrs. Take this service for **Vieng Phouka**. To **Luang Prabang**, 1 morning departure, 8 hrs. To **Vientiane**, morning and afternoon, 21hrs. To get to **Nong Khiaw**, you need to go via Udomxai (leave early).

### Vieng Phouka

Buses and *songthaew* depart for **Houei Xai**, a few times daily from the market, usually in the morning, 5 hrs. It is also possible to catch buses to **Luang Namtha**, 4 hrs, and **Udomxai**.

### Boten

A variable service to **Luang Namtha**, 2 hrs; and **Udomxai**, 4-6 hrs.

**friendly town amid gorgeous scenery with accessible hilltribe communities**

Many visitors consider this peaceful valley to be one of the highlights of the north. Lying at the terminus of the highway in the far northwest corner of Laos, it is a natural point to stop and spend a few days recovering from the rigours of the road, before either heading south or moving on to China. This area is a border region that has been contested by the Chinese, Lao and Thai at various points in the last few centuries. While it is now firmly Lao territory, there is a sense that the Chinese have invaded by stealth as their economic presence is extremely evident. There are also several NGOs, as well as bilateral and multilateral development operations in the area. The only way to get to Muang Sing is by bus or pickup from Luang Namtha. The road is asphalt and the terrain on this route is mountainous with dense forest.

### Sights

Muang Sing itself is little more than a supremely picturesque village, situated on an upland plateau, where golden rattan huts glow among misty blue-green peaks. The town features some interesting old wooden and brick buildings and, unlike nearby Luang Namtha and several other towns in the north, it wasn't bombed close to oblivion during the struggle for Laos. The **old French fort**, built in the 1920s, is off limits to visitors, as it is occupied by the Lao army, but the relocated market is certainly worth a look if you're up very early in the morning; it starts about 0600 and begins to wind down after 0800. Along with the usual array of plastic objects, clothes and pieces of hardware, local silk and cotton textiles can be purchased. Numerous hill peoples come to the market to trade, including Akha and Hmong tribespeople, along with Yunnanese, Tai Dam and Tai Lue.

The **Muang Sing Ethnic Museum** ① *in the centre of town, daily 0800-1200 and 1300-1600*, is a beautiful old wooden and brick building. It houses a range of traditional tools, ethnic clothes, jewellery, instruments, religious artefacts and household items, like the loom. The building was once the royal residence of the Cao Fa (Prince), Phaya Sekong. Most Buddhist monasteries in the vicinity are Tai Lue in style. The most accessible is **Wat Sing Chai**, on the main road.

### Around Muang Sing

From Muang Sing, trek uphill past **Stupa Mountain Lodge** for 1 km to reach **That Xieng Tung**, the most sacred site in the area. The stupa was built in 1256 and is believed to contain the Buddha's adam's apple. It attracts lots of pilgrims in November for the annual **full moon festival**. Originally a city was built around the stupa but everyone migrated down to lower lands. There is a small pond near the stupa, which is believed to be auspicious: if it dries up it is considered bad luck for Muang Sing. It is said that the pond once dried up and the whole village had no rice and starved. Most tourism operators will run treks to the stupa and a stop at **Nam Keo waterfall**, a large cascade with a 10-m drop, 7 km from the guesthouse. It's a nice place for a picnic. The local tourism authority runs treks to the falls. Bring good shoes.

## Ethnic minority villages

The area around Muang Sing is home to many minorities who have been resettled, either from refugee camps in Thailand or from highland areas of Laos. The town is predominantly Tai Lue but the district is 50% Akha, with a further 10% Tai Neua. The population of the district is said to have trebled between 1992 and 1996 and, as a result, it is one of the few places in northern Laos where hilltribe villages are readily accessible. The main activity for visitors is to hire bicycles and visit the villages that surround the town in all directions; several guesthouses have maps of the surrounding area and trekking is becoming increasingly popular. However, please do not undertake treks independently as it undermines the government's attempts to make tourism sustainable and minimize the impact on the culture of local villages.

## Muang Long

The small, predominantly Akha market town Muang Long is being developed as a trekking centre. Set at the bottom of a flat narrow valley with limestone cliffs rising steeply from the riverside, there is great potential but it remains relatively undeveloped. The **Muang Long Tourism Office** ⓘ *look out for the blue sign next to the Long Administration office, www.muanglongtourismoffice.weebly.com*, can arrange treks from one to five days.

## Xieng Kok

On the 13-14 and 28-29 of each month at **Xieng Kok** a market is held to which all the local minorities come. The Muang Sing tourism office organizes tuk-tuk tours. Otherwise there is little to attract visitors to this sleepy backwater.

## Listings Muang Sing

### Tourist information

Muang Sing Tourism Office
*Ban Xiengchai, T086-400015, www. luangnamtha-tourism-laos.org. Mon-Fri 0800-1130 and 1330-1700, Sat-Sun 0800-1000 and 1500-1700.*
Offers a wide variety of treks. There is a small bank opposite the market. Internet is available at the tourism office and Wi-Fi is becoming more widely available at guesthouses.

### Where to stay

$ Adima Guesthouse
*Near Ban Oudomsin, 8 km north of Muang Sing towards the Chinese border, 600 m off the main road, T020-2239 3398.*
A little hard to get to but the location is extremely scenic with views over the paddy fields and hills. Peaceful bungalows constructed in traditional Yao and Akha style (some with shared bathroom), bathrooms with squat toilets, plus a lovely open-air restaurant serving good food. A place to get away from it all.

### $ Phou Lu Bungalows
*At the southern end of town,*
*T030-5511 0326.*
Spacious wooden double bungalows
with 4-poster beds, small balconies
with bamboo seats, set around a
grassy compound with restaurant
and massage service.

### $ Taileu Guesthouse
*On the main road, T030-511 0354.*
Above the restaurant there are 8 very
basic rattan rooms with bamboo-style,
4-poster beds (the rickety backpacker
version not the romantic type), squat
toilets and temperamental hot water
heated by solar power. The guesthouse
owners are lovely people, speak good
English and run one of the best places
to eat in town.

## Restaurants

It is highly recommended that you eat
some of the delicious ethnic food while
you're in Muang Sing as there aren't
many other places where you will be
able to sample these meals.

### $$-$ Adima Guesthouse
*See Where to stay.*
Western offerings, such as the usual
backpacker pancakes or fried eggs,
as well as some Lao-inspired meals.

### $ Muang Sing View Restaurant
*Just off the main road.*
A bamboo walkway leads to this rustic
restaurant which enjoys the best views
in Muang Sing overlooking the paddy
fields and the valley. All the usual Lao
staples are served.

### $ Taileu Guesthouse and Restaurant
*See Where to stay, T081-212375.*
The most popular place to eat due to
its indigenous Tai Lue menu. Try baked

aubergine with pork, soy mash and
fish soup. Try their local piña colada
with *lao lao*, their *sa lo* (Muang Sing's
answer to a hamburger) or one of the
famous *jeow* dishes. The banana flower
soup is fantastic. This is an eating
experience you won't find elsewhere
in Laos. Noi, the owner, is very friendly.
Highly recommended.

## What to do

### Trekking
Trekking has become a delicate issue
around Muang Sing as uncontrolled
tourism was beginning to have a
detrimental effect on some of the
minority villages. Luckily some sensible
procedures have been put in place
to ensure low-impact tourism. The
**Muang Sing Tourism Office** (see Tourist
information, above) has a wide variety of
treks on offer from 1 to 3 days.
**Exotissimo**, *T086-400016, akhaexp@
gmail.com, www.exotissimo.com*. In
cahoots with **GTZ**, a German aid agency,
**Exotissimo** has launched more expensive
but thoroughly enjoyable treks such as
the 'Akha Experience', which include tasty
meals prepared by local Akha people.
Advertised as a 3-day trek, it can be
organized as a 1- and 2-day trek too.

## Transport

### Bicycle
Available for rent from a couple of
guesthouses in town – to go further
afield a mountain bike is definitely
preferable. Bikes are usually set out the
front when they are available, so keep
an eye out for the better ones.

### Boat
It is sometimes possible to charter boats
from **Xieng Kok** downstream on the

Mekong to **Houei Xai**, 3-4 hrs, but the price can be rather steep.

**Bus/truck/songthaew**
The bus station is across from the new morning market, 500 m from the main road. To **Luang Namtha**, by bus or pickup, 2 hrs. It is also possible to charter a *songthaew* or tuk-tuk to Luang Namtha. *Songthaew* to **Xieng Kok**, 3 hrs. To **Muang Long**, 2 hrs.

## Along the Mekong
border region, ideal for nature lovers

**Houei Xai (Houay Xai)** → *Phone code: 084. Colour map 1, B1.*
*Most passengers arrive at the passenger ferry pier, close to the centre. The vehicle ferry pier is 750 m further north (upstream). The bus station is at the Morning Market, 3 km out of central Houei Xai. The immigration office is at the boat terminal and the airport, daily 0800-1800.*

This town is in the heart of the Golden Triangle and used to derive its wealth from the narcotics trade on the heroin route to Chiang Mai in Thailand. Today trade still brings the town considerable affluence, although it is rather less illicit: timber is ferried across the Mekong from Laos to the Thai town of Chiang Khong and, in exchange, consumer goods are shipped back. Sapphires are mined in the area and, doubtless, there is also still some undercover heroin smuggling.

Houei Xai is a popular crossing point for tourists travelling to and from Thailand and a considerable amount of money flows in from the numerous guesthouses and restaurants that have been built here. However, few people spend more than one night in the town.

**Sights** Although the petite, picturesque town is growing rapidly as links with Thailand intensify, it is still small and easy enough to get around on foot. **Wat Chom Kha Out Manirath**, in the centre of town, is worth a visit for its views. The monastery was built at the end of the 19th century but, because it is comparatively well endowed, there has been a fair amount of re-building and renovation since then. There is also a large former French fort here called Fort Carnot, currently used by the Lao army (and consequently out of bounds), which is to be redeveloped as a tourist spot by the LNTA.

The **Morning Market** can be entertaining, particularly for first-time visitors who have entered from Thailand, as this will be their first experience of a Lao market. There is little of note about the produce on display but local tribespeople come from their villages to sell things here. To get there, take a tuk-tuk to the small outlying village of Houei Xai (10,000 kip).

## BORDER CROSSING
### Houei Xai–Chiang Khong (Thailand)

Now that the Thai Friendship bridge has been built here, the border crossing is a very simple affair.

The new crossing is 10 km south of the town. To reach it, take a tuk-tuk to the Laos Immigration office from where a shuttle bus will deliver you to the Thai immigration office on the other side.

Thai immigration is open daily 0800-1800. A one-month Thai visa is available at the border. Buses and taxis travel from Chiang Kong to Chiang Rai Airport where there are connections to Bangkok. From Chaing Khong there are regular buses to Chiang Rai, 0600-1700, and Chiang Mai, 0630.

Crossing into Laos, immigration is open daily 0730-1730, but expect to pay a small overtime fee at the weekend or after 1600. Tourist visas (30 days) are available at the border. There is also a bank at the Lao border (daily 0830-1600).

### ★ Bokeo Nature Reserve Gibbon Experience
*Office on the main Sekhong Rd in Houay Xai, T084-212021, www.gibbonexperience.org.*

Most visitors who stick around Houei Xai do so to visit the Gibbon Experience, a thrilling, exciting and unmissable three-day trip into Bokeo Nature Reserve where a number of treehouses have been built high in the jungle canopy and linked with a course of interconnected ziplines. The experience of staying in one of these treehouses and being awoken by singing soprano gibbons is truly awe-inspiring, as is ziplining through the mist high above the jungle canopy.

In the morning well-trained guides take visitors for hikes to see if they can spot the elusive gibbons and other animal and plant species. Such species include the giant squirrel, one of the largest rodents in the world, and the Asiatic black bear, whose numbers are in decline due to hunting for their bile and gall bladders.

First and foremost this is a very well-run conservation project. It was started to help reduce poaching, logging, slash-and-burn farming and the destruction of primary forest by working with villagers to transform the local economy by making a non-destructive living from their unique environment. Already the Gibbon Experience has started to pay dividends: the forest conservation and canopy visits can generate as much income year on year as a local logging company could do only once.

Alongside the 'Classic' experience there is now a 'Waterfall Gibbon Experience' which takes people deeper into the reserve, trekking for two to three hours per day along the Nam Nga River. The waterfall tree house has a freshwater swimming hole at the bottom, the other shows sunsets overlooking several valleys. This option gets consistently excellent feedback from guests.

### Ban Nam Chan and Ban Nam Keun

**Ban Nam Chan** is a pleasant Chinese-speaking village, about 17 km from Houei Xai. The Lanten tribespeople who live here are famous for their textiles: the women wear black, kaftan-style dresses and shave their eyebrows and wear a headpiece once they are married; the men wear black shirts and blue trousers. Along the way, the road passes Hmong villages.

**Ban Nam Keun**, a small traditional village on the high plateau not far from the main town, is worth a visit for its natural beauty.

## Pakbeng → *Colour map 1, C2.*

This long thin strip of a village is perched halfway up a hill, with fine views over the Mekong. Its importance lies in its location at the confluence of the Mekong and Nam Beng rivers. There is not much to do here but it's a good place to stop (and is the obligatory stop) on the slow boat between Houei Xai and Luang Prabang. The village is worth a visit for its traditional atmosphere and the friendliness of the locals, including various minorities. Just downstream from the port is a good spot for swimming in the dry season, but be careful as the current is strong. There are also a couple of monasteries in town. The locals organize guided treks to nearby villages. Electricity is now available 24 hours and internet is widely available.

## Hongsa and around

From Pakbeng you can take a boat downriver to the small town of **Tha Suang** and then catch a *songthaew* (one hour), through beautiful jungled hills, to the valley of Hongsa. Hongsa district is renowned for its working elephants. The town is usually just a jump-off point for excursions to nearby **Vieng Ghiaw** (see below). **Hongsa Tourism** office ⓘ *T020-5577 8142.* ▸▸ *See What to do, page 143.*

## Vieng Ghiaw

The men of Vieng Ghiaw have a long tradition as *mahouts* (elephant handlers), training elephants specifically for use in the local timber trade. The village is surrounded by overgrown, ruined city walls, believed to be hundreds of years old, and an extensive moat system that spans several kilometres. The predominantly Tai Lue village features traditional stilt houses, made of solid Maidu (an Asian rosewood) and designed to house both elephants and humans, with a large spacious area underneath so that the *mahout* can step straight off his veranda onto the elephant's back. Locals are actively involved in the preservation of these unique houses and are hoping, through sponsorship, to keep their village homes rather than replacing them with ugly concrete equivalents. Displayed beneath the veranda are miscellaneous items, usually weaving looms or elephant saddles, which symbolize the family's social status. The Tai Lue use a variety of saddles, separate ones for training, hunting, weddings or religious celebrations. The village is also well known for its textiles, which are woven by the Tai Lue women.

**Lao** National Tourism State Bokeo
*On the main street up from immigration,*
*T084-211162. Mon-Fri 0800-1130 and*
*1330-1600.*
Can offer limited advice.

### Where to stay

#### Houei Xai

**$ BAP Guesthouse**
*On the main Sekhong Rd, T084-211083,*
*bapbiz@live.com.*
One of the oldest guesthouses in town
consisting of a labyrinth of additions
and add-ons as their business has
grown over the years. A range of rooms;
the newer tiled ones with hot-water
bathrooms are the best.

**$ Sabaydee**
*On the riverfront, T020-5692 9458.*
Big, tiled rooms, with en suite hot
showers and Western toilets. Good
value and recommended.

**$ Taveensinh Guesthouse**
*Northwest end of the town, T084-211502.*
A good budget choice with clean
rooms and great communal balconies
overlooking the river and friendly
family in charge.

#### Pakbeng

During peak season, when the slow
boat arrives from Luang Prabang, about
60 people descend on Pakbeng at the
same time. As the town doesn't have
an endless supply of great budget
guesthouses, it is advisable to get
someone you trust to mind your bags,
while you make a mad dash to get the

best room in town. There are a number
of shack-like bamboo lodgings running
up the hill.

**$$$$-$$$ Pakbeng Lodge**
*On the hillside above the river, T081-*
*212304, www.pakbenglodge.com.*
A wooden and concrete construction,
built in traditional Lao style, this
stunning guesthouse includes 20 rooms
with fan, toilet and hot water. Good
restaurant and wonderful views.
Breakfast is included. 10 new deluxe
rooms were due to open at the time
of writing. Wi-Fi available. Elephant
activities can be arranged.

**$$$ Luangsay Lodge**
*About 1 km from the centre of town,*
*www.mekong-cruises.com.*
This is the most beautiful
accommodation in Pakbeng. An
attractive wooden pathway curves
through luscious tropical gardens
to several wooden bungalows with
fantastic balconies and large windows
overlooking the river and misty
mountains. Hot-water bathrooms and
romantic rooms make this a winner.
Great restaurant. Book in advance as it
tends to get booked up by customers on
the **Luangsay Cruise** especially in high
season but Sun and last-minute deals
are possible. Breakfast and dinner is
included. Highly recommended.

**$ Monsovanh Guesthouse**
*On the main road.*
One of the most popular choice and
rightly so thanks to the good location,
clean rooms and welcoming owner.
Very good breakfasts at the **Monsovanh**
bakery across the road.

## Hongsa

### $ Jumbo Guesthouse
*300 m from the bus station, T020-5685 6488, www.lotuselephant.com.*
The nicest place to stay, with 5 rooms and lots of elephant-focused activities arranged. Run by the helpful Monica who also cooks great Asian and European cuisine. She doesn't have a menu, instead asking her guests what they fancy and rustling something up based on that and what she can find at the market. A special find.

## Restaurants

### Houei Xai

### $$-$ Riverside
*Just off the main road, near the* **Houay Xai Guesthouse***, T084-211064.*
Huge waterfront restaurant on large platform. Perfect position for taking in the sunset. Great shakes. Extensive menu that's a mixture of Lao and Thai food. The curries are quite good. Usually live music is played here, some of it decidedly off-key.

### $ BAP Guesthouse
*See Where to stay.*
Wide range of dishes including pancakes, croissants and eggs.

### $ Nutpop
*On the main road, T084-211037.*
A pleasant little garden restaurant, set in an atmospheric lamp-lit building. Good Lao food – fried mushrooms and good curry. Excellent fish.

### Pakbeng
Restaurants serve breakfast (baguettes, pancakes and coffee) really early. The eco-lodges have pretty upscale restaurants, and there are several more modest restaurants lining the main road towards the river; all seem to have the same English menu, basic Lao dishes, eggs and freshly made sandwiches. The local market has an array of dishes from *feu* through to frogs.

### $ Kopchaideu Restaurant
*Overlooking the Mekong.*
This restaurant has a wide selection of Indian dishes with a few Lao favourites thrown in. Great shakes, naan bread and fantastic service – the pick of the bunch.

## Festivals

### Hongsa
**Mid-Feb**  **Elephant Festival**. See Sayaboury, page 146, for details.

## What to do

### Houei Xai
**Tour operators**
**Gibbon Experience**, *T084-212021, www.gibbonexperience.org*. This unique ecotourism operation provides the rare opportunity to see or hear the soprano-singing, black-cheeked crested gibbons. See page 140 for details.

### Pakbeng
**Elephant trekking**
Contact **Pakbeng Lodge**, *see Where to stay*.

**Massage**
Massage is offered in several places around town.

### Hongsa
**Elephant trekking**
Elephant treks can also be organized through **Jumbo Guesthouse**. See Where to stay.

### Houei Xai

**Lao National Tourism State Bokeo** (see page 142) can advise on the sale of boat, bus, pickup and other tickets but limited English is spoken. You are better off approaching the travel agencies around the immigration centre many of which sell bus and boat tickets. See page 113 for information on boat travel between Houei Xai and **Luang Prabang**.

### Boat

The passenger ferry pier is close to the centre of town. The vehicle ferry pier is 750 m further north (upstream). The **BAP Guesthouse** is a good place to find out about boat services. For services across the Mekong to Thailand, see Border crossings, page 332.

The 2-day trip down the Mekong to **Luang Prabang** is a Southeast Asian rite of passage. The slow boat to **Pakbeng** is raved about by many travellers. However, in peak season it can be packed. Bring something soft to sit on, a good book to read and a packed lunch. If you can get enough people together you can charter your own boat – ask for advice at the tourist office as they may be able to arrange it much more cheaply than if you go direct. The trip in reverse usually has fewer passengers.

For a luxury option there is the lovely **Luangsay Cruise**, T084-212092, www.luangsay.com, opposite Lao immigration, which makes a 2-day/1-night cruise down the river in comfort with cushioned deckchairs, a bar, wooden interior, and plenty of food. Stops are made to visit riverside villages. Guests stay at the beautiful **Luangsay Lodge** in Pakbeng. Accommodation and meals are included.

Speedboats are a noisy, dangerous alternative to the slow boats.

### Bus/truck/songthaew

The bus station is at the Morning Market, 3 km out of central Houei Xai. Trucks, buses and minivans run to **Vieng Phouka**, 5 hrs; **Luang Namtha**, 7 hrs; **Udomxai**, 12 hrs; **Luang Prabang**, 12 hrs; and **Vientiane**, 20 hrs.

### Pakbeng
### Boat

Times and prices are always changing so it's best to check before you travel. There is a slow boat to **Houei Xai** and **Luang Prabang**. You can also take a boat downriver to **Tha Suang**, 2 hrs and then catch a *songthaew* from here to **Hongsa** or arrange a private pickup through the **Jumbo Guesthouse** in Hongsa, see Where to stay.

### Bus/truck/songthaew

Buses and *songthaew* leave about 2 km from town in the morning for the route north to **Udomxai**, 6-7 hrs. Direct *songthaew* to Udomxai are few and far between, so take one to Muang Houn and then catch a more frequent service from there. The road to Udomxai passes through spectacular scenery.

Sayaboury is not on many visitors' agendas, although the annual elephant festival is staged in this province (see page 146). Transport difficulties have given Sayaboury a charming forgotten atmosphere. It may be the capital of a province covering over 16,000 sq km – equivalent to the area of Hawaii or Northern Ireland – with 300,000 inhabitants, but it doesn't feel like it.

The town has an attractive setting on the Nam Houn – a tributary of the Mekong – and a number of monasteries; those of note are **Wat Thin**, **Wat Pha Phoun**, **Wat Natonoy** and **Wat Sisavang Vong**, named after the king who reigned during the de facto Japanese occupation of French Indochina. The province is mountainous with Phu Khao Mieng, Laos' ninth highest peak, at just over 2000 m.

Gluttons for punishment or very adventurous travellers may want to take the seven- to 10-hour *songthaew* trip from Sayaboury to Hongsa (see page 141). The trip passes through stunning scenery and sometimes includes the chance to see working elephants en route but it is a bone-jarringly bumpy trip on unsealed roads, which, in the rainy season, are often flooded.

### Pak Lai → *Colour map 2, B1.*
Pak Lai is not very much more than a convenient place to stop on the long river journey between Vientiane and Luang Prabang and it grew up as a boating equivalent to a truck stop. There are a sprinkling of colonial shopfronts and old wooden Lao houses, a couple of guesthouses, a few restaurants and shops, post office and a branch of the Lao Development Bank.

Pak Lai does, however, enjoy a footnote in Laos' colonial history which is worth recounting. In 1887 Luang Prabang was attacked by a band of Chinese Haw and northern Tai bandits. Auguste Pavie, the newly appointed French vice consul, rescued King Unkham from his burning palace and escaped downstream to Pak Lai. Here they remained while the old and frail king recovered from the journey and Pavie researched the early history of Lane Xang. This piece of quick-thinking indebted the king to Pavie and therefore also to the French. Within five years of this heroic rescue Laos was French and the Siamese had lost control of the country.

## Listings Northwest Laos

### Tourist information

**Sayaboury** Provincial Tourism Department
*T030-518 0095.*

### Where to stay

**Sayaboury**

**$ New Sayaboury Hotel**
*Near the market.*
Large, 3-storey hotel with clean, fair-sized rooms boasting fan, en suite

bathroom and hot water. For a few extra dollars you can get a/c. Recommended.

## Pak Lai

**$ Lamdouan Guesthouse**
*To the west of the boat landing, along the river road, T020-9980 3451.*
Very friendly, family-run guesthouse offering basic rooms with shared facilities.
$ There is a good little restaurant beside the boat landing that serves *feu* and *pad gow*.

## Restaurants

### Sayaboury
There are restaurants, along with the usual noodle shops and stalls on streets leading off the market. None are particularly noteworthy. Simple Chinese and Lao dishes.

## Festivals

### Sayaboury
**Mid-Feb** **Elephant Festival**. Check www.elefantasia.org. Alternating between the districts of Sayaboury, Paklay and Hongsa, the annual elephant festival is gaining momentum in this least-visited area of the country. Originally organized by **Elefant Asia** which has now stepped back to allow the local organization of the event. Recommended.

## Transport

### Sayaboury
**Bus**
There are 2 bus terminals, the South bus station, 2 km southeast of town, and the North bus station, 2 km north of town. It is now possible to reach **Vientiane** by road, but doing it by boat, or a combination of the 2, is preferable, but you'll need plenty of time because finding a boat is not always easy. One option is to catch a vehicle to Pak Lai, on the Mekong, where it is possible to catch a boat downstream to Vientiane. There are several buses to **Pak Lai**, daily, 4 hrs. In the wet season (Jun/Jul-Oct/Nov) travel is difficult and sometimes impossible.

You can catch a *songthaew* north to **Tha Deua** on the Mekong, 23 km, from where a ferry crosses to **Pak Khon** and then catch a bus on to **Luang Prabang**, 4 hrs.

### Pak Lai
**Boat**
There are irregular connections by slow boat (downriver) to **Vientiane**, 8 hrs.

**Songthaew**
*Songthaew* terminate 3 km out of town; share a tuk-tuk to the centre. *Songthaew* run to **Sayaboury**, 4 hrs.

# Xieng Khouang
## Province

Apart from the historic Plain of Jars, Xieng Khouang Province is best known for the pounding it took during the war. Many of the sights are battered monuments to the plateau's violent recent history. Given the time it takes to make the return trip and the fact that the jars themselves aren't as visually arresting as some sights in Laos, many travellers consider the destination a stretch too far. However, for those interested in modern history and seeing some of the country's less visited areas, it's one of the most fascinating areas of Laos and gives a real insight into the resilient nature of the Lao people. The countryside, particularly towards the Vietnam border, is very beautiful – among the country's best – and the jars, too, are interesting by dint of their very oddness and the mystery that surrounds them. In the late afternoon light the sight of them spread out across the rolling landscape is nothing less than other-worldly.

★ Phonsavanh is the main town of the province today – old Xieng Khouang having been flattened – and its small airstrip is a crucial transport link in this mountainous region. Surrounding the town are huge mountains, among them Phu Bia, one of the country's highest. The town itself is notable mainly for its ugliness. It was established in the mid-1970s and sprawls out from a heartless centre with no sense of plan or direction. While Phonsavanh will win no beauty contests, it does have a rather attractive 'Wild West' atmosphere.

South of Phonsavanh, on two small hills, a pair of white and gold monuments can be seen. (The road to the memorials is marked Ban Yone Temple.) It is worth the short hike up, if only for the views they afford of the surrounding countryside.

## Essential Xienh Khouang Province

### Finding your feet

The region's main town is Phonsavanh, which has an airport and is a good base from which to explore the surrounding area. The most direct route by road from Luang Prabang to Xieng Khouang Province is to take Route 13 south to Muang Phou Khoun and then Route 7 east. You might want to take travel sickness tablets as it's quite a bumpy trip. An alternative, scenic, albeit convoluted, route is via Nong Khiaw (see page 114), from where there are pickups to Pak Xeng and Phonsavanh via Vieng Thong on Route 1 or Nam Nouan. Public transport throughout the province is limited and sporadic. A car with driver is the easiest way of touring the area.

### When to go

It is cold at higher elevation, such as Phonsavanh, from November to March. Several jumpers and a thick jacket are required.

The **Vietnamese war memorial**, on the west side, was built to commemorate the death of over one million Vietnamese troops during the war against the anti-Communists. It contains the bones of Vietnamese soldiers and is inscribed 'Lao Vietnamese Solidarity Forever'. It is the more interesting of the two for its golden socialist statues in strident pose and socialist murals in relief.

The UK-based **Mines Advisory Group (MAG) UXO Visitor Information Centre** ⓘ *on the main road in the centre of town, Mon-Fri 0800-2000, Sat-Sun 1600-2000*, is currently engaged in clearing the land of Unexploded Ordnance. It has an exhibition of bombs, interesting photographs and information on the bombing campaign and ongoing plight of Laos with UXO. Usually there are members of staff on hand to explain exactly how the bombs were used. All T-shirts sold here help fund the UXO clearance of the area and are a very worthwhile souvenir.

Opposite the MAG centre is the **Xieng Khuang UXO Survivors Center** ⓘ *www.laos.worlded.org, daily 0900-2100*, detailing the work of World Education Laos in preventing UXO accidents and aiding UXO survivors.

Just before the bus station on the way into town is **Mulberries** ⓘ *Route 7, T020-5552 1408, www.mulberries.org, tours Mon-Sat 0800-1600*, where you can visit a silk farm, see the sericulture process in action and buy a wide range of exquisite silk goods in the shop.

## Listings Phonsavanh

### Tourist information

**Xieng Khouang Provincial Tourism** *Department, 2 km from the town centre, signposted, T061-312217, xkgtourism@yahoo.com.*
Some members of staff speak a bit of English. As well as having the largest collection of bomb paraphernalia in town, the office has interesting displays and can provide useful leaflets, as well as up-to-date bus timetables.

### Where to stay

**$$ The Hillside Residence (aka Nearn Phou)**
*On the track to the Vansana Resort, T061-213300, www.the-hillside-residence.com.*
Family-run guesthouse. Rooms are decorated with textiles and some offer great views. The 1st-floor balcony is a great place to kick back and the restaurant is reasonable. A nice option.

**$$ Maly Hotel**
*Down the road from local government offices, T061-312031.*
All rooms have hot water and are furnished with a hotchpotch of local artefacts, including a small cluster bomb casing on the table. The more expensive, much larger rooms on the upper floors have satellite TV, out-of-place baths in large bathrooms, a sitting area, fireplace and hairdryers. There is also a restaurant and tour desk. The former owner spent his teenage years in a cave at Xam Neua.

**$$ Vansana Resort**
*On a hill about 1 km out of town, T061-213170, www.vansanahotel-group.com.*
Rather dated, but offers big rooms equipped with telephone, TV, minibar, and tea/coffee-making facilities, and has good views of the countryside. The best room is the smart suite with polished wooden floors and textile decoration, or opt for one of the rooms upstairs, which have free-form bathtubs and picturesque balcony views. The restaurant offers Lao and international cuisine.

**$ Nice Guesthouse**
*On the main road, T020-5561 6246, naibhoj@hotmail.com.*
Clean, decent-sized rooms with hot water and comfortable beds. Offers reasonable value and friendly service.

### Restaurants

**$$-$ Craters**
*Main street, T020-7780 5775.*
Modern, Western-style restaurant offering range of burgers, pizza and sandwiches. Comfortable cane sofas, good music, attentive service. Also has delectable but pricey cocktails.

# BACKGROUND
## Xieng Khouang Province

Xieng Khouang Province has had a murky, blood-tinted, war-ravaged history. The area was the most bombed province in the most bombed country, per capita, in the world, as it became a crucial strategic zone that both the US and Vietnamese wanted to control. The town of Phonsavanh has long been an important transit point between China to the north, Vietnam to the east and Thailand to the south and this status historically made the town a target for neighbouring countries. What's more, the plateau of the Plain of Jars is one of the flattest areas in northern Laos, rendering it a natural battleground for the numerous conflicts that ensued from the 19th century to 1975. As a result, the region holds immense appeal for those interested in the modern history of the country.

The earliest known settlers in this area were believed to be of the ethnic Tai origin and a Phuan kingdom was established in the region in the 14th century. The kingdom suffered numerous sackings by the Vietnamese over hundreds of years, until, in 1832, they invaded Phonsavanh, executing the Phuan king and turning the area into an Annan vassal state. The region was incorporated into the kingdom of Lane Xang by King Fa Ngum briefly in the 16th century but was more often than not ruled by the Vietnamese (who called it Tran Ninh) because of its proximity to the border. The Chinese Haw also ravaged Phonsavanh in the 19th century, an event that, along with the sacking of Luang Prabang, became a catalyst for the government's acceptance of French protection.

Under the French, Xieng Khouang supported tea plantations and many colonial settlers took to the temperate climate of the province. Once the French departed, massive conflicts were waged in 1945-1946 between the Free Lao Movement and the Viet Minh. The Pathet Lao and Viet Minh joined forces and, by 1964, had a number of bases dotted around the Plain of Jars. From then on chaos ensued, as Xieng Khouang got caught in the middle of the war between the Royalist-American and Pathet Lao-Vietnamese (see also page 155). The extensive US bombing of this area was to ensure it did not fall under Communist control of Pathet Lao. The Vietnamese were trying to ensure that the US did not gain control of the area from which they could launch attacks on North Vietnam.

During the 'Secret War' (1964-1974) against the North Vietnamese Army and the Pathet Lao, tens of thousands of cluster bomb units (CBUs) were dumped on Xieng Khouang Province. Other bombs, such as the anti-personnel plastic

$ Bamboozle! Restaurant and Bar
*Main street opposite Nice Hotel,*
*T020-779 928 959.*
A top choice for Lao or Western fair in a good atmosphere. Along with **Craters**,

this is one of the most ocular options in town.

$ Nisha Indian
*Main street.*
Great Indian restaurants can be found in the oddest of place in Laos, and this

'pineapple' bomblets, were also used. As 30% of the original CBUs did not explode, these cluster bombs continue to kill and maim today. The Plain of Jars was also hit by B-52s returning from abortive bombing runs to Hanoi, which jettisoned their bomb loads before heading back to the US air base at Udon Thani in northeast Thailand. One bombing raid destroyed 1600 buildings in Xieng Khouang town alone. Suffice to say that, with over 580,944 sorties flown (one-and-a-half times the number flown in Vietnam), whole towns were obliterated and the area's geography was permanently altered.

Today, as the **Lao Airlines** plane begins its descent towards the plateau, the meaning of the term 'carpet bombing' becomes clear. On the final approach to the town of Phonsavanh, the plane banks low over the cratered paddy fields, affording a T-28 fighter-bomber pilot's view of his target, which in places has been pummelled into little more than a moonscape.

There is no official figure on the number of dead but, since over 80% of the population is believed to have inhabited the northern and southern provinces targeted by US bombing, some sources estimate 300,000 Lao were killed – 9-10% of the country's total population at the time.

Today, hundreds of thousands of bomblets – and equally lethal impact mines, which the Lao call *bombis* – remain buried in Xieng Khouang's grassy meadows. Because the war was 'secret', there are few records of what was dropped where, and even when the unexploded ordnance (UXO) has been uncovered their workings are often a mystery – the Americans used Laos as a testing ground for new ordnance so blueprints are unavailable.

Uncle Sam has, however, bequeathed to local people an almost unlimited supply of twisted metal. Bombshells and flare casings can frequently be seen in Xieng Khouang's villages where they are used for everything from cattle troughs and fences, to stilts for houses and water-carriers. In Phonsavanh steel runway sheets make handy walls, while plants are potted out in shell casings.

Xieng Khouang remains one of the poorest provinces in an already wretchedly poor country. The whole province has a population of only around 250,000, a mix of different ethnic groups, predominantly Hmong, Lao and a handful of Khmu. Government attempts to curtail shifting cultivation and encourage the Hmong to settle have not been very successful, largely because there are no alternative livelihoods available. Travelling through the province there is a sense not just that the American air war caused enormous suffering and destruction, but that the following decades have not provided much in the way of economic opportunities.

is no exception. A very good choice of north and south Indian food. The service can be rather slow, but the wait is worth it.

**$ Simmaly**
*Main street, T061-211013.*
What this place lacks in atmosphere it makes up tenfold with food. Great service and massive portions.

## Shopping

There are a multitude of shops at the town's market. The **dry market** is beside the town bus station and sells a good selection of local handicrafts including textiles and silver. Most everyday items, from shoes to biscuits can also be purchased here. West of the centre of town is the **Chinese market**, which stocks a good variety of ethnic clothes and jewellery as well as lots of cheap tacky imported products. Behind the post office is a **fresh produce market** with a gamut of fruit and vegetables on offer. The **Navang Craft Center**, behind the new hilltop Phou Vieng Kham hotel, daily 0730-2000, specializes in crafts made of Fijian cypress wood. Silk goods are sold at **Mulberries**, see page 149, a silk farm on the outskirts of Phonsavanh.

## Festivals

**Dec  National Day** on 2 Dec is celebrated with horse-drawn drag-cart racing. Also in Dec is **Hmong New Year** (movable), which is celebrated in a big way in this area. Festivities centre on the killing of a pig and then offering the head to the spirits. Boys give cloth balls, known as *makoi*, to girls they've taken a fancy to.

## What to do

**Tour operators**
There is no shortage of tour operators in Phonsavanh and most guesthouses can also arrange tours and transport. Most of the travel agencies are located within a block of each other on the main road. **Indochina Travel**, *on the main road, T061-312409, www.indochinatravelco.com.*

This is a comparatively expensive but well-regarded company offering minivan tours. It works out a lot cheaper if you can organize a group.

## Transport

**Air**
Xienh Khouang Airport is 4 km from Phonsavanh. **Lao Airlines**, T061-312027 (airport T061-312177), runs flights to **Vientiane**, daily; check www.laoairlines. com for current schedules.

**Bus**
The bus station is 4 km west of Phonsavanh on Route 7, T030-517 0148; a tuk-tuk to/from the centre costs 10,000 kip. From the main bus station outside of town (T030-517 0148): to **Luang Prabang**, 8 hrs; **Vientiane**, 6 daily, 9-10 hrs, also a VIP bus (with a/c and TV) daily; **Vang Vieng**, 6 VIP buses daily, 14 hrs; and **Xam Neua**, daily, 10 hrs. Buses also travel to **Vinh** (Vietnam), 10 hrs, and **Hanoi**, 18 hrs.

Buses leave from the new market (T061-312178): to **Muang Kham**, 1 hr.

Buses from the Namngam market (near the tourist office, T020-5587 5207): to **Muang Khoun**, 45 mins; and **Nam Nouan**, 4 hrs (change here for transport west to **Nong Khiaw**).

**Car with driver/songthaew**
Hiring a car with driver is the easiest way of touring the area. A full car to the **Plain of Jars** will could be combined with a trip to the hot springs, west of Muang Kham.

**Motorbike**
**Happy Motorbike for Rent** (next to Craters), rents motorbike and also bicycles.

**intriguing landscape of monoliths; one of Laos' most iconic sights**

★The undulating plateau of the Plain of Jars (also known as Plaine de Jarres, or **Thong Hai Hin**), stretches for about 50 km east to west, covering an area of 1000 sq km at an altitude of 1000 m. In total there are 136 archaeological sites in this area, containing thousands of jars, discs and deliberately placed stones. Of these only three are currently open to tourists. Note that the plateau can be cold from December to March.

It is recommended that you hire a guide, for at least a day, to get an insight into the history of the area and take you around the jar sites. There are many places in Phonsavanh offering tours of the jars and it is possible to either join together with a group or pay extra for your own private tour – the latter is recommended if you want to see everything at your own pace.

**Tip...**
If you have time, try to visit at least two of the sites. Site One has the largest concentration of jars, as well as the biggest, but also sees the most visitors; Site Two spread is spread over two hills and has great views; Site Three is the most peaceful site, atop a small hill with views of farmland and villages.

# Plain of Jars

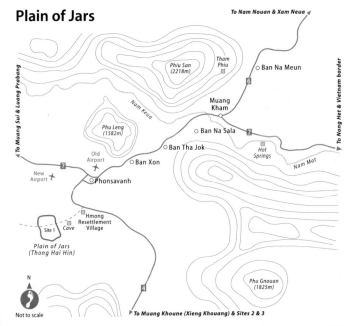

To Nam Nouan & Xam Neua

To Muang Sui & Luang Prabang

To Nong Het & Vietnam border

Phiu San (2218m)

Tham Phiu

○ Ban Na Meun

**6**

Nam Keua

Muang Kham

Phu Leng (1582m)

○ Ban Na Sala

**7**

Old Airport

○ Ban Tha Jok

Hot Springs

New Airport

○ Ban Xon

Nam Mat

**7**

○Phonsavanh

Hmong Resettlement Village

Cave

Site 1

Plain of Jars (Thong Hai Hin)

Phu Gnouan (1825m)

N

**4**

Not to scale

▶To Muang Khoune (Xieng Khouang) & Sites 2 & 3

# BACKGROUND
## Plain of Jars

Most of the jars are between 1 m and 2.5 m high, around 1 m in diameter and weigh about the same as three small cars. The largest are about 3 m tall. The jars have long presented an archaeological conundrum, leaving generations of theorists nonplussed by how they got there and what they were used for. Local legend relates that King Khoon Chuong and his troops from southern China threw a stupendous party after their victory over the wicked Chao Angka and had the jars made to brew outrageous quantities of *lao lao*. However attractive this alcoholic thesis, it is more likely that the jars are in fact 2000-year-old funeral urns. The larger jars are believed to have been for the local aristocracy and the smaller jars for their minions.

Some archaeologists speculate that the cave below the main site was hewn from the rock at about the same time as the jars themselves and that the hole in the roof possibly indicates that the cave was used for cremation or that the jars were made and fired in the cave. But this is all speculation and the jars' true origins and function remain a mystery. In fact, the stone from which the jars at Site One are made doesn't seem to come from that area. Instead, using the evidence of some half-hewn jars made of the same stone found near Site Two and Site Three, archaeologists have postulated that the jars were carved here and then transported to Site One.

Tools, bronze ornaments, ceramics and other objects have been found in the jars, indicating that a civilized society was responsible for them but no-one has a clue which one, as the artefacts bear no relation to those left behind by other ancient Indochinese civilizations. Some of the jars were once covered with round lids and there is one jar, in the group facing the entrance to the cave, which is decorated with a rough carving of a dancing figure.

Over the years, a few jars have been stolen and a number have been transported by helicopter down to Vientiane's Wat Phra Kaeo and the backyard of the National Museum (see pages 40 and 41). Local guides will claim that despite four or five B-52 bombing raids on the plain every day for five years during the Secret War (see box, page 150), the jars remained mysteriously unscathed. However, several bomb craters and damaged jars at the main site show this to be a fanciful myth. During heavy fighting on the plain in the early 1970s, the Pathet Lao set up a command centre in the cave next to the jars and then posed among the jars for photographs (which can be seen in the Revolutionary Museum in Vientiane). Around the entrance to the cave are numerous bomb craters, as the US targeted the sanctuary in a futile attempt to dislodge the Communists.

A vast aviation fuel depot was built next to the jars, early in the 1990s, to supply the huge new airbase just to the west. The base, designed by Soviet technicians, is the new headquarters for the Lao Air Force, although why the government needs a large airbase here remains a mystery and something of a political minefield.

## Secret war on the Plain of Jars

The Plain of Jars occupies an important place in modern Lao history as it became one of the most strategic battlegrounds of the war. For General Vang Pao's Hmong, it was the hearthstone of their mountain kingdom; for the royalist government and the Americans it was a critical piece in the Indochinese jigsaw; for Hanoi it was their back garden, which had to be secured to protect their rear flank. From the mid-1960s, neutralist forces were encamped on the Plain (dubbed 'the PDJ' during the war). They were supported by Hmong, based at the secret city of Long Tien, to the southwest. US-backed and North Vietnamese-backed forces fought a bitter war of attrition on the PDJ; each time royalist and Hmong forces were defeated on the ground, US air power was called in to pummel from above. In mid-February 1970, American Strategic Air Command, on presidential orders, directed that B-52 Stratofortress bombers should be used over the PDJ for the first time. Capable of silently dumping more than one hundred 500-lb bombs from 40,000 ft, they had a devastating effect on the towns and villages of the plain but a minimal effect on Communist morale. Even if the B-52s had managed to wipe out North Vietnamese and Pathet Lao forces, the US-backed troops were unable to reach, let alone hold, the territory. Hanoi had garrisons of reinforcements waiting in the wings.

On the plain, the B-52 proved as ineffective a weapon as it would later on the Ho Chi Minh Trail. As US bomber command turned its attention to the trail, the Pathet Lao seized the upper hand and retook the PDJ. The Communists were beaten back onto the surrounding hills by Vang Pao's forces and American bombers but they kept swarming back and, by March 1972, the North Vietnamese Army had seven divisions in Laos supporting the Pathet Lao. The so-called 'Mountain of Courage' – the hill behind the new airport to the northwest – was the scene of particularly hard fighting. It was here that the royalists, encamped on Phu Kheng, were trapped on two fronts by the Communists. When the Pathet Lao retook Xieng Khouang for the last time in 1973, they consolidated their position and bided their time.

### Site One

Some 334 jars survive, mainly scattered on one slope at so-called 'Site One' or **Thong Hai Hin**, 10 km southwest of Phonsavanh. This site is closest to Phonsavanh and has the largest jar – along with a small café. A path, cleared by MAG, winds through the site, with a warning not to walk away from delineated areas as UXO are still around. There are also information boards on UXO in the area. Each of the jars weighs about a tonne, although the biggest, called **Hai Cheaum**, is over 2 m tall and weighs over six tonnes. Folklore suggests that the jar is named after a Thai-Lao liberator, who overthrew Chao Angka. Further downhill is another smattering of jars, some of which feature carvings. The smallish cave in the hill to the left was used by the Pathet Lao as a hideout during the war and may have been the ancient kiln in which the jars were fired (see Background box, page 154). People leave cigarettes burning here in memory of those who lost their lives and it can be quite a poignant experience to visit it.

## Site Two

True jar lovers should visit Site Two, known as **Hai Hin Phu Salatao** (literally 'Salato Hill Stone Jar Site'), and Site Three (see below). Site Two is 25 km south of Phonsavanh and features 90 jars spread across two hills. The jars are set in a rather beautiful location, affording scenic 360-degree views over the surrounding countryside. Most people miss this site, but it is in fact the most atmospheric because of the hilltop location. On the second hill, trees have grown through the centre of the jars, splitting them four ways; butterflies abound here.

## Site Three

A further 10 km south of Site Two, Site Three, also called **Hai Hin Laat Khai**, is the most peaceful of all the sites, set in verdant green rolling hills, Swiss-cheesed with bomb craters. To get to the site you have to walk through some rice paddies, past a burbling brook and cross the small bamboo bridge. There are more than 130 jars at this site, which are generally smaller and more damaged than at the other sites. There's also a very small, basic restaurant here, serving *feu*.

Close by is **Ban Xieng Dee**, a friendly village, home to a monastery featuring some Buddha images, which were badly damaged during the war. Villagers will lead treks to the nearby **Lang waterfall**.

## Muang Khoune (old Xieng Khouang) → Colour map 1, C5.
**more notable for its history than its sights; combine with a day trip to Plain of Jars**

The old town of Xieng Khouang – now rebuilt and renamed Muang Khoune – was destroyed during the war, between 1964 and 1969, and now the population is reduced to a mere 14,000. Prior to the bombing, the town was extremely picturesque, similar to Luang Prabang, with over 400 old colonial buildings and 30 wats and pagodas, but today, reduced to little more than a row of wooden Lao houses and a market area, it holds nothing in the way of aesthetic charm, and a sense of impermanence pervades the town. However, while Muang Khoune itself is spectacularly unimpressive, its position, surrounded by mountains, is noteworthy.

## Sights

Those excited about the prospect of visiting a unique collection of 500-year-old wats must, for the most part, be content with piles of bricks. There is virtually nothing left of the 16th-century **Wat Phia Wat** (at the far end of town on the right-hand side by the road), except the basement and several shrapnel-pocked Buddha statues, including a large, seated Buddha which is believed to be over 600 years old. The once-picturesque wat underwent a series of renovations in 1930 only to

## BACKGROUND
## Muang Khoune

Xieng Khouang was founded by Chao Noi Muang and was a stronghold for the Xieng Khouang royal family. In 1832 the Hmong mountain state was annexed by Vietnam and renamed Tran Ninh; the king was marched off to Vietnam and publicly executed in Hué' while the population of Xieng Khouang was forced to wear Vietnamese dress.

Many important temples were built here in the distinctive Xieng Khouang style but these were completely obliterated by the American bombing. The religious architecture of the province was one of Laos' three main architectural styles (Luang Prabang and Vientiane styles being the other two). The town was also the main centre for the French in this area during the colonial period and remnants of French colonial architecture are still in evidence.

Xieng Khouang was most heavily bombed during 1969 and 1970, when US air power was called in to reverse the success of the Communists' dry season offensive on the Plain of Jars. In his book *The Ravens*, Christopher Robins interviews several former US pilots who describe the annihilation of the town in which 1500 buildings were razed, together with another 2000 across the plain. Three towns, he says, "were wiped from the map. By the end of the year (1970) there would not be a building left standing". During this time most villagers left their homes and lived in caves or in the forest, subsisting on rice from China and Vietnam. So incessant was the bombing and strafing that peasants took to planting their rice fields at night. One brave woman recalled, "I would have to get the rice at two or three in the morning so as not to be seen. I would carry it on my back, sometimes 100 kg, it was so heavy that I was doubled over, my head almost touching the ground."

The town, now not much more than a village, was rebuilt after 1975 and renamed Muang Khoune.

be bombed into oblivion by the Americans. The half-hearted attempt at further renovation is barely noticeable. Walking up the hill, the remains of the French colonial governor's house, built in the 1930s, can be seen, with some old tile floors still in place and a hospital, patched together Lao style.

Two stupas perch on a pair of hills rising above the town. **That Chompet** is a stump of its former self and is relatively overgrown. A better alternative is the 16th-century **That Foun**, which is quite sizeable and similar to That Dam in Vientiane (see page 40). It is said to contain relics of the Indian emperor Asoka but this legend should be taken with a large pinch of *nam pa*. It may, however, explain why the heart of the stupa has been hollowed out, as thieves have searched, apparently in vain, for buried treasure, in particular old Buddha images said to have been hidden here.

**Wat Si Phoum**, opposite the market below the main road, was also destroyed by the war and now a new inelegant wat has been built next to the ruined *that*. There is a small monastery attached.

## Restaurants

There are a number of simple Lao places to choose from in Muang Khone.

**$ Manivanh**
*T020-2234 5396.*
Good soup and fried rice/noodles dishes. There's also good *pho* opposite the market.

## Shopping

The market in Muang Khoune sells the bare essentials. Head to the Black Tai village, about 500 m northwest of town, to buy local handicrafts and scarves.

## Transport

Buses to **Phonsavanh** depart daily from the Morning Market, 45 mins.

## West of Phonsavanh

remote town with nearby caves to explore; worth a day trip

### Nong Tang (formerly Muang Sui)

Nong Tang lies 45 km west of Phonsavanh on Route 7. The town was formerly known for its vast array of old Buddhist temples and traditional Lao architecture but its fate was sealed once it became a primary landing site for US planes. The town was later razed by the North Vietnamese Army. It is part of a district called Phu Kut, an area known for Hmong insurgency. There aren't many sights in the actual town and a day trip from Phonsavanh should be more than sufficient to take in the outlying caves and picturesque **Nong Tang Lake**. The lake is crowned by limestone karst formations and believed to be very deep.

The caves around Nong Tang make the trip worthwhile; an entrance fee is paid at **Buddha Cave** (Tham Pha), a large honeycomb network of labyrinthine passages, grottoes and caverns that is said to house over 1000 Buddha images, many dating back 1200 years. Another nearby cave was used by the Vietnamese army as a hospital and is still known as **Hospital Cave**. **Water Cave**, named after the water that falls through its roof, isn't as interesting as the other caves. Nearby is the large **Stupa Cave** (Tham That), which contains the ruins of an old stupa believed to be several hundred years old. Within walking distance is **Coffin Cave**, nestled high up in a limestone cliff.

Route 7 heads east from Phonsavanh towards Muang Kham and the border with Vietnam (see box, page 160). The journey is characterized by attractive rolling hills and grassy meadows in the wet season but becomes very barren in the dry season, especially where the bomb craters have pock-marked the landscape. The area is an abject lesson in the potentially destructive nature of some forms of shifting cultivation. Some authorities estimate that up to 100,000 ha of forest were being destroyed in this region by slash-and-burn agriculture before the government implemented a policy to minimize the practice. The difficulty is that minority shifting cultivators – especially the Hmong – often farm land that has already been logged by commercial timber firms (for the simple reason that it is easier to cultivate) and then find themselves blamed for the destruction.

About 12 km east of Phonsavanh is the village of **Ban Xon**, which lays claim to two famous daughters, Baoua Kham and Baoua Xi, who are reported to have shot down a US B-52 with small arms fire. War historians are very sceptical about this claim but a Lao popular song was nonetheless written about them. The ballad is said to extol the beauty and courage of the women of Xieng Khouang.

The only way to visit the minority villages en route to Muang Kham is by hiring a taxi.

### Hmong villages
Route 7 winds its way down off the plateau along the Nam Keua, a fertile area where Hmong villagers grow rice and maize. About 25 km east of Phonsavanh is the **Hmong market**, held on Sundays from 0400 to 1000. Hundreds of people come in from surrounding villages to the colourful market to sell local produce, animals and handicrafts. Many of the older people wear traditional attire.

Seven kilometres further east is the roadside Hmong village of **Ban Tha Jok**, where there are some old Hmong houses that use old bomb casings as stilts but you must walk away from the main road to see them; it is well worth it.

If you wish to visit a more traditional Hmong settlement, leave your vehicle at Ban Na Sala Mai on the main road and walk south for 5 km, up a pleasant valley to **Ban Na Sala**. This is a very beautiful village, perched in the hills. During the war, the Pathet Lao occupied the hills surrounding this village, so the US army was not able to go anywhere near it. Ban Na Sala is one of the best places in Laos to see the creative architectural and household application of war debris. Many people have utilized the bomb casings to construct their houses.

### Tham Phiu
*East of Muang Kham, off Route 7, just after the Km 183 post. A rough track leads down to an irrigation dam, built in 1981. To get to Tham Phiu it is necessary to take a guide, so hire a driver in Phonsavanh, especially as UXO still litters the area.*

## BORDER CROSSING

### Nong Het–Nam Khan (Vietnam)

Nong Het is 60 km east of Muang Kham. It is deep in Hmong country and an important trading post with Vietnam, a few kilometres away at Nam Khan. Few tourists use this crossing, although trucks and *songthaew* ply between Phonsavanh and the border daily, four to five hours, US$4-5. There are also buses via Nong Het from Phonsavanh's bus station Tuesday and Friday at 0630, US$10. Lao visas (30 days) available border for US$30-42; Vietnamese visas are required in advance.

This site will only really be of interest to true history buffs. Evidence of the dirty war can be seen in the area immediately surrounding Muang Kham. The intensity of the US bombing campaign under the command of the late General Curtis Le May was such that entire villages were forced to take refuge in caves. (Curtis Le May is infamously associated with bragging that he wanted to bomb the Communists "back into the Stone Age".) In Tham Phiu, a cave overlooking the valley, 374 villagers from nearby Ban Na Meun built a two-storey bomb shelter and concealed its entrance with a high stone wall. They lived there for a year, working in their rice fields at night and taking cover during the day from the relentless bombing raids.

On the morning of 24 November 1968 two T-28 fighter bombers took off from Udon Thani air base in neighbouring Thailand and located the cave mouth which had been exposed on previous sorties. It is likely that the US forces suspected that the cave contained a Pathet Lao hospital complex. Indeed, experts are at odds whether this was a legitimate target or an example of collateral damage. The first rocket destroyed the wall; the second, which was fired as the planes swept across the valley, carried the full length of the chamber before exploding. There were no survivors and 11 families were completely wiped out; in total 437 people died, many reportedly women and children. Local rescuers claim they were unable to enter the cave for three days, but eventually the dead were buried in a bomb crater on the hillside next to the cave mouth.

Today there is an official memorial halfway up the steps but nothing inside the cave, just the eerily black walls. The interior of the cave was completely dug up by rescue parties and relatives and today there is nothing but rubble inside. It makes for a poignant lesson in military history and locally it is considered a war memorial.

Further up the cliff is another cave, **Tham Phiu Song**, which didn't suffer the same fate. Visitors are welcome to explore but will need to take a torch.

# Hua Phan Province

Hua Phan Province is one of the most isolated areas of the country. More than 20 ethnic groups, mostly mountain-dwellers, inhabit the province, whose character has been shaped over the centuries by a variety of shifting rulers: it was part of the Tai Neua Kingdom, then integrated into the Annamese state of Ai Lao and also experienced stints as a Siamese protectorate and French colonial outpost.

Until recently, Hua Phan remained relatively sheltered from the free market ethos that has spilled into towns along the Thai and Chinese borders, and memories of the period when it was the base for the revolutionary struggle are still close to the surface. Traders from China and Vietnam are more common these days but Hua Phan is still known in Laos as the 'revolutionary province'.

Hua Phan is spectacularly beautiful but largely overlooked by tourists. Local authorities hope that the area's large tourism potential will help to alleviate poverty here and they have teamed up with NGOs to develop tourism infrastructure. The Nam Nern Night Safari in the Nam Et-Phou Louey National Protected Area is one of the very best tours in the country and together with the US-Based Wildlife Conservation Trust, the local authorities are looking to open more tours to the area. The recently opened Indochina War Airbase, known as Lima Site 36, looks set to attract those who are interested in the country's recent history.

Xam Neua is a provincial capital that some will take to and others will want to skip on the way to Vieng Xai. It is set against a picture-perfect mountain backdrop, amid forested hills and rice fields. A river flows through the middle along which it's possible to take a stroll. However, the town itself was obliterated during the war and rebuilt after 1973, so it offers little in the way of historic sights and is largely unattractive. The once buzzing central market has been bulldozed to make way for a Vietnamese-owned hotel that was being constructed at the time of writing. The new market lacks the atmosphere of the old and is now largely filled with cheap imported clothing, but it still offers some silks woven in the surrounding area which are regarded as some of the very best in the nation.

## Essential Hua Phan Province

### Finding your feet

Tourists are often put off visiting Hua Phan by the long bus haul to get there, but considering the road passes through gorgeous mountain scenery, the trip is well worth the endeavour. Xam Neua is the main town and there three main sealed roads to get there: Route 6 from the south, linking Xam Neua with Phonsavanh; Route 1 from Vieng Thong and the west, and Route 6A from the Vietnamese border. Due to the upgrading of Route 6, it is now possible to make the journey between Phonsavanh and Xam Neua in a day without an overnight stop in Nam Nouan en route, but always check on road conditions before setting off. There is also an airport at Xam Neua.

### When to go

Summer is pleasant in Xam Neua but temperatures at night reach freezing in winter and you should bring a pullover, even in summer. The area is at its most picturesque in October, when the rice is almost ready for harvest.

## Sights

The new **market** is worth a visit and the area around it remains a good place to see the province's mixture of cultures and peoples – Hmong, Yao, Tai Dam (Black Tai), Tai Khao (White Tai), Tai Neua (Northern Thai) and other ethnic groups – who can all be found buying and selling various commodities. Examples of the distinctive weaving of Xam Neua and Xam Tai can be found for reasonable prices, although nowadays this is rare and hidden among stalls stacked with goods trucked in from China and Vietnam. Loudspeakers in the market area blast music and propaganda from 0600.

The province is known for its weaving and many of the houses in the blocks surrounding the market have looms on their verandas. There are also several **weaving workshops** with four or five looms each; some of these still use traditional vegetable dyes rather than the aniline (chemical) dyes that have become the norm in other areas. Information can be found at the tourist office.

# BACKGROUND
## Hua Phan Province

Together with Phongsali Province, Hua Phan was the base for left-wing insurgency from the late 1940s until the final victory of the Pathet Lao over the royalist forces in 1975. Members of the Lao Issara, who had fled to Vietnam after French forces smashed the movement in 1946, infiltrated areas of northeast Laos in 1947-1949 under the sponsorship of the Viet Minh. The movement coalesced when Prince Souphanouvong, who had fled to Thailand, arrived in Hanoi and organized a conference in August 1950 at which the Free Lao Front and the Lao Resistance Government were formed. Thereafter, the Pathet Lao adopted strategies developed by the Viet Minh in Vietnam, who in turn drew on the strategies of Mao Zedong and the Chinese Communists: establishment of bases in remote mountain areas; use of guerrilla tactics; exploitation of the dissatisfaction of tribal minorities, and mobilization of the entire population of liberated areas in support of the revolutionary struggle. By the time of the Geneva Agreement of 1954, following the French defeat at Dien Bien Phu, Communist forces effectively controlled Hua Phan and Phongsali provinces, a fact acknowledged in the terms of the settlement, which called for their regroupment inside these provinces pending a political settlement. The Pathet Lao used the breathing space and the succession of coalition governments during the late 1950s and early 1960s to reorganize their operations. The Lao People's Revolutionary Party was formed at Xam Neua in 1955 and the Neo Lao Hak Sat, or National Front, was established in 1956.

While Party President Prince Souphanouvong spent a good deal of time in Vientiane, participating in successive coalition governments between 1958 and 1964, Secretary-General Kaysone Phomvihane remained in Hua Phan overseeing the political and military organization of the liberated zone. The beginning of the American bombing campaign in 1964 forced the Pathet Lao leadership to find a safe haven from which to direct the war. Vieng Xai was chosen because its numerous limestone karsts contained many natural caves which could be used for quarters, while their proximity to each other inhibited attack from the air. American planes tried to dislodge the Communists from their mountain hideout but, protected in their caves, they survived the onslaught. Nevertheless, phosphorous rockets and napalm caused many casualties in the less-fortified caves. After the war, senior members of the Royal Lao Government were sent to re-education camps in the province.

## Tourist information

**Houa Phanh Provincial Tourist office**
*Pathee Rd, a couple of blocks back
from the river, T064-312567, www.
houaphantourism.com. Mon-Fri 0830-
1200 and 1300-1600.*
A very well-run outfit with lots of
information on what to see and do in
the province. It can organize a car with
driver/guide or for visiting Vieng Xai
caves or Hintang Archaeological Park.
Well worth a visit, although the opening
hours are erratic.

## Where to stay

Wi-Fi is available in most hotels
and guesthouses.

**$ Boun Home**
*In the lane around the corner from
Shuliyo, T064-312223.*
Offers clean and pleasant rooms, with
private bathrooms and hot showers.
Strong Wi-Fi connection and a very
useful information folder with details
of transport and tourism sites.

**$ Chittavanh Hotel**
*By the river around the corner from
Kheamxam, T064-312265.*
Good service, including a free airport
or bus station pick-up and free Wi-
Fi. Some of the smartest rooms in
town, which also have river views.
Restaurant. A good option

**$ Kheamxam Guesthouse**
*On the corner by the river, T064-312111.*
Has a wide range of fairly well-
appointed large rooms, some with
a/c and TV, with spacious hot-water
bathrooms and beds with soft pillows.

Also has cheaper options with no en
suite. No Wi-Fi.

## Restaurants

Sam Neua is not geared toward foreign
tourists, but alongside the restaurants
listed below, you'll find plenty of good
Beerlao and barbecue places dotted
around town with no signs or menus
written in English. Noodle soup is also
readily available, with the shack-like
eatery opposite the Tourism Division
serving good chicken and beef varieties.

**$ Chittavanh Restaurant**
*See Where to stay.*
Great Lao food, particularly *feu*.

**$ Dan Nao Muang Xam**
*A block back from the river, near the
bridge, T020-2234 8895.*
Most foreign visitors to town seem
to eat here, probably because of the
English menu complete with pictures,
but also because it does a solid range
of Lao food and a few Western options.
The fried rice with egg is a good choice.

## Transport

### Air
The tiny airport complete with
amusingly diminutive control tower
is 3 km from the centre of town. **Lao
Airlines** flies direct to **Vientiane**.

### Bus/truck/songthaew
There are 2 bus stations. The Nathong
(T030-312238) and the Phoutanou up
the hill (T030-516 0974).
  From Nathong bus station: there
are regular *songthaew* to **Vieng
Xai**, 50 mins, early morning to late

## BORDER CROSSING
## Na Maew–Nam Xoi (Vietnam)

Route 6A heads east from Xam Neua to the border crossing between Na Maew (Laos) and Nam Xoi (Vietnam), which was opened to tourists in 2004. You'll need to get your Laos or Vietnam visa in advance. The border is open 0730-1130 and 1330-1700. It may be necessary to pay a processing or overtime fee.

The trip to the border is two hours from Vieng Xai. *Songthaew* leave Vieng Xai at 0640 from the main Xam Neua–Na Maew road, 1 km from the centre of Vieng Xai, 20,000 kip. It is also possible to take a *songthaew* from Xam Neua station at 0630-0715 (three to four hours), 30,000 kip, or to charter one to the border from Xam Neua for about US$50.

Footprint has received several complaints about difficulties with unethical tourism operators on the Vietnamese side of this border charging a fortune for transport. A motorbike taxi to Quan Son should cost around US$10. If you get really stuck on the Vietnam side contact Mr Pham Xuan Hop in Na Maew, T0084-9923 7425, who may be able to organize minivan rental (US$42-50 to Quan Son).

There are two guesthouses in Na Maew (Phucloc Nha Tru and Minhchien); they both offer rudimentary facilities for US$3-5 per night).

A bus runs from Na Maew to Thanh Hoa Tue, Thu and Sat at 1130, US$8 but it's advisable to check all transport details in Xam Neua, at the bus station or with the provincial tourism office.

afternoon. Also to **Xam Tai**, 5 hrs; **Na Meo** (the Vietnam border), 3 hrs; and **Thanh Hoa** (Vietnam), daily, 11 hrs.

From Phoutanou bus station: to **Vieng Thong**, 6 hrs; **Phonsavanh**, 8 hrs; **Luang Prabang**, 12 hrs; and **Vientiane**, 24 hrs, VIP bus,18 hrs.

**Motorbike and minivan hire**
Motorcycles can be rented from Meuangxam Travel Service, T020-5565 7479, www.meuangxamtravel.com, which also offers a taxi and minibus rental service that is worth considering

if you are travelling in a group. For example, the trip to Vieng Xay to see the caves is 1,000,000 kip.

The **Provincial Tourism Office** (see Tourist information, opposite) also offers motorcycle rental and minibus hire. A minibus to **Na Meo** for the Vietnam border crossing is 1,000,000 kip.

**Tuk-tuk**
It is possible to hire a tuk-tuk for a visit to the **Nameuang hot springs** or to **Vieng Xai**, 31 km. Alternatively a taxi will cost around 14,000 kip.

South of Xam Neua are the Houiyad falls, located amid undulating hills in a stunning river valley, and surrounded by fields, rice paddies and ethnic minority villages. The falls themselves don't rank highly in the Lao waterfall stakes but make a nice half-day picnic trip from Xam Neua.

Nearby **Ban Houaiyad** is renowned for making belts from aluminium gathered from crashed aircrafts, although these days recycled cans are used instead. A few kilometres away are the **Nameuang hot springs** ① *22 km south of Xam Neua, off Route 6; at the junction follow the unpaved road for 3 km*, which feature a small bathing pool and various washrooms.

Continuing south on Route 6 towards Nam Nouan, the **Saleuy waterfall** makes a pleasant stop. At over 15 m wide in places, water gushes down the sloping rock face hemmed in on either side by dense forest. A swing bridge at the bottom and the top allows for a steep walking circuit affording great views. However, the path is not well maintained making it difficult to find the way.

Two kilometres south of the falls is the small village of **Ban Saleuy** where it's now possible to stay in very simple homestays with roll-out mattresses. A half-day guided trek can also be arranged here taking in **Tad Seua** (Tiger Falls) and **Tad Mou** (Board Falls). This is a great way to see some of the temperate forest of Laos and get well off the beaten path. Stays here can be arranged at the Xam Neua tourist office or in the village itself.

## Sao Hintang

*Off Route 6, 130 km north of Phonsavanh, 57 km south of Xam Neua and 36 km north of the junction with Route 1 at Phou Lao. At the faded billboard-sized sign in Ban Liang Sat, turn up the dirt road heading east. About 3 km up the road is a sign for the Kechintang Trail, a 90-min walking trail that takes you to some of the sites. The first is visible from the road after a further 3 km, with Site two located another 3 km after that. For further information contact the tourist office in Xam Neua where cars can be rented for this trip; it might make sense as the site is not well signposted and the stones are not always easy to see.*

The **Hintang Archaeological Park** features hundreds of ancient upright stone pillars, menhirs and discs, gathered in Stonehenge-type patterns over a 10-km area, surrounded by jungle. The megaliths have been cut into narrow blades, up to 2 m tall, and stand one behind the other, with the tallest usually in the middle. According to local sources they are at least 1500 years old. Interspersed between the stone sites are burial chambers dug deep into the bedrock. These were originally covered with large stone discs, up to 7 m wide, and could only be accessed via a narrow vertical chimney.

The enigmatic stones are as mysterious as the Plain of Jars: no-one is quite sure who, or even which ethnic group, is responsible for erecting them and they have become steeped in legend. It is believed that the two sites are somehow linked, as they are fashioned from the same stone and share some archaeological similarities. In 1931, the sites were surveyed and partially excavated by an archaeological team, led by Madeleine Colani, although, by this time, the contents of the chambers had already been raided or simply washed away. The exploration uncovered a number of objects – funerary urns, ceremonial stones, bronze bracelets and ceramic pendants – that give credence to the theory that the stone park was an ancient burial site.

While travelling along Route 6 to the park keep your eyes peeled for the numerous roadside **fox-holes**. These small bolt-holes were used as air-raid shelters during the US bombardment of the area. A large number actually expand into large bunkers capable of accommodating 10-12 people.

## East of Xam Neua
### small villages with a strong weaving tradition

### Xam Tai
Hua Phan Province is known as a 'cradle' of traditional Lao weaving. The province's remoteness means that the diversity of designs produced here is second to none and techniques that have become rare elsewhere are still practised here. The premier centre for weaving is Xam Tai (local pronunciation, Xam Teua), 100 km southeast of Xam Neua, close to the Vietnamese border. You can try to charter a pickup to Xam Tai from the market, or hire a car through the tourist office but be aware that the road is in a poor state and there is no guesthouse at Xam Tai.

## Vieng Xai (Viengsay) → Colour map 1, B6.
### fascinating cave city; off the beaten track and well worth the detour

★The village of Vieng Xai lies 31 km east of Xam Neua on a road that branches off Route 6 at Km 20. The trip from Xam Neua is possibly one of the country's most picturesque journeys, passing terraces of rice, pagodas, copper- and charcoal-coloured karst formations, dense jungle with misty peaks and friendly villages dotted among the mountains' curves.

The village area is characterized by lush tropical gardens, a couple of smallish lakes and spectacular limestone karsts, riddled with natural caves that proved crucial in the success of the left-wing insurgency in the 1960s and 1970s.

Although it takes only one day to see the caves, it is worth spending some more time exploring the area and at least staying overnight. The valley contains many other poignant reminders of the struggle, although the war debris is less obvious here than in Xieng Khouang.

**Tip...**
Most visitors to Vieng Xai stay in Xam Neua and make a day trip to see the caves, but this is a great shame, for Vieng Xai is a wonderful place for an early morning bike ride and to watch the sun go down over the karst scenery.

# BACKGROUND
## Vieng Xai

From 1964 onwards, Pathet Lao operations were directed from the cave systems at Vieng Xai, which provided an effective refuge from furious bombing attacks. The village of Vieng Xai grew from four small villages consisting of less than 10 families into a thriving hidden city concealing over 20,000 people in in the 100 plus caves in the area. The Pathet Lao leadership renamed the area Vieng Xai, meaning 'City of Victory' and it became the administrative and military hub of the revolutionary struggle.

A conservation survey of the area in 1982 identified over 95 caves of historical significance. Included in these was a former hospital complex approximately 15 km from Vieng Xai and a school for children of government officials at Ban Bac. A separate cave complex at Hang Long, 25 km from Xam Neua, housed the provincial government during the war years but is now completely abandoned. Other caves, called 'embassy caves', were intended for VIPs from other countries, with individual caves set aside for Russia, Vietnam, Cuba and China. Locals make unsubstantiated suggestions that King Sihanouk from Cambodia also spent a long time hiding out in Vieng Xai during the war.

## Visiting the caves

There are six main caves open to visitors, five of which were formerly occupied by senior Pathet Lao leaders (Prince Souphanouvong, Kaysone Phomvihan, Nouhak Phounsavanh, Khamtai Siphandon and Phoumi Vongvichit). The sixth cave is the hospital cave. The caves have a secretive atmosphere, with fruit trees and frangipani decorating the exteriors. Each one burrows deep into the mountainside and features 60-cm-thick concrete walls, encompassing living quarters, meeting rooms, offices, dining and storage areas.

All the caves are within walking distance of the village, but it is best to cycle. Tickets are sold at the **Vieng Xai Caves Visitor Centre** ⓘ *on the edge of town, signposted, T064-314321, daily 0800-1200 and 1300-1600; guided tours are conducted in English at 0900 and 1300, with compulsory guide.* If you arrive outside of these hours, you can pay extra for your own tour. Tours last between three and four hours and are usually conducted by bicycle, which can be rented from the office.

A new set of excellent 90-minute audio tours, including personal memories of local people, has been launched. A taster can be heard on www.visit-viengxay.com. The visitor centre has historical information, photographs and Communist gifts on display.

## Tham Souphanouvong

Off the small roads that head out of town towards the caves, is a mossy path flanked by large grapefruit trees which leads to Tham Souphanouvong. This cave was home to Prince Souphanouvong, the 'Red Prince' and son of the Queen of Luang Prabang. To the right of the path stands a pink stupa, the tomb of the prince's son, who was beaten to death with a hammer by infiltrators a few kilometres away in 1967, at the age of 28. Souphanouvong's stunning garden, bursting with a rainbow of flowers and dripping with fruit, was planted in 1973-1974 and is a memorial to his son and a metaphor for the war. An old bomb crater has been ingeniously concreted into a pool, referred to as the broken heart; a head, shoulders and neck have been landscaped around the heart. The whole area is surrounded by a sea of red plants, to symbolize all the blood lost during the war. Be careful near the far entrance of the cave as occasionally rocks have fallen. Souphanouvong and Phoumi's caves both feature a 'garage cave' at the base of the karst, a cavity in the limestone large enough to accommodate a car.

## Tham Kaysone Phomvihane

Kaysone Phomvihane's cave is reached by mossy steps cut into the cliff face and is over 100 m long. The cavern is surrounded by blossoming bushes and large frangipani trees. Like the other caves here, it has a suite of rooms, including a bedroom, meeting room and library. A few of Kaysone's books are on display; it's no surprise that the collection includes Lenin, Marx, Engels, Ho Chi Minh and an economic text from Vietnam. Also on display are a few gifts from foreign dignitaries, including a lacquer-ware vase from Vietnam and a bust of Lenin (a framed picture of Che Guevara given to Kaysone by Fidel Castro has been removed due to water damage).

The cave's construction started some time prior to 1963 but Kaysone and Co moved in in 1974. Kaysone rarely left the cave and allowed only the most important of visitors inside, mostly other Communist leaders. About 10 people lived in the cave: Kaysone, his children, a doctor, intelligence officer, cook and bodyguards. At the start of the war Kaysone's wife relocated to Yunnan, China, where she was head of a school. These days she lives in Vientiane. The Americans knew of Kaysone's whereabouts but were unable to attack the cave directly or infiltrate it, due to its position and to the large numbers of Pathet Lao soldiers that were mounted on the summit. The cave remained Kaysone's official residence until 1973, when he relocated to the building in front of the cave. In 1975 he left the cave and moved to Vientiane.

An interesting feature of Kaysone's cave is a long, narrow passage which connects the living quarters to a large meeting area which includes emergency accommodation for dozens of guests.

## Tham Than Khamtai Siphandon

Khamtai Siphandone's cave, the former military headquarters, is slightly different from the others. The first thing you'll notice is a set of three bomb craters within metres of the entrance to the cave. The craters, now overgrown, are so close together they almost touch. Possibly inspired by their arrival, the entrance is shielded by an enormous, tapering slab of concrete, 4.5 m high and nearly 2 m wide at the base. Inside, the cave is darker and more claustrophobic than the others, with no outside areas. The attendant may or may not lead you through a thick steel door at the bottom of some stairs well inside the cave. It gives access to a staircase which descends steeply before ending in a sheer drop of several metres, and connects to a number of military caves including the army administration. There is a longish tunnel which connects to **Tham Xang Lot** (Elephant Cave) but this is sometimes inaccessible.

## Tham Xang Lot

A small distance from Khamtai's cave and included in its entry price, is the large and obvious entrance to what is known as Tham Xang Lot, or 'cave that an elephant can walk through'. Once used as an enclosure to keep animals such as elephants and monkeys, during the war this natural cavern was also used as a theatre, complete with stage, arch, orchestra pit and a concrete floor with space for an audience of several hundred. At the opposite end from the stage, a long passage featuring a number of stalactites and lit by daylight connects to the theatrette below Khamtai's cave. It is hard to imagine now, but this damp, dark area once entertained numerous dancers, symphonies, circuses and foreign dignitaries from Romania, Bulgaria, Vietnam and China. As one local recalls: "I snuck in for a look and an orchestra was playing. I got so excited but was trying to contain myself because I was worried that the grenade in my pocket would go off." At times up to 2000 soldiers were hidden in the two caves.

## Other caves

The **Artillery Cave**, set halfway up a hillside, offers phenomenal views. The cave was a military installation purposefully set up to conceal fighters who would return fire during US bombing raids. **Phoumi Vongvichid's Cave**, home to the former Minister of Education and Public Health, also houses the enclosure of Sithon Kommadam, of the Lao Theung minority, who was reputedly immune to bullets. **Nouhak Phoumsavan's Cave** has been recently opened to the public. The cave was home to the former President of Laos.

## Vieng Xai village

The village itself was built in 1973, when the bombing finally stopped and the short-lived Provisional Government of National Union was negotiated. Today the former capital of the liberated zone is an unlikely sight: surrounded by rice fields at the dead end of a potholed road, it features street lighting, power lines, sealed and kerbed streets and substantial public buildings. Nonetheless it is truly one of the most beautiful towns in Laos. The 'Garden of Eden'-type village is dotted with fruit trees and hibiscus and is flanked by amazing karst formations and dotted with man-made lakes (reputedly formed from bomb craters).

Just before the market and truck stop, a wonderful socialist-realist statue in gold-painted concrete pays tribute to those three pillars of the revolution: the farmer, the soldier and the worker; the worker has one boot firmly planted on a bomb inscribed 'USA'.

The police station is situated just behind the disused department store on the town square. ATMs located near the market. The small hospital is on the main road into town.

## Around Vieng Xai

There is a spectacular **waterfall** and another cave site, 8 km before Vieng Xai. About 3 km after the turn-off from Route 6, a swift stream passes under a steel and concrete bridge. A path just before the bridge leads off to the left, following the river downstream. It takes just a few minutes to reach the top of the waterfall, but the path leads all the way to the bottom, about 20 minutes' walk. Swimming is not advised.

## Listings Vieng Xai (Viengsay)

### Where to stay

**$ Naxay Guesthouse**
*Close to Prince Souphanouvong's cave, T064-314336.*
Now re-built, these are large, smart bungalows, well located for visiting the caves.

**$ Naxay Guesthouse 2**
*Opposite Vieng Xai Cave Visitor Centre, T064-314336.*
The best option with 11 clean if a little aged bungalows with warm showers, comfortable beds and Western-style toilet, set in a leafy compound. If nobody is there when you arrive, try around the corner at **Naxay Guesthouse** where the staff are normally found. Recommended.

**$ Say Mon Yen/Xailomyen Guesthouse**
*By the lake, T030-516 1399.*
13 small somewhat tired rooms over the lake with tiny bathrooms. There are lovely views from the vast restaurant which may or may not be serving food.

### Restaurants

There are a few basic food stalls scattered around town offering noodle soup, *larb khoai* (buffalo) or *larb ngoa* (beef). Several of the guesthouses have restaurants, including **Xailomyen**, which does a range of fish, pork, noodle and egg dishes and also offers a lovely view over the lake. A very tasty *pho* is served at an outdoor joint complete with *pétanque* pitch about 100 m north of the school – look for orange and blue chairs and the *pétanque* area.

**$ Nha Hang Viet**
*Just down the road from Sabaidee, T064-5550 9874.*
This basic Vietnamese joint serves up fairly average food including fried rice, fried beef and stir fried morning glory.

**$ Sabaidee Restaurant**
*On the corner by the market, T064-5557 7202.*
Run by the very affable Prakash since 2012, this Indian and Lao restaurant offers excellent Indian dishes and also some Lao staples. Highlights include the *masala papad*, 'chilly' chicken and a sublime *brinjal bharta*. Be prepared for a long wait for the Indian dishes however, as everything is prepared fresh. Also rents bicycles. Recommended.

### Transport

Pickups and passenger trucks leave from in front of the market in Vieng Xai to **Xam Neua** throughout the day, but the service is haphazard. You may be able to charter your own truck – ask at the Indian restaurant, **Sabaidee**, for help. A taxi from to Xam Neua will cost around 150,000 kip. To catch the bus to **Vietnam**, wait at the main road and cross your fingers that there is a seat free.

## West on Route 1

*few sights but abundant natural beauty*

### Nam Nouan (aka Nam Nern 2 and Sop Lao)

The junction of Route 1 and Route 6 is known as **Phou Lao**; just to the south is the larger settlement of Nam Nouan, which is also known locally as Nam Nern 2 and also Sop Lao. This is a staging post where travellers bound for Xam Neua or Nong Khiaw will invariably find themselves. The through traffic for Xam Neua is relatively frequent and most buses/*songthaew* from Phonsavanh stop on their way through. To get a connecting bus to Nong Khiaw is a little more complicated as Nam Nouan is 7 km south of the junction between routes 1 and 6, which is at a village called **Ban Sam Nyay**. You can get to the actual junction town by *songthaew* or by asking one of the locals for a lift on a motorbike. Most buses to/from Nong Khiaw stop at this junction settlement not Nam Nouan.

This is a pleasant Khmu village with very little in the way of amenities. If you are coming from Nong Khiaw you will probably arrive disorientated and dishevelled at some ungodly hour. Locals may try to charge you an extortionate rate to get a pickup to Nam Nouan; if that is the case you may be able to grab a lift with someone on a motorbike for about US$5-6.

### Vieng Thong (aka Muang Hiam)

Vieng Thong, also known as Muang Hiam, lies 158 km west of Xam Neua on Route 1 and is a reasonable stopover for those journeying to or from Nong Khiaw. The town itself has little to offer but the surrounding countryside is nothing short of spectacular. The Nam Khan River flows through the town, straight from Luang Prabang, so it's a shame no tour operators have yet capitalized on what could be an amazing journey between the two areas.

**Vieng Thong Tourist Information Office** ① *opposite the bus station*, can book accommodation and arrange a guide for the Nakout Historical Area. There is a bank next to **Heungkhamxay guesthouse** which has an ATM and money exchange service.

### Around Vieng Thong

North of town are the **Vieng Thong hot springs** ① *10,000 kip*, which offer great respite from what can be quite a tiring journey. The local population have been using the bathing and washing clothes here for centuries and the area in front of the tourist centre remains preserved for local use. Behind this, there are several baths that can be filled for tourists to wallow in, or you can choose to relax in the more natural retention pool. Further back, a path bordered by many different plants and flowers follows the piping hot stream (take care) up to the source of the spring where the bubbling water gives off a strong smell of ammonia.

## ON THE ROAD
## The Indochina War base Lima Site 26

Until 2014 this former secret airbase was off-limits to tourists and many maps did not show the road leading to it. However, it has been opened up in the hope of bringing more people to this little visited part of Laos.

The French first used the wide Nakhang Valley to construct an airstrip during the First Indochina War, but it was during the Second Indochina War (Vietnam War) that the site saw most of the action when it functioned as an important support center for the Royal Lao Government (RLG) supported by the USA and Hmong paramilitaries – also referred to as the 'Secret Army'.

The base was known by the Americans as Lima Site 36 and it was used by the CIA's Air America for its covert operations to attack Pathet Lao controlled areas in the northern provinces, particularly Hou Panh.

After continuous attacks during February 1969 which weakened defences, North Vietnamese forces approached the base from a completely unanticipated direction that caught the defenders by surprise, and on 1 March 1969, the base was captured.

Evidence of the former military base can still be found. The airstrip is still clearly visible, and around it there are three 10,000-litre fuel tanks and the remains of road work equipment. Further north, hidden in the overgrowth, a shell launcher is located.

The area is highly contaminated with UXO, including land mines and stocks of ammunition that were not destroyed, and unexploded ordnance left over from the shelling of the site and ground battles.

### Visiting Lima Site 26

It is now possible to stay in the fascinating village of Ban Nakout where the locals have constructed a simple but comfortable village lodge. Ban Nakout was established in 1865 when seven families moved there from Xieng Khouang. The village is 100% Tai Phuan and practises Buddhism.

In 1964, when the Nakhang area became an important military base, the villagers abandoned their homes and hid in the forest. When they returned they rebuilt their village using leftovers from the war, including oil drums and bomb shells.

Tours can be booked via the tourism office in Vieng Thong (see opposite page).

On the road to the hot springs is the excellent **Nam Et-Phou Louey Visitor Centre** where visitors can learn more about the efforts being made to protect the local environment. The staff can also give information on the half-day self-guided trek out to the **Hokdon waterfall**. The trek takes walkers past the Forest School which educates high school children about the need to protect the habitat. It then ends at the hot springs – a great way to revive weary limbs.

## ON THE ROAD

## ★The Nam Nern Night Safari

The Nam Nern Night Safari was set up by the Wildlife Conservation Society together with the local authorities in 2012 and has since won awards for its responsible tourism model and been featured in the *New York Times* Top 52 things to do in 2014. It is one of the top two-day experiences available in Laos.

It begins in the small village of Son Loua (aka Nam Nerm 2) which is most easily reached from Vieng Thong. After learning about the endangered wildlife in the Nam Et-Phou Louey National Protected Area and the efforts being made to stop illegal poaching, visitors are taken up the Nam Nern River in a long-tail boat. When the river is higher in October and November this river journey is quite exciting in itself, thanks to the rapids the boat is expertly guided over. Along the way there is an abundance of birdlife, including eagles and kingfishers.

After lunch at the base camp, the boat forges further upstream to a salt lick where you may spot animals such as deer. After collecting firewood and local plants to cook with dinner, visitors dine on the bank of the river next to a roaring fire.

The boat is then guided downstream with the engines cut, as the guides use head torches to point out wildlife such as sambar deer, slow loris and monitor lizards. Floating silently downstream in the pitch darkness is an unbeatable experience.

The next morning a tour of the base camp village precedes breakfast which is followed by a final thrilling journey back to the village to end the trip.

Back on dry land guests fill out a form detailing the wildlife seen; this relates directly to the bonus the participating villages will receive from the tour. The theory is that by paying more depending on the volume of wildlife seen, poaching will decrease and wildlife populations will begin to build.

Many local agents, including **Tiger Trail**, **Buffalo Tours** and **Green Discovery**, can book this tour (see Tour operators, page Variable), or it can be booked direct in Vieng Thong at the NPA visitor centre or the tourist office by the bus station. Full details at www.namet.org.

### Nam Et-Phou Louey National Protected Area

Just 10 km beyond Vieng Thong is Laos' largest protected area, the Nam Et-Phou Louey National Protected Area. Camera trap studies conducted in recent years by the Wildlife Conservation Society have discovered a vast array of large mammals here, including tiger, guar, bear, leopard, macaque, wild pig and deer. See the box, above, for details of the excellent Nam Nern Night Safari here.

## Where to stay

### Nam Nouan

**$ Nam Nern Guesthouse**
*2 mins along the road from the market.*
Now rebuilt, this tidy but simple
guesthouse has large rooms with
en suite squat toilet bathrooms and
comfortable beds. Good Wi-Fi.

### Vieng Thong

**$ Dokkhoun Guesthouse**
*Right next to Heungkhamxay,*
*T064-810017.*
Offers a similar level of accommodation
to **Heungkhamxay**. Good quality for the
price and well located.

**$ Heungkhamxay Guesthouse**
*Near the market, T064-810033.*
Basic, but clean en suite rooms and
a strong internet connection. The
owners have limited English but are
very welcoming.

> **Tip...**
> For drinks and a light meal with a
> view, head to the bar down the track
> at the end of the bridge as you enter
> town. It's run by a very welcoming
> husband and wife team and offers
> a great vista overlooking the paddy
> fields and ice cold beers.

## Restaurants

### Vieng Thong

The small places around the bus station
serve sticky rice and various dishes
which you can peruse and order by
the plate, including vegetables, beef
and chicken.

**$ Nha Hang 669**
*Opposite **Heungkhamxay** guesthouse*
*near the market.*
This is a ramshackle noodle and rice shop
run by a Vietnamese woman. Serves
reasonable fried beef in the evening and
a good beef noodle soup in the morning.

**$ Tontavenh**
*Opposite the market, T020-5557 9975.*
Serves Lao food and is popular with the
few tourists that come through town.

## Transport

### Vieng Thong

The bus station is on the road opposite
the market. It is home to 3 or 4 small
eateries where basic Lao food can be
found. Buses leave from here for **Xam
Neua**, 5-6 hrs; **Nong Khiaw**, 5 hrs, and
**Luang Prabang**, 8-9 hrs.

The routes in both directions out of
town are classic northern Laos, with
seemingly no flat or straight sections
as the road undulates through fantastic
scenery. Try and bag a window seat and
enjoy the fine vistas.

# Central Laos

some of the country's best scenery, without the crowds

Laos' central provinces, sandwiched between the Mekong (and Thailand) to the west and the Annamite Mountains (and Vietnam) to the east, are some of the least visited in the country.

Travellers entering Laos from Vietnam cross the border via Lak Xao or Xepon but few choose to linger. This is a shame because the scenery here is stunning, with dramatic limestone karsts, enormous caves, beautiful rivers and forests. In particular, the upland areas to the east, off Route 8 and Route 12, are a veritable treasure trove of attractions, mottled with scores of caves, lagoons, rivers and unusual rock formations.

Tourists will require some degree of determination to explore this part of the country, as the infrastructure is still being developed, but it is far better than it was just a few years ago.

The Mekong towns of Thakhek and Savannakhet are also elegant and relaxed. If you are short on time, Thakhek is the best stopover point for the central provinces, and there is also some fantastic rock climbing nearby.

**Best** for
Caves ▪ Rock climbing ▪ Wilderness

# Footprint
## picks

⭐ **Boat trip through Kong Lor Cave**, page 182
Float along the Nam Hinboun River as it travels through this awe-inspiring cave.

⭐ **The limestone caves off Route 12**, page 192
Explore underground caverns in the limestone landscape, especially the beautiful Buddha Cave.

⭐ **Savannakhet**, page 198
Enjoy the town's crumbling colonial charm, great local food and relaxed Mekong riverfront.

⭐ **Song Sa Kae sacred forest**, page 207
Trek to the sacred forest and cemetery within Dong Phou Vieng National Protected Area.

**Footprint picks**

1 **Boat trip through Kong Lor Cave**, page 182
2 **The limestone caves off Route 12**, page 192
3 **Savannakhet**, page 198
4 **Song Sa Kae sacred forest**, page 207

# Paksan to
# Lak Xao

East of Paksan adventurous visitors will encounter some of the county's most stunning landscapes. This region contains a maze of limestone karst peaks, studded with thousands of caves, and a beautiful river flanked by pristine jungle. The magical Kong Lor Cave, a river cave running straight through the centre of a mountain for 6 km and the principal tourist attraction in the region, could be straight out of *Lord of the Rings*. *Phone code: 054.*

## Paksan and around → *Colour map 2, B4.*

*somewhat dishevelled but characterful town*

In the mid-1990s people used to stop in Paksan (Paxsan) to break the journey south (or north) but, now that road upgrading has shortened the journey between Vientiane and Thakhek to a bearable five to six hours, the town's one purpose in life – as far as most tourists were concerned – has been rendered obsolete. However, you might still find yourself stranded here on your way to Vientiane from the Vietnamese border at Lak Xao.

If you do find yourself here, there are a couple of interesting sights. Dating back to 1933, **Wat Prah Bat** is an important pilgrimage site for Lowland Lao. The stupa boasts a footprint of the Buddha as well as one of the largest drums in Laos. Overlooking the Mekong is the more modern **Phonsane Temple**, which isn't anything spectacular in itself but has become famous for its annual **Naga Fireball Festival** (see Festivals, below).

For those travellers who are beginning to feel 'templed out', there are exhilarating opportunities to explore the province's natural heritage by boat, canoe or kayak (see below).

### Pak Kading

Some 50 km east of Paksan, Pak Kading is a small whistlestop of a town where the **Nam Kading River** flows into the Mekong. The picturesque Nam Kading is known as a local fishery goldmine and is one of the most pristine rivers in the country. There is little to do here, but it is possible to hire a boat for a very pretty ride upstream where everyday life on the river plays out as it has for years.

## Essential Paksan to Lak Xao

### Finding your feet

Route 13 is the main north–south road which hugs the Mekong and the border with Thailand, south of Vientiane. The other main highway in this region is Route 8, which runs from Ban Lao to the Vietnamese border at Nam Phao, passing through the dramatic karst scenery of the Annamite Mountains with a viewpoint for the Phu Phu Man Limestone Forest (see page 181). Daily buses from Vientiane ply this route. Paksan is the main town and transport hub with buses passing through every couple of hours.

### Best places to stay

**Sainamhai Resort**, Ban Na Hin, page 183
**Phoutthavong Guesthouse**, Lak Xao, page 185

### When to go

November to March is the cool, dry season, with visitor numbers peaking November/December when the rivers are high enough to make river travel easy but it is not too hot. The towns along the Mekong south of Vientiane receive less rain than other parts of the country. The **Fireball Festival**, at the Phonsane Temple in Paksan takes, place in October.

## Listings Paksan and around

### Where to stay

#### Paksan

Accommodation seems insufficient, given the number of backpackers that pass through Pakse.

#### $ B&K Guesthouse
*Across the river, 1st road on the right, T054-212638.*
The town's best option. The friendly owners of this establishment speak good English and offer fruit from their own trees on arrival (in season). Clean, pleasant rooms and en suite bathrooms. Also has a very good restaurant attached.

#### $ Paksan Hotel
*On the main road, opposite the post office, T054-791333.*
Well-appointed, Vietnamese-run hotel with clean rooms. There's a variety of different options, from small tiled rooms to quite spacious rooms with massive windows.

### Restaurants

#### Paksan
There are many small restaurants and noodle shops along the main drag. Few have English menus.

#### $ Saynamxam Restaurant
*At the north end of the bridge.*
In a town very short on options, this has a fairly decent menu.

#### Ban Lao
There is a small market at the intersection, with several *feu* restaurants.

## BORDER CROSSING
## Paksan–Beung Kan (Thailand)

This crossing is for the more intrepid travellers and is seldom used. If you intend to use it, check information in advance. The Thai border is 2 km from Paksan on the Mekong, where there's a small port and immigration office, open daily 0800-1200 and 1330-1630. Visas are not available at the border and need to be arranged in advance. Boats to Beung Kan on the Thai side leave when they are full, usually about every 30 minutes. You can also charter a boat. From Beung Kan there are irregular buses to Udon Thani and Bangkok.

## Festivals

### Paksan
**Jul** (movable)  Every year **Wat Prah Bat** hosts a full moon festival.
**Mid-Oct** (movable)  The famous **Naga Fireball Festival (Bang Fai Phayanuk)**, at the Phonsane Temple, sees small colourful fireballs shoot out of the river.

## Transport

### Paksan
**Bus**
The bus stop is next to the Morning Market. To **Vientiane**, 7 daily in the morning, 1-2 hrs. In the other direction, most buses from Vientiane to southern destinations ply through the town every couple of hours, so it's just a matter of waiting at the bus stop/market to pick up a lift: to **Thakhek**, 190 km, 4-5 hrs, or on to **Savannakhet** 320 km, 8 hrs. To reach the Vietnam border at **Nam Phao** (see box, page 184), catch one of the border-bound buses that starts from the southern terminal in Vientiane or travel by pickup to **Lak Xao**, 5-6 hrs, for onward transport (see below). These *songthaew* depart between 0500 and 0600.

### Ban Lao
There is a small transport terminus at the intersection. If a bus/*songthaew* happens to dump you here, your best bet is to hop on one of the northbound buses to Vientiane or a southbound bus to **Thakhek**, **Savannakhet** and **Pakse**. *Songthaew* generally scurry through from early in the morning to well into the afternoon, on their way to **Ban Na Hin** (for Kong Lor Cave) and **Lak Xao**.

## East on Route 8
a colossal cave amid some of Laos' most stunning scenery

After leaving the north–south Route 13, take Route 8 east towards Lak Xao. This road leads into the hills, with tremendous views over a karst landscape of jagged pinnacles cutting through a patchwork of forest, conjuring a somewhat daunting, Gothic fairytale image. Two-thirds of the way to Ban Na Hin, on the right-hand side, look out for **Phu Phu Man Limestone Forest**, a cluster of sharp limestone pillars, saw-toothing across the countryside. There is a small lookout point at Km 54; most *songthaew* passengers won't mind if you stop for a minute to take a picture.

## Ban Na Hin (Ban Khoun Kham)

Ban Na Hin, also known as Khoun Kham ('Gateway to Kong Lor') is a real end-of-the-earth town, low on charm but redeemed by the phenomenal landscapes surrounding it. Its two raisons d'être are as a transit point for Nam Theun II dam operations and for visitors to Kong Lor cave to the south. Ban Na Hin has quite a large market where you can buy fresh fruit and vegetables, bread and other supplies; if you haven't got a torch, it's a good idea to pick one up here. There are also a few cheap *feu* shops dotted around the market's periphery.

There isn't a whole lot more here but just outside of town is **Namsanam waterfall**. Take the signposted path on the left-hand side of Route 8, beside a colourful monastery. The trek to the falls is roughly 3 km through pleasant countryside. The two-tiered, 70-m-tall falls are magnificent and flow year round. There are reputed to be wild elephants in the area around the falls but the likelihood of seeing one is very slim. The provincial tourism office has built an **information centre** on Route 8, just before the turn-off to the waterfall. Apparently local guides do exist but you will probably find the waterfall before you find a guide.

## Towards Tham Kong Lor

From Ban Na Hin it is possible to travel to Tham Kong Lor by boat or by road; both journeys pass through stunning scenery.

The boat trip starts in **Ban Napur**, a couple of kilometres south of Ban Na Hin, and runs along the Nam Hinboun River to either **Ban Phonyang**, where eco-lodge **Sala Hin Boun** is located (see Where to stay, opposite) or to **Ban Kong Lor**, the closest village to the caves, where you can find a homestay and the new **Sala Kong Lor Lodge** (see page 184). It's a fascinating journey with excellent views of impressive limestone cliffs along the way and classic riverside scenes with people fishing and bathing. Take some padding as the wooden seats, even if they are cushioned, can be uncomfortable. Beyond Ban Phonyang the river route to Tham Kong Lor is gorgeous, with small fish skipping out of the water, languid buffalo bathing, kids taking a dip and ducks floating by – all surrounded by a *Lord of the Rings* fantasyland of cliffs and rocky outcrops.

Ban Kong Lor can also be reached by pickup or *songthaew* from Ban Na Hin but the road sometimes gets flooded.

## ★ Tham Kong Lor (Kong Lor Cave)

*Entrance fee at cave site 5000 kip; 100,000 kip to go through the cave (maximum 3 people per boat). See Towards Tham Kong Lor, above, and Transport, page 184, for information on getting to Tham Kong Lor.*

Tham Kong Lor is sensational and should not be missed. The Nam Hinboun River has tunnelled through the mountain, creating a giant rocky cavern, 6 km long, 90 m wide and 100 m high, which opens out into blinding bright light at **Ban Natan** on the other side. The cave is apparently named after the drum makers who were believed to craft their instruments here. It is also home to possibly the largest living cave-dwelling spider in the world, the giant huntsman, which has a leg span of 30 cm. However, it is unlikely you will have a run in with the massive arachnid as they are very rare. Fisherman will often come into the cave to try their luck as it is believed that 20-kg fish lurk below the surface.

At the start of the cave, you will have to scramble over some boulders while the boatmen carry the canoe over the rapids, so wear comfortable shoes with a good grip. A torch or, better still, a head-lamp, is also recommended. It is eerie travelling through the dark, cool cave, with water splashing and bats circulating. There are a few minuscule rapids inside and the cave's surface is riddled with nooks and crannies. About two-thirds of the way through the cave is an impressive collection of stalagmites and stalactites.

It is possible to continue from Ban Natan, on the other side of Kong Lor, into the awesome **Hinboun gorge**. This is roughly 14 km long and, for much of the distance, vertical cliffs over 300 m high rise directly from the water on both sides. The discovery of some valuable religious documents indicates the historical significance of the gorge both during the Vietnamese War and much earlier. There is no white water but the river frequently flows quite fast. More impressive scenery then follows until the village of **Paktuk**, close to Route 13 where any journey can be continued. ▸▸ *The cave can also be visited as part of the 400-km 'loop' from Thakhek,* *see page 195.*

## Listings East on Route 8

### Where to stay

**Ban Na Hin**

**$ Inthapanya Guesthouse**
*At the far end of the village.*
This wooden built guesthouse has reasonable clean rooms, a/c and internet. A decent budget option.

**$ Sainamhai Resort**
*4 km outside town, T020-2249 8989.*
Set on the river next to a small village, this welcoming little resort offers accommodation set among beautiful gardens along the Namhai River. There are 8 well-kept bungalows each with great views. Friendly staff run a very good restaurant on-site. This is a great place for families, with a play area and a *pétanque* pitch. Call the resort for free pick-up from Ban Na Hin. They can also arrange trips to Kong Lor Cave. Recommended.

**Towards Tham Kong Lor**
There are 2 guesthouses on Route 13 in Ban Lao, just past the Route 8 intersection, which are passable. Homestays are available in Ban Kong Lor and Ban Natan.

**$$-$ Sala Hin Boun**
*Ban Phonyang, 10 km from Kong Lor Cave, T020-7775 5220, www.salalao.com.*
The best option. It enjoys a scenic location on the riverbank amongst karst rock formations and has 10 well-equipped and very pleasant rooms in 2 bungalows. The manager will arrange for a boat to pick you up in Ban Na Hin (aka Ban Khoun Kham) advance notice. A tour to Kong Lor for 2-3 people with picnic lunch can be arranged.

## BORDER CROSSING

## Nam Phao–Cau Treo (Vietnam)

The border is 30 km east of Lak Xao, at Nam Phao (Laos), a legal crossing point since 1997. There are buses to the border from Vientiane (via Paksan, see page 181). *Songthaew* leave Lak Xao market every hour and take about 50 minutes to the border. The border is open 0800-1800. Be prepared for slow service around lunchtime and an overtime fee at weekends. You need to organize Vietnamese visas in advance (ideally in Vientiane) as they aren't issued at the border. Once in Vietnam transport can be caught to Vinh from where buses service all the major cities. Arriving from Vietnam, 30-day Laos visas are issued at the border.

**$$-$ Sala Kong Lor Lodge**
*1.5 km from Kong Lor Cave, near Ban Tiou, T020-7776 1846, www.salalao.com.*
Lodge with 4 small huts with twin beds and several superior rooms.

### Transport

**Ban Na Hin**
**Bus/songthaew**
There is a small transport terminus at the Route 13/Route 8 intersection in **Ban Lao** (also known as Tham Beng or Vieng Kham) for north–south buses between Vientiane and Thakhek, Savannakhet or Pakse. *Songthaew* generally pass through here from early in the morning to well into the afternoon to Ban Na Hin. This trip along Route 8 is about 60 km.

To get to **Kong Lor Cave** cave from Ban Na Hin, a pickup is usually on hand to take passengers as far as **Ban Kong Lor**, the closest village to the caves, from where it's possible to hire a boat to take you into the cave. There is also one public *songthaew* a day making the journey to Ban Kong Lor.

**Boat**
To **Kong Lor Cave**, boats run from **Ban Napur**, a couple of kilometres south of Ban Na Hin, to **Ban Phonyang**, 2-3 hrs, or **Ban Kong Lor** (closer to the cave), and onto the cave, a further 1 hr.

If you are staying at **Sala Hin Boun**, see Where to stay, they will send a boat to Ban Napur to collect you.

## Lak Xao (Lac Sao) → *Colour map 2, B5.*

**transit town for Kong Lor cave loop**

Lak Xao is a relatively new town. It was established by the army's Bolisat Phathana Khet Phoudoi (BPKP or Mountainous Area Development Company) back in 1968 in a remote and sparsely populated area close to the border with Vietnam, and still retains a frontier atmosphere. It is sometimes called Muang Kham Keut, which is confusing because there is another Kham Keut, 30 km to the west of town. (This was the original settlement and is worth a visit as it is over 500 years old.)

## ON THE ROAD
## The Mlabri – spirits of the yellow leaves

The elusive Mlabri 'tribe', which occupies the forests around Lak Xao as well as parts of Thailand, represents one of the few remaining groups of hunter gatherers in Southeast Asia. They are also known as the Phi Tong Luang or 'Spirits of the Yellow Leaves'; when their shelters of rattan and banana leaves turn yellow they take this as a sign from the spirits that it is time to move on. Traditionally the Mlabri hunted using spears. If they were stalking larger game, they would brace the weapon against the ground, rather than throwing it, and allow the charging animal to impale itself on the point. In this way, the Mlabri were able to kill the great *saladang* wild buffalo (*Bos gaurus*), as well as bears and tigers. Smaller game was more common, however, and this was supplemented with tubers, nuts, honey and other forest products to provide a balanced diet.

Many of the Mlabri's traditions are already on the verge of extinction. The destruction of the forest means that the Mlabri have been forced to lead more sedentary lives, turning to settled agriculture in place of hunting and gathering, while inter-marriage with other tribes is reducing their number. As recently as the 1980s, a Mlabri was displayed in a cage in a Bangkok department store. Today, many of the few Mlabri that remain have been forced to become cheap labourers for groups such as the Hmong.

This part of Laos was once one of the richest in terms of wildlife. However, the area was extensively logged prior to the building of the building of the controversial **Nam Theun II dam**; it remains heavily scarred today, although logging is less invasive. It is believed that Lak Xao was once a mini fiefdom controlled by an old Lao general, who logged the town into oblivion. Another threat to the forests and fauna is the area's great hydropower potential.

There's a bank and post office in the town. The **Lak Xao Wildlife Centre** used to operate here, trying to protect animals displaced by the logging and dam construction. Unfortunately the centre has now closed.

## Listings Lak Xao (Lac Sao)

### Where to stay

There are several reasonably pleasant places to stay in Lak Xao.

**$ Phoutthavong Guesthouse**
*Just west of the station, off the main road, T054-341074.*

Spotless rooms with a/c or fans, tiled floor, polished wooden furniture and white paintwork at odds with the dusty atmosphere of the town. Recommended.

**$ Vongsouda Guesthouse**
*300 m north of the main road away from the station, T054-341035.*

Quite a nice guesthouse with a/c and en suite bathrooms with Western toilets and hot water. Clean and airy lobby too, but the real selling point is the large veranda outside the main entrance where you can sit and relax with a drink. Motorbike hire also available.

## Restaurants

The main street has a few simple restaurants and a number of noodle stalls.

## Transport

*Songthaew* depart for **Paksan**, every hour from 0700 daily, 5-6 hrs, and **Thakhek**, every hour 0730-1200 daily. If you wish to leave after midday, go to Ban Lao and pick up a lift from there. Buses leave for **Vientiane** at 0500,

0600 and 0800, 6-8 hrs. These buses go via **Ban Lao** (Vieng Kham). There is a scheduled bus for **Thakhek** daily at 0730, 5-6 hrs.

The road up into the mountains is excellent, partly because there is a hydro-power dam here and also because of the need to establish and maintain good transport links with neighbouring countries.

Pickups depart from the Lak Xao market throughout the day to the Vietnam border 32 km away, at **Nam Phao**, 1 hr. Often tour buses to Vietnam leave from the **Phou Doi Hotel**, so it is worth checking if you can get on board, as it is an infinitely more comfortable mode of transport. There is also a minivan service from Lak Xao market to **Chung Thom**, near Vinh, daily in the late morning.

# Thakhek
## & around

Thakhek is sometimes translated as Indian (*khek* or *khaek*) Port (*tha*), although it probably means Guest (*khaek*) Port after the large number of people who settled here from the north. During the royalist period through to the mid-1970s it was a popular weekend destination for Thais who came here in droves to gamble. After the Communist victory, when Laos effectively shut up shop, everything went very quiet. The recent recovery of commercial traffic has brought some life back to this small settlement, though it remains a quiet town. The third Friendship Bridge to Thailand was completed here in 2011 making the town a major international border point.

Thakhek is the most popular stopover point in the central provinces, although it is still not considered a primary tourist destination. However, the region encompasses some of the most beautiful scenery in Laos: imposing jagged mountains, bottle-green rivers, lakes and caves. Tourism infrastructure is improving and a trip to this area will prove a highlight of most visitors' holidays to Laos, particularly the stunning karst scenery and impressive trip out to Buddha Cave, or the popular route known as the 'Loop' (see page 195). Rock climbing has also taken off here thanks to the opening of the Green Climber's Home. *Phone code: 052. Colour map 2, B5.*

# Essential Thakhek and around

## Finding your feet

It takes four to five hours to travel from Paksan to Thakek along the north–south Route 13. The other major road is Route 12 which heads east from Thakhek and connects with Vietnam's Highway 15. This road forms part of the 400-km motorbike 'Loop' taking in the impressive karst landscape of the Mahaxai area and a number of impressive caves.

Boats run across the border to Thailand from Thakhek (see border box, page 191), but the nearby bridge is now a more common means of making the crossing.

### Tip...

Don't miss the 'Loop' if you're a road trip fan, but be sure to hire quality wheels for the journey and give your motorbike a thorough inspection before heading out. Be aware that during the rainy season (September/October) some of the roads may be impassable. Good information about the 'Loop' can be found at **Thakhek Travel Lodge**, see page 190.

## Time required

The area could be traversed in a day but it's worth allowing a few extra days for the worthwhile detours. Three to five days to do the 'Loop' by motorbike.

## Sights

There are few officially designated sights in Thakhek but many visitors consider it to be a gem of a settlement. Quiet and elegant, with some remaining Franco-Chinese architecture, including a simple fountain square, it has a fine collection of colonial-era shophouses, a breezy riverside position and a relaxed ambience. What locals regard as the central business district at the river end of **Kouvoravong Road** is wonderful for its faded elegance. Other visitors, in contrast, look more critically at the dusty streets, seeing pockets of squalor, dilapidated buildings and an uncharacteristic atmosphere of disinterest among the locals.

Thakhek is small enough to negotiate on foot or by bicycle. A number of places organize motorbike hire (see Transport, page 192). ▸▸ *For details of the town's three markets, see Shopping, page 190.*

### That Sikhot

*6 km south of Thakhek, daily 0800-1800, 5000 kip.*

That Sikhot or **Sikhotaboun** is one of Laos' holiest sites. It overlooks the Mekong and the journey downstream from Thakhek, along a quiet country road, reveals bucolic Laos at its best. The *that* was restored in 1956 but is thought to have been built by Chao Anou at the beginning of the 15th century, around the same time as That Inheng in Savannakhet Province (see page 205). The *that* houses the relics of Chao Sikhot, a local hero, who founded the old town of Thakhek.

That Sikhot consists of a large gold stupa raised 29 m on a plinth, with a viharn upstream commissioned in 1970 by the last King of Laos.

# BACKGROUND

## Thakhek

The origins of Thakhek can be traced back to the Cambodia-based kingdoms of Chenla and Funan, which reached their heyday in the seventh century AD. But modern Thakhek was founded in 1911-1912, under the French, clearly evident in the architecture. Apart from Luang Prabang, this is probably the most outwardly French-looking town in Laos, particularly with the fading pastel hues of the villas around the town's fountain area.

### Kong Leng lake
*33 km northeast of Thakhek.*

This stunning lake is usually incorporated into hikes as there isn't direct road access to the site. It is steeped in legend, for locals believe an underground kingdom lies beneath the surface. As a result, you must request permission to swim in this lake from the local village authority and you can swim only in the designated swimming zone. Fishing is not permitted. The beautiful green waters of the lake morph into different shades season to season due to the dissolved calcium from the surrounding limestone outcrops. It is very difficult to get to the lake independently and sometimes the track is completely inaccessible except on foot. The Tourist Information Centre in Thakhek organizes excellent treks to the lake.

## Listings Thakhek and around

### Tourist information

**Tourist Information Centre**
*Vientiane Rd, in a signposted chalet-like building, T052-212512, Mon-Fri 0800-1130 and 1330-1630, Sat-Sun 0800-1130 and 1400-1700.*
Has particularly helpful staff. This is a good stop-off place for advice. Proceeds from the tours go to poor, local communities.

### Where to stay

**$$$-$$ Hotel Riveria**
*Setthathirat Rd, T051-250000, www. hotelriveriathakhek.com.*
This huge white building is the 1st structure that arrivals from Thailand will see. Situated right on the riverfront, it offers comfort at a price; go for the superior deluxe which is a good size. There's a restaurant, pool and gym and Wi-Fi is available in the lobby. The views of the karst landscape are beautiful from the upper floors.

**$$-$ Inthira Hotel**
*Chao Anou Rd, close to the fountain, T051-251237, www.inthira.com.*
A stylish small hotel with some very attractive rooms that are warmly decorated; however, the standard rooms are extremely cramped, so opt for the deluxe. Restaurant and Wi-Fi available.

**$ Southida Guesthouse**
*Chao Anou Rd (a block back from the river), T051-212568.*

Very popular guesthouse in the centre of town. Clean comfortable rooms with a/c, TV, and hot water; cheaper with fan. Very helpful staff; often booked up as this is a solid budget option.

### $ Thakhek Travel Lodge
*2 km from the centre of town, T030-530 0145, travell@laotel.com.*
Popular guesthouse set in a restored old house. Fantastic outdoor seating area and with nightly open fire creating a very social atmosphere and making it a good place to get tips for the 'Loop'. There's also an excellent logbook for those intending to travel independently around the 'Loop' and motorcycle hire can be arranged. The rooms are rather basic, but people only tend to stay here as a quick stop before and after their motorcycle adventure.

## Restaurants

Thakhek is not a place to come to for its cuisine, but you will find the usual array of noodle stalls (try the one in the town 'square', which also sells good fruitshakes). Warm baguettes are also sold on the square in the morning. The best place to eat is at one of the riverside restaurants on either side of the square. Otherwise, most of the restaurants are attached to the hotels and guesthouses.

### $ Kaysone Restaurant
*In the centre of town, T051-212563.*
Although from the outside this looks like someone's backyard, inside is a sprawling restaurant compound. *Sindat*, Korean barbecue, and fantastic ice cream. Karaoke on site.

### $ Lao-named restaurant
*On the corner of Ounkham Rd and the east–west street leading to Wat Nabo.*

English menu with Lao and Western dishes, mainly centred on seafood. Popular with local expats.

### $ Phoukanna
*Vientiane Rd.*
Big choice of Western and Lao dishes plus new noisy bar.

### $ Sabaidee
*1 km towards the river from **Travel Lodge** (see below), T051-251245. Closed 1500-1700.*
Serves great backpacker fare (burgers, salads, sandwiches) plus a range of Lao dishes on cheery red-checked tablecloths. Book exchange and CNN on TV.

### $ Sukiyaki
*Vientiane Rd, T020-5575 1533.*
A pokey but exceptionally friendly restaurant where you can barbecue your own meal on the tables.

### $ Thakhek Travel Lodge
*See Where to stay.*
The food in the lodge's restaurant is not all good but recommended is the Hawaii curry and barbecue (which needs to be ordered in advance). The service, on the other hand, is unacceptably slow and haphazard.

## Bars

**Boua's Place** on the Mekong is great for a sunset drink. There are a lot of drinking holes strung along the front here.

## Shopping

### Markets
There are 3 markets in Thakhek. The largest, **Talaat Lak Saam**, is at the bus terminal, 4 km east of town and is a good place to pick up odds and ends, with tuk-tuks ferrying market-goers to and fro (10,000 kip). **Talaat Lak Song** is

## BORDER CROSSING
### Thakhek–Nakhon Phanom (Thailand)

With the construction of the third Friendship bridge 16 km north of Thakek, this is now a very simple border crossing with a bus taking passengers straight across and efficient service, particularly on the Thai side. There's a customs and immigration office on the Lao side open daily 0800-1730. From Nakhon Phanom, scheduled buses depart for Udon Thani and Bangkok. Arriving from Thailand, 30-day Lao visas are available at the border.

at the eastern end of Kouvoravong Rd, 1.5-2 km from the centre. It is a mixed, mainly dry goods market, although basketry and handcrafted buffalo bells are also sold. North on Chaoanou Rd is the **Talaat Nabo**. A new night market has opened in the fountain area.

### What to do

The tourist office (page 189) is very helpful and organizes the following treks and excursions: 3-day trip to Kong Lor Cave, 770,000 kip per person for 2; to Phou Hin Poun for lakes and caves, 600,000 kip per person for 2; to Buddha Cave, 300,000 kip per person for 2. Also runs Route 12 trips.

**Green Climbers Home**, *12 km east of Thakek, see website for directions, T020-5966 7532, www.greenclimbershome.com. Oct-May*. An absolute heaven for seasoned climbers and those who want to learn. 10 bungalows and 2 dorm rooms set among some breathtaking karst scenery. Basic ' just climb' half-day courses start at 130,000 kip and 2-day courses on rope work and skills start at 300,000 kip. Climbing routes are 12-40 m long and range from 3+ to 8a+/8b. **Thakek Travel Lodge**, *see Where to stay, T020-2220 5070*. The owner, Mr Ku is a wealth of information about travelling

the 'Loop' and has many contacts. Motorbikes can be rented from his lodge daily from 0700-1100 and 1500-1930. He recommends riders take 4 days. He will help out in an emergency and advises on no-go times; for example, in Sep and Oct during the rains.

### Transport

**Bus/truck**
Thakhek's **main bus station** is 4 km northeast of town, T051-251519. It is a large station with a mini-market and is open throughout the night and offers inter-provincial and international buses. Frequent daily connections from 0400-1200 northbound to **Vientiane**, 346 km, 6 hrs; the VIP bus also dashes through town in the morning at around 0900. Frequent scheduled buses to **Paksan**, 0400-1200, 190 km, 4-5 hrs; it is also possible to pick up a bus to Paksan en route to Vientiane. Get off at **Ban Lao** for connections along Route 12.

Southbound buses to **Savannakhet**, from 1030, every 30 mins daily, 139 km, 2½-3 hrs; to **Pakse**, every hour 1030-2400 daily, 6-7 hrs; Pakse VIP bus leaves at 2400; also to **Sekong**, 3 daily; to **Attapeu**, 1500 and 2300 daily; to **Don Khong**, 2300 daily, 15 hrs.

**Buses to Vietnam** To **Vinh** daily; to **Dong Hoi**, Mon, Wed, Sat and Sun;

to **Hué**, Wed, Thu, Sat and Sun. Also services to **Hanoi**.

The **local bus station** is at Talaat Lak Sarm and services towns and villages within the province. From here *songthaew* depart hourly between 0900 and 1300 to **Mahaxai**, 45 km, 2-3 hrs; **Nakai**, 0800-1600, 77 km, 2-4 hrs; **Na**

**Phao** (Vietnam border) 142 km, 6-7 hrs; and **Na Hin**, 45,000 kip. There is also a *songthaew* to **Kong Lor** village.

**Motorbike hire**
Bikes can be rented from **Thakhek Travel Lodge** and the **Provincial Tourism Office**.

## Excursions off Route 12

spectacular karst scenery; a trip to the Buddha Cave is a must

The caves along Route 12 can be visited on day trips from Thakhek, although some are difficult to find without a guide and access may be limited in the wet season. Some sights have no English signposts but locals will be more than happy to point you in the right direction.

### Tham Xang (Tham Pha Ban Tham)

*9 km northeast of town. Follow Route 12 for about 7 km until you pass the bridge, then turn right (difficulties can arise in the wet season due to flooding).*

This is the closest cave to Thakhek. It is considered an important Buddhist shrine and contains a number of Buddhist artefacts, including some statues and a box containing religious scripts. The Buddhist component, however, pales into insignificance compared to the 'elephant head' that has formed from calcium deposits. Locals herald it as a miracle and in the Lao New Year they sprinkle water on it. Visitors will need a torch to find the formation along a small passage at the right-hand corner of the cave, behind the golden Buddha

### ★Tham Pha (Buddha Cave)

*Ban Na Khangxang, off Route 12, 18 km from Thakhek. Boat 5000 kip and entrance to the cave 2000 kip. Women will need to hire a sinh (sarong) at the entrance, 3000 kip.*

A trip out here is highly recommended not just for the cave itself, which is impressive in its own historical right, but for the surrounding villages, pristine waterways and wonderful karst scenery. A farmer hunting for bats accidentally stumbled across Buddha Cave (also knowns as Tham Pa Fa – Turtle Cave) in April 2004. On climbing up to the cave's mouth, he found 229 bronze Buddha statues, believed to be over 450 years old, and ancient palm leaf scripts. The Buddhas were part of the royal collection believed to have been hidden here when the Thais ransacked Vientiane. Since its discovery, the cave has become widely celebrated, attracting pilgrims from as far away as Thailand, particularly around **Pi Mai** (Lao New Year). In the wet season it is possible to bathe in the beautifully clear waters surrounding the cave, though women will need to wear a *sinh* (sarong). A wooden ladder and ugly concrete steps have been built to access the cave but it is still quite difficult to get to, as the road from Thakhek is in poor condition.

### Tha Falang (Vang Santiphap – Peace Pool)
*To get there, follow Route 12 until Km 13, and then turn north on a track for 2 km. In the wet season it may be necessary to catch a boat from the Xieng Liab Bridge.*

This lovely emerald billabong is surrounded by pristine wilderness and breathtaking cliffs. The swimming pool, created by the Nam Don River, was a favourite French picnic spot during the colonial period and it's a nice place to spend the afternoon or break your journey if you're doing the 'Loop' (see page 195). The water is less pleasant in the dry season, when it can become a bit stagnant.

### Tham Xiang Liab
*Turn off Route 12 at Km 14 (1 km past the turn-off for Tham Xang) and follow the track south to reach the cave.*

Tham Xiang Liab was the first cave in the province to be officially opened to tourists. The 200-m-long cave sits at the foot of a 300-m-high limestone cliff, with a small swimming hole (in the dry season) at the far end. It is not easy to access the interior of the cavern on your own; in the wet season it can only be navigated by boat, as it usually floods. This cave, called 'sneaking around cave', derived its name from a legend of an old hermit who used to meditate here with his beautiful daughter. A novice monk fell in love with the hermit's daughter and the two love birds planned sneaky trysts around this cave and Tham Nan Aen (see below). When the hermit found out he flew into a rage and did away with the novice monk; the daughter was banished to the cave for the rest of her life. There are limestone formations on the roof of the cave and experts have suggested that there may be some cave drawings hidden among the shadows.

### Tham Sa Pha In
*Follow route 12 to Km 17; beyond the narrow pass turn to the left (north) and follow the path for 400 m.*

This little-visited cave contains a small lake, reputed to be 75 m long, and a couple of interesting Buddhist shrines. Swimming in the lake is strictly prohibited as the auspicious waters are believed to have magical powers.

### Nam Don Resurgence/Khoun Nam Don
*Close to Ban Na, off Route 12 at Km 14, 25 km northeast of Thakhek.*

This beautiful lagoon is located within a cave and shaded by a sheer 300-m-tall cliff. The lagoon offers about 20 m of swimming then filters off into an underground waterway network, believed to extend for 3 km. In 1998 French surveyors found a rare species of blind cave fish 23 m below the surface here. If you follow the cave wall round, there is another entrance which offers a good vista of the turquoise pool below. A trip to Nam Don Resurgence can be done in conjunction with the

‘Loop’ but requires a few hours. It is also a bit tricky to find on your own so you might need to ask the locals or recruit a local guide. During the wet season, access is often only by boat. The Provincial Tourism Office (see page 189) runs some good tours which include this sight.

## Tham Nan Aen
*South of Route 12, at Km 18, a path leads 700 m to the cave entrance.*

Tham Nan Aen is the giant of the local caverns at 1.5 km long and over 100 m high. It has multiple chambers and the entrances are illuminated by fluorescent lighting; it also contains a small underground freshwater pool.

## Mahaxai
Mahaxai is a beautiful small town 50 km east of Thakhek on Route 12. The sunset here is renowned but even more stunning is the surrounding scenery of exquisite valleys and imposing limestone bluffs. A trip to Mahaxai could be combined with a visit to one or more of the spectacular caves along Route 12 and some river excursions to see the Xe Bang Fai gorges or to run the rapids further downstream.

## Listings Excursions off Route 12

### Where to stay

**Mahaxai**

**$ Mahaxai Guesthouse**
*Just north of town.*
These simple bungalows are just the ticket for those on the ‘Loop’, especially as the attached restaurant serves good food. Each individual bungalow has a small balcony ideal for sipping a cold *Beerlao*.

### Restaurants

**Mahaxai**
Food is generally of a high quality in the local noodle shops and foodstalls.

### Transport

**Mahaxai**
*Songthaew* leave from the station in the morning.

**three- to five-day motorbike trip from Thakhek to Kong Lor Cave**

**Route 12 and the 'Loop'** → *Colour map 2, B5/6.*
*Contact Thakhek Travel Lodge (see What to do, page 191) for excellent information about the 'Loop' route and for motorbike hire.*

The impressive karst landscape of the Mahaxai area is visible to the northeast of town and can be explored on a popular motorbike tour from Thakhek, known as the 'Loop'. This is a magnificent trip which runs from Thakhek along Route 12 to Mahaxai, then north to Lak Sao, west along Route 8 to Ban Na Hin and then south back to Thakhek on Route 13, taking in caves and other beautiful scenery along the way. The circuit should take approximately three days but allow four to five, particularly if you want to sidetrack to Tham Kong Lor and the other caves.
▶▶ *For details of excursions off Route 12, see page 192.*

**Distances** The whole 'Loop' covers an area over 400 km (without the side-trips). This includes 50 km from Thakhek to the petrol station before the turn-off to Mahaxai; 45 km between the petrol station and Nakai; 75 km between Nakai and Lak Xao; 58 km between Lak Xao and Ban Na Hin; 41 km between Ban Na Hin and

# Around Thakhek: The Loop

Ban Lao and then 105 km between Ban Lao and Thakhek. The trip between Ban Lao and Ban Na Hin offers some spectacular views.

**Equipment** If on a motorbike pack light: include a waterproof jacket, a torch, a few snacks, a long-sleeved shirt, sunglasses, sun block, closed-toe shoes, a *sinh* or sarong (to use as a towel, to stop dust and – for women – to bathe along the way), a phrase book and a good map. It is a bumpy, exhausting but enjoyable ride. All of the sites are now well signposted in English. Most sites charge a parking fee for motorbikes.

## Nakai Nam Theun National Protected Area
important protected area with tourism infrastructure

The Nakai Plateau was once a royal hunting ground, but today it is part of a National Protected Area (NPA). Over 3700 sq km of stunning landscape have been designated for protection, making it the largest area of its type in Laos and some of the most pristine wilderness remaining in Southeast Asia.

Gradually rising from the Nakai Plateau, the heavy jungle looms up into the Annamite Mountain range, bordering Vietnam. Although numbers are dwindling, there is a great wealth of rare and endangered flora and fauna in this region, including elephants, tigers, the giant muntjac, Asiatic black bears, Malayan sun bears, clouded leopards and the very rare saola (or spindlehorn). At the time of writing, tours were planned for the area – visit the Thakek tourism office for details.

# Savannakhet
## Province

Savannakhet Province has the highest provincial population in Laos. It consists of 15 districts, with 826,000 inhabitants dispersed within its boundaries. Like most provinces in the country, it comprises a kaleidoscope of ethnicities, including the Lao, Phouthai, Thaidam, Katang, Chali, Lava, Souai, Pako, Kaleng, Mangkong and Tai. The cultural diversity is even more visible in Savannakhet city, which has large Chinese and Vietnamese populations. Vietnamese and Thai merchants sell their products throughout the city, while the ubiquitous colonial houses and fading shopfronts are an ever-present reminder of its French influence. Due to its proximity to both Thailand and Vietnam, Savannakhet is considered an important economic corridor. The province has several natural attractions, although the majority are a fair hike from the provincial capital. *Phone code: 041.*

★Situated on the banks of the Mekong and at the start of the Route 9 to Danang in Vietnam, Savannakhet – or Savan as it is usually known – is an important river port and the gateway to the south. It is also an important trading centre with Thailand.

Across the Mekong, high-rise Mukdahan in Thailand may be cocking a snook at its poorer neighbour to the east, but Savannakhet has got a lot to offer that Mukdahan has bulldozed away in the name of modernization. It feels as though the countryside never left Savan: goats and chickens graze and wander around the urban area and a large portion of the town's French colonial buildings still stand, moulding gently in the tropical climate. With a good lick of paint, Savannakhet could scrub up well and, although it's not quite Luang Prabang, it certainly shares many of the same characteristics. In 2010, the authorities recognized the value of its historic core and planned a 30 billion kip investment to preserve its colonial-era architecture. Whether this will last long is questionable. A new Japanese-sponsored bridge across the Mekong to Mukdahan is now open, a development that may change the town's character. Tuk-tuks, locally known as 'Sakaylab' (as in Skylab), criss-cross town.

## Essential Savannakhet Province

### Finding your feet

There is an airport at Savannakhet, which receives flights from Vientiane and Bangkok. By bus, it takes three hours to travel from Vientiane to Savannakhet (125 km) along the main north–south highway, Route 13. Route 9 cuts through the region from east to west and is served by daily buses between Savannakhet and Danang in Vietnam, via the border at Xepon. Just south off Route 9 is the Dong Phou Vieng National Protected Area and Ho Chi Minh Trail, though getting to the latter is not easy and should only be attempted with a 4WD in the dry season (November to March).

### Tip...
The Eco Guide Unit (see page 203) is a great source of information.

### Sights

Like any town of this size, Savan has quite a number of wats; none are particularly notable but most are quite beautiful. **Wat Sounantha** on Nalao Road has a three-dimensional raised relief on the front of the *sim*, showing the Buddha in the *mudra* of bestowing peace, separating two warring armies. **Wat Sayaphum** on the Mekong is rather more attractive and has several early 20th-century monastery buildings. It is both the largest and oldest monastery in town, although it was only built at the end of the 19th century. Some monks at **Wat Sayamungkhun** speak a bit of English and are pleased to talk about their 50-year-old monastery. There is a large temple school here and, if you arrive during lessons, you may get roped into some impromptu English teaching.

Savan's **colonial architecture** can be seen throughout the central part of town. Perhaps the most attractive area is the square east of the old immigration office between Khanthabouli and Phetsalath roads. Simuang Road, near the Catholic church, is also rewarding in this regard.

Evidence of Savan's diverse population is reflected in the **Chua Dieu Giac**, a Mahayana Buddhist pagoda at the intersection of Soutthanu and Phetsalath

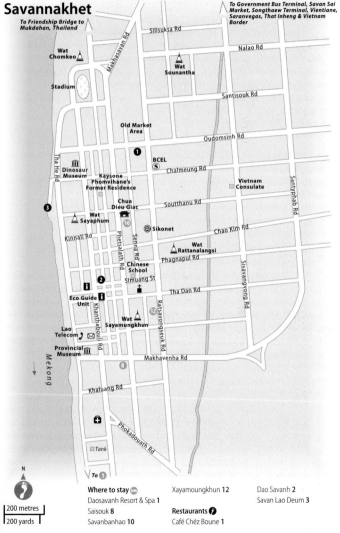

**Savannakhet**

To Friendship Bridge to Mukdahan, Thailand

To Government Bus Terminal, Savan Sai Market, Songthaew Terminal, Vientiane, Saranvegas, That Inheng & Vietnam Border

Silisuksa Rd
Nalao Rd
Wat Chomkeo
Wat Sounantha
Stadium
Santisouk Rd
Old Market Area
Oudomsinh Rd
BCEL
Dinosaur Museum
Chalmeung Rd
Vietnam Consulate
Kaysone Phomvihane's Former Residence
Chua Dieu Giac
Soutthanu Rd
Wat Sayaphum
Sikonet
Chao Kim Rd
Kinnali Rd
Wat Rattanalangsi
Chinese School
Phagnapul Rd
Simuang St
Tha Dan Rd
Eco Guide Unit
Lao Telecom
Wat Sayamungkhun
Provincial Museum
Makhavenha Rd
Khaluang Rd
Phokadouath Rd
Tank
To

Mekong
Tha He Rd
Makhasavan Rd
Phetsalath Rd
Khanthabouli Rd
Senna Rd
Ratsavongseuk Rd
Sisavangvong Rd
Santyphab Rd

N
200 metres
200 yards

**Where to stay**
Daosavanh Resort & Spa 1
Saisouk 8
Savanbanhao 10

Xayamoungkhun 12

**Restaurants**
Café Chéz Boune 1

Dao Savanh 2
Savan Lao Deum 3

## BACKGROUND
### Savannakhet

Savannakhet was established in 1642 by Prince Thao Keosimphali, the son of King Luang of Phonsim. The prince relocated the majority of families from Ban Phonsim, 18 km east of Savannakhet, to the modern-day town, naming the new fiefdom Ban Thahae (Mineral Port Village). The name was later changed to Souvannaphoum and, in 1883, was adapted to Savannakhet by French colonizers. In 1989, US servicemen arrived in Savannakhet, searching for the remains of men missing in action (MIAs) and the whole town turned out to watch their arrival at the airport. Not realizing that the Lao bear absolutely no animosity towards Americans, the men kept their heads down and refused to disembark until the crowds dispersed. During the war against the Pathet Lao the Royal Lao Air Force operated out of Savannakhet and, towards the end of the conflict, even headquartered here.

roads that serves the town's Vietnamese population. In deference to Theravada tradition, the *chua* has a *that* in the courtyard. There's also a Chinese school close to the Catholic church. The church, which dominates the historic centre, holds Mass at 0800 on Sunday.

Unfortunately, the beautiful French colonial building housing the local museum has closed. The **Provincial Museum** ⓘ *Khanthabouli Rd, Mon-Sat 0800-1200 and 1330-1600, 5000 kip*, now has a purpose-built building. The museum has plenty of propaganda-style displays but little that is terribly enlightening, unless you are interested in the former revolutionary leader Kaysone Phomvihane.

Another attraction is the **Dinosaur Museum** ⓘ *Khanthabouli Rd, south of the stadium, T041-212597, daily 0800-1200 and 1300-1600, 5000 kip*, which houses a collection of four different dinosaur and early mammalian remains, and some fragments of a meteorite that fell to earth over 100 million years ago. The first fossils in the region were unearthed in 1990 by a team of French and Lao scientists. All exhibits are accompanied by explanations in Lao and French; some staff speak good English and French and are happy to explain their work. A DVD in French explains the discoveries.

In the near future, the local tourism authority intends to open up a few more local sights to visitors, including Kaysone Phomvihane's former residence and the Thonglahasinh factory, where you can learn about the processes of natural silk-dyeing (which are surprisingly interesting). The town's night market is also to be developed, along with a Savannakhet historic trail, so that travellers can visit the ethnic minority groups near Muang Phin (where there is a downed helicopter and a wonderful socialist-realist Lao-Vietnamese statue), the *lao lao*-making village of Ban Nong Yang and the bombed out bridge at Tad Hai. At Ban Makhong, some women have embroidered American bombers into their skirts.

Savannakhet's newest attraction is the architecturally kitsch **Savan Vegas Hotel & Casino** (see page 202). If you're passing, it's worth a diversion to see the mammoth white elephant statues supporting the building.

## Tourist information

**Provincial Tourism Office**
*Chaleun Meuang Rd, T041-212755.*
*Mon-Fri 0800-1200 and 1300-1600.*
One of the least helpful in the country.
Much better is the nearby **Eco Guide
Unit** (see page 203). The tourism
office has at least produced a series of
useful leaflets including a worthwhile
self-guided walking tour of the historic
quarter, called *Savannakhet Downtown*,
distributed at guesthouses, the tourism
office and the Eco Guide Unit.

## Where to stay

Savannakhet has a good selection
of places to stay for US$5 and
upwards but rock-bottom budget
accommodation is scarce.

**$$$ Daosavanh Resort & Spa Hotel**
*1 km south of the historic centre,*
*T041-252188, www.daosavanh.com.*
A newer resort with attractive
rooms (those with Mekong views
cost more), super mattresses, rain
shower in bathrooms, great pool
and Wi-Fi, though bathrooms need
much better ventilation. It's a little
stuck out of the centre but great for
the spa and pool. Let's hope they
preserve the lovely French colonial
building, the former provincial
museum, which is in the grounds.

**$$ Phonepasut**
*Santisouk Rd, 1 km from town centre
in quiet street, T041-212158.*
Motel-like place with 2 courtyards,
restaurant and pool (US$10 for non-
residents to use). The rooms are clean,
with hot water in the bathrooms, a/c

and satellite TV. Friendly and well run
with business support services.

**$$ Sala Savanh**
*A block south of the Catholic church,*
*T041-212445, www.salalao.com.*
A small hotel (5 spacious rooms) in an
historic building that used to be the
Thai consulate. There is original tiling
throughout. This is an old building with
no soundproofing so you would be wise
to opt for the upstairs rooms. Friendly
management and excellent location.

**$$-$ Hoongthip**
*Phetsarath Rd, T041-212262,*
*hoongtip@laotel.com.*
Dark rooms with big en suite bathrooms,
a/c and satellite TV. The new rooms are
large but austere with bathtubs in the
en suites. Breakfast included. Other
services include sauna, and car hire
with driver. Wi-Fi in lobby.

**$ Nongsoda**
*Tha He Rd, T041-212522.*
If you're not put off by the oodles of
white lace draped everywhere, you'll
find clean rooms with a/c and en suite
bathrooms with wonderfully hot water.
During the low season the hotel drops
its room rate. Motorbike hire (80,000 kip)
and bike hire (10,000 kip) also available.

**$ Saisouk**
*Makhavenha Rd, T041-212207.*
A real gem, this new guesthouse has
good-sized twin and double rooms
which are immaculately furnished
and spotlessly clean, with a/c in some
rooms, communal bathrooms and cold
water. It's beautifully decorated with
interesting *objets d'art* and what look
like dinosaur bones. There are plenty of

chairs and tables on the large verandas. It is efficiently run by very friendly staff who speak English. Homely.

## $ Savanbanhao Hotel
*Senna Rd, T041-212202,*
*sbtour@laotel.com.*
Centrally located hotel comprising 4 colonial-styles houses set around a quiet but large concrete courtyard, with a range of rooms. There are cheaper rooms in '4th class' (not musty, contrary to appearances). The more expensive rooms have en suite showers and hot water. Some a/c. Large balcony. **Savanbanhao Tourism Co** is attached (see What to do, below). Good choice for those who want to be in and out of Savannakhet, quickly, with relative ease.

## $ Xayamoungkhun
*85 Rasavongseuk Rd, T041-212426.*
An excellent little guesthouse with 16 rooms in an airy colonial-era villa. Central with a largish compound. Range of very clean rooms available, with hot water, a/c and fridge in the more expensive ones. Friendly owners. Second-hand books available. Recommended.

## Restaurants

Several restaurants on the riverside serve good food and beer. The market also has stalls offering decent fresh food, including excellent Mekong river fish. **Phengsy** coffee shop at the bottom of the square is a great people-watching spot and serves good coffee too.

## $$$ Bungva Lake Restaurant
*On Bung Va Lake. Daily 0800-2200.*
Stilted restaurant in the lake, with individual dining rooms. Enjoy fresh seafood washed down with *Beerlao*. A lovely way to pass the afternoon.

## $$$-$ Dao Savanh
*Simuang St, T041-260888.*
*Open 0700-2200.*
A newcomer to the restaurant scene, this place occupies a restored French colonial building and provides good but pricey food. It's worth splashing out on a set menu (65,000-95,000 kip). Sit at one of the outdoor tables for views of the central square.

## $$-$ Savan Lao Deum
*Old ferry pier, T041-252125.*
This lovely place has taken over the old ferry pier area. The attractive wooden restaurant juts out onto the river on a floating veranda. It's a particularly good venue for a sunset drink. The food is delicious, too, especially steamed fish and herbs. You might like to try some of the more adventurous options: fried tree ant eggs, grilled buffalo skin and roasted cicadas. The service is exceptional.

## $ Café Chéz Boune,
*Opposite the old market, T041-215190.*
*Open 0700-2300.*
This place provides good travellers' fare in attractive surrounds.

## Bars and clubs

There are several large discos/beer gardens in Savannakhet, most of which stage live bands and are open 7 days a week. **Seven** on Ratsavongseuk Rd is especially popular with young Lao.

## Entertainment

**Savan Vegas Casino**, *T041-252200, www.savanvegas.com.* At the city roundabout, dominated by dinosaur statues, a sign reads 'Welcome to Lao

Vegas'. If you want to play, it's Thai baht only; if you want to stay, the comfortable rooms overlook the casino hall; there's a spa and pool too.

## Festivals

**Feb  Than Ing Hang** (movable) similar to the festival at Wat Phou, Champasak (see page 229).

## Shopping

**One District One Product**, *Km 6, T020-5554 0226, not too far from Savan Vegas.* A large warehouse with all sorts of handicrafts and wares on sale.
**Talaat Savan Sai (Central Market)**, *behind the government bus station, north of town. Daily 0700-1700.* The central market has moved from its former location to a new site in the north of town. Though not as convenient for tourists, the spanking new building, built and managed by a Singaporean company, comes complete with parking spaces and one of the few escalators in Laos. You'll find the usual selection of meat, vegetables, fruit, dry goods, clothes, fabrics and baskets, plus an abundance of gold and silversmiths.

There is a branch of **Lao Cotton** on Ratsavongseuk Rd.

## What to do

### Spa

**Champa Savanh Spa**, *at the Daosavanh Resort, T041-252188 ext 402, www. daosavanhhtl.com. Open 1300-2200.* This spa offers a broad range of treatments. Go for the kitsch waterfall experience and steam rooms and then make use of the large swimming pool.

See also **Savan Vegas**, under Entertainment, above.

### Swimming

Non-guests can use the pool at the **Daosavanh Resort** (see Where to stay) for 50,000 kip. It has an attractive sala in which to lounge after your swim.

### Trekking

**Savanbanhao Tourism Co**, *at the Savanbanhao Hotel (see Where to stay), T041-212944, sbhtravel@yahoo.com. Mon-Sat 0800-1200 and 1330-1630.* Provides trips to most sights in the vicinity as well as bus tickets to Vietnam.
**Savannakhet Eco Guide Unit**, *Rasphanit Rd, T041-214203, www. savannakhet-trekking.com. Mon-Fri 0800-1130 and 1330-1700, Sat-Sun 0800-1130 and 1400-1700.* This unit, run by Oudomsay Thongsavath, operates excellent ecotours and treks to the national parks in the area. There are several keen and enthusiastic English-speaking guides to take tourists out to see the local ethnic culture and sights. Highly worthwhile treks have been established, with proceeds filtering down to local communities.

Note that some treks only operate Nov-Mar. Tours include 1- to 5-day treks (with homestay) to Dong Phou Vieng NPA, Phu Xang Hae NPA, Dong Natad protected area to see the honey collection (Feb-Mar), tree oil extraction, Nom Lom Lake and the ancient ruins of Meuang Kao. Also runs 1-day cycling trips to Dong Natad and Bungva Lake takes in That Ing Hang and village visits; and a 2-day cycling trip takes in a homestay at Ban Phonsim. The minimum price for a 1-day trekking tour for 2-3 people is US$26, including transport, food, water and a guide. Book in advance. The office can also arrange guides and drivers for other trips. Highly recommended.

# BORDER CROSSING
## Dansavanh–Lao Bao (Vietnam)

The Vietnam border is 236 km east of Savannakhet (45 km from Xepon). Getting through customs and dealing with potential obstacles on the other side means that it's impossible to state how long it may take to get into Vietnam itself. Buses leave Savannakhhet for the border at throughout the morning and take four to five hours. There are buses that run from Savannakhet to Dong Ha, Hué and Danang, but for some you will need to change buses at the border.

The Lao border post is at Dansavanh, from where it is about 500 m to the Vietnamese immigration post and a further 3 km to Lao Bao, the first settlement across the border; motorbike taxis are available. We have received reports of long delays at this border. Don't be surprised if formalities take one hour – and keep smiling! The problem is at the Vietnamese end but those with a Vietnamese visa (required) should be OK. The closest Vietnamese consulate is in Savannakhet. Lao immigration can also issue 30-day tourist visas. Expect to pay 'overtime fees' on the Lao side if you come through on a weekend.

## Transport

### Air
**Lao Airlines** (T041-212140) flies to **Vientiane** and **Bangkok** 3 times a week. A tuk-tuk from the airport is 20,000 kip.

### Bus/truck
The government bus terminal is on the northern edge of town, near the Savan Xai market, T041-213920. A tuk-tuk to the centre should cost about 10,000 kip. Just west of the bus station is the *songthaew* terminal, where vehicles depart to provincial destinations.

From the bus station, frequent northbound buses depart daily to **Vientiane** (0600-1130), 457 km on a good road, 9 hrs, 80,000 kip. Most of the Vientiane-bound buses also stop at **Thakhek**, 125 km, 2½-3 hrs, 25,000 kip; **Paksan**, 5-6 hrs, 55,000 kip; and **Pak Kading**, 7-8 hrs, 55,000 kip. There are also specially scheduled morning buses to **Thakhek**.

Southbound buses to **Pakse** depart daily at 0700, 0900, 1030, 1230, 1730, 6-7 hrs, 35,000 kip; buses in transit from Vientiane to Pakse will usually also pick up passengers here. A VIP bus leaves at 2130, 8 hrs, 95,000 kip. To **Don Khong**, 1900 daily, 9-10 hrs, 75,000 kip; to **Salavan**, 1230 daily, 8-10 hrs, 60,000 kip; to **Attapeu**, 0900 and 1900 daily, 9-12 hrs, 70,000 kip. This road is also in pretty good condition.

Eastbound buses depart daily to: **Xepon** at 0700, 0800, 1000, 1100, 1230, 4 hrs, 30,000 kip; and **Lao Bao** (Vietnam border, see Border crossing, above), at 0630, 0900 and 1200 daily, 6 hrs, 40,000 kip.

**To Vietnam** A bus departs at 2200 daily for destinations within Vietnam, including **Hué**, 13 hrs, 90,000 kip; **Danang**, 508 km, 13 hrs, 110,000 kip; and **Hanoi**, 24 hrs, 200,000 kip on Tue and Sat; there are additional services at 1000 (VIP bus to Hué). Luxury Vietnam-bound buses can be arranged through the **Savanbanhao Hotel** (see Where to stay), 90,000 kip. Although buses claim to be direct, a bus change is required at the border. Buses leave on even days at 0800 and arrive in Hué at 1600.

**To Thailand** For buses to the border at **Mukdahan**, Thailand, see Border crossing, page 207.

### Car, motorbike and bicycle hire
Cars and drivers can be hired from the **Savanbanhao Hotel** (see Where to

stay). Some of the guesthouses rent bicycles for 10,000 kip and motorbikes for 50,000-80,000 kip.

### Tuk-tuk and saamlor
Most tuk-tuks charge around 10,000 kip per person for a local journey. There is one traditional old bicycle *saamlor* still operating in town. Track down the old man that runs it for a leisurely jaunt around the colonial core.

## Around Savannakhet
*flora and fauna, architecture and local culture*

### That Inheng
*12 km northeast of Savannakhet, 0800-1800, 5000 kip.*

That Inheng is a holy 16th-century *that* or stupa. It was built during the reign of King Sikhottabong at the same time as That Luang in Vientiane, although local guides may try to convince you it was founded by the Indian emperor Asoka over 2000 years ago. Needless to say, there is no historical evidence to substantiate this claim. The wat is the site of an annual festival at the end of November akin to the one celebrated at Wat Phou, Champasak (see page 229).

The regular tuk-tuks that ferry people between Savannakhet and Xeno will usually take you to That Inheng (100,000 kip return). Otherwise, take a shared *songthaew* to Xeno and ask to hop off at That Inheng. They will usually take you all the way, but if they drop you at the turning it is only a 3-km walk from the road. Alternatively, hire a bicycle in town and cycle out here. Another option is to travel by the **Bungva Lake**, 7 km outside of Savannakhet, and stop for lunch at the lakeside restaurant.

### Salt works
*In the village of Ban Nateuy, 18 km from town. Visits by prior appointment, T041-212255.*

The salt works make for a good excursion. About 90% of Lao salt is produced here, either in large open saltpans or in an interesting Heath-Robinson contraption where the saline solution is pumped into small metal trays over wood fires in open sheds. You will see grilled fish encrusted in salt sold from stalls along the Mekong in Savannakhet.

### Champone District
*A tuk-tuk will do the round-trip for US$40, divided amongst passengers. Otherwise contact the local tourist office, who should be able to hook you up with a guide/driver.*

An increasingly popular excursion, particularly for nature and wildlife enthusiasts, is a day trip to Champone District, the location of Hai Suey Lake, the Monkey Forest, Hotay Pidok Library (a repository of palm leaf books written in Burmese

Pali) and Don Deng Turtle Lake. A number of villages in the area provide an insight into local farming life. These include Ban Kengok, a typical village surrounded by beautiful countryside.

Take Route 13 south towards Pakse and turn left at Km 35; follow this road for approximately 20 km until you reach **Ban Sokuan**, a friendly village that's a good place to break the journey. **Hai Suey Lake**, the largest lake in Savannakhet Province, is 4 km further on. Boats will do short trips on the lake for about 5000 kip. Another 7 km beyond Ban Sokuan is **Ban Dong Meun**, known as the **Monkey Forest**. If travelling independently ask locals to point you in the right direction. The monkeys reign supreme from their forested habitat, not far from Champone River, and locals have attached many superstitions to their presence, such as imminent death if you hit a monkey.

From Monkey Forest it is another 30 km south, via the Ban Nong Lan Chanh intersection, to **Ban Dong Deng** and **Turtle Lake** (0800-1800, 10,000 kip). There are more monkeys than turtles but they are still reasonably visible. Locals revere these soft-shelled turtles (*paa faa*), and it is believed that certain residents can summon the creatures from the waters with a special call.

## Ban Houan Hine

*75 km south of Savannakhet. Buses take Route 13 south, 60 km from Savan, and then turn right onto a track for a further 15 km (signposted 'Stone House Pillars').*

Ban Houan Hine, or Stone House, was built between the sixth and the end of the seventh centuries. It does not begin to compare with the better known Wat Phou outside Champasak but a visit here can be combined with a visit to **That Phone**, a hilly Buddhist *that* en route. It was previously possible to travel by boat down the Mekong to this lesser-known Khmer site but, again, improvements in road conditions coupled with the usual tourist's disposition to press on elsewhere, has meant this is no longer an option and public transport is now by road.

## East on Route 9

outstanding natural beauty rewards the adventurous

### Xepon (Sepon) to the Vietnamese border → *Colour map 3, A3.*

It is possible to cross into Vietnam by taking Route 9 east over the Annamite chain of mountains to **Lao Bao** (just over the border) and from there to the Vietnamese town of Dong Ha and the cities of Hué and Danang (see box, page 204). The largest place on the Lao side of the frontier is **Xepon**. At first glance it might seem that there's not much to see and do in Xepon but as there is a government guesthouse here, travellers very occasionally use it as a stopping place en route to Vietnam. There is a **tourist office** in the town office, which can organize a boat trip to a traditional Lao village, 2½ hours away.

The area around Xepon, particularly **Ban Dong**, 20 km east of the town, intersected the Ho Chi Minh Trail (see below) and was devastated during the war. It remains littered with unexploded ordnance and war remnants.

## BORDER CROSSING
### Savannakhet–Mukdahan (Thailand)

Crossing the border into Mukdahan via the Friendship Bridge is now straightforward. Buses leave the terminal in Savannakehet throughout the day, last bus 1900. It takes 10 minutes. The bus will pick you up on the other side of Lao immigration to take you on to the Thai authorities. There are regular buses to Ubon Ratchathani from Mukdahan, three hours; and also to Bangkok. Lao visas (30 days) are available at the border with one passport photo. If you are coming from Thailand and miss the regular connecting bus to Savannakhet, you can hire a *songthaew*. There are ATMs at both borders.

### Around Xepon

The waterfall of **That Salen** is 25 km north of Xepon. The owner of **Vieng Xai Guesthouse** will be able to get you there (fit visitors have been known to hire bicycles). The other waterfall, **Sakoy**, is about 4 km away by river, or 15 km by main road towards Vietnam. Wide without being high, it's nevertheless a great place for a picnic, and some travellers have pitched camp here, situated as it is by the small village of **Ban Sakoy**, surrounded by coconut trees.

### ★Dong Phou Vieng National Protected Area

The Savannakhet Eco Guide Unit (see page 203) runs excellent treks through the Dong Phou Vieng National Protected Area (NPA), south of Route 9, which is home to wildlife such as Siamese crocodiles, Asian elephants, the endangered Eld's deer, langurs and wild bison (most of which you would be incredibly lucky to see). Located within the NPA is a **Song Sa Kae** (sacred forest and cemetery), revered by the local Katang ethnic group, who are known for their buffalo sacrifices. The well-trained local guides show how traditional natural produce is gathered for medicinal, fuel or other purposes. The tours are exceptionally good value and homestays are included. Most of the tours only run during the dry season.

### Ho Chi Minh Trail

This is an enticing prospect for some visitors but getting here is not easy from Savannakhet and should only be attempted in the dry season, November to March being the ideal time. It is necessary to hire a jeep or 4WD in order to cross the rivers because many of the bridges are broken, so your best bet is to organize a tour from Savan, although you could also travel with a guide on public buses, staying overnight in Xepon, the nearest town to the trail. A guide, arranged through the **Savannakhet Eco Guide Unit** (see page 203), will charge US$130 per day for two to nine people for a vehicle plus US$12 per day per guide. The easiest access point to the trail is **Ban Tapung**. On the way, stops include the downed helicopter at **Muang Phin** and the American-bombed bridge at **Tad Hai**, its fallen carcass (1967) still there to see in the river. At **Ban Dong**, the Lamson 719 war museum is under construction. Old weapons and tanks will be displayed.

## ON THE ROAD

### Ho Chi Minh Trail

Throughout the Vietnam War, Hanoi denied the existence of the Ho Chi Minh Trail and, for most of it, Washington denied dropping 1.1 million tonnes of bombs on it – the biggest tonnage dropped per sq km in history. The North Vietnamese Army (NVA) used the trail, really a 7000-km network of paths and roads – some two-lane carriageways, capable of carrying tanks and truck convoys – to ferry food, fuel and ammunition to South Vietnam. Bunkers beneath the trail housed cavernous workshops and barracks. Washington tried everything in the book to stem the flow of supplies down the trail.

The Viet Minh had used it as far back as the 1950s in their war against the French. By 1966, 90,000 troops were pouring down the trail each year, and four years later, 150,000 infiltrators were surging southwards using the jungle network. Between 1966 and 1971, the trail was used by 630,000 communist troops. At any given time, the trail was guarded by 25,000 NVA troops and studded with artillery positions, anti-aircraft emplacements and SAM missiles.

The trail wound its way through the Annamite mountains, entering Laos at the northeast end of the 'Panhandle', and heading southeast, with several access points into Cambodia and south Vietnam.

The US airforce started bombing the trail as early as 1964 in Operation Steel Tiger and B-52s first hit the Mu Gia pass on the Ho Chi Minh Trail in December 1965. Carpet-bombing by B-52s was not admitted by Lao Prime Minister Prince Souvanna Phouma until 1969, by which time the US was dispatching 900 sorties a day to hit the trail.

## Listings East on Route 9

### Where to stay

#### Xepon

**$ Nangtoon Guesthouse**
*Route 9, 2 km from Xepon, T041-214894.*
Rooms with either fan or a/c and hot water in the bathrooms. Outstanding value. Recommended.

**$ Vieng Xai Guesthouse**
*In town on Route 9, T041-214895.*
A big house, wooden upstairs and concrete down. The rooms are very clean, with a shared bathroom. The friendly owners speak a little English.

### Restaurants

#### Xepon

On the west side of the market there is a reasonable restaurant called **Bouphan**, which does good eggs, *feu* and coffee.

### Transport

#### Xepon

*Songthaew* depart from the market to **Savannakhet** at 0800 daily, 30,000 kip. There are numerous *songthaew* from the market to **Lao Bao**, 45 km, 1 hr, 20,000 kip but you'll need to get there

In an effort to monitor NVA troop movements, the US wired the trail with tiny electronic listening devices, infra-red scopes, heat- and smell-sensitive sensors, and locational beacons to guide fighter-bombers and B-52s to their target. The NVA carefully removed these devices to unused lengths of trail, urinated on them and retreated, while preparing to shoot down the bombers.

Creative US military technicians hatched countless schemes to disrupt life on the trail: they bombed it with everything from Agent Orange (toxic defoliant) to Budweiser beer (an intoxicating inebriant) and washing up liquid (to turn the trail into a frothing skid-track). In 1982 Washington admitted to dumping 200,000 gallons of chemical herbicides over the trail between 1965 and 1966. The US also dropped chemical concoctions designed to turn soil into grease and plane-loads of Dragonseed – miniature bomblets which blew the feet off soldiers and the tyres off trucks. Nothing worked.

The US invasion of Cambodia in May 1970 forced Hanoi to further upgrade the trail. This prompted the Pentagon to finally rubberstamp a ground assault on it, codenamed Lamson 719, in which south Vietnamese and US forces planned to capture the trail-town of Tchepone, east of Savannakhet, inside Laos. The plans for the invasion were drawn up using maps without topographical features.

In February 1971, while traversing the Annamite range in heavy rain, the South Vietnamese forces were routed, despite massive air support. They retreated, leaving the trail intact, 5000 dead and millions of dollars-worth of equipment behind. Abandoned vehicles, bomb casings and even gutted choppers and bombers can still be seen along the trail. There is more war debris here than on the Plain of Jars as trucks cannot easily enter the area to pick it up.

by 0700 to ensure a space. It's also possible to jump on the various buses from Savannakhet to **Vietnam**, which pass through Xepon, the cheapest option being the service to Lao Bao (see above).

# Southern
## Laos
from somnolent Mekong islands to the cool Bolavan Plateau

Laos' southern provinces offer a varied array of enticements and a different character from the north of the country. Base yourself in the region's unofficial capital, Pakse, to explore the many attractions of Champasak Province, including the romantic, pre-Angkorian ruins of Wat Phou and Ban Kiet Ngong, with its opportunities for elephant trekking.

Inland from Pakse is the Bolaven Plateau, an area that was earmarked by the French for settlement and coffee production. The rivers running off the plateau have created a series of spectacular waterfalls, including towering Tad Fan and stunning Tad Lo.

A highlight of any trip down south is Siphandon, where the Mekong divides into myriad channels and 'Four Thousand Islands'. The idyllic, palm-fringed Don Khone, Don Deth and Don Khong provide perfect places to relax and absorb riverine life, as fisherman cast nets amongst lush green islets and children frolic on the sand bars.

**Best** for
Beaches ▪ Dolphins ▪ Khmer ruins ▪ Waterfalls

# Footprint
## picks

★ **Champasak**, page 222

A sleepy riverside town where colonial-era buildings sit alongside traditional Lao wooden houses.

★ **Don Daeng Island**, page 223

Life on this tranquil river island continues much as it has done for centuries.

★ **Wat Phou**, page 225

Laos' own mini-Angkor is worth taking a day to explore.

★ **Xe Pian National Protected Area**, page 229

One of Laos' most important nature reserves, with extensive wetlands home to rare wildlife.

★ **Tad Lo**, page 236

A base for exploring the Bolaven Plateau; take a picnic at the enchanting Tad Yeung falls.

★ **Four Thousand Islands (Siphandon)**, page 249

Best explored by bicycle, these idyllic islands are a traveller haven.

Gulf of Tonkin

VIETNAM

THAILAND

SAVANNAKHET

SALAVAN

SEKONG

CHAMPASAK

ATTAPEU

CAMBODIA

N

| 20 km |
| 20 miles |

**Footprint** picks

# Pakse (Pakxe)
## & around

Pakse is the largest town in the south and is strategically located at the junction of the Mekong and Xe Don rivers. Pakse is a busy commercial town, built by the French early in the 20th century as an administrative centre for the south. The town has seen better days but the tatty colonial buildings lend an air of old-world charm. Pakse is a major staging post for destinations further afield, such as the old royal capital of Champasak, famed for its pre-Angkor, seventh-century Khmer ruins of Wat Phou. The town's colonial ebb is quickly succumbing to Thai and Vietnamese influences, with whole areas now dominated by Vietnamese shops and businesses.

Champasak Province used to include Champasak, Sedon and Sitandon provinces. The governor's office was located in Ban Muang in Sedon prior to French settlement in the area. Pakse's appointment as a French administrative outpost in 1905 spurred the relocation of all major government offices and businesses across the three provinces to Pakse and an amalgamation of provincial authorities.

Close to Pakse are various ecotourism projects where elephant treks, birdwatching and homestays can easily be arranged. *Phone code: 031. Colour map 3, B2.*

Pakse, by anyone's standards, is not a seething metropolis, which, of course, is much of its charm. But this is starting to change now that infrastructure has improved and Pakse is firmly linked into the Thai economy; it has become a major crossroads between the two countries. A strong Vietnamese influence is also apparent.

## Essential Pakse and around

### Finding your feet

Pakse is southern Laos' transport hub: from here you can get to anywhere in the southern region, and travel between smaller towns in the region often requires a connection through Pakse. Although it is not on the border with Thailand, Pakse is the largest Lao town close to the border crossing at Chongmek. From the Thai side, *songthaew* continue on to Ubon Ratchathani in Thailand. There is also an airport at Pakse which has domestic connections with Vientiane as well as international flights from Thailand, Vietnam and Cambodia.

Tuk-tuks and *saamlors* are the main means of local transport and can be chartered. The main tuk-tuk 'terminal' is at the Daoheung market, although they can easily be picked up in the guesthouse area. Cars, motorbikes and bicycles are available for hire from hotels and tour companies. Note that the town's roads are numbered as if they were highways: No 1 Road through to No 46 Road.

### Best places to stay

**The River Resort**, Champasak, page 223

**Kingfisher Ecolodge**, Xe Pian National Protected Area, page 230

There's not that much to see in Pakse, so far as official sights are concerned. However, those who are charmed by slightly dishevelled mid-20th-century architecture will find plenty to photograph here. There is a lot of good food on offer in the form of barbecue meats and beer snacks along the Xe Don River and some excellent Vietnamese options in the Vietnamese area. This is also a great place to observe early morning alms giving in a much more low key way than Luang Prabang. Finally, Pakse is a good place to base yourself to visit destinations further afield, including Tad Lo, Tad Fan and Wat Phou. Facilities such as post office, Telecom office, internet and tourist information are readily available.

### Champasak Historic Museum

*No 13 Rd (the main highway) running east out of town, close to the stadium, T031-212501. Daily 0830-1130 and 1330-1600. 10,000 kip.*

This museum opened in 1995 and displays pieces recovered from Wat Phou, handicrafts from the Lao Theung of the Bolaven Plateau, weaponry, musical instruments and a seemingly endless array of photographs of plenums, congresses and assemblies and of prominent Lao dignitaries opening hydropower stations and widget factories. The charming Lao guides who show visitors around speak only limited English, and the labels are not very informative, but it's still a treat for museum aficionados. Opposite the museum is a *that*-like **Heroes Monument**.

### Wat Luang

There are 40 wats in town but none figures particularly high in the wat hall of fame. Wat Luang, in the centre of town, is the oldest. It was built in 1830, but was reconstructed and redecorated in 1990 at a cost of 27 million kip. The *sim* now sports a kitsch pink and yellow exterior complete with gaudy relief work. Lots of monks can be found loitering around the premises, as this is one of the main centres where they practise English. The hefty doors were carved locally. The compound was originally much larger but, in the 1940s, the chief of Champasak Province requisitioned the land to accommodate a new road. To the right of the main entrance stands a **stupa** containing the remains of Khatai Loun Sasothith, a former prime minister who died in 1959. To the right of the *sim* is the **monks' dormitory**, which dates from the 1930s; the wooden building behind the *sim* is the **monastic school**, the biggest in southern Laos, and on the left of the entrance is the **library**, built in 1943. These earlier structures are, needless to say, the finest – at least for Western sensibilities. The compound backs onto the Xe Don.

There are many more Lao monasteries in town. For those who desire a change there is also a Vietnamese Mahayana Buddhist **Linh Bao Tu Pagoda** on No 46 Road, and a church on No 1 Road.

### Boun Oum Palace

Situated on the road north towards Paksong, the Boun Oum Palace is now the Champasak Palace Hotel and by far the largest structure in town. Before Thai hotel interests bought the place, it was the half-finished palace of the late Prince Boun Oum of Champasak, the colourful overlord of southern Laos and a great collector of objets d'art. He began constructing the house of his dreams in 1968, with the intention of creating a monument with more than 1000 rooms. However, the prince was exiled to France before his dream was realised. Looking at the hotel it is hard not to conclude that his exile was wholly for the best, at least architecturally.

## Muang Khao

Muang Khao lies on the opposite bank of the Mekong to Pakse and, as the name suggests (it means 'Old Town'), was established before its larger sibling across the water. Once the French concentrated their attentions on Pakse, Muang Khao was neglected and fell into decline. As a consequence it has a quaintness that is largely absent from Pakse. Most people come here on their way to the Lao–Thai border at Chongmek, but it has some attractive buildings which are worth a closer look.

## Ban Saphai
*5 km off Route 13, 15 km northwest of Pakse.*

This specialist silk-weaving village is 15 km north of town on the banks of the Mekong. Here a group of about 200 women weave traditional Lao textiles on hand

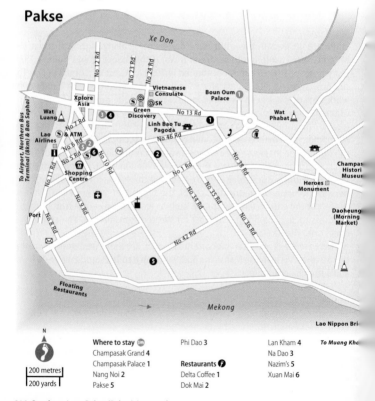

**Pakse**

Where to stay
Champasak Grand 4
Champasak Palace 1
Nang Noi 2
Pakse 5

Phi Dao 3

Restaurants 🍴
Delta Coffee 1
Dok Mai 2

Lan Kham 4
Na Dao 3
Nazim's 5
Xuan Mai 6

*To Muang Khao*

looms. The designs, like the classic *lao mut mee*, show clear similarities with those of northeastern Thailand, where the population is also Lao. However, there are also some unique designs. Prices vary according to the quality and the intricacy of the design. There is also an unusual statue of Indra, Ganesh and Parvati at the local wat.

## Listings Pakse *map p216*

### Tourist information

**Champasak Provincial Tourism Office**
*No 11 Rd, T031-212021. Daily 0800-1130 and 1330-1630.*
They have some fantastic ecotours on offer to unique destinations; some are offered in conjunction with local travel agents, such as **Green Discovery** (see page 220). They also have maps, bus times and a wide range of tourist information. Good, English-speaking staff. Well worth a visit.

### Where to stay

**$$$ Champasak Grand**
*Near the Japanese Bridge, T031-255111, www.champasakgrand.com.*
Gargantuan new business hotel with large rooms, ranging from deluxe to executive suites. Being slightly out of town, the large windows give superb views of the Mekong and the surrounding hills. Also has a good pool and lays on an impressive buffet breakfast. Good value for money.

**$$$-$$ Champasak Palace**
*No 13 Rd, T031-212263, www.champasak-palace-hotel.com.*
This is a massive chocolate box of a hotel with 55 rooms and lit up like a Christmas tree. It was conceived as a palace for a minor prince, complete with bellhops in traditional uniforms. The hotel has lost much of its original character but some classic touches remain: wooden shutters, some art deco furniture and lovely tiles. If you want to kick back for a day or 2, splash out on the King suite for the kitsch factor, jacuzzi and private balcony.

### $$$-$$ Pakse Hotel
*No 5 Rd, T031-212131,*
*www.paksehotel.com.*

The **Pakse Hotel** has a definite charm – a little worn and already feeling like it's from a bygone era, it is nevertheless a firm favourite. The French owner, Mr Jérôme, has integrated local handicraft decorations and rosewood accents. The eco-rooms are good value and the deluxe rooms are a welcome bonus. Breakfast is included and Wi-Fi available. There's also an atmospheric rooftop restaurant with a perfect view over the city.

### $ Nang Noi
*No 5 Rd, T 030-956 2544,*
*bounthong1978@hotmail.com.*

Opened in 2011, **Nang Noi** offers some of Pakse's best budget digs, with kitsch bedcovers covering comfy beds. Some rooms come with peaceful balconies, so ask to see a few first. The family rooms include a/c at extra cost. Run by a very welcoming Lao/Vietnamese husband and wife team who offer a laundry service, tours and bus bookings. Motorcycles can be rented.

### $ Phi Dao Hotel
*125/13 Rd, T031-215588,*
*phidaohotel@gmail.com.*

Vietnamese-owned with very friendly staff. All rooms are decorated in relaxing cream tones with flatscreen TV and fridge, offering good value. Spotless, tiled bathrooms. The big twin rooms at the front have large balconies. Most doubles have a window, but some twins do not, so be sure to check. Also has a decent café-cum-restaurant on the ground floor.

## Restaurants

A string of open-air restaurants line the Mekong from the boat landing, many serving sindat and fish dishes. There are also many great river front beer verandas-cum-restaurants along the Xe Don River – some are quiet; others, such as the very popular **Topa**, get quite raucous later in the evening with a good party atmosphere and live music. Various low-key Vietnamese restaurants can be found by wandering along Rd 46 east of the hospital – expect excellent *pho* noodle soup, *bun thit nuong* (vermicelli with herbs and marinated pork) and good *nem* (spring rolls). For a cheap meal of rice with various toppings look for the *'com'* signs. There are a couple of fantastic *sindat* (barbecue) places near the Da Heung market that are extremely popular with the locals.

### $$ Na Dao
*Opposite the Champasak Grand Hotel near the bridge.*

A cosy French restaurant serving a range of classics and some fusion dishes. Good wine list and a welcoming ambiance.

### $$ Pakse Hotel
*See Where to stay.*

The fantastic rooftop restaurant has atmospheric lighting and offers a range of Lao dishes plus pretty good pizza, delicious chicken curry soup and some delectable cocktails including gin fizz and great mojitos from 1600.

### $$-$ Dok Mai
*Rd 24, T020-9800 8652.*

A real find, this intimate Italian serves a broad range of excellent pasta dishes and some good salads. Try the eggplant with parmesan dish – it's superb. The house wines are good value. The owner is very welcoming and does a great job of making diners feel right at home. A lovely spot and highly recommended.

### $ Delta Coffee
*Rd 13, opposite the Champasak Palace Hotel, T020-5534 5895.*
This place is a real find if you are craving some Western comfort food. The menu is tremendously varied and offers everything from pizza and lasagne to Thai noodles. The coffee is brilliant too, and staff are exceptionally friendly.

### $ Lan Kham
*In front of Lan Kham hotel.*
Longstanding beef noodle joint serving up a solid rendition of the Vietnamese classic until lunchtime. Pancakes and baguettes can be had from a stall next door. Free Chinese tea. Recommended.

### $ Nazim's Restaurant
*In a new location on Rd 12, T031-252912.*
An excellent Indian restaurant with a fantastic choice of meat dishes. The service is a little slow as dishes are prepared fresh.

### $ Xuan Mai
*Near Pakse Hotel, T031-213245.*
Vietnamese restaurant with outdoor kitchen and eating area. Serves good shakes and fresh spring rolls.

### Cafés and bakeries
Crusty baguettes are available across town; they're great for breakfast with wild honey and fresh Bolaven coffee. Low-key coffee shops are found on every street serving coffee strong and on ice.

### Café Sinouk
*Corner Rd 11, www.sinouk-cafe.com.*
This new French-style café is charming and the staff are great. The outside view is a non-event but inside is comfortable seating, framed black-and-white photos, and a range of patisserie and jams, honey and teas to buy in attractive packaging.

## Shopping

### Markets
**Central market**, the closest thing to a shopping centre in town remains half-filled with vendors mostly selling clothes. The initial plans were for it to be a pan-Asian centre, stocking Thai, Japanese, Vietnamese and Lao goods but this is yet to happen.
**Daoheung market**, *opposite the Champasak Museum.* Even for Southeast Asia this is a major agglomeration of stalls and traders. It is best to get here between 0730 and 0800 when the place is in full swing. Although it continues to function throughout the day, it does so in a rather detached fashion. Most people come here just to look but there are some fun things to buy: tin cans, clay pots, textiles and sarongs.

### Textiles
Traditional handwoven silk cloth is available in the **Daoheung market** (see above). There is a good handicraft shop opposite the small park near Wat Luang, which sells lovely woven baskets, wooden carvings and good-quality embroidery. The **Pakse Hotel** (see Where to stay) stocks some good products.

Serious textile shoppers may wish to visit the village of **Ban Saphai** where the embroidery is actually produced (see page 216). The *mut mee ikat* designs are similar to those produced across the border in the northeastern or Isan region of Thailand. However, here in Laos it is more likely that the design will be produced using home-produced silk (in Thailand, silk yarn is often interwoven with imported thread) and coloured using natural rather than aniline dyes.

## What to do

### Golf
There are 2 golf courses in the area.

### Massage and sauna
There is a small sauna and massage centre at the **Champasak Palace Hotel**, and a good massage place right across the road from the **Pakse Hotel**.

### Tour operators
There are a number of tour agencies in town, all of which will arrange tours to local sites like Wat Phou, Phu Asa, Siphandon, Bolaven Plateau and Champasak. Most of the hotels arrange day tours; of these the best is **Wat Phou Travels** at the Pakse Hotel. The **Provincial Tourism Office** (see page 217) also offers a variety of trips including a new 3-day trip to Phou Xieng Thong National Protected Area. **Green Discovery**, *T031-252908, www. greendiscoverylaos.com*. Offers a range of adventure tours and ecotourism treks around Champasak province including Ban Kiet Ngong, Bolaven waterfalls, Xe Pian trekking, Siphandon trip, Wat Phou trip and trekking in Dong Hua Sao National Protected Area. Highly recommended.
**Sabaidy 2 Guesthouse**, *T031-212992, www.sabaidy2tour.com*. Mr Vong and crew offer a wide range of tours around a variety of provincial sites, very good value and recommended for visitors who are only around for 1-2 days. The 1-day Bolaven tour is popular with backpackers. Mr Vong contributes to a school project charity

in the province: www.kokphungtai-primaryschool-fund.com.
**Vat Phou Mekong Cruises**, *www. vatphou.com*. Offers a 3-day/2-night cruise that starts and finishes in Pakse taking in Wat Phou, the Oum Muong ruins at Huei Thamo, 4000 Islands and Pha Pheng waterfall on the Cambodian border.
**Xplore Asia**, *opposite Jasmine Restaurant, Rd 13, T031-212893, www. xplore-laos.com*. Offers a variety of tours and useful tour services (including a minivan service to Siphandon).

## Transport

### Air
The airport is 2 km northwest of town; cross the bridge over the Xe Don River, next to Wat Luang, and continue straight up No 13 Road; take a tuk-tuk from town. There is a small café and BCEL exchange inside the terminal building. There are domestic flights **Vientiane** several times a week, as well as international flights to **Bangkok**, **Ho Chi Minh City** and **Siem Reap** and **Phnom Penh**. There is a **Lao Airlines** office west of the BCEL by the river in Pakse, open Mon-Fri.

### Boat
Public boats to **Champasak** leave from the main pier daily at 0800, 2 hrs. It is also possible to charter a boat, at quite a cost.

### Bus/songthaew
You can charter a tuk-tuk to the airport, northern bus station, southern bus station or the VIP station – most guesthouses will help.

**Northern terminal** Km 7 on Route 13 north, T031-251508, for buses to the north. Hourly departures daily 0730-

1630 to **Savannakhet**, 250 km, 5 hrs; **Thakhek**, 7-8 hrs; and **Vientiane**, 16-18 hrs. Local buses can be painfully slow due to the number of stops they make. For those heading to **Vientiane** it makes more sense to pay a couple of extra dollars and get on the much quicker and more comfortable VIP bus at the VIP station.

**Southern terminal** Km 8 south on Route 13, T031-212981, for buses to the south. There are regular connections with **Champasak**, 1030-1400 (1-2 hrs). If you are travelling to **Wat Phou** (see page 225), take the Champasak bus and ask for 'Ban Lak Sarm Sip' (translates as 'village 30 km'), where there is a signpost and you turn right and travel 4 km towards **Ban Muang** (2-3 km) on the eastern side of the Mekong. In the village people sell tickets for the ferry (extra charge for motorbikes) across to **Ban Phaphin**, on the western side of the Mekong, 2 km north of Champasak; from here walk or take a tuk-tuk into town. The ferry runs regularly from 0630-2000, or you can charter a ferry direct from Ban Muang to the boat landing in Champasak itself.

Buses travelling through from **Vientiane** provide the main means of transport to other destinations in the south, so can be slightly off kilter.

*Songthaew* run east to the **Bolaven Plateau**: to **Paksong**, at 0930, 1000, 1230, 3 hrs; **Tad Fan**, 5 morning departures, 1 hr; and **Ban Kiet Ngong**, at 1200, 2 hrs.

Buses/*songthaew* leave for **Siphandon** (**Muang Khong**) in the far south at 0830, 1030, 1130, 1300, 1430 and 1600, 3-4 hrs; for **Ban Nakasang** (the closest port to Don Deth/Don Khone) several departures at 0700, 0800, 0900, 1130, 1200, 1430 and 1400, 3-4 hrs.

Several of the buses to Ban Nakasang also stop at **Ban Hat Xai Khoune** (the stop-off for Don Khong). Make sure that you let the bus/*songthaew* driver know that you are going to Ban Nakasang or Ban Hat Xai Khoune rather than saying the name of the islands.

A quicker more comfortable option to Siphandon is to take the minivan service to **Don Deth/Don Khong** offered by Pakse operators, 2-2½ hrs. This is highly recommended and, once you have paid all the fees involved with local transport, it costs about the same.

**VIP Khiang Kai/international terminal** (with neighbouring **Seangchaolearn terminal**), on the edge of the hotel area, is where you'll most likely arrive if travelling from Vientiane or from across the border. A VIP sleeping bus with comfy beds, duvet, cake and films leaves at 0830 arriving in **Vientiane** at 0600 (stopping en route to **Thakhek**). The beds are double, so unless you book 2 spaces you might end up sleeping next to a stranger. If you are tall ask for a bed towards the back of the bus.

**To Vietnam** Buses leave for Vietnam via the **Bo Y** border, see box, page 246. Guesthouses and agents offer varying schedules. To **Danang**, 0700 and 1900, 18 hrs; to **Hué**, 0700 and 1900, 15½ hrs; to **Dong Ha**, 0700 and 1900, 14 hrs; to **Lao Bao**, 1700, 11 hrs.

**To Cambodia** Buses run to **Stung Treng** at 0830, 4½ hrs; to **Kratie**, 0800, 6½ hrs; to **Kampong Cham**, 0800, 9½ hrs; to **Phnom Penh**, 0800, 13½ hrs; and to **Seam Reap**, 0800, 17 hrs.

**To Thailand** VIP buses to **Ubon** (Thailand) leave at 0830 and 1530, 3 hrs. Laos visas are available on arrival at the Chongmek border crossing if you're coming in from Thailand, though, don't expect the bus to wait for you. Buses for **Bangkok** leave at 1530. A combination of minibus and sleeper train to **Bangkok** can also be booked departing Paske at 1300 or 1500 and arriving Bangkok at 0730 or 0550.

## Motorbike and bicycle hire
The **Lankham Hotel**, on Rd 13, rents out bicycles, standard small motorbikes and larger dirt bikes.

## Private transport
For out-of-town journeys, hotels such as the **Pakse Hotel** and **Champasak Palace**, and tour companies such as **Xplore-Asia** charter cars and minibuses (with driver). A private *songthaew* from Pakse to **Champasak** (with ferry and tuk-tuk included) can be arranged.

## Champasak and around
underrated charming town close to Wat Phou

★The appealing agricultural town of Champasak, which stretches along the west bank of the Mekong for 4 km, is the nearest town to Wat Phou and a good base from which to explore the site and the surrounding area. Although the trip to Wat Phou can be done in a day from Pakse (it is about 40 km south of Pakse), the sleepy town of Champasak is quaint and charming and now offers a couple of quality mid- and upper-end accommodation options.

### Sights
Champasak is dotted with stunning colonial buildings. The former residence of Champasak hereditary Prince Boun Oum and former leader of the right-wing opposition, who fled the country in 1975 after the Communist takeover, is quite possibly the most magnificent colonial building in Laos. It is not open to tourists but worth a look from the outside.

Champasak is known for its wooden handicrafts and you'll find vases and other carved ornaments for sale near the jetty. About 15 km southwest of Champasak is **Don Talaat**, which is worth a visit for its weekly market (Saturday and Sunday).

### Um Muang (Tomo Temple)
*45 km south of Pakse off Route 13, accessible via the main road south from Pakse to Ban Thang Beng, Km 30, from where a track (vehicle access possible) leads 4 km to Ban Noi. From the village it is a 1-km walk to the temple. It is possible to hire a car or tuk-tuk from Pakse. If you go by bus, you need to get off at Ban Huaytomo. Chartering a boat from Ban Muang, Champasak or Dong Daeng, is also possible.*

Also known as Muang Tomo and Oup Moung, Um Muang is a lesser-known temple complex built at about the same time as Wat Phou on the opposite (east) bank of the Mekong. In colonial days, Um Muang was a stopping point for ships travelling upriver from Cambodia. Its main treasure is a ninth-century Khmer-era temple complex built at roughly the same time as Wat Phou. The temple is thought to have been built by Yasarvoman I and is dedicated to Shiva's companion, Rudani. The site comprises an assortment of ruins, surrounded by jungle. A seven-headed sandstone *naga* greets you as you approach the site from the Mekong.

Like Wat Phou, the main temple is built of laterite and its carvings are in similar style to those of the bigger complex upriver. It is thought, in fact, that the laterite blocks used in the construction of Wat Phou were taken from Um Muang. There are also the ruins of a second building, more dilapidated and moss-covered, making it difficult to speculate about its function, and, hidden in the jungle, are the remains of two *baray*. Um Muang is not on the same scale and nowhere near as impressive as Wat Phou but stumbling across a sixth-century Khmer temple in the middle of the jungle is nonetheless a worthwhile experience. Despite the presence of seemingly abandoned tourist facilities, it's still an atmospheric spot. With great slabs of laterite protruding from the undergrowth and ancient sandstone carvings lying around the bushes, there is no doubt that a great deal about the site remains undiscovered.

Some of the best artefacts from the temple are exhibited in the museum in Pakse (see page 214).

## ★Don Daeng Island

This idyllic river island sits right across from Champasak and is accessed by a cheap boat ride. It stretches for 8 km and is the perfect place for those wishing to see quintessential village life, with basket weaving, fishing and rice farming, with little hustle and bustle. There is a path around the island that can be traversed on foot or by bicycle. A crumbling ancient brick stupa, built in the same century as Wat Phou, is in the centre of the island and there are a few ancient remnants from the construction in **Sisak village**. The inhabitants of **Pouylao village** are known for their knife-making prowess.

There is a lovely sandy beach on the Champasak side of the island, perfect for a dip. If you would like to stay overnight, **La Folie Lodge** is a beautiful spot (see Where to stay, below).

## Listings Champasak and around

### Tourist information

**Champasak District Visitor Information Centre**
*Mon-Fri (daily in high season) 0800-1230 and 1400-1630.*
Can arrange boats to Don Daeng, guides to Wat Phou and tours to surrounding sights.

### Where to stay

**Champasak**

**$$$ The River Resort**
*14a Rd, T020-5685 0198, www. theriverresortlaos.com.*
A class apart from the neighbouring offerings, this superb US-owned resort comprises 24 rooms across 12 split level modernist villas. Each is decorated in

white with blue Lao and Thai ethnic fabrics and bamboo furnishings. All suites include indoor and outdoor showers and the more expensive ones have sweeping Mekong views that are worth every penny. An infinity pool looks over the river next to an open-air restaurant. Private river boat cruises as well as private dining can be arranged. Also has a lovely spa *sala*. Polished service. Highly recommended.

**$$ Inthira Champakone Hotel**
*Diagonally opposite Vong Pasued,*
*T031-511011, www.inthirahotels.com.*
This is a lovely hotel with a friendly Lao manager. The spacious twin rooms in the courtyard come with outdoor rain showers and wooden floors. There are also 2-storey duplex suits, each with mezzanine bed area, balcony, shower room and bathroom. The bar is the only place in town with Beerlao on tap.

**$ Anouxa Guesthouse**
*1 km north of the roundabout,*
*T031-213272.*
A wide range of accommodation from dingy bamboo structures with cold water to wooden bungalows through to concrete rooms with hot water and either a/c (extra) or fan. The concrete villas are the best, with a serene river vista from the balconies. The restaurant, overlooking the river, is one of the best in town. However, service can be slow and the lower-end rooms are rather poor. Bikes and motorbikes for hire.

### Don Daeng Island

**$$$$-$$$ La Folie Lodge**
*T030-5347603, www.lafolie-laos.com.*
24 rooms housed in lovely wooden bungalows, each with private balcony overlooking the river. The lodge

has a stunning pool surrounded by landscaped tropical gardens. The restaurant serves good wine and a cocktail selection. Bicycle hire and pool use is available to non-guests for a fee. It's a luxurious base from which to explore the island.

**$ Homestays** are offered in a community lodge and at 17 homes in Ban Hua Don Daeng. The wooden lodge has 2 common rooms, sleeping 5 people with shared bathrooms and dining area. Meals are 20,000 kip. Contact the **Champasak Tourism Office** for details.

## Restaurants

### Champasak
Most restaurants are in the guesthouses; all are cheap.

**$ Anouxa Guesthouse**
*See Where to stay.*
Has a restaurant set over the river, with a small but good menu. The fish dishes are especially good. Also offers a selection of wines. Service can be very slow.

**$ Inthira Champakone Hotel**
*See Where to stay.*
The **Inthira** does Western burgers and pizzas as well as Asian dishes in handsome surroundings. The iced coffee is fabulous.
For higher-end dining, head to **The River Resort** (see Where to stay)

## What to do

### Champasak
**Champasak Spa**, *T020-5649 9739, www. champasak-spa.com. Daily 1000-1200 and 1300-1900.* This new venture, run by a French couple, is lovely. It aims to be sustainable and they plan to hand it

over to local management after training is complete. The massages are simply divine (opt for coconut oil) and the service exceptional. The foot massage is perfect after a morning at the ruins. Booking advised after 1600.

### Don Daeng Island

The tourist office in Pakse organizes a 2-day biking and long-tail boat trip around Don Daeng that departs from Pakse and takes in Wat Phou. It is possible to hire bikes from **La Folie Lodge** (see Where to stay) to explore the island.

## Transport

### Champasak

Transport to Champasak is by minibus, tuk-tuk or boat. The ferry from Ban Muang (on the eastern side of the Mekong) runs regularly to **Ban Phaphin** (on the western side, 2 km north of Champasak). From Ban Phaphin, tuk-tuks run into town. Alternatively, charter a ferry from Ban Muang directly to the boat landing in Champasak.

A more upmarket option from Pakse is to take a cruise which stop at **Wat Phou**, the Oum Muong ruins at **Huei Thamo**, **4000 islands** and **Pha Pheng waterfall** on the Cambodian border.

To get to **Wat Phou**, either take a tuk-tuk or hire a bicycle at one of the guesthouses and cycle the 8 km.

There are buses and *songthaew* to **Pakse**, as well as daily boats (2 hrs), all of which leave in the morning. Ask at your guesthouse for details and arrange your ticket through them. The ferry from **Ban Phaphin** (2 km north of Champasak) to **Ban Muang** runs 0630-2000.

From Champasak, it is also possible to get a *songthaew* to **Siphandon**, which leaves in the morning, and a boat to **Don Daeng**.

## Wat Phou

**Angkor Wat's little brother**

★Wat Phou lies at the foot of the Phou Pasak, 8 km southwest of Champasak and is the most significant Khmer archaeological site in Laos. With its teetering, weathered masonry, it conforms exactly to the Western ideal of the lost city. The mountain behind Wat Phou is called **Linga Parvata**, as the Hindu Khmers thought it resembled a lingam – albeit a strangely proportioned one. Although construction of the original Hindu temple complex was begun in the fifth and sixth centuries, much of what remains today is believed to have been built in the 10th to 11th centuries. Wat Phou was a work in progress and was constructed and renovated over a period spanning several hundred years.

### Visiting Wat Phou

Wat Phou is best visited as a day trip from Champasak or Pakse. You can get a tuk-tuk from Champasak, though most tourists prefer to cycle the 8 km – bicycles are available at most guesthouses.

The official website is www.vatphou-champassak.com. The site is open daily 0800-1800. Admission is 35,000 kip and goes towards restoration of the wat

# Wat Phou

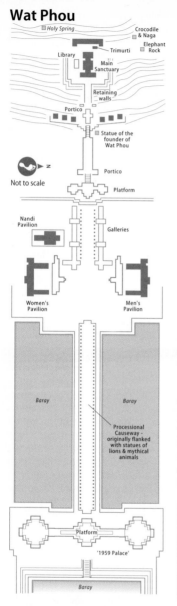

Holy Spring
Crocodile & Naga
Elephant Rock
Trimurti
Library
Main Sanctuary
Retaining walls
Portico
Statue of the founder of Wat Phou
Portico
Platform
Nandi Pavilion
Galleries
Women's Pavilion
Men's Pavilion
Baray
Baray
Processional Causeway - originally flanked with statues of lions & mythical animals
Platform
'1959 Palace'
Baray

Not to scale

(entering the site before hours or staying after hours incurs an extra 10,000 kip fee). It is possible to enter at 0600 by paying 40,000 kip at the main gate. A bus service that must rank as the most expensive per metre in Southeast Asia is now available to transport visitors 500 m from the gate to the main site for 15,000 kip.

There is also the Wat Phu Exhibition Centre (closes 1600) at the entrance, a good museum with a fantastic array of artefacts (entrance to the centre is included in admission to the temple). A guide for the museum and the wat area itself costs 100,000 kip per group.

A few times a year a full moon event is held when there is an atmospheric exploration of the site with lights – check the listed website for dates.

### Exploring the site

**Processional causeway** The king and dignitaries would originally have sat on a platform above the 'tanks' or *baray* and presided over official ceremonies or watched aquatic games. In 1959 a palace was built on the platform so the king had somewhere to stay during the annual **Wat Phou Festival** (see page 229). A smaller house had been for the king's entourage. These have now been dismantled. A long avenue leads to the pavilions. The **processional causeway** was probably built by Khmer King Jayavarman VI (1080-1107), and

> **Tip...**
> The site can get busy so try to visit early in the morning or late in the afternoon. It is also cooler during these times and the light is better for photography. There is little shade so take lots of water and a sunhat.

may have been the inspiration for a similar causeway at Angkor Wat. This grand approach to the temple would originally have been flanked by statues of lions and mythical animals, but few traces of these remain.

**Tip...**
Make sure you climb all the way to the top – it's well worth the effort for the wonderful views over the whole site. Wear sturdy shoes as the steps are quite steep in places.

**Pavilions** The sandstone pavilions, on either side of the processional causeway, were added after the main temple and are thought to date from the 12th century (in all probability from the reign of Suryavarman II). Although crumbling, with great slabs of laterite and collapsed lintels lying aesthetically around, both pavilions are remarkably intact and, as such, are the most photographed part of the temple complex. The pavilions were probably used for segregated worship by pilgrims, one for women (left) and the other for men (right). The porticoes of the two huge buildings face each other. The roofs were thought originally to have been poorly constructed with thin stone slabs on a wooden beam-frame and later replaced by Khmer tiles.

Only the outer walls of the pavilions now remain but there is enough still standing to fire the imagination: the detailed carving around the window frames and porticoes is well-preserved. The laterite used to build the complex was brought from **Um Muang**, also called Tomo Temple, a smaller Khmer temple complex located a few kilometres downriver (see page 222), but the carving is in sandstone. The interiors were without permanent partitions, although it is thought that rush matting was used to divide areas, and furniture was limited – reliefs depict only low stools and couches. At the rear of the women's pavilion are the remains of a brick construction, which is believed to have been the queen's private quarters. Brick buildings were very costly at that time.

**Nandi Pavilion and temple** Above the main pavilions is the Nandi Pavilion, a small temple with entrances on two sides. It is dedicated to Nandi, the bull (Siva's vehicle), and is a common feature in Hindu temple complexes. There are three chambers, each of which would originally have contained statues – these have been stolen. As the hill begins to rise above the Nandi temple, the remains of six brick temples follow the contours, with three on each side of the pathway. All six are completely ruined and their function is unclear. Archaeologists and Khmer historians speculate that they may have been Trimurti temples. At the bottom of the steps is a portico and statue of the founder of Wat Phou, Pranga Khommatha. Many of the laterite paving stones and blocks used to build the steps have holes notched down each side; these would have been used to help transport the slabs to the site and drag them into position.

**Main sanctuary** The main sanctuary, 90 m up the hillside and orientated east–west, was originally dedicated to Siva. The rear section (behind the Buddha statue) is part of the original sixth-century brick building. Sacred spring water

### Wat Phou

Linga Parvata provides an imposing backdrop to the crumbling temple ruins, many of which date from the fifth and sixth centuries, making them at least 200 years older than Angkor Wat. At that time, the Champasak area was the centre of power on the lower Mekong. The Hindu temple only became a Buddhist shrine in later centuries. The French explorer, Francis Garnier, discovered Wat Phou in 1866 and local villagers told him the temple had been built by 'another race'. Unfortunately, not much is known about Wat Phou's history. Ruins of a palace have been found next to the Mekong at Cesthapoura (halfway between Wat Phou and Champasak – now an army camp) and it is thought the sixth-century Chenla capital was based there.

Archaeologists and historians believe most of the building at Wat Phou was the work of the Khmer king, Suryavarman II (1131-1150), who was also responsible for starting work on Angkor Wat, Cambodia. The temple remained important for Khmer kings even after they had moved their capital to Angkor. They continued to appoint priests to serve at Wat Phou and sent money to maintain the temple until the last days of the Angkor Empire.

was channelled through the hole in the back wall of this section and used to wash the sacred linga. The water was then thrown out, down a chute in the right wall, where it was collected in a receptacle. Pilgrims would then wash in the holy water. The front of the temple was constructed later, probably in the eighth to ninth century, and has some fantastic carvings: apsaras, dancing Vishnu, Indra on a three-headed elephant (the former emblem of the kingdom of Lane Xang) and, above the portico of the left entrance, a carving of Siva, the destroyer, depicted tearing a woman in two.

The Hindu temple was converted into a Buddhist shrine, either in the 13th century during the reign of the Khmer king Jayavarman VII or when the Lao conquered the area in the 14th century. A large Buddha statue now presides over its interior. There is also a modern Buddhist monastery complex on the site.

**Around the sanctuary** To the left of the sanctuary is what is thought to be the remains of a small library. To the right and to the rear of the main sanctuary is the **Trimurti**, the Hindu statues of Vishnu (right), Siva (central) and Brahma (left). Behind the Trimurti is the holy spring, believed by the Khmers to have possessed purificatory powers. Some of the rocks beyond the monks' quarters (to the right of the temple) have been carved with the figures of an elephant, a crocodile and a *naga*. They are likely to have been associated with human sacrifices carried out at the **Wat Phou Festival**; it is said the sacrifice took place on the crocodile and the blood was given to the *naga*. Present-day visitors to the festival in February (see Festivals, below) should note that this practice has now stopped!

## Around Wat Phou

If you are particularly interested in archaeology, and haven't had your fill at Wat Phou, there are several other ancient sites that can be visited in the surrounding area, though they are all in a state of disrepair. **Ho Nang Sida**, just 1 km south of Wat Phou (accessible by *saamlor* and tuk-tuk), is an understated ruined temple, overgrown with jungle and strewn with piles of rubble and rocks. The temple, called Lady Sida Hall, is believed to have sat on an ancient highway that linked Angkor Wat to Wat Phou; it was probably used as a hospital.

One kilometre south of Ho Nang Sida is **Hong Nan Tao**, another set of ancient ruins, built under Jayavarman VII and used as a shrine (not accessible by larger vehicles). Another 3 km along the route are three ancient stupas.

## Listings Wat Phou map p226

### Festivals

**Late Jan-early Feb Phu Asa (Ban Kiet Ngong)** The Elephant Festival sees lots of elephants gather from all over the province and *mahouts* dressed in traditional costume. There's a procession to the top of Phu Asa.

**Feb Wat Phou Festival** lasts for 3 days around the full moon of the 3rd lunar month (usually Feb). Pilgrims come from far and wide to leave offerings at the temple.

In the evening there are competitions – football, boat racing, bullfighting and cockfighting, Thai boxing, singing contests and the like. There is also some pretty extravagant imbibing of alcohol.

A *Son et Lumière* of sorts has been arranged at each full moon in the dry season with thousands of lamps lighting the archaeological site. For further information before heading to Champasak ask at the tourist office in Pakse or at the **Pakse Hotel.**

## Xe Pian National Protected Area

out-of-the-way park, leading the way in ecotourism

★The Xe Pian National Protected Area has a rich variety of birdlife, including large water birds and great hornbills, and is home to sun bears, Asiatic black bears and the yellow-cheeked crested gibbon. The best time for birdwatching is December-February.

### Visiting Xe Pian National Protected Area

Ban Kiet Ngong is the base for exploring the area. From Pakse it takes about 1½ hours by motorbike. From Pakse follow Route 13 until you get to the Km 48 junction with Route 18 at Thang Beng village (the Xe Pian National Protected Area office is here). Follow Route 18 east for 7 km, turn right at the signpost for the last 1.5 km to Ban Kiet Ngong. To organize an elephant trek go to the Eco-Guide Unit at the **Champasak Provincial Tourism Office** in Pakse (see page 217), or the **Kingfisher Ecolodge**, if you are staying there (see Where to stay, page 230).

## Sights

North of Xe Pian, the village of **Ban Kiet Ngong** is at the **Kiet Ngong Wetland**, the largest wetland in southern Laos. Here you'll find a community-based project which offers elephant trekking, wetland walks, canoeing trips and homestay accommodation.

The villagers have traditionally been dependent on elephants for agricultural work for centuries, and these days elephants are also used for treks (see What to do, below) to the amazing fortress of **Phu Asa**. Located 2 km from Kiet Ngong at the summit of a small jungle-clad hill, this ancient ruined fortress is an enigmatic site that has left archaeologists puzzled. It consists of 20 stone columns, 2-m high, arranged in a semi-circle – they look a bit like a scaled-down version of Stonehenge.

The **Kiet Ngong Village Elephant Festival** is held annually in late January or early February. It takes place in the village and on the curious archaeological remains at Phu Asa, which provides a fascinating backdrop.

## Listings Xe Pian National Protected Area

### Where to stay

**$$$-$$ Kingfisher Ecolodge**
*1 km east of Kiet Ngong, T030-534 5016,*
*www.kingfisherecolodge.com.*
A bonafide eco-lodge facing the wetlands. The set of 6 glass-fronted bungalows are very romantic, complete with 4-poster beds. There are also 4 attractive thatched rooms with nearby shared bathroom. The restaurant, set on the 2nd floor of the lodge, has stunning views over the Pha Pho wetlands. Elephant-related activities can be arranged, as well as massage. The owners are very helpful. Highly recommended.

**$ Homestay**
*Ban Kiet Ngong.*
The villagers offer basic homestay accommodation with meals. You can book at the **Kiet Ngong Visitor Centre** or at the tourism office in Pakse (see page 217).

### Restaurants

Eating in Ban Kiet Ngong is very basic and, with the exception of nearby **Kingfisher Ecolodge**, you will have to rely on the local food available – generally *feu* and noodle soup, rustled up on the spot.

**$$ Kingfisher Ecolodge**
*See Where to stay.*
This genuine eco-lodge includes an excellent restaurant with lovely views. The menu includes a range of Western and Lao dishes. Also stocks wine.

### What to do

**Elephant treks and birdwatching**
There are several 2- to 3-day trekking/homestay trips offered in the area. These include elephant treks across the **Xe Pian** forests, wetlands and rocky outcrops; treks from Kiet Ngong Village to the top of **Phu Asa** (this takes about 2 hrs; the elephant baskets can carry 2 people); and birdwatching trips. There is a 2-day canoe/trekking/

homestay trip called the **Ban Ta Ong Trail** with guides trained in wildlife and the medicinal uses of plants. Many tour operators in Pakse can also organize trips to the area. Contact the **Provincial Tourism Office** in Pakse (see page 217) for complete information. **Green Discovery**, *see page 220*. Offers a 2-day camping excursion into the protected area, taking visitors deep in to the jungle; and the more challenging 3-day camping **Kiet Ngong-Ta Ong Trail** which includes a homestay and an elephant ride. These tours are designed to ensure that local communities reap the rewards of tourism in a sustainable fashion and are highly recommended.

**Kingfisher Ecolodge**, *see Where to stay*. One of the best contacts for advanced internet bookings, can arrange 1-day courses for you to train to be a bona fide elephant rider with a traditional *mahout* (elephant keeper).

## Transport

*Songthaew* run to the 4000 Islands or ask a private tourist bus running south to stop at the **Ban Kiet Ngong** junction. **Kingfisher Ecolodge** can arrange transport to the village, but call in advance. The easiest way is to hire a private tuk-tuk or car via an agent.

# Bolaven Plateau

The French identified the Bolaven Plateau, in the northeast of Champasak Province, as a prime location for settlement by hardy French farming stock. It is named after the Laven minority group that resides in the area. The soils are rich and the upland position affords some relief from the summer heat of the lowlands. Fortunately, their grand plans came to nought and, although some French families came to live here, they were few in number and all left between the 1950s and 1970s as conditions deteriorated. The area also suffered another setback during the war years, when the major surrounding towns were completely destroyed by US bombing campaigns. Even so, the area was developed as a coffee-, rubber-, tea- and cardamom-growing area. The cool breeze of the plateau, with an average altitude of 600 m, offers much respite from the stifling heat of the surrounding lowlands, particularly in April and May.

Today it is inhabited by a colourful mix of ethnic groups, such as the Laven, Alak, Tahoy and Suay, many of whom were displaced during the war. There are numerous villages dotted between the small settlement of Tha Teng and Salavan. The premier attraction in the area is the number of roaring waterfalls plunging off the plateau. Today, Tad Lo and Tad Fan are popular tourist destinations, while grand Tad Yeung makes a perfect picnic destination. The plateau also affords excellent rafting and kayaking trips. A trip to a coffee or tea plantation also provides an interesting insight into the region.

The main town on the Bolaven Plateau is Paksong, a small market town 50 km east of Pakse. It was originally a French agricultural centre, popular during the colonial era for its cooler temperatures. Paksong was yet another casualty of the war and was virtually destroyed. The area is famous for its fruit and vegetables; even strawberries and raspberries can be cultivated here.

The town occupies a very scenic spot. However, the harsh weather in the rainy season changes rapidly, making it difficult to plan trips around the area. The town consists of little more than a couple of blocks of old shops and a big produce market, which acts as a trading centre for many of the outlying villages of the plateau.

### Waterfalls around Paksong

Just 17 km from Paksong are the twin falls of **Tad Mone** and **Tad Meelook**. Once a popular picnic spot for locals, the area is now almost deserted and the swimming holes at the base of the falls are an idyllic place for a dip. To reach the falls take Route 23 northeast of Paksong towards Tha Teng and Salavan, until you reach a signposted turning; follow the road for about 3.5 km to reach the falls.

Not far from Paksong, 1 km off the road to Pakse, is **Tad Fan**, a dramatic 120-m-high waterfall, which is believed to be one of the tallest cascades in the country. The fall splits into two powerful streams roaring over the edge of the cliff and plummeting into the pool below, with mist and vapour shrouding views from above. The fall's name derives from the species of barking deer which formerly surrounded the area and local legends talk of large numbers of the species falling to their death.

Around 2 km from Tad Fan and 1 km from the main road is **Tad Yeung** (pronounced 'Tad N'Yeung'). Set amongst beautiful coffee plantations and sprinkled with wooden picnic huts, these falls are possibly the best on the

# BACKGROUND
## Bolaven Plateau

The fertile farmland of the Bolaven Plateau has given Salavan Province a strong agricultural base, supporting coffee, tea and cardamom plantations. The road from Paksong to Pakse is known as the Coffee Road. Coffee was introduced to the area by French settlers in the 1920s and 1930s, who then made a quick exit as the bombing escalated in the 1960s. It is mainly exported via Pakse to Thailand, Singapore and Vietnam. Fair Trade has also catapulted the coffee into the UK and US markets. Tea grown in this area, however, is for local use. The Bolaven also has the perfect climate for durians; villages (particularly on the road from Paksong to Pakse) are liberally dotted with durian trees. The fruit is exceptionally rich and creamy with a pungent smell and in the peak season, between May and July, can be bought from roadside stalls.

Thanks to its fertility, the plateau is now rapidly repopulating and new farms are springing up. One can see evidence of the government's relocation policy everywhere on the plateau, where villages have been moved from higher lands to the lower lands, with the end goal of minimizing slash-and-burn agriculture and providing people better access to infrastructure, markets and other facilities. As a result, many new farming practices and produce have been steadily introduced. Towards Salavan, lots of banana plantations are cropping up and, between Paksong and Tha Teng, many small-time village operations are producing cabbage and corn crops, often sold roadside.

During the bombing of the Ho Chi Minh Trail (see box, page 208), to the east, many hilltribes and other ethnic minority groups also migrated to the Bolaven, which consequently has become an ethnographic goldmine with more than 12 obscure minority groups living in the area, including the Katu, Alak, Tahoy, Suay, Ya Houne, Ngai and Suk. Most of the tribes are of Indonesian (or Proto-Malay) stock and have very different facial characteristics from the Lao; they are mainly animist (see page 299) in belief.

plateau. Packing a picnic in Pakse and bringing it along for an afternoon trip is recommended. The cascades plummet 50 m to a pool at the bottom, which is possible to swim in, in the dry season. During the wet season the waterways create numerous little channels and islands around the cascades. Behind the main falls sits a cave – however it is best to get someone to guide you here. There is a slippery walkway from the top of the falls to the bottom, where you can swim.

The falls sit on the edge of the **Dong Hua Sao National Protected Area** and access via the falls is one of the only ways to explore the area. Previously, it was inhabited by a number of rare species now dwindling in number. It is believed that a local population of tigers still resides in the protected area but the chances of spotting one are minimal.

Trekking is offered around the waterfall but is quite difficult in the wet season due to slipperiness and leaches, so it's best to hire one of the guides at the **Tad**

**Fan Resort**. If you follow the track to the left off the main road at Ban Lak, Km 38, at the end of the track, a path leads down to a good viewpoint halfway down the horseshoe-shaped gorge. The magnificent falls offer stunning views but if you wish to swim you should trek further along to **Tad Gniang**, 2 km east of Tad Fan. Tad Gniang, named after the wild stags that populate the area, is only recommended for a dip during the dry season (October to the end of March). There is a charge of 2000 kip per person to visit the falls, plus an additional 3000 kip per motorbike. Tours to Tad Fan and Tad Gniang can be organized through most travel agents in Pakse (see page 220).

Thirty-six kilometres northeast of Pakse is **Paseum Waterfall** and **Utayan Bajiang Champasak** ⓘ *T031-251294*, a strange ethnic theme park. The large compound features the small cascades, restaurant, model ethnic village, gardens and plenty of trails in between.

## Listings Paksong (Pakxong) and around

### Where to stay

$ Borlavan Guesthouse
*Route 23, 2 km north of the market, beyond Paksong town.*
The new brick and wood building has a cabin feel and is surrounded by coffee trees, corn fields and a flower garden. The simple rooms are clean and bright (with pink floral sheets) with en suite bathrooms but no hot water. The very friendly owner speaks English.

#### Waterfalls around Paksong

$$ Tad Fan Resort
*Opposite Tad Fane falls, T020-5553 1400, www.tadfane.com.*
Perched on the opposite side of the ravine from the Tad Fane falls, this resort offers a series of wooden bungalows with nicely decorated rooms and en suite bathrooms, with hot-water showers. The 2nd floor of the excellent open-air restaurant has a distant view of the falls and serves a wide variety of good Lao, Thai and Western food. Great service. Treks to the top of falls and the Dan-Sin-Xay Plain can be arranged.

### Restaurants

There is a small string of barbecue restaurants, past the market away from Route 23. The market also has a large restaurant section and there's a row of Vietnamese restaurants along Route 23 near the bank.

### What to do

To organize kayaking and rafting trips to the Bolaven Plateau, contact **Green Discovery**, in Pakse, see page 220.

### Transport

**Bus**
Regular connections to **Pakse**'s southern bus terminal 0830-1530, 1½ hrs. For the onward journey to **Tad Fan** ask the *songthaew* to stop at Km 38 and follow signs. Also buses to **Attapeu**, daily 0830 and 1200, 3½-4½ hrs.

## Tha Teng and around

**dusty truck stop with little to keep travellers long**

On the Bolaven Plateau, at the junction of Routes 23 and 16 between Salavan (45 km), Sekong (48 km) and Paksong (37 km), is Tha Teng, a village that was levelled during the war. Before that, it was the home of Jean Dauplay, the Frenchman who introduced coffee to Laos from Vietnam in 1920.

There isn't much to see in the town itself – essentially it's just a big roundabout, affording stunning views. There is, however, an excellent ethnic minority market starting at about 0600 daily, to which villagers come to sell produce from their plots.

## Listings Tha Teng and around

### Where to stay

**$ Viphavanh Guesthouse**
*1 km east on Route 16 towards Sekong,*
*T034-211970.*
One of the few options in town. Basic, but it does the job.

### Transport

**Bus/songthaew**
All transport departs from the market. To **Salavan**, 0730 and 0830 daily, 1½ hrs; to **Sekong**, 0730, 1 hr; to **Pakse**, 0530, 0630, 0730 and 0830 daily, at least 2 hrs (87 km). Due to its location many unscheduled buses pass through Tha Teng, running between Pakse, Salavan and Sekong, or Salavan, Paksong and Attapeu. *Songthaew* leave intermittently (mostly in the morning) for various destinations in the vicinity.

## Tad Lo and around → *Colour map 3, B3. Phone code: 031.*

**tranquil backpacker haven with lots of waterfalls**

★Tad Lo is a popular, extremely pretty little village on the edge of the Bolaven Plateau, 30 km from Salavan, and nestled alongside three rolling cascades. The Xe Xet (or Houei Set) flows through Tad Lo, crashing over two sets of cascades: **Tad Hang**, the lower series of waterfalls, is overlooked by the **Tad Lo Lodge** and (see Where to stay, page 238), while **Tad Lo**, the upper series, is a short hike away. The Xe Xet is yet another of the area's rivers that has been dammed to produce hydropower for export to Thailand.

There are several places to stay in this idyllic retreat, good hiking, fantastic waterfalls and elephant trekking.In the vicinity of Tad Lo there are also several villages, which can be visited in the company of a local villager. The area has become particularly popular with the backpacker set, many of whom prefer to stay here rather than in Pakse.

## Visiting Tad Lo

The turning for Tad Lo is Ban Houei Set on Route 20 between Pakse and Salavan. Catch a bus or *songthaew* from either town; most drivers know Tad Lo and will stop at Ban Houia Set (2½ hours from Pakse and under an hour from Salavan). There is a sign here indicating the way to Tad Lo – a 1.8-km walk along a dirt track and through the village of Ban Saen Wang. Usually you can get a tuk-tuk to Tad Lo for around 10,000 kip.

## Trekking

The two-day trek to **Phou Tak Mountain** involves a stay in an ecolodge near a mixed Katu/Souay village. The **Tad Soung trek** is a fairly demanding day out giving awesome views across the plateau. There is also a five-day trek to the **Xe Sap National Protected Area**, involving sleeping in hammocks and the chance to see deer and many bird species.

All the guesthouses in Tad Lo also arrange guided treks. Elephant treks can be arranged from the **Tad Lo Lodge**.

## Around Tad Lo

There are two Alak villages, **Ban Khian** and **Tad Soung**, close to Tad Lo; the latter is approximately 10 km away from the main resort area and has the most panoramic falls in the vicinity.

The Alak are an Austro-Indonesian ethno-linguistic group. Their grass-thatched huts, with rounded roofs, are not at all Lao in style and are distinct from those in neighbouring Lao Theung villages. Most fascinating is the Alak's seeming obsession with death. The head of each household carves coffins out of logs for himself and every member of his family (even babies), then stacks them, ready for use, under their rice storage huts. This tradition serves as a reminder that life expectancy in these remote areas is around 40 and infant mortality around 100 per 1000 live births; the number one killer here is malaria.

Katou villages such as **Ban Houei Houne** (on the Salavan–Pakse road) are famous for their weaving of a bright cloth used locally as a *pha sinh* (sarong). This village also has an original contraption to pound rice: on the river below the village are several water-wheels which power the rice pounders. The idea originally came from Xam Neua and was brought to this village by a man who had fought with the Pathet Lao.

## Listings Tad Lo and around

### Tourist information

**Tourist Information Centre**
*Just after the turn onto the main guesthouse road, T020-5445 5907, kouka222@hotmail.com.*

Excellent centre managed by Kouka, which runs a variety of treks from 1 to 5 days.

## Where to stay

**$$ Tad Lo Lodge**
*By the falls, T034-211889,*
*souriyavincente@yahoo.com.*
The hotel reception is on the east
side of the falls, with chalet-style
accommodation, some built almost
on top of the waterfalls, on the
opposite side. The accommodation is
comfortable, with cane rocking chairs
on the balconies overlooking the falls.
Rates include breakfast, during which
it's possible to watch the elephants
being brought down to the water for
their morning dip – quite a special
experience. The restaurant serves
plenty of Lao and Thai food.

**$ Fandee**
*Main guesthouse road, www.fandee-*
*guesthouse.com.*
Run by Frenchman Louis since 2013,
this is the first place you'll see on the
'main' road of guesthouses. Lovely
wooden bungalows, a cool chill-out
area with plenty of hammocks and
black and white films projected for the
tourists and the community to enjoy.
Fandee translates as 'good dream' –
a very apt name.

**$ Green Garden**
*Just beyond Palamei Guesthouse (clearly*
*signed).*
This is a very laid-back spot set among
trees. The communal area has fantastic
West African-style rosewood chairs.
Food is available and don't miss the
home-made cookies with freshly
ground Arabica coffee. The Czech
owner, Martin, is learning the art of
coffee-roasting on his wok. The 3 basic
rooms are in a building modelled on
a Katu spirit house while the lone

bungalow is like a home away from
home, with a small outdoor kitchen.

**$ Palamei Guesthouse**
*Just past the turning to the falls,*
*T030-962 0192, palamei.guesthouse@*
*gmail.com.*
Run by Mr Poh, this family place has
absolutely beautiful views over rice
paddies from the large bungalows at the
rear. Mr Poh has 19 kids, some of whom
are adopted, so this is a great place to
feel part of a Lao family. Breakfast and
lunch are served, and in the evening
guests can eat with the whole family
and even learn to cook. Free transport
to the bus station 2 km away. Also sells
bus tickets and organizes guided treks,
which Mr Poh himself sometimes runs.
A very special spot.

**$ Sipaseuth Guesthouse & Restaurant**
*Right next to the bridge, T020-5430 4380.*
Wooden bungalows right on the
riverbank are slightly rundown but
have fans and en suite bathrooms. The
restaurant serves good Lao food with
great view. Very friendly owners. Trekking
organized; private transport arranged.

## Restaurants

**$ Chom**
*Main guesthouse road, T055-667900.*
A simple joint with wooden bench-style
seating in the open-air. A very solid
range of Lao food although during
daytime hours it is limited. Also home
to one of the country's most laid-back
dogs. Recommended.

**$ Sabai Sabai**
*Next to Chom.*
Run by a Lao/Spanish couple who like to
party, this place offers Spanish classics as
well as pizza and some lethal cocktails.

**$ Tee Na Restaurant**
*Opposite Chom, no phone.*
Very friendly service and extremely
good larb (minced meat salad) and
spring rolls (the fresh version, not the
fried) in the most basic of surrounds.
Also offers a homestay and laundry
service. Bungalows set to open.
Recommended.

**$ Tim Guesthouse**
*Main guesthouse road.*
Once the most popular place in town,
this place still does a good range of
food but the atmosphere can now be
a little lacking.

## Festivals

**Mar  Buffalo ceremony**  This Ta Oy
ceremony takes place in a village near
Tad Lo on the first full moon in Mar. It is
dedicated to the warrior spirit, who is
asked for protection.
**Apr**  Annually just before Lao New Year
there is a **full moon sacrifice** by Nghe
and Katu people in villages around Tad
Lo. It is important to employ a guide if
you wish to visit the festivities in order
to ensure local customs are respected.

## What to do

### Elephant trekking
This is an excellent way to see the area
as elephants can go where jeeps cannot.
It is also a thrill being on the back of an
elephant. **Tad Lo Lodge** (see Where to
stay) organizes treks throughout the
day; 2 people per elephant.

### Trekking
The best place to head for information
on tours in the area is the **Tourist
Information Centre** (see page Variable).
All the local guesthouses run treks to
Ban Khian and Tad Soung, but Mr Poh
at **Palamei Guesthouse** (see Where to
stay) is particularly recommended.

## Transport

### Bus
There are buses from Ban Houei Set
(1 km north of Tad Lo) to **Pakse**, hourly
until 1630, plus a VIP sleeping bus to
**Vientiane** or **Thakek**. Buses also run
to **Salavan** but times are sporadic. For
information and tickets, contact the
Tourist Information Centre.

## Salavan (Saravan) and around → *Colour map 3, B3. Phone code: 034.*
**dusty frontier town with spectacular but inaccessible mountain scenery**

The capital of one of the most beautiful provinces in Laos, the old French town
of Salavan (also Saravan and Saravane) lies at the northern edge of the Bolaven
Plateau and acts as a transport hub and trading centre for the agricultural
commodities that are produced on the plateau. The Xe Don River, which enters the
Mekong at Pakse, flows along the edge of town.

Salavan itself is no beauty, but it is charming with no pretensions. Pigs and buffalo
wander along the roads, children play in the streets and shops sell such practical
goods such as anvils, bicycle tyres, lengths of wire, transmission parts and brightly
coloured functional plastic objects.

# BACKGROUND
## Salavan

The area around Salavan was an important Champasak kingdom outpost called Muang Mam and populated by mostly Mon-Khmer ethnic groups. In 1828 the Siamese renamed the area Salawan, which has evolved into the current name.

Salavan changed hands several times during the American war in Indochina, as the Pathet Lao and forces of the Royal Lao Government (RLG) fought for control of this critical town, which is located on a strategic flank of the Ho Chi Minh Trail. The two sides, with the RLG supported by American air power, bombed and shelled the town in turn as they tried to dislodge one another, and Salavan was all but obliterated. (There is a crude painting of the battle on display in the **Champasak Museum** in Pakse; see page 214.) Until just a few years ago, you would still come across piles of war scrap, including unexploded bombs, shells and mortars in the streets. Now that these have been cleared, reminders of the war are largely confined to the memories of the town's older residents (most of the population is under 30) and the pages of books. The consequences of the shelling and bombing today is that Salavan is a provincial capital with scarcely an ounce of physical beauty and almost no evidence of its French-era origins, with the single exception of the post office.

Like Xieng Khouang, another critical town to the north, Salavan had one of the most beautiful temples in the country, **Wat Chom Keoh**, which was destroyed in an air raid in 1968. (The wat was commemorated on a postage stamp in the 1950s.)

Tourists are welcomed but not wooed; there are few handicrafts or postcards in sight. In the cool of the evening, when the locals have stopped work and are relaxing, talking, cooking and playing, the town seems – despite the legacy of the war – to epitomize a more innocent past. If you happen to be walking past the market at 1700 or thereabouts, you may even find yourself invited to join the locals in a game of pétanque.

### Sights

Today all that remains of **Wat Chom Keoh** are two forlorn and shell-pocked corner-posts, one ruined chedi and a dilapidated wat building decaying still further in the grounds of the Salavan general hospital. The daily **market** in the centre of town is worth a visit, mainly because the only other sight is the **handicraft centre**. In past years the market was an environmentalist's nightmare: all manner of wild creatures, including some endangered species, were sold here, either for the cooking pot or for the trade in live wild animals. Today the frisson of such sights is, fortunately, no longer on offer. There's the usual array of frogs and fish, and perhaps a wild bird, squirrel or lizard, but not much else. The post office in the heart of town is the sole building to provide an architectural window into the town's past.

## Ban Nong Boua

Ban Nong Boua, a beautiful lake near the source of the Xe Don, lies 18 km east of Salavan town. It is famed for its crocodiles (although apparently now only two remain), which move into the river in the dry season but usually stay out of sight. The locals have a number of cultural beliefs surrounding the crocodiles, so a donation – perhaps in order to offer a pig to the crocs, which the residents will actually consume themselves – is likely to be expected before they will escort you to the lake. The road to Ban Nong Boua is too rough to be negotiated by tuk-tuk, which means it is necessary to charter a jeep or other sturdy vehicle. There are two river crossings along the way, so any vehicle that won't fit in a small boat or isn't large enough to brave the waters won't make it there. In the wet season it is advisable to travel by boat.

Ban Nong Boua is also rumoured to be a starting point for climbing **Phou Katae**, the 1588-m-high mountain that looms over Salavan from the south. However, *falangs* aren't welcome to climb it, either because of the American airstrip from the war that is supposedly up there, or because of the logging operations on the other side, which are not entirely legal.

Access to both Ban Nong Boua and Phou Katae is very difficult and is only recommended for the tougher independent traveller. There is no accommodation near the mountain but it may be possible to sleep at the nearby temple if you have a mosquito net.

## Around Salavan

**Tahoy**, northeast of Salavan along Route 15, is a major centre of the Tahoy minority ethnic group. There are 30,000 Tahoy spread across the two adjoining provinces but the largest population lives here. Aside from being an interesting cultural insight into the Tahoy culture, the town is also renowned for war junk, as the Ho Chi Minh Trail (see box, page 208) dissected the area. Locals believe that there is a large tiger population in the area and tales are rife of people being eaten by a tiger. However, it would seem that the tigers aren't very forthcoming, as even tiger specialists have difficulty tracking them.

**Toum Lan** is a Katong village 46 km north of Salavan, notable for its longhouse and traditional weaving (ask Mr Bousasone at **Saise Guesthouse** for details). They celebrate the **Lapup** festival, where buffaloes are sacrificed around the full moon in March. During the rainy season it is difficult to access the site. A bus leaves for Toum Lan at 1430 (15,000 kip) and returns at 0700. Accommodation may be possible in the village (10,000 kip).

The **Paseum waterfall** lies 81 km from Salavan on Route 20. It is a beautiful spot but is dominated by the resort that sits on the site. The proprietor has relocated a small ethnic village from their homes to the resort premises in order to make a distinctly dubious 'ethnic museum', where the villagers show tourists their 'traditional way of life'. As tourists approach, the villagers change out of their jeans and into traditional attire before running around, beating drums and playing traditional music.

## Coffee Road

Heading south from Salavan, Route 20 reaches Ban Beng after 26 km (4 km from Tad Lo). Turn south (right if coming from Tad Lo or Pakse) onto Route 23, known as the 'Coffee Road'. From here the road climbs up to the lower slopes of the Bolaven Plateau. From Ban Beng, the road is poor as far as Tha Teng, although there are indications that upgrading is in the pipeline. From Tha Teng to Sekong, however, the road is paved and very scenic. The area is still largely forested with a sparse population concentrated along the road and mainly cultivating coffee. Buses and trucks usually stop at the local market centre of **Ban Tha Teng**.

Towards Sekong the land is more intensively cultivated; there is even some irrigated rice. This is also an area of resettlement with a number of new villages carving out a small area of civilized space in the forest. The large logging yard and saw mill at **Ban Phon**, about 12 km north of Sekong, demonstrates the local economy's dependence on timber.

## Listings Salavan (Saravan) and around

### Tourist information

Tourist office
*T034-211528.*

### Where to stay

**$ Chindavone**
*Near the market, T034-211065.*
There are 2 types of room on offer here. The more expensive ones are beautifully decorated and bamboo-clad twins or doubles, with a/c, en suite bathroom, writing table, TV, and 'chill out' area; the cheaper rooms are basic, with fan and no en suite. Restaurant attached. Recommended.

**$ Thiphaphone**
*Next to **Chindavone** on the market side, T034-211063.*
Clean (but somewhat musty) basic rooms with wooden walls and decent mattresses on the beds. Some rooms have a/c, TV and hot water, others only have fans. Spotless bathrooms; some en suite, some communal.

### Restaurants

Most restaurants in Salavan serve the same range of dishes. Along the road to Pakse near the handicraft centre are a number of barbecue joints offering whatever parts of a pig can be found, including just the fat. By the market towards the road to Pakse are a number of restaurants offering Korean grilled meat, the Lao buffet, *khao piak* and *feu*, among other things. The road into town makes a 90° turn to the left; just beyond is a small road on the right heading towards the Xe Don and Sekong. There are a few decent little restaurants here.

### Entertainment

Salavan lacks any sort of bars but there are plenty of beer garden-style places where the *Beerlao* flows and large groups gather.

## Shopping

The **handicraft centre** near the market has a selection of locally made textiles, baskets and other products. Basketry and traditional textiles can be found in and around the **market**.

## Transport

Most buses coming from Pakse turn off Route 23 and travel to Salavan via Route 20, a new and comparatively fast road that goes past the turning to Tad Lo (see page 236). They often also stop for a while at the small market town of Ban Lao Ngam on the Houei Tapoung (46 km from Salavan, 79 km from Pakse). Some buses, though, take the longer and rougher route via Paksong (Route 23).

## Bus/truck

The bus terminal is 2 km west of the town centre. Salavan is by no means a tourist hub, which means the reliability of buses is dicey at best. Regular buses depart for **Pakse**, 3 hrs; **Sekong**, 2 daily, 98 km, 4 hrs; to **Khong Xedon**, 1 per morning, 76 km, 3½ hrs; to **Lao Ngam** (via **Tad Lo**), 4 daily, 1 hr; to **Ta Oy**, 1 per morning, 84 km, 6 hrs; to **Savannakhet**, early morning 4-5 hrs; to **Tha Teng**, mid-morning; to **Vientiane**, 1 morning service 8 hrs. Trickier destinations to get to from Salavan include **Attapeu** (you have first to go by bus to Sekong, then find a bus to Attapeu) and **Lao Bao** (the best way to get here is via Savannakhet and then along Route 9).

## Sekong (Xekong) and around → *Colour map 3, B4. Phone code: 038.*

*transit stop with little infrastructure and very few tourists*

Sekong (or Xekong) is a new town and capital of the province of the same name. It is located on the Kong River at the eastern edge of the Bolaven Plateau, about 100 km south of Salavan and a similar distance north of Attapeu, and was created comparatively recently from areas formerly part of Attapeu and Salavan. Much of Sekong's population voluntarily moved from Dakchung, close to the Vietnamese border, in the early 1980s, when the government created the new province and established better facilities.

For the moment, anyone travelling between Salavan and Attapeu (but probably not vice versa) must stay overnight here as the first bus from Salavan does not arrive until the last Pakse-bound bus for Attapeu has already departed (see Transport, page 245). As roads improve and journey times drop, however, it may become possible to make this trip without spending a night in Sekong.

Those hoping to chance upon an unknown gem of a town will be disappointed. In theory Sekong ought to be a good base to explore the people and scenery of the Bolaven Plateau but there is simply no tourist infrastructure to make that possible. The only reason to come here, other than out of sheer perversity, is to take a boat down the Xe Kong to the much more attractive town of Attapeu (see Transport, page 245).

The **market**, centred on the bus terminal, has some rather pathetic wild animals, such as giant flying squirrels, for sale – more, in fact, than Salavan which has an infamous reputation in this regard. There is a **wat** behind the market. A reminder of the war is the number of UXO that still litter the area. The **UXO office** ⓘ *near the Ministry of Finance*, has set up a little exhibition and welcomes tourists.

## Towards Attapeu

Travelling by road to Attapeu, about 25 km south of Sekong near the Alak village of Ban Mun Hua Mung, the Xe Nam Noi River crashes over a series of waterfalls: 100 m east of the bridge is **Tad Houakone**, while signposted 4 km downstream is **Tad Phek**; in between are a number of smaller falls. Those tempted to swim in the falls, should dip in the higher pool as the Pa Pao (a nasty piranha-like blowfish) is rumoured to live in the lower pools. A track leads from one to the other; during the dry season you can walk downriver between the two. A tuk-tuk can be hired for a day to see these sights, but you may be better off trying to hire a motorbike from one of the locals.

The road between Sekong and Attapeu, along the eastern edge of the imposing Bolaven Plateau, has finally been completed. The spectacular 120-m-high **Tad Sekatamtok waterfall** tumbles from the Xe Nam Noi about 16 km from the junction (Km 52) with the new road towards Paksong and Pakse. Local sources call this the highest waterfall in the country. Unlike its closest counterpart, Tad Fan, this fall comprises one giant surge burgeoning over the cliff-top, certainly securing its ranking as one of the country's most spectacular.

Along the road to Attapeu are clearings where new villages have been created for the 'upland' Lao. In a bid to resettle these people, the government provided land, aid and resources for building and a space by the banks of the Xe Kong to grow vegetables and other crops to sell.

Eight kilometres from Attapeu is the village of **Ban Ta Hin**, where locals glaze earthenware pots with a mixture made from black sticky rice and a type of local hardwood, *mai seuak*. Archaeologists discovered the same glaze used at Angkor.

## Listings Sekong (Xekong, Muang Lamam) and around

### Tourist information

**Tourist office**
*Just off the main road entering town,*
*T038-211361.*

### Where to stay

**$ Hongkham**
*On the main road, T038-211606.*
In a town short on options, this hotel is a good bet, with large, clean rooms, free internet and an attached restaurant that serves a reasonable breakfast.

### Restaurants

There is not a huge choice here, but there are noodle shops in and around the market and a range of grilled meats on offer.

**$ Khamting Restaurant**
*Next to Phathip.*
Popular spot with tourists and locals.

**$ Phathip Restaurant**
*Opposite the Sekong Hotel.*
Owned by Nang Tu, a Vietnamese woman with considerable culinary expertise. The huge platters are a treat, especially the Vietnamese options. An amazing range of dishes on offer considering the location, plus the menu is written in a variety of languages. The front of the menu boasts all sorts of information about the area.

## Transport

**Boat**
Locals do not advise taking a boat along the Xe Kong River from Sekong to **Attapeu**. The river is dangerous and narrow in parts and the boats are not built for tourist transport. People have died on this stretch.

**Bus/truck**
The bus station is 2.5 km out of town; some also stop on the highway near the hospital. To **Salavan**, twice daily, 98 km, 3-4 hrs; to **Pakse** (via **Paksong**), early morning 4-6 hrs; to **Attapeu**, 1 per morning, 2-3 hrs

---

**wilderness area with ecotourism potential**

---

Attapeu has an altogether different character from the Bolaven Plateau, as the province is predominantly Lao Loum rather than comprised of ethnic minority groups. Attapeu Province was formerly administered under the Lane Xang Kingdom, King Saysetthathirath moved operations in 1571, later dying in the small town. Attapeu suffered greatly between 1964 and 1975, and evidence of this destruction is clear, particularly in the eastern corner along the Ho Chi Minh Trail, where the land is so cratered that some expats refer to it as 'moon-land'.

There are two National Protected Areas (NPAs) in Attapeu: the **Dong Ampham Forest**, and the eastern portion of the **Xe Pian** (see page 229), covering almost 250,000 ha in total. The NPAs are home to numerous animal and plant species. You'll see giant logging trucks growling along the southern highway, transporting enormous trees, but visitor access to the sites is very difficult and tourism infrastructure is incredibly poor, rendering them almost impossible for a quick visit. For information on the province, visit the tourism office in Attapeu town.

**Health warning**  Malaria is quite a serious problem in this Attapeu Province and precautions should be taken to avoid being bitten. Make sure you also take the correct prophylaxis (see page 337).

### Attapeu town
Attapeu is an attractive, leafy town positioned on a bend in the Xe Kong, at the confluence of the Xe Kaman. Once referred to as the Golden Land for its gold deposits, Attapeu prides itself on the old provincial saying that "Attapeu people traded gold for chickens, while Salavan sold their own elephants to buy fire".

According to ML Manich in his *History of Laos*, Attapeu should really be called Itkapü, which translates as 'buffalo dung', due to a misunderstanding between the original population and incoming Lao Loum people. The French, in their turn, transliterated Itkapü as Attapeu. For a pile of dung the town, however, is remarkably picturesque. For those in the ecotourism sector, Attapeu and its surrounding are heralded as the next up-and-coming place in Laos. For now, though, it is relatively free of the tourist hordes.

Apart from an unremarkable monastery, **Wat Luang**, dating from the 1930s, Attapeu is not over-endowed with obvious sights of interest. However, it is a pleasant place to walk around, with traditional wooden Lao houses with verandas and some French buildings. The people are friendly and traffic is limited. Vegetables are grown on the banks of the Xe Kong. Attapeu was fought over by the Pathet Lao and RLG, so it is a surprise that the town remains as attractive as it is. It was the only capital that was never taken by the RLG and is consequently far more attached to the early years of the Lao PDR than the rest of the country; the local tourism authorities seem more intent on providing patriotic propaganda than real tourist information. Despite being one of the poorest provinces in Laos, Attapeu is developing fast due to improved infrastructure and the 2006 border opening at Bo Y (see right), which has increased both trade and traffic to and from Vietnam.

### Nongfa Lake

The real treasure of Attapeu is Nongfa Lake, which was 'discovered' in 1930. The crystal-clear blue lake shares many of its attributes with the beautiful volcanic lake of Yaek Loam in Cambodia. The shores are surrounded by pristine wilderness and mountains and the lake is considered an auspicious site by the local population. Although no conservationists have officially surveyed the lake, the government has done its own survey. Official tourist brochures proclaim, proudly, that the lake is so large that "a shot of an AK47 rifle from one edge of the lake never reaches the other".

Most locals can't pinpoint exactly how to get to the lake, so it's best to organize a trip with the tourism authorities. The lake is within the confines of the Dong Ampham National Protected Area, where the provincial tourism authorities run treks. It can also be reached via 4WD. Although trails exist in the area much of the infrastructure remains undeveloped for tourist visits. It may take several days to find this little gem and the trip must not be undertaken without a well-informed guide.

## East of Attapeu

The sleepy town of **Xaisetha** (Saisettha), which stretches along the north bank of the Xe Kaman, lies 12 km east of Attapeu along Route 18. There is regular transport from the east bank of the Xe Kong across from Attapeu. A further 18 km along Route 18, 30 km in all from Attapeu, is the Alak village of **Pa-am**, which sits directly on the Ho Chi Minh Trail. War memorabilia freaks might be interested in the Soviet surface-to-air missile launcher (still apparently live), abandoned there by the Vietnamese. It will cost you 5000 kip for a peek through the fence surrounding it.

## West of Attapeu

The Lao Loum village of **Ban Mai** lies 50 km southwest of Attapeu. From Ban Mai it is 6 km to Ban Hinlat and, a further 6 km on, is the **Xe Pha waterfall**, which lies on the Se Pian. The falls are around 23 m high and 120 m wide. And another 9 km on from here, on the same river, are the **Xe Pang Lai falls**, the most stunning in the area.

From Ban Mai it is also possible to access the 20-m-wide **Tad Samongphak** on a one-hour boat ride up the Se Pian. You may need a guide between the falls; ask locally, the tourism office is the best starting point. It should be possible to arrange accommodation in either village.

## Listings Attapeu Province

### Tourist information

**Attapeu Provincial Tourism Office**
*In the provincial hall, northwest of the town centre, T036-211056.*
Has large-scale relief maps of the area, good for hiking on or around the Bolaven Plateau, and informative brochures on all there is to do in Attapeu. If intending to explore the countryside hereabouts, it is best to ask here for a guide.

### Where to stay

**$ Dokchampa**
*Main road, T036-211846.*
The most charming option in town, at least from the exterior, this is an old wooden house with a wide variety of rooms, some of which are en suite, so ask to see a few. Has the feel of staying in a home rather than a hotel.

**$ Vhang Namyen Hung Heuang**
*On the river, T030-901 1580.*
A well-kept option with rooms offering good beds, TVs and a/c.

### Restaurants

Attapeu is a small town and finding an open restaurant after 2100 can be difficult. Most places serve the local breakfast speciality *feu* 0700-0800. Just up from **Souksomphone Guesthouse**, towards the wat, are a few places selling good Lao food in pots. There are also noodle shops in the same area and by the boat jetty on the south side of town.

**$ Sabaydy Attapeu Restaurant**
*On the riverbank.*
This is the prettiest place to eat in town with a large outdoor area right on the river making it a great place for a sundowner. Try the grilled fish.

**$ Thi Thi Restaurant**
*Between Wat Luang Muang Mai and*
*the bridge, T031-211054.*
Vietnamese food, with lots of seafood
and standard fried rice.

## Transport

### Bicycle
Basic bikes can be hired from
some guesthouses.

### Boat
An alternative way to get to **Ban Mai** is
to charter a boat to Xe Nam Sai and pick
up a connection from there.

It is possible to travel upriver from
Attapeu to **Sekong**, but it would take
much longer than downriver and be
quite expensive.

### Bus/truck
The main bus station is at the market
3 km northwest of town. It is chaotic
and inefficient. Although there are daily
connections with the main tourist hubs,
departure times are a source of great
debate. To **Pakse**, from the market,
4 times daily, in the morning, 5-6 hrs;
to **Sekong**, afternoon service, 2-3 hrs;
to **Vientiane**, 2 per morning, up to
24 hrs; to **Savannakhet**, early morning,
10-12 hrs. To get to **Salavan** you will
have to transfer at Tha Teng. There are
3 daily buses to **Ban Mai**, 0800, 1200
and 1400 daily, 1 hr.

# Islands of
the south

★This area, locally known as Siphandon, 'The 4000 Islands', is an idyllic picture-perfect ending to any trip to Laos. The three main islands offer something for all tourists: the larger Don Khong is great for exploring traditional Lao rural life; Don Deth is a backpacker haven and perfect if you want to while away the days with a good book in a hammock; and Don Khone is better for those wanting to take in some tourist sites such as the Li Phi falls or colonial ruins. These are just three of the many islands littered across the Mekong right at the southern tip of Laos near the border with Cambodia. Half of the islands are submerged when the Mekong is in flood. Just before the river enters Cambodia it divides into countless channels. The distance between the most westerly and easterly streams is 14 km – the greatest width of the river in its whole 4200-km course. The river's volume is swelled by the Kong, San Srepok and Krieng tributaries, which join just upstream from here. Pakha, or freshwater dolphins, can sometimes be spotted in this area between December and May, when they come upstream to give birth to their young, but they are increasingly endangered. *Phone code: 031. Colour map 3, C2/3.*

## Essential Islands of the south

### Finding your feet

The easiest way to get to all three major Siphandon islands (Don Khong, Don Deth and Don Khone) from Pakse is by private minivan, arranged by tour operators in Pakse. The most luxurious way is aboard the **Vat Pho**, www.vatphou.com, a boutique riverborne hotel that does a three-day/two-night cruise from Pakse to Champasak and Wat Phou to Don Khong returning to Pakse.

Using public transport, take a bus or *songthaew* from Pakse to Ban Hat Xai Khoune from where ferries make the short crossing to Don Khong; or further south, at Ban Nakasang, where boats shuffle tourists to Don Deth and Don Khone. Once on the islands, most guesthouses can help arrange private boats for exploring. It's possible to walk between Don Deth and Don Khone across the bridge, for which there is a small charge (also used as a ticket for Li Phi Falls). The islands are small and can be easily navigated by foot on by bicycle.

### When to go

The best time to visit the area is during the dry season (November to March), when the waters recede and the islands can be clearly seen. This is also the best time to spot the rare freshwater dolphins as they come up the river to breed.

### Time required

The islands are small and the main sights could be seen within a day or two, but it's best to allow a few days to really relax and enjoy the pace of island life.

### Route 13 to Ban Hat Xai Khoune

The bus journey south from Pakse to Ban Hat Xai Khoune on Route 13 is 120 km. The trip is worthwhile for the contrast it offers to conditions in northeastern Thailand, just 20 km or so west. Much of the area is still forested (large quantities of Lao timber are trucked to Thailand via Chongmek, west of Pakse and villages are intermittent even on this road, the national artery for north–south communications. Paddy fields sometimes appear to be fighting a losing battle against the encroaching forest and most houses are roofed in thatch rather than zinc. At **Ban Hat Xai Khoune** boats wait to transport passengers across the Mekong to Don Khong and Muang Khong (see below). Further along, at Ban Nakasang, boats shuffle tourists to Don Deth and Don Khone.

### Don Khong
#### a gentle pace of life and pleasant countryside

Don Khong is the largest of the Mekong islands at 16 km long and 8 km wide. It's a tremendous place to relax or explore by bicycle. Visitors might be surprised by the smooth asphalt roads, electricity and general standard of amenities that exist on the island but two words explain it all – Khamtai Siphandone – Laos' former president, who has a residence on the island. The island was also electrified about five years before the surrounding mainland areas and it is not unusual to see heavily armed personnel cruising around the place.

### Muang Khong

Don Khong's 'capital' is Muang Khong, a small former French settlement.

'Muang' means city but, although Muang Khong is the district's main settlement, it feels more like a village than a town, with only a few thousand inhabitants. Pigs and chickens scrabble for food under the houses and just 50 m inland the houses give way to paddy fields.

There are two wats in the town. **Wat Kan Khong**, also known as Wat Phuang Kaew, is visible from the jetty: a large gold Buddha in the *mudra* of subduing Mara garishly overlooks the Mekong. Much more attractive is **Wat Chom Thong** at the upstream extremity of the village, which may date from the early 19th century but which was much extended during the colonial period. The unusual Khmer-influenced *sim* may

Tip...
There are no banks on the islands but some guesthouses change money. Mr Phao of **Phao's Riverview** on Don Deth will take you by boat to Ban Khinak, north of Ban Nakasang, where there is a Visa and MasterCard ATM. There are internet cafés on Don Deth and Don Khone and many restaurants and guesthouses have Wi-Fi. If you need to make an international call, it's cheapest to call via the net. Guesthouses may let you call from their mobiles, at US$4 or more a minute.

be gently decaying but it is doing so with style, and the wat compound, with its carefully tended plants and elegant buildings, is a peaceful and relaxing place. The *naga* heads on the roof of the main *sim* are craftily designed to channel water, which issues from their mouths. The old *sim* to the left of the main entrance is also notable, although it is usually kept locked because of its poor condition.

For early risers the **morning market** in Muang Khong is also worthwhile – if only to see the fish before they are sold to the restaurants here and consigned to the cooking pot. Note that the market only really operates between 0530 and 0730. If you are getting up for the market, it is worth setting the alarm clock even earlier to get onto the banks of the Mekong before 0600, when the sun rises over the hills to the east, picking out the silhouettes of fishermen in their canoes.

All of the guesthouses can arrange bicycle hire. Some places hire motorbikes too. There is a **Lao Agriculture Promotion** bank in Muang Khong; hours are erratic. **Pon's Hotel** and **Pon's Arena Khong Hotel** advance cash against Visa and Mastercard for a fee.

## Exploring the island

Most people come to Muang Khong as a base for visiting the **Li Phi** and **Khong Phapheng Falls** (see page 259) in the far south of Laos. However, these trips, alongside dolphin-watching trips are much easier to arrange from Don Deth or Don Khone. But the island is a destination in itself, and offers a great insight into Lao rural life without all the hustle and bustle found in more built-up areas. To a certain extent – apart from electricity, a sprinkling of cars and a couple of internet terminals – time stands still in Dong Khong.

The island is worth exploring by bicycle and deserves more time than most visitors give it. The coastal area is flat (though the interior is hilly) and the roads are quiet and the villages and countryside offer a glimpse of traditional Laos. Most people take the southern 'loop' around the island, via **Ban Muang Saen Nua**, a distance of about

25 km (two to three hours by bike). The villages south of Ban Muang Saen Nua are wonderfully picturesque with buffalos grazing in the field and farmers tending to their rice crops. Unlike in other parts of Laos the residents here are fiercely protective of their forests and illegal logging incurs very severe penalties.

About 6 km north of Ban Muang Saen Nua is a hilltop wat which is arguably Don Khong's main claim to national fame. **Wat Phou Khao Kaew** (Glass Hill Monastery)

# Mekong islands

is built on the spot where an entrance leads down to the underground lair of the *nagas*, known as **Muang Nak**. This underground town lies beneath the waters of the Mekong, with several tunnels leading to the surface – another is at That Luang in Vientiane. Lao legend has it that the *nagas* will come to the surface to protect the Lao whenever the country is in danger. Some people believe that the Thais tricked the Lao to build *thats* over the holes to prevent the *nagas* coming to their rescue – the hole at Wat Phou Khao Kaew is covered.

**Tham Phou Khiaw** is tucked away among the forests of the **Green Mountain** in the centre of the island. It's a small cave, containing earthenware pots. Buddha images and other relics and offerings litter the site. Every Lao New Year (April) townsfolk climb up to the cave to bathe the images. Although it's only 15 minutes' walk from the road, finding the cave is not particularly straightforward except during Lao New Year when it is possible to follow the crowds. Head 1.5 km north from Muang Khong on the road until you come to a banana plantation, with a couple of wooden houses. Take the pathway just before the houses through the banana plantation and at the top; just to the left, is a small gateway through the fence and a fairly well-defined path. Head up and along this path and, after 300 m or so, there is a rocky clearing. The path continues from the top right corner of the clearing for a further 200 m to a rocky mound that rolls up and to the left. Walk across the mound for about 20 m, until it levels out, and then head back to the forest. Keeping the rock immediately to your right, continue round and after 40 m there are two upturned tree trunks marking the entrance to the cave.

On the northern tip of the island is a sandy beach, though swimming is generally not advised due to parasites in the water and potentially strong currents. Word on the ground is that Lao's former President Siphandone is building a resort here. In nearby **Ban Houa Khong**, approximately 13 km north of Muang Khong, is the former president's modest abode set in traditional Lao style.

## Listings Don Khong *map p252*

### Where to stay

Most guesthouses now have Wi-Fi.

**$$$-$$ Pon Arena Hotel**
*40 m north of the main street, T020-221 8166, www.ponarenahotel.com.*
There are 2 distinct properties, one on the river and another set in a garden across the road. The less expensive garden rooms may lack the Mekong view, but they are larger and the garden view is pleasant. All rooms are very tastefully decorated with high ceilings. Some rooms have tiny balconies. Wi-Fi throughout. Breakfast served on the upstairs veranda.

**$$$-$ Senesothxeune Hotel**
*100 m to the left of the main ferry point, T030-526 0577, www.ssxhotel.com.*
Tastefully designed, modern interpretation of colonial Lao architecture. Beautiful fittings, including carved wooden fish above each entrance and brass chandeliers. Splurge a little for the superior room with private balcony. The restaurant menu is mainly

confined to Asian dishes. The hotel is run by a very friendly team. Recommended.

## $ Pon's River Guesthouse
*T031-214037.*
Same owner as **Pon Arena Hotel**. The large, spotless a/c rooms are very good value, with hot showers, mosquito nets and comfortable beds. Mr Pon, who speaks French and English, is very helpful and well-informed. He can arrange motorbike and bike rental, as well as trips to the Cambodian border, to Don Deth and Don Khon and back to Pakse. The restaurant is still the most popular on the island.

## $ Rattana
*Next to the boat landing.*
While the service here is very slack, the upstairs rooms do represent very good value with the cheapest river views in town. Bathrooms have tiny shower areas, but are otherwise adequate. A good budget option, but for hospitality and advice, head to **Pon's**.

## $ Villa Khang Kong
*Set back from the main road, near the ferry point, T031-213539.*
Fantastic traditional Lao wooden building recently painted in black and white. A great veranda and communal lounging area. Spacious clean rooms, with or without a/c. No river views.

## Restaurants

In the low season most restaurants will only be able to fulfil about half of the menu options and some will be devoid of other diners. Local fish with coconut milk cooked in banana leaves, *mok pa*, is truly a divine local speciality and makes a trip to the islands worthwhile in itself – order in advance.

## $$ Pon's Arena
*See Where to stay.*
Serves a broadly similar menu to everywhere else in town but adds a more refined setting, dim lighting and cheesy background music.

## $ Souksan Chinese Restaurant
*Next to Pon's, on stilts over the river.*
Attractive place with a stunning, unobscured view of the river. Good local fish, tasty honeyed chicken and basil pork with chilli.

## $ Pon's Hotel and Restaurant
*See Where to stay.*
Good atmosphere and busy when everywhere else is dead. Excellent food, try the chicken curry or the fish soup. The *mok pa* here is excellent, order 2 hrs in advance. Very popular. Service can be rather haphazard when busy.

## Festivals

**Dec** A 5-day **Boat Racing festival** takes place early in the month, on the river opposite Muang Khong. It coincides with **National Day** on 2 Dec and is accompanied by a great deal of celebration, feasting and drinking.

## What to do

All the guesthouses in Don Khong run tours to Don Deth and Don Khone, taking in the Phaphaeng Falls and dolphin watching.

## Transport

### Boat
**Pon's Hotel** (reliable and recommended) and others can arrange boats to **Don Deth** or **Don Khone**. There are also several boatmen on the

riverfront who are more than happy to take people for the right price.

**Bus/truck**
*Songthaew* and buses head to **Pakse** at 0630, 0700, 0800, 0830, 3-4 hrs. Or cross to Ban Hat Xai Khoune and then try for transport south.

The minibus service back to **Pakse** can be organized by Mr Pon, 2 hrs.

Drop-off at Ban Muang for **Champasak** possible. Guesthouses also arrange transport to the Cambodian border and beyond to **Siem Reap**, to **Phnom Penh**, **Kratie** and **Stung Treng**.

**Motorbike and bicycle**
Many of the guesthouses including **Pon's** and **Senesothxene** offer motorbikes and bicycles.

## Don Deth, Don Khone and around
### beautiful and relaxed backpacker hub

The islands of Don Khone and Don Deth are the pot of gold at the end of the rainbow for most travellers who head to the southern tip of Laos, and it's not hard to see why. After the transport headaches around the Bolaven Plateau and the architectural wonder of Wat Phou, the bamboo huts that stretch along the banks of these two staggeringly beautiful islands are filled with contented travellers in no rush to move on. Don Deth is more of a backpacker haven, while Don Khone has been able to retain a more authentically Lao charm. Travelling by boat in this area is very picturesque: the islands are covered in coconut palms, flame trees, stands of bamboo, kapok trees and hardwoods; the river is riddled with eddies and rapids and it demands a skilled helmsman to negotiate them. In the distance, a few kilometres to the south, are the Khong Hai Mountains, which dominate the skyline and delineate the frontier between Laos and Cambodia.

### Ban Nakasang
Ban Nakasang, the jumping-off point for Don Khone and Don Deth, is not the most pleasant of Lao towns. However, it has a thriving market, where most of the islanders stock up on their goods, so it's worth having a look around before you head off to the islands, particularly if you need to pick up supplies.

### Don Deth
This island has really woken up to tourism and the riverbank is peppered with cheap-as-chips bamboo huts and restaurants geared to accommodate the growing wave of backpacker travellers that floods south to stop and recoup in this idyllic setting. A good book, hammock and icy beverage are the orders of the day here, but those with a bit more energy should explore the truly stunning surroundings. It's a great location for watching sunrises and sunsets, for walking through shady palms and frangipani trees and for swimming off the beaches, which attract the hordes in the dry season. Away from the picturesque waterfront, the centre of the island comprises rice paddies and farms; you should take care not to harm crops when exploring the island.

The national tourism authorities have been coordinating with locals to ensure that the beautiful island doesn't become 'Vang Vieng-ified', so you'll find no *Friends* DVDs here, although 'happy' shakes have started to appear. The islands got electricity in 2009 although not everyone has signed up to the 24-hour connection; there are no cars (except for the odd truck and tourist open-sided buses) and few other modern conveniences. Internet has made its way to the island, however, and it's still possible to get mobile phone coverage. Most guesthouses run tours to the falls/dolphins. The dwindling population of dolphins appears between December and May. If you do take a boat out make sure you keep your distance from them.

A few entrepreneurial types are starting to promote adventure tourism here. Kayaking and rafting trips can be organized. Several guesthouses also have tubes

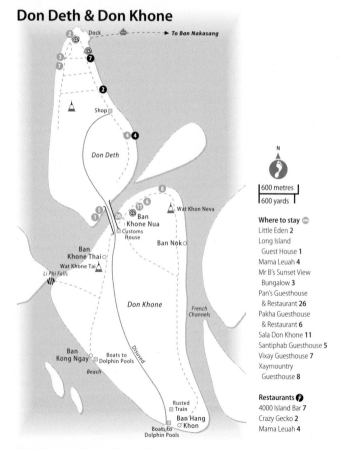

# Don Deth & Don Khone

600 metres
600 yards

**Where to stay**
Little Eden 2
Long Island
 Guest House 1
Mama Leuah 4
Mr B's Sunset View
 Bungalow 3
Pan's Guesthouse
 & Restaurant 26
Pakha Guesthouse
 & Restaurant 6
Sala Don Khone 11
Santiphab Guesthouse 5
Vixay Guesthouse 7
Xaymountry
 Guesthouse 8

**Restaurants**
4000 Island Bar 7
Crazy Gecko 2
Mama Leuah 4

## BACKGROUND
## Don Deth, Don Khone and around

For those who have travelled on the lazy upper reaches of the Mekong, huge roaring waterfalls might seem rather out of character. But here, near the Cambodian border, the geology changes and the river is punctuated by rapids and the Khone Falls. The name Khone is used loosely and there are in fact two impressive cascades in the area: the Li Phi (or Somphamit) Falls and Khong Phapheng Falls – the latter are the largest in Southeast Asia and reputedly the widest in the world. Francis Garnier was impressed when he ascended the Khone cataract in 1860, his boatmen hauling their vessels "through a labyrinth of rocks, submerged trees, and prostrate trunks still clinging to earth by their many roots".

The French envisaged Don Deth and Don Khone as strategic transit points in their grandiose masterplan to create a major Mekong highway from China. In the late 19th century, ports were built at the southern end of Don Khone and at the northern end of Don Deth and a narrow-gauge railway line was constructed across Don Khone in 1897 as an important bypass around the rapids for French cargo boats sailing upriver from Phnom Penh. In 1920, the French built a bridge across to Don Deth and extended the railway line to Don Deth port. This 5-km stretch of railway has the unique distinction of being the only line the French ever built in Laos. Although the lucrative Chinese supply line was never properly realised, the route remained operational until 1940.

A colonial-style customs house still stands in the shadow of the impressive railway bridge on Don Khone. On the southern side of the island lie the rusted corpses of the old locomotive and boiler car. Before pulling into Ban Khone Nua, the main settlement on Don Khone, Don Deth's original 'port' is on the right, with what remains of its steel rail jetty.

for rent. The river's current here is probably the strongest in all of Laos, so it is definitely inadvisable to go tubing in the wet season and probably not a good idea at any other time. It is also inadvisable to go by yourself; there is a huge set of falls at the bottom of Laos. Swimming, visiting the falls and other activities all need to be undertaken with the utmost caution as several tourists have drowned here.

### Don Khone and Li Phi Falls
From the railway bridge, follow the southwest path through **Ban Khone Thai** and then wind through the paddy fields for 1.7 km (20 minutes' walk) to **Li Phi Falls** ⓘ *aka Somphamit or Khone Yai falls, 10,000 kip entry fee, paid at the bridge.* These are a succession of raging rapids, crashing through a narrow rocky gorge. In the wet season, when the rice is green, the area is beautiful; in the dry season, it is scorching. From the main vantage point on a jagged, rocky outcrop, the falls aren't that impressive, as a large stretch of them are obscured. 'Phi' means ghost, a reference, it is believed, to the bodies that floated down the river from the north during the war.

## ON THE ROAD

## The Mekong: mother river of Southeast Asia

The Mekong River forms the heart and soul of mainland Southeast Asia, a sinuous thread that binds Vietnam, Cambodia and Laos geographically, historically, culturally and economically.

Its source in eastern Tibet was only pinpointed in 1995. From here the giant river plies 4500 km through six countries, cutting through almost the entire length of Laos, dissecting Cambodia, and plunging into Vietnam's Mekong Delta before emptying into the South China Sea. The river is the 12th longest river in the world and is the 10th largest by volume of water dispersed into the ocean.

French explorer Francis Garnier commented that: "no other river, over such a length, has a more singular or remarkable character". The Mekong has indeed woven itself into the cultural fabric of the region and shaped its history, from the ancient Funan settlement in the Mekong Delta, through to the Khmer Empire, which established its capital at Angkor and relied on the river for transport and agriculture. After several expeditions the French, in the mid-19th century, developed grandiose plans to transform the Mekong into a river highway from China. (The plans were thwarted upon discovering that the Mekong could not be traversed.) The river later played an integral role in the Vietnam War for the transportation of Viet Cong supplies.

The river has been a major purveyor of culture, ushering in various religions, arts and customs and folklore, including colourful boat races and annual water festivals, which celebrate the Mekong and its importance to agriculture. Nor is the river free from superstition or strange phenomena. In Laos

It's best to visit Li Phi around June or July, when all the fishermen are putting out their bamboo fish traps. Every year Cambodia's Tonlé Sap lake reverses its flow sending millions of fish up the Mekong into Laos. During this time, each fish trap can catch 1000-2000 kg of fish in a day. In theory, enough fish are caught in these two short months to feed half the population of Laos, although most of the catch is exported to Thailand.

### Dolphin spotting

The Mekong, south of Don Khone, is one of the few places in the world where it is possible to see freshwater dolphins. They can be spotted from December to May, from the French pier at the end of the island, not far from the village of **Ban Hang Khon**. The walk across Don Khone from the railway bridge is some 4 km and bicycles can be hired. (A much better bicycle route is to head north round the tip and down to Hang Khon, 45 minutes; the disused railway bridge is not a comfortable ride for bikes as it's rocky.) However the dolphins reside in deep-water pools and catching a glimpse of them is more likely if you're in a boat (from **Ban Kong Ngay** or **Ban Hang Khon**.

thousands of people gather each year to witness *naga* fireballs rising from the river's surface.

Today, the Mekong is instrumental in the region's future prosperity, with more than 60 million people in Southeast Asia dependent on the river and its tributaries for their economic and physical survival. Agriculture, particularly the farming of rice, relies on the river's annual flood-drought cycle. During the monsoon, the river swells to around 30 times its original size, depositing rich fertilizing sediments along the floodplains and riverbanks.

Fish are an important part of the Lao diet, constituting around 80% of many people's protein requirement. The river is home to between 770 and 1300 species of freshwater fish, including the world's largest, a giant 300 kg catfish (the size of a grizzly bear). It also shelters the endangered Irrawaddy dolphin.

However, it is unclear how much longer the Mekong can be relied on to support millions of Vietnamese, Cambodian and Lao people. In the last decade, more than 100 large dam proposals have been tabled for the Mekong Basin, while China, the source of up to 45% of the lower Mekong's water, has embarked on a massive programme for the construction of eight new dams. Two of these have been completed and are already having a detrimental effect, altering the river's natural ebb and flow. Lao also has major dams planned including one mainstream one in the Siphandon region. Whether it goes ahead or not is undecided as opposition to the project is massive. Chainarong Setthachua, director of South East Asia Rivers Network has said that: "Not only is the water the lowest in its history, it is also fluctuating; sometimes up, sometimes down. This comes from dam operations in China." The Mekong River Commission (MRC) agrees, pointing out that, in places, the river has reached rock-bottom levels.

## Khong Phapheng Falls

ⓘ *Ban Thatko, 10,000 kip entry fee for foreigners. There are a number of food and drinks stalls. Guesthouses on Don Deth and Don Khone organize trips to the falls and will usually be booked in conjunction with a trip to see the dolphins (this will cost extra). Boats can no longer go direct to the falls, so most tours will include a tuk-tuk ride from Ban Nakasang.*

About 36 km south of Ban Hat Xai Khoune at Ban Thatko, a road branches off Route 13 towards Khong Phapheng Falls, which roar around the eastern shore of the Mekong for 13 km. One fork of the road leads to a vantage point, where a large wooden structure on stilts has a fantastic head-on view of the falls. When you see the huge volume of white water boiling and surging over the jagged rocks below, it is hard to imagine that there is another 10 km width of river running through the other channels. A perilous path leads down from the viewpoint to the edge of the water. Be careful here. Unsurprisingly, the river is impassable at this juncture, as an 1860s French expedition led by adventurers Doudart de Lagrée and Francis Garnier discovered. Another road leads down to the bank of the Mekong, 200 m away, just above the lip of the falls; at this deceptively tranquil spot, the river is gathering momentum before it plunges over the edge. It was said that a tongue of rock once extended from the lip of the falls, and the noise of Khong Phapheng – literally 'the voice of the Mekong' – crashing over this outcrop could be heard many miles away. The rock apparently broke off during a flood surge but the cascades still make enough noise to justify their name.

## Listings Don Deth, Don Khone and around *maps p252 and p256*

### Tourist information

The **Provincial Tourism Office** in Pakse (see page 217) is responsible for the islands. While on the islands, you will need to ask your guesthouse owner or one of the travel operators.

### Where to stay

#### Don Deth
#### Sunset side

**$$-$ Little Eden**
*Hua Det, T020-7773 9045, www. littleedenguesthouse-dondet.com.*
Very close to the island tip and a small hike from the main drop-off dock, this place offers the best view of the stunning sunsets. Miss Noy and her husband Mathieu offer 16 excellent rooms which are the island's most upmarket lodgings. The restaurant, serving top-notch Asian and European dishes, is in a prime position with awesome views.

**$ Mr B's Sunset View Bungalow**
*Near the northern tip, T020-5418 1171.*
The bungalows and grounds themselves are a bit lacklustre, however the views are great and the staff are helpful.

**$ Vixay Guest House**
*A short walk from Mr B's, T020-7645 1331.*
The extremely affable Mr Vixay offers small bungalows and a reasonable restaurant with great views. The cheaper riverside options come with

squat toilets and cold showers, while the more expensive western en suites are set slightly back from the view. The attached restaurant serves great food. Bike hire. Recommended.

#### Sunrise side

**$ Long Island Guest House**
*Next to Santiphab, T020-5567 9470.*
Run by the friendly Mr Kham, a local English teacher who gives classes on site. 4 simple, clean rattan bungalows with hot water showers line the river. Reached via a quaint path linking it with the paddy fields, lit by hanging bulbs at night. A restaurant is being built, with plans for Lao cooking lessons. Wi-Fi.

**$ Mama Leuah**
*A few properties along from Mr Tho, T020-5907 8792, www.mamaleuah-dondet.com.*
Ultra basic bungalows that prove ever popular for 3 key reasons: the wonderful, river front garden setting; the ultra-accommodating hosts, Lutz (German) and Pheng (Lao); and the best kitchen on the island. All bungalows have squat toilets, some shared, some private. Number 7 at the end is the pick of the bunch. Recommended for those seeking ambience, not creature comforts.

**$ Mr Phao's Riverview**
*On the riverfront, T020-5656 9651.*
7 relatively new wooden bungalows with lovely carved furniture offering lodgings

a notch above the nearby options. Some rooms have showers. Mr Phao is one of the friendliest folk on the island and super helpful. If he has time he will take guests across to opposite Aan island where there is a wat.

### $ Santiphab Guesthouse
*Far end of the island next to the bridge, T020-5461 4231, www. santiphab-don-det.com.*
Alongside the older rattan bungalows, some newer half-wood bungalows have been added. Idyllic setting, flanked by the Mekong on one side and rice paddies on the other. Good for those who want seclusion but also quick access to Don Khone. Very cheap restaurant serves tasty fare including a good peppery fried vegetables with chicken and great iced coffee. A friendly, timeless place with plenty of cute cats milling around. Small general store next door.

## Don Khone

### $$$-$$ Sala Don Khone
*T030-525 6390, www.salalao.com.*
Various options are available here, including rooms in the former French hospital built in 1927, each with beautiful tiling and 4 poster beds. In addition, traditional Luang Prabang-style houses have been built in the grounds, with 8 twin rooms, all with en suite hot shower and toilet. On the river itself a series of rafts provide floating rooms, each with plenty of small touches that make them special. Also has a wonderful deck and a fine pool.

### $$-$ Pan's Guesthouse
*About 250 m from the bridge, T030-534 6939.*
These wooden bungalows are exceptionally good value for money.

The 6 riverside bungalows with hot water, fan and comfy mattresses are simple but comfortable and ultra clean. The cushioned seating on the balconies is a real plus. The owner is one of the most helpful hosts in Siphandon. Highly recommended for those on a limited budget. Breakfast included.

### $ Pakha Guesthouse
*20 m past Auberge, T020-5584 7522.*
The main track splits this guesthouse in 2, with half the rooms directly on the river and the remainder facing paddy fields to the rear. River rooms are fan only and are joined by a long, peaceful balcony, meaning this is a better spot for meeting fellow travellers than seeking privacy. The paddy facing rooms are larger and come with a/c. The restaurant does a good papaya salad and roasted fish in salt.

### $ Xaymountry Guesthouse
*Near the old school, no phone.*
This huge, beautiful stilt house is home to a range of budget rooms; those at the rear are rather small, but the recently refurbished front rooms offer good value. The veranda area is a peaceful spot for breakfast and the owner is very welcoming.

## Restaurants

### Ban Nakasang
2 small thatched beachside restaurants serve good chicken *feu*. In the rainy season they move further up the bank. There are also food and drinks stalls on the right as you get off the boat.

### Don Deth
Most people choose to eat at their guesthouses; most of which all have pretty much the same menu, but there are now a few places worth seeking out.

### $$-$ Little Eden
*See Where to stay.*

A large menu with some good Western and Lao dishes thanks to the Belgian/Lao couple who own it. Superb views.

### $ 4000 Island Bar
*T020-7793 5802, www.4000islandbar.com.*

This is a big hit with the backpacker set as much for the views as for the great Indian food. Also serves Western fodder.

### $ Crazy Gecko
*A few mins past the main strip.*

An intimate little over-water eatery with lots of funky decorative touches. Serves a simple menu of Lao and Western dishes. Decent wine by the glass. Recommended.

### $ Mama Leuah
*See Where to stay.*

Perhaps the best kitchen on the island, the chef, Lutz, is rightly proud of his cuisine which draws rave reviews. Lutz learned his trade in Thailand, so expect good green and red curries along with a solid pad Thai. The muesli is also a hit as are his German classics. Vegetarians will be pleased to see a great pumpkin burger on the menu.

### Don Khone

### $$ Auberge Sala Don Khone
*See Where to stay.*

There's a beautiful view from the restaurant and some good options on the menu.

### $ Pakha Guesthouse
*See Where to stay.*

Ms Noy's steamed fish makes this a good lunch pit stop. No river views, but she will serve food on one of the river bungalow balconies when they're not too busy.

### $ Pan's Restaurant
*See Where to stay.*

Across from the guesthouse, this is a fantastic, cheap option serving up brilliant home-made meals. The fish here is outstanding.

## Shopping

### Don Deth

There isn't much to buy here. A small grocery store just down from the port has a few essential items and snacks but is not very well stocked. If you're in desperate need of any items, you are better off making a quick trip to Ban Nakasang to pick up things from the market there. Most guesthouse owners go to Ban Nakasang on an almost daily basis and will usually agree to buy things for you if you pay them 5000 kip or so.

## What to do

### Don Khone and around
### Boat trips

Boats can be hired for day trips to the islands, including one where the rice pots are made. Ask at **Mr Pan's**.

### Dolphin watching

It is possible to hire a boat to try and spot the dolphins from Kong Ngay, 90,000 kip, maximum 3 people to a boat. Further south, at Ban Hang Khon, it's slightly less expensive – maximum 3 people. Plenty of outfits offer Phapheng tours and dolphin watching. Costs reduce the larger the group of people.

### Fishing and kayaking

Most tour operators are able to arrange a day out fishing – prices start from around 75,000 kip per person (4 people). 2-hr sunset boat tours are also on offer.

## Swimming

There is a sandy beach on Don Khone where many travellers like to take a dip. However, in the wet season this can be particularly dangerous as there is a nasty undercurrent and tourists have drowned here, so be careful. The other thing to consider when bathing is the possibility of picking up the parasite called schistosomiasis, also known as bilharzia.

### Transport

Ban Nakasang
**Boat**
To **Don Deth** and **Don Khone**, 15-20 mins. To **Don Khong**, 2 hrs. Between **Don Khone** and **Don Deth** a few mins.

**Bus/songthaew**
Decent buses depart from Ban Nakasang's market, hourly 0600-1000 daily, northbound for **Pakse**; some continue onwards to **Vientiane**; get off at **Ban Hat Xai Khoune** for the crossing to **Don Khong**. Xplore-Asia, www.explore-asia.com, runs tourist buses to **Pakse**; the same minivan will stop at **Ban Muang** for **Champasak**.

Agencies can also arrange bus tickets for destinations further afield such as **Ubon Ratchathani** or **Bangkok**.

**To Cambodia** To get to **Don Kralor** (on the Cambodian border) most guesthouses can organize the trip in a minivan. Cambodian visas are available on the border and Lao visas are now also available. To **Don Kralor**, the largest town on the other side of the Cambodian border, 2 hrs. Tickets can also be bought to more distant destinations in Cambodia. For the Cambodia border, see box, above.

Don Deth, Don Khone and around
**Boat**
For scheduled boat transport, see page 254. Almost every guesthouse can arrange tours, transport and tickets. Tour operators offer tickets for transport out of Siphandon down to Cambodia or back up to other parts of Laos.

To **Ban Nakasang** the 1st boat is the market boat, leaving at 0630.

There are 2 ways to get to **Don Khong** from Ban Nakasang, either by boat, 2 hrs, or by bus. Although it's slower and more expensive, the boat trip is one of the loveliest in Laos.

# Background
# Laos

# History

Scholars of Lao history, before they even begin, need to decide whether they are writing a history of Laos; a history of the Lao ethnic group; or histories of the various kingdoms and principalities that have, through time, been encompassed by the present boundaries of the Lao People's Democratic Republic. Historians have tended to confront this problem in different ways without, often, acknowledging on what basis their 'history' is built. It is common to see 1365, the date of the foundation of the kingdom of Lane Xang, as marking the beginning of Lao history. But, as Martin Stuart-Fox points out, prior to Lane Xang the principality of Muang Swa, occupying the same geographical space, was headed by a Lao. The following account provides a brief overview of the histories of those peoples who have occupied what is now the territory of the Lao PDR.

Archaeological and historical evidence indicates that most Lao originally migrated south from China. This was followed by an influx of ideas and culture from the Indian subcontinent via Myanmar (Burma), Thailand and Cambodia – something which is reflected in the state religion, Theravada Buddhism.

Being surrounded by large, powerful neighbours, Laos has been repeatedly invaded over the centuries by the Thais (or Siamese) and the Vietnamese – who both thought of Laos as their buffer zone and backyard. They too have both left their mark on Lao culture. In recent history, Laos has been influenced by the French during the colonial era, the Japanese during the Second World War, the Americans during the Indochinese wars and, between 1975 and the early 1990s, by Marxism-Leninism.

It is also worth noting, in introduction, that historians and regimes have axes to grind. The French were anxious to justify their annexation of Laos and so used dubious Vietnamese documents to provide a legal gloss to their actions. Western historians, lumbered with the baggage of Western historiography, ignored indigenous histories. And the Lao People's Revolutionary Party uses history for its own ends too. The official three volume *History of Laos* is being written by Party-approved history hacks. The third volume (chronologically speaking) was published in 1989 and, working back in time, the first and second thereafter. As Martin Stuart-Fox remarks in his *A History of Laos*, "the communist regime is as anxious as was the previous Royal Lao government [pre-1975] to establish that Laos has a long and glorious past and that a continuity exists between the past and the present Lao state". In other words, Laos has not one history, but many. Take your pick.

## First kingdom of Laos
Myth, archaeology and history all point to a number of early feudal Lao kingdoms in what is now South China and North Vietnam. External pressures from the Mongols under Kublai Khan and the Han Chinese forced the Tai tribes to migrate south into what had been part of the Khmer Empire. The mountains to the north and east served as a cultural barrier to Vietnam and China, leaving the Lao exposed to influences from India and the West. There are no documentary

records of early Lao history (the first date in the Lao chronicles to which historians attach any real veracity is 1271), although it seems probable that parts of present-day Laos were annexed by Lannathai (Chiang Mai) in the 11th century and by the Khmer Empire during the 12th century. But neither of these states held sway over the entire area of Laos. Xieng Khouang, for example, was probably never under Khmer domination. This was followed by strong Siamese influence over the cities of Luang Prabang and Vientiane under the Siamese Sukhothai Dynasty. Laos (the country) in effect did not exist, although the Laos (the people) certainly did.

The downfall of Sukhothai in 1345 and its submission to the new Siamese Dynasty at Ayutthaya (founded in 1349) was the catalyst for the foundation of what is commonly regarded as the first truly independent Lao Kingdom – although there were semi-independent Lao *muang* (city states, sometimes transliterated as *meuang*) existing prior to that date.

### Fa Ngum and Lane Xang

The kingdom of Lane Xang (Lan Chang) emerged in 1353 under Fa Ngum, a Lao prince who had grown up in the Khmer court of Angkor. Fa Ngum is clearly an important man – that is, if the amount of space devoted to his exploits in the

## ON THE ROAD
### Kings of Lane Xang

| | |
|---|---|
| Fa Ngum | 1353-1373 |
| Samsenthai | 1373-1416 |
| Lan Kamdaeng | 1417-1428 |
| Phommathat | 1428-1429 |
| Mun Sai | 1429-1430 |
| Fa Khai | 1430-1433 |
| Khong Kham | 1433-1434 |
| Yukhon | 1434-1435 |
| Kham Keut | 1435-1441 |
| Chaiyachakkapat-Phaenphaeo (aka Sao Tiakaphat) | 1441-1478 |
| Suvarna Banlang (aka Theng Kham) | 1478-1485 |
| Lahsaenthai Puvanart | 1485-1495 |
| Sompou | 1497-1500 |
| Visunarat | 1500-1520 |
| Pothisarath | 1520-1548 |
| Setthathira | 1548-1571 |
| Saensurin | 1572-1574 |
| Mahaupahat (under Burmese control) | 1574-1580 |
| Saensurin | 1580-1582 |
| Nakhon Noi (under Burmese control) | 1582-1583 |
| Interregnum | 1583-1591 |
| Nokeo Koumone | 1591-1596 |
| Thammikarath | 1596-1622 |
| Upanyuvarat | 1622-1623 |
| Pothisarat | 1623-1627 |
| Mon Keo | 1627 |
| Unstable period | 1627-1637 |
| Sulinya Vongsa | 1637-1694 |

Lao chronicles is anything to go by. There is more written about him than there is about the following two centuries of Lao history. It is also safe to say that his life is more fiction than fact. Fa Ngum was reputedly born with 33 teeth and was banished to Angkor after his father, Prince Yakfah, was convicted of having an incestuous affair with a wife of King Suvarna Kamphong. In 1353 Fa Ngum led an army to Luang Prabang and confronted his grandfather, King Suvarna Kamphong. Unable to defeat his grandson on the battlefield, the aged king is said to have hanged himself and Fa Ngum was invited to take the throne. Three years later, in 1356, Fa Ngum marched on Vientiane – which he took with ease – and then on

Vienkam, which proved more of a challenge. He is credited with piecing together Lang Xang – the Land of a Million Elephants (or, if not accented, the Valley of Elephants) – the golden age to which all histories of Laos refer to justify the existence (and greatness) of the country.

In some accounts Lang Xang is portrayed as stretching from China to Cambodia and from the Khorat Plateau in present-day Northeast Thailand to the Annamite mountains in the east. But it would be entirely wrong to envisage the kingdom controlling all these regions. Lane Xang probably only had total control over a comparatively small area of present-day Laos and parts of Northeast Thailand; the bulk of this grand empire would have been contested with other surrounding kingdoms. In addition, the smaller muang and principalities would themselves have played competing powers off, one against another, in an attempt to maximize their own autonomy. It is this 'messiness' which led scholars of Southeast Asian history to suggest that territories as such did not exist, but rather zones of variable control. The historian OW Wolters coined the term *mandala* for "a particular and often unstable political situation in a vaguely defined geographical area without fixed boundaries and where smaller centres tended to look in all directions for security. *Mandalas* would expand and contract in concertina-like fashion. Each one contained several tributary rulers, some of whom would repudiate their vassal status when the opportunity arose and try to build up their own network of vassals".

Legend relates that Fa Ngum was a descendant of Khoum Borom, "a king who came out of the sky from South China". He is said to have succeeded to the throne of Nanchao in 729, aged 31, and died 20 years later, although this historical record is, as they say, exceedingly thin. Khoum Borom is credited with giving birth to the Lao people by slicing open a gourd in Muong Taeng (Dien Bien Phu, Vietnam) and his seven sons established the great Tai kingdoms. He returned to his country with a detachment of Khmer soldiers and united several scattered Lao fiefdoms. In those days, conquered lands were usually razed and the people taken as slaves to build up the population of the conquering group. (This largely explains why today there are far more Lao in northeastern Thailand than in Laos – they were forcibly settled there after King Anou was defeated by King Rama III of Siam in 1827) The kings of Lane Xang were less philistine, demanding only subordination and allegiance as one part of a larger *mandala*.

Luang Prabang became the capital of the kingdom of Lane Xang. The unruly highland tribes of the northeast did not come under the kingdom's control at that time. Fa Ngum made Theravada Buddhism the official religion. He married the Cambodian king's daughter, Princess Keo Kaengkanya, and was given the Pra Bang (a golden statue, the most revered religious symbol of Laos), by the Khmer court.

It is common to read of Lane Xang as the first kingdom of Laos; as encompassing the territory of present-day Laos; and as marking the introduction of Theravada Buddhism to the country. On all counts this portrait is deeply flawed. As noted above, there were Lao states that predated Lane Xang; Lane Xang never controlled Laos as it currently exists; and Buddhism had made an impact on the Lao people before 1365. Fa Ngum did not create a kingdom; rather he brought together various pre-existing *muang* (city states) into a powerful *mandala*. As Martin Stuart-Fox writes, "From this derives his [Fa Ngum's] historical claim to hero status as the founder of the Lao Kingdom." But, as Stuart-Fox goes on to explain, there was no central authority and rulers of individual *muang* had considerable autonomy. As a result the "potential for disintegration was always present".

After Fa Ngum's wife died in 1368, he became so debauched, it is said, that he was deposed in favour of his son, Samsenthai (1373-1416), who was barely 18 when he acceded the throne. He was named after the 1376 census, which concluded that he ruled over 300,000 Tais living in Laos; *samsen* means, literally, 300,000. He set up a new administrative system based on the existing *muang*, nominating governors to each that lasted until it was abolished by the Communist government in 1975. Samsenthai's death was followed by a period of unrest. Under KingChaiyachakkapat-Phaenphaeo (1441-1478), the kingdom came under increasing threat from the Vietnamese. How the Vietnamese came to be peeved with the Lao is another story which smacks of fable more than fact. King Chaiyachakkapat's eldest son, the Prince of Chienglaw, secured a holy white elephant. The emperor of Vietnam, learning of this momentous discovery, asked to be sent some of the beast's hairs. Disliking the Vietnamese, the Prince dispatched a box of its excrement instead, whereupon the Emperor formed an army of an improbably large 550,000 men. The Prince's army numbered 200,000 and 2000 elephants. (Considering that the population of Lane Xang under Samsenthai was said to be 300,000 this beggars statistical belief. Still, it is a good story.) The massive Vietnamese army finally prevailed – two Lao generals were so tired that they fell off their elephants and were hacked to pieces – and entered and sacked Luang Prabang. But shortly thereafter they were driven out by Chaiyachakkapat-Phaenphaeo's son, King Suvarna Banlang (1478-1485). Peace was only fully restored under King Visunarat (1500-1520), who built Wat Visoun in Luang Prabang.

**Increased prominence and Burmese incursions**  Under King Pothisarath (1520-1548) Vientiane became prominent as a trading and religious centre. The king married a Lanna (Chiang Mai) princess, Queen Yotkamtip, and when the Siamese King Ketklao was put to death in 1545, Pothisarath's son claimed the throne at Lanna. He returned to Lane Xang when his father died in 1548. Once again an elephant figured in the event: Pothisarath was demonstrating his prowess in the art of elephant lassoing when he was flung from his mount and fatally crushed. Asserting his right as successor to the throne, he was crowned Setthathirat, in 1548 and ruled until 1571 – the last of the great kings of Lane Xang.

At the same time, the Burmese were expanding East and in 1556 Lanna fell into their hands. Setthathirat gave up his claim to that throne, to a Siamese prince, who ruled under Burmese authority. (He also took the Phra Kaeo – Thailand's famous 'Emerald' Buddha and its most sacred and revered image – with him to Luang Prabang and then to Vientiane. The residents of Chiang Mai are reputed to have pleaded that he leave it in the city, but these cries fell on deaf ears. The Phra Kaeo stayed in Vientiane until 1778 when the Thai general Phya Chakri 'repatriated' it to Thailand.) In 1563 Setthathirat pronounced Vieng Chan (Vientiane) the principal capital of Lane Xang. Seven years later, the Burmese King Bayinnaung launched an unsuccessful attack on Vieng Chan itself.

Setthathirat is revered as one of the great Lao kings, having protected the country from foreign domination. He built Wat Phra Kaeo (see page 40) in Vientiane, in which he placed the famous Emerald Buddha brought from Lanna. Setthathirat mysteriously disappeared during a campaign in the southern province of Attapeu in 1574, which threw the kingdom into crisis. Vientiane fell to invading Burmese the following year and remained under Burmese control for seven years. Finally the anarchic kingdoms of Luang Prabang and Vientiane were reunified under Nokeo Koumane (1591-96) and Thammikarath, king of Lane Xang (1596-1622).

## Disputed territory

From the time of the formation of the kingdom of Lane Xang to the arrival of the French, the history of Laos was dominated by the struggle to retain the lands it had conquered. Following King Setthathirat's death, a series of kings came to the throne in quick succession. King Souligna Vongs, crowned in 1633, brought long awaited peace to Laos. The 61 years he was on the throne are regarded as Lane Xang's golden age. Under him, the kingdom's influence spread to Yunnan in South China, the Burmese Shan States, Issan in Northeast Thailand and areas of Vietnam and Cambodia.

Souligna Vongsa was even on friendly terms with the Vietnamese: he married Emperor Le Thanh Ton's daughter and he and the Emperor agreed the borders between the two countries. The frontier was settled in a deterministic – but nonetheless amicable – fashion: those living in houses built on stilts with verandas were considered Lao subjects and those living in houses without piles and verandas owed allegiance to Vietnam.

During his reign, foreigners first visited the country – the Dutch merchant Gerrit van Wuysthoff arrived in 1641 to assess trading prospects – and Jesuit missionaries too. But other than a handful of adventurers, Laos remained on the outer periphery of European concerns and influence in the region.

**The three kingdoms** After Souligna Vongsa died in 1694, leaving no heir, dynastic quarrels and feudal rivalries once again erupted, undermining the kingdom's cohesion. In 1700 Lane Xang split into three: Luang Prabang under Souligna's grandson, Vientiane under Souligna's nephew and the new kingdom of Champasak was founded in the south 'panhandle'. This weakened the country and allowed the Siamese and Vietnamese to encroach on Lao lands. *Muang*, which previously owed clear allegiance to Lane Xang, began to look towards Vietnam or Siam. Isan muang in present day Northeast Thailand, for example, paid tribute to Bangkok; while Xieng Khouang did the same to Hanoi and, later, to Hué. The three main kingdoms that emerged with the disintegration of Lane Xang leant in different directions: Luang Prabang had close links with China, Vientiane with Vietnam's Hanoi/Hué and Champasak with Siam.

By the mid-1760s Burmese influence once again held sway in Vientiane and Luang Prabang and before the turn of the decade, they sacked Ayutthaya, the

## ON THE ROAD
### Prince Souvanna Phouma

Prince Souvanna Phouma was Laos' greatest statesman: an architect of independence and helmsman of catastrophe. He was prime minister on no less than eight occasions for a total of 20 years between 1951 and 1975. He dominated mainstream politics from independence until the victory of the Pathet Lao in 1975. But he was never able to preserve the integrity of Laos in the face of much stronger external forces. "Souvanna stands as a tragic figure in modern Lao history," Martin Stuart-Fox writes, a "stubborn symbol of an alternative, neutral, 'middle way'."

He was born in 1901 into a branch of the Luang Prabang royal family. Like many of the Lao elite he was educated abroad, in Hanoi, Paris and Grenoble, and when he returned to Laos he married a woman of mixed French-Lao blood. He was urbane, educated and arrogant. He enjoyed fine wines and cigars, spoke French better than he spoke Lao, and was a Francophile – as well as a nationalist – to the end.

In 1950 Souvanna became a co-founder of the Progressive Party and in the elections of 1951 he headed his first government which negotiated and secured full independence from France.

Souvanna made two key errors of judgement during these early years. First, he ignored the need for nation building in Laos. And, second, he under-estimated the threat that the Communists posed to the country. With regard to the first of these misjudgements, he seemed to believe – and it is perhaps no accident that he trained as an engineer and architect – that Laos just needed

capital of Siam. Somehow the Siamese managed to pull themselves together and only two years later in 1778 successfully rampaged through Vientiane. The two sacred Buddhas, the Phra Bang and the Phra Kaeo (Emerald Buddha), were taken as booty back to Bangkok. The Emerald Buddha was never returned and now sits in Bangkok's Wat Phra Kaeo.

King Anou (an abbreviation of Anurutha), was placed on the Vientiane throne by the Siamese. With the death of King Rama II of Siam, King Anou saw his chance of rebellion, asked Vietnam for assistance, formed an army and marched on Bangkok in 1827. In mounting this brave assault, Anou was apparently trying to emulate the great Fa Ngum. Unfortunately, he got no further than the Northeast Thai town of Korat where his forces were driven back. Nonetheless, Anou's rebellion is considered one of the most daring and ruthless rebellions in Siamese history and he was lauded as a war hero back home.

King Anou's brief stab at regional power was to result in catastrophe for Laos – and tragedy for King Anou. The first US arms shipment to Siam allowed the Siamese to sack Vientiane, a task to which they had grown accustomed over the years. (This marks America's first intervention in Southeast Asia.) Lao artisans were frogmarched to Bangkok and many of the inhabitants were resettled in to be administered efficiently to become a modern state. He appeared either to reject, or to ignore the idea that the government first had to try and inculcate a sense of Lao nationhood. The second misjudgement was his long-held belief that the Pathet Lao was a nationalist and not a Communist organization. He let the Pathet Lao grow in strength and this, in turn, brought the US into Lao affairs.

By the time the US began to intervene in Lao affairs in the late 1950s, the country already seemed to be heading for catastrophe. But in his struggle to maintain some semblance of independence for his tiny country, he ignored the degree to which Laos was being sucked into the quagmire of Indochina. As Martin Stuart-Fox writes: "He [Souvanna] knew he was being used, and that he had no power to protect his country from the war that increasingly engulfed it. But he was too proud meekly to submit to US demands – even as Laos was subjected to the heaviest bombing in the history of warfare. At least a form of independence had to be maintained."

When the Pathet Lao entered Vientiane in victory in 1975, Souvanna did not flee into exile. He remained to help in the transfer of power. The Pathet Lao, of course, gave him a title and then ignored him as they pursued their Communist manifesto. Again, Martin Stuart-Fox writes: "Souvanna ended his days beside the Mekong. He was to the end a Lao patriot, refusing to go into exile in France. The leaders of the new regime did consult him on occasions. Friends came to play bridge. Journalists sought him out, although he said little and interviews were taped in the presence of Pathet Lao minions. When he died in January 1984, he was accorded a state funeral."

From Martin Stuart-Fox's *Buddhist Kingdom, Marxist State: the Making of Modern Laos* (White Lotus, 1996).

Northeast Siam. Rama III had Chao Anou locked in a cage where he was taunted by the population of Bangkok. He died soon afterwards, at the age of 62. The cause of his death has been variously linked to poison and shame. One of his supporters is said to have taken pity on the king and brought him poison. Other explanations say that he wished himself dead or that he choked to death. Whatever the real cause, before he died, the disconsolate Anou put a curse on Siam's monarchy, promising that the next time a Thai king set foot on Lao soil, he would die. To this day no Thai king has crossed the Mekong River. When the agreement for the supply of hydroelectric power was signed with Thailand in the 1970s, the Thai king was invited to open the Nam Ngum Dam, a feat he managed to achieve from a sandbank in the middle of the Mekong.

**Disintegration of the kingdom** Over the next 50 years, Anou's Kingdom was destroyed. By the time the French arrived in the late 19th century, the virtually unoccupied city was subsumed into the Siamese sphere of influence. Luang Prabang also became a Siamese vassal state, while Xieng Khouang Province was invaded by Chinese rebels – to the chagrin of the Vietnamese, who had always considered the Hmong mountain kingdom (they called it Tran Ninh), to be their exclusive source of slaves. The Chinese had designs on Luang Prabang too and in order to quash their expansionist instincts, Bangkok dispatched an army there in 1885 to pacify the region and ensure the north remained firmly within the Siamese sphere of influence. This period was clearly one of confusion and rapidly shifting allegiances. In James McCarthy's book of his travels in Siam and Laos, *Surveying and Exploring in Siam* (1900), he states that an old chief of Luang Prabang remarked to him that the city had never been a tributary state of Annam (North Vietnam) but had formerly paid tribute to China. He writes:

"The tribute had consisted of four elephants, 41 mules, 533 lbs of nok (metal composed of gold and copper), 25 lbs of rhinoceros' horns, 100 lbs of ivory, 250 pieces of home-spun cloth, one horn, 150 bundles of areca palm nuts [for betel 'nut' chewing], 150 cocoanuts [sic] and 33 bags of roe of the fish *pla buk* [the] giant Mekong cat fish."

The history of Laos during this period becomes, essentially, the history of only a small part of the current territory of the country: namely, the history of Luang Prabang. And because Luang Prabang was a suzerain state of Bangkok, the history of that kingdom is, in turn, sometimes relegated to a mere footnote in the history of Siam.

## The French and independence

Following King Anou's death, Laos became the centre of Southeast Asian rivalry between Britain, expanding east from Burma and France, pushing west through Vietnam. In 1868, following the French annexation of South Vietnam and the formation of a protectorate in Cambodia, an expedition set out to explore the Mekong trade route to China. Once central and north Vietnam had come under the influence of the Quai d'Orsay in Paris, the French became increasingly curious about Vietnamese claims to chunks of Laos. Unlike the Siamese, the French – like the British – were concerned with demarcating borders and establishing explicit areas of sovereignty. This seemed extraordinary to most Southeast Asians at the time who could not see the point of spending so much time and effort mapping space when land was so abundant. However, it did not take long for the Siamese king to realize the importance of maintaining his claim to Siamese territories if the French in the east and the British in the south (Malaya) and west (Burma) were not to squeeze Siam to nothing.

However, King Chulalongkorn was not in a position to confront the French militarily and instead he had to play a clever diplomatic game if his kingdom was to survive. The French, for their part, were anxious to continue to press westwards from Vietnam into the Lao lands over which Siam held suzerainty. Martin Stuart-Fox argues that there were four main reasons underlying France's desire to expand West: the lingering hope that the Mekong might still offer a 'back door' into China; the consolidation of Vietnam against attack; the 'rounding out' of their Indochina possessions; and a means of further pressuring Bangkok. In 1886, the French received reluctant Siamese permission to post a vice consul to Luang Prabang and a year later he persuaded the Thais to leave. However, even greater humiliation was to come in 1893 when the French, through crude gunboat diplomacy – the so-called Paknam incident – forced King Chulalongkorn to give up all claim to Laos on the flimsiest of historical pretexts. Despite attempts by Prince Devawongse to manufacture a compromise, the French forced Siam to cede Laos to France and, what's more, to pay compensation. It is said that after this humiliation, King Chulalongkorn retired from public life, broken in spirit and health. So the French colonial era in Laos began.

What is notable about this spat between France and Siam is that Laos – the country over which they were fighting – scarcely figures. As was to happen again in Laos' history, the country was caught between two competing powers who used Laos as a stage on which to fight a wider and to them, more important, conflict.

**Union of Indochina** In 1893 France occupied the left bank of the Mekong and forced Thailand to recognize the river as the boundary. The French Union of Indochina denied Laos the area which is now Isan, northeast Thailand, and this was the start of 50 years of colonial rule. Laos became a protectorate with a *résident-superieur* in Vientiane and a vice-consul in Luang Prabang. However, as Martin Stuart-Fox points out, Laos could hardly be construed as a 'country' during the colonial period. "Laos existed again", he writes, "but not yet as a political entity in its own right, for no independent centre of Lao political power existed. Laos was but a territorial entity within French Indochina." The French were not interested in establishing an identifiable Lao state; they saw Laos as a resource-rich appendage to Vietnam. Though they had grand plans for the development of Laos, none of them came to anything. Unlike Cambodia to the south, the French did not perceive Laos to have any historical unity or coherence and therefore it could be hacked about and developed or otherwise, according to their whim, as if it were a piece of brie.

In 1904 the Franco-British convention delimited respective zones of influence. Only a few hundred French civil servants were ever in Vientiane at any one time and their attitude to colonial administration – described as 'benign neglect' – was as relaxed as the people they governed. To the displeasure of the Lao, France brought in Vietnamese to run the civil service. But for the most part, the French colonial period was a 50-year siesta for Laos. The king was allowed to stay in Luang Prabang, but had little say in administration. Trade was left to the Chinese and the Vietnamese. A small, French-educated Lao élite did grow up and by the 1940s had become the core of a laid-back Lao nationalist movement.

**Japanese coup** Towards the end of the Second World War, Japan ousted the French administration in Laos in a coup in March 1945. The eventual surrender of the Japanese in August that year gave impetus to the Lao independence movement. Prince Phetsarath, hereditary viceroy and premier of the Luang Prabang Kingdom, took over the leadership of the Lao Issara, the Free Laos Movement (originally a resistance movement against the Japanese). They prevented the French from seizing power again and declared Lao independence on 1 September 1945. Two weeks later, the north and south provinces were reunified and in October, Phetsarath formed a Lao Issara government headed by Prince Phaya Khammao, the governor of Vientiane.

France refused to recognize the new state and crushed the Lao resistance. King Sisavang Vong, unimpressed by Prince Phetsarath's move, sided with the French, who had their colony handed back by British forces. He was crowned the constitutional monarch of the new protectorate in 1946. The rebel government took refuge in Bangkok. Historians believe the Issara movement was aided in their resistance to the French by the Viet Minh – Hanoi's Communists.

**Independence** In response to nationalist pressures, France was obliged to grant Laos ever greater self government and, eventually, formal independence within the framework of the newly reconstructed French Union in July 1949. Meanwhile, in Bangkok, the Issara movement had formed a government-in-exile, headed by Phetsarath and his half-brothers: Prince Souvanna Phouma (see box, page 270) and Prince Souphanouvong. Both were refined, French-educated men, with a taste for good wine and cigars. The Issara's military wing was led by Souphanouvong who, even at that stage, was known for his Communist sympathies. This was due to a temporary alliance between the Issara and the Viet Minh, who had the common cause of ridding their respective countries of the French. Within just a few months the so-called Red Prince had been ousted by his half-brothers and joined the Viet Minh where he is said to have been the moving force behind the declaration of the Democratic Republic of Laos by the newly formed Lao National Assembly. The Lao People's Democratic Republic emerged – albeit in name only – somewhere inside Vietnam, in August 1949. Soon afterwards, the Pathet Lao (the Lao Nation) was born. The Issara movement quickly folded and Souvanna Phouma went back to Vientiane and joined the newly formed Royal Lao Government.

By 1953, Prince Souphanouvong had managed to move his Pathet Lao headquarters inside Laos and with the French losing their grip on the north provinces, the weary colonizers granted the country full independence. Retreating honourably, France signed a treaty of friendship and association with the new royalist government and made the country a French protectorate.

**The rise of Communism**
**French defeat** While all this was going on, King Sisavang Vong sat tight in Luang Prabang instead of moving to Vientiane. But within a few months of independence, the ancient royal capital was under threat from the Communist Viet Minh and Pathet Lao. Honouring the terms of the new treaty, French commander General Henri Navarre determined in late 1953 to take the pressure off Luang Prabang by confronting the Viet Minh who controlled the strategic approach to the city at Dien Bien Phu. The French suffered a stunning defeat which presaged their withdrawal from Indochina. The subsequent occupation of two north Lao provinces by the Vietnam-backed Pathet Lao forces, meant the kingdom's days as a Western buffer state were numbered. The Vietnamese, not unlike their previous neighbours, did not respect Laos as a state, but as a extension of their own territory to be utilized for their own strategic purposes during the ensuing war.

With the Geneva Accord in July 1954, following the fall of Dien Bien Phu in May, Ho Chi Minh's government gained control of all territory north of the 17th parallel in neighbouring Vietnam. The Accord guaranteed Laos' freedom and neutrality, but with the Communists on the threshold, the US was not prepared to be a passive spectator: the demise of the French sparked an increasing US involvement. In an operation that was to mirror the much more famous war with Vietnam to the East, Washington soon found itself supplying and paying the salaries of 50,000 royalist troops and their corrupt officers. Clandestine military assistance grew, undercover special forces were mobilized and the CIA began meddling in Lao politics. In 1960 a consignment of weapons was dispatched by the CIA to a major in the Royal Lao Army called Vang Pao – or VP, as he became known – who was destined to become the leader of the Hmong.

**US involvement: the domino effect**  Laos had become the dreaded first domino, which, using the scheme of US President Dwight D Eisenhower's analogy, would trigger the rapid spread of Communism if ever the country fell. The time-trapped little kingdom rapidly became the focus of superpower brinkmanship. At a press conference in March 1961, President Kennedy is said to have been too abashed to tell the American people that US forces might soon become embroiled in conflict in a far-away flashpoint that went by the name of 'Louse'. For three decades Americans have unwittingly mispronounced the country's name as Kennedy decided, euphemistically, to label it 'Lay-os' throughout his national television broadcast.

**Coalitions, coups and counter-coups**  Even though it was headed by the neutralist, Prince Souvanna Phouma, the US-backed Royal Lao Government of independent Laos ruled over a divided country from 1951 to 1954. The US played havoc with Laos' domestic politics, running anti-communist campaigns, backing the royalist army and lending support to political figures on the right (even if they lacked experience or political qualifications). The Communist Pathet Lao, headed by Prince Souphanouvong and overseen and sponsored by North Vietnam's Lao Dong party since 1949, emerged as the only strong opposition. By the mid-1950s, Kaysone Phomvihane, later prime minister of the Lao PDR, began to make a name for himself in the Indochinese Communist Party. Indeed the close association between Laos and Vietnam went deeper than just ideology. Kaysone's father was Vietnamese, while Prince Souphanouvong and Nouhak Phounsavanh both married Vietnamese women.

**Government of National Union**  Elections were held in Vientiane in July 1955 but were boycotted by the Pathet Lao. Souvanna Phouma became prime minister in March 1956. He aimed to try to negotiate the integration of his half-brother's Pathet Lao provinces into a unified administration and coax the Communists into a coalition government. In 1957 the disputed provinces were returned to royal government control under the first coalition government. This coalition government, much to US discontent, contained two Pathet Lao ministers including Souphanouvong and Phoumi Vongvichit. This was one of Souvanna Phouma's achievements in trying to combine the two sides to ensure neutrality, although it was only short-lived. In May 1958 elections were held. This time the Communists'

Lao Patriotic Front (Neo Lao Hak Xat) clinched 13 of the 21 seats in the Government of National Union. The Red Prince, Souphanouvong and one of his aides were included in the cabinet and former Pathet Lao members were elected deputies of the National Assembly.

Almost immediately problems which had been beneath the surface emerged to plague the government. The rightists and their US supporters were shaken by the result and the much-vaunted coalition lasted just two months. Driven by Cold War prerogatives, the US could not abide by any government that contained Communist members and withdrew their aid, which the country had become much dependent upon. Between 1955 and 1958 the US had given four times more aid to Laos than the French had done in the prior eight years and it had become the backbone of the Lao economy. If Laos was not so dependent on this aid, it is quite plausible that the coalition government may have survived. The National Union fell apart in July 1958 and Souvanna Phouma was forced out of power. Pathet Lao leaders were jailed and the right-wing Phoui Sananikone came to power. With anti-Communists in control, Pathet Lao forces withdrew to the Plain of Jars in Xieng Khouang Province. A three-way civil war ensued, between the rightists (backed by the US), the Communists (backed by North Vietnam) and the neutralists (led by Souvanna Phouma, who wanted to maintain independence from both the US and Communist countries).

**Civil war** CIA-backed strongman General Phoumi Nosavan thought Phoui's politics rather tame and with a nod from Washington he stepped into the breach in January 1959, eventually overthrowing Phoui in a coup in December and placing Prince Boun Oum in power. Pathet Lao leaders were imprisoned without trial. Confusion over Phoumas, Phouis and Phoumis led one American official to comment that it all "could have been a significant event or a typographical error".

Within a year, the rightist regime was overthrown by a neutralist *coup d'état* led by General Kong Lae and Prince Souvanna Phouma was recalled from exile in Cambodia to become prime minister of the first National Union. Souvanna Phouma incurred American wrath by inviting a Soviet ambassador to Vientiane in October. With US support, Nosavan staged yet another armed rebellion in December and sparked a new civil war. In the 1960 general elections, provincial authorities were threatened with military action if they did not support the right-wing groups and were rigged to ensure no Pathet Lao cadres could obtain a seat in office. In August 1960 paratroop neutralist Kong Le staged a successful coup d'état; however, with US funding, the rightists were able to assemble formidable troops in Savannakhet and marched to Vientiane, retaking the capital in mid-December. Kong Lae backed down, Souvanna Phouma shuffled back to Phnom Penh and a new rightwing government was set up under Boun Oum. By this stage, the Pathet Lao had consolidated considerable forces in the region surrounding the Plain of Jars and, with support from the Vietnamese, had been able to expand their territorial control in the north. This represented a major crisis to the incoming Kennedy administration that Stuart Martin-Fox (1996) describes as "second only to Cuba".

# Vietnam War

CHINA

NORTH VIETNAM

LAOS

○ Dien Bien Phu
HANOI □   Haiphong ○

Xam Neua ○

*Gulf of Tonkin*

○ Luang Prabang
Phonsavanh ○
*Plain of Jars*

VIENTIANE □

Mekong River

Ho Chi Minh Trail

Demilitarized Zone (22-7-54)

THAILAND

Khe Sanh ○   ○ Quang Tri

*Hamburger Hill* □ Hué

○ Pakse   *Boloven Plateau*

Danang ○

My Lai ○

Kontum ○
○ Pleiku
*Ia Drang Valley*   Qui Nhon ○

CAMBODIA

SOUTH VIETNAM

Mekong River

Ho Chi Minh Trail

Dalat ○

*Cam Ranh Bay*

PHNOM PENH □

Tay Ninh ○
○ Cu Chi   Bien Hoa ○
Vung Tao ○
SAIGON □

Sihanoukville ○

Can Tho ○   Ap Bac ○

*South China Sea*

*Gulf of Thailand*

Ca Mau ○

N

100 km
100 miles

**Zurich talks and the Geneva Accord** The new prime minister, the old one and his Marxist half-brother finally sat down to talks in Zurich in June 1961, but any hope of an agreement was overshadowed by escalating tensions between the superpowers. In 1962, an international agreement on Laos was hammered out in Geneva by 14 participating nations and accords were signed, once again guaranteeing Lao neutrality.

By implication, the Geneva Accord denied the Viet Minh access to the Ho Chi Minh Trail. But aware of the reality of constant North Vietnamese infiltration through Laos into South Vietnam, the head of the American mission concluded that the agreement was "a good bad deal".

Another coalition government of National Union was formed under the determined neutralist Prince Souvanna Phouma (as prime minister), with Prince Souphanouvong for the Pathet Lao and Prince Boun Oum representing the right. A number of political assassinations derailed the process of reconciliation. Moreover, antagonisms between the left and the right, both backed financially by their respective allies, made it impossible for the unfunded neutralists to balance the two sided into any form of neutrality. It was no surprise when the coalition government collapsed within a few months and fighting resumed. This time the international community just shrugged and watched Laos sink back into the vortex of civil war. Unbeknown to the outside world, the conflict was rapidly degenerating into a war between the CIA and North Vietnamese jungle guerrillas.

## Secret War

**The war that wasn't** In the aftermath of the Geneva Accord, the North Vietnamese, rather than reducing their forces in Laos, continued to increase their manpower on the ground. With the Viet Minh denying the existence of the Ho Chi Minh Trail, while at the same time enlarging it, Kennedy dispatched an undercover force of CIA men, green berets and US-trained Thai mercenaries to command 9000 Lao soldiers. By 1963, these American forces had grown to 30,000 men. Historian Roger Warner believes that by 1965 "word spread among a select circle of congressmen and senators about this exotic program run by Lone Star rednecks and Asian hillbillies that was better and cheaper than anything the Pentagon was doing in South Vietnam." To the north, the US also supplied Vang Pao's force of Hmong guerrillas, dubbed 'Mobile Strike Forces'. With the cooperation of Prince Souvanna Phouma, the CIA's commercial airline, Air America, ferried men and equipment into Laos from Thailand (and opium out, it is believed). Caught between Cold War antagonisms it was impossible to maintain a modicum of neutrality as even the most staunch neutralist, Souvanna Phouma, began to become entangled. As Robbins argues, by the early 1960s, Sovanna Phouma – trying to reinforce the middle way – had given permission "for every clandestine manoeuvre the United States made to match the North Vietnamese. In turn Souvanna demanded that his complicity in such arrangements be kept secret, lest his position in the country become untenable." Owing to the clandestine nature of the military intervention in Laos, the rest of the world – believing that the Geneva settlement had solved the foreign interventionist problem – was oblivious as to what was happening on the ground. Right up until 1970, Washington never admitted to any activity in Laos beyond 'armed reconnaissance' flights over northern provinces. Richard Nixon, for example, claimed that "there are no American ground combat troops in Laos".

Meanwhile the North Vietnamese were fulfilling their two strategic priorities in the country: continued use of the Ho Chi Minh trail (by this stage the majority of North Vietnamese munitions and personnel for the Viet Cong was being shuffled along the trail) and ensuring that the Plain of Jars did not fall under the control of the right, where the US could launch attacks on North Vietnam. This latter goal amounted to supporting the Pathet Lao in their aim to hold onto as much territory as possible in the north. The Pathet Lao, in turn, were dependent on the North Vietnamese for supplies – both material and manpower. As Martin Stuart-Fox (1996) argues, "Pathet Lao leaders were not in a position after 1964 to reach any settlement that might have disadvantaged their Vietnamese mentors. Genuine Lao neutrality was out of the question for the Pathet Lao. It had to be subverted for the sake of the Vietnamese revolution." With both the US bankrolling the Royalist right and the Vietnamese puppeteering the Pathet Lao, within the country any pretence of maintaining a balance in the face of Cold War hostilities was shattered for neutralists like Souvanna Phouma.

Souvanna Phouma referred to it as 'the forgotten war' and it is often termed now the 'non-attributable war'. The willingness on the part of the Americans to dump millions of tonnes of ordnance on a country which was ostensibly neutral may have been made easier by the fact that some people in the administration did not believe Laos to be a country at all. Bernard Fall wrote that Laos at the time was "neither a geographical nor an ethnic or social entity, but merely a political convenience", while a Rand Corporation report written in 1970 described Laos as "hardly a country except in the legal sense". More colourfully, Secretary of State Dean Rusk described it as a "wart on the hog of Vietnam". Perhaps those in Washington could feel a touch better about bombing the hell out of a country which, in their view, occupied a sort of political never-never land – or which they could liken to an unfortunate skin complaint.

Not everyone agrees with this view that Laos never existed until the French wished it into existence. Scholar of Laos Arthur Dommen, for example, traces a true and coherent Lao identity back to Fa Ngum and his creation of the kingdom of Lane Xang in 1353, writing that it was "a state in the true sense of the term, delineated by borders clearly defined and consecrated by treaty" for 350 years. He goes on:

"Lao historians see a positive proof of the existence of a distinct Lao race (*sua sat Lao*), a Lao nation (*sat Lao*), a Lao country (*muong Lao*) and a Lao state (*pathet Lao*). In view of these facts, we may safely reject the notion, fashionable among apologists for a colonial enterprise of a later day, that Laos was a creation of French colonial policy and administration".

American bombing of the North Vietnamese Army's supply lines through Laos to South Vietnam along the Ho Chi Minh Trail in East Laos (see box, page 208) started in 1964 and fuelled the conflict between the Royalist Vientiane government and the Pathet Lao. The neutralists had been forced into alliance with the Royalists to avoid defeat in Xieng Kouang Province. US bombers crossed Laos on bombing runs to Hanoi from air bases in Thailand and gradually the war in Laos escalated. In his book *The Ravens* (1987), Christopher Robbins sets the scene:

"Apparently, there was another war even nastier than the one in Vietnam and so secret that the location of the country in which it was being fought was classified. The cognoscenti simply referred to it as 'the Other Theater'. The men who chose to fight in it were hand-picked volunteers and anyone accepted for a tour seemed to disappear as if from the face of the earth."

America's side of the secret war was conducted from a one-room shack at the US base in Udon Thani, 'across the fence' in Thailand. This was the CIA's Air America operations room and in the same compound was stationed the 4802 Joint Liaison Detachment – or the CIA logistics office. In Vientiane, US pilots supporting Hmong General Vang Pao's rag-tag army, were given a new identity as rangers for the US Agency for International Development; they reported directly to the air attaché at the US embassy (see box, page 155). Robbins writes that they "were military men, but flew into battle in civilian clothes – denim cutoffs, T-shirts, cowboy hats and dark glasses ... Their job was to fly as the winged artillery of some fearsome warlord, who led an army of stone age mercenaries in the pay of the CIA and they operated out of a secret city hidden in the mountains of a jungle kingdom ..." He adds that CIA station chiefs and field agents "behaved like warlords in their own private fiefdoms."

The most notorious of the CIA's unsavoury operatives was Anthony Posepny – known as Tony Poe, on whom the character of Kurtz, the crazy colonel played by Marlon Brando in the film *Apocalypse Now*, was based. Originally, Poe had worked as Vang Pao's case officer; he then moved to North Laos and operated for years, on his own, in Burmese and Chinese border territories, offering his tribal recruits one US dollar for each set of Communist ears they brought back. Many of the spies and pilots of this secret war later re-emerged in covert and illegal arms-smuggling rackets to Libya, Iran and the Nicaraguan Contras.

By contrast, the Royalist forces were reluctant warriors: despite the fact that civil war was an ingrained tradition in Laos, the Lao went to great lengths to avoid fighting each other. One foreign journalist, reporting from Luang Prabang in the latter stages of the war, related how Royalist and Pathet Lao troops, encamped on opposite banks of the Nam Ou, agreed an informal ceasefire over Pi Mai (Lao New Year), to celebrate the king's visit to the sacred Pak Ou Caves (see page 99). Most Lao did not want to fight. Correspondents who covered the war noted that without the goading of their respective US and North Vietnamese masters, many would have gone home. Prior to the war, one military strategist described the Lao forces as one of the worst armies ever seen, adding that they made the [poorly regarded] "South Vietnamese Army look like Storm Troopers". "The troops lack the basic will to fight. They do not take initiative. A typical characteristic of the Laotian Army is to leave an escape route. US technicians attached to the various training institutions have not been able to overcome Lao apathy". (Ratnam, P, *Laos and the Superpowers*, 1980.)

Air Force planes were often used to carry passengers for money – or to smuggle opium out of the Golden Triangle. In the field, soldiers of the Royal Lao Army regularly fled when faced with a frontal assault by the Vietnam People's Army (NVA). The officer corps was uncommitted, lazy and corrupt; many ran opium-smuggling rackets and saw the war as a ticket to get rich quick. In the south, the Americans considered Royal Lao Air Force pilots unreliable because they were loath to bomb their own people and cultural heritage.

**The air war**  The clandestine bombing of the Ho Chi Minh Trail (see box, page 208) caused many civilian casualties – so-called collateral damage – and displaced much of the population in Laos' eastern provinces. A whole gamut of military devices and defoliants were used to destroy Lao territory and, although there are not really any official casualty figures in circulation, it is estimated that between a sixth and a 10th of the population were killed. By 1973, when the bombing stopped, the US had dropped more than two million tonnes of bombs on Laos – equivalent to some 700 kg of explosives for every man, woman and child in the country. It is reported that up to 70% of all B-52 strikes in Indochina were targeted at Laos. To pulverize the country to this degree 580,994 bombing sorties were flown.

The bombing intensified during the Nixon administration: up to 1969 less than 500,000 tonnes of bombs had been dropped on Laos; from then on nearly that amount was dropped each year. In the 1960s and early 1970s, more bombs rained on Laos than were dropped during the Second World War – the equivalent of a plane load of bombs every eight minutes for nine years. This campaign cost Americans more than US$2 million a day but the cost to Laos was incalculable. The activist Fred Branfman, quoted by Roger Warner in *Shooting at the Moon*, wrote: "Nine years of bombing, two million tons of bombs, whole rural societies wiped off the map, hundreds of thousands of peasants treated like herds of animals in a Clockwork Orange fantasy of an aerial African Hunting safari."

The war was not restricted to bombing missions – once potential Pathet Lao strongholds had been identified, fighters, using rockets, were sent to attempt to destroy them. Such was the intensity of the bombing campaign that villagers in Pathet Lao-controlled areas are said to have turned to planting and harvesting their rice at night. Few of those living in Xieng Khouang Province, the Bolovan Plateau or along the Ho Chi Minh Trail had any idea of who was bombing them or why. The consequences were often tragic, as in the case of Tham Phiu Cave (see page 159).

In *The Ravens*, Robbins tells of how a fighter pilot's inauspicious dream would lead the commander to cancel a mission; bomber pilots hated dropping bombs and when they did, aluminium canisters were brought back and sold as scrap. After the war, the collection and sale of war debris turned into an industry for tribes' people in Xieng Khouang Province and along the Ho Chi Minh Trail. Bomb casings, aircraft fuel tanks and other bits and pieces that were not sold to Thailand have been put to every conceivable use in rural Laos. They are used as cattle troughs, fence posts, flower pots, stilts for houses, water carriers, temple bells, knives and ploughs. The bomb craters are often turned into fish ponds.

But the bombing campaign has also left a more deadly legacy – of unexploded bombs and anti-personnel mines. Today, over 30 years after the air war finally ended, over 500,000 tonnes of deadly unexploded ordnance (UXO) is believed to still be scattered throughout nine of Laos' 13 provinces. Most casualties are caused by cluster bombs, or 'bombis' as they have become known. Cluster bombs are carried in large canisters called Cluster Bomb Units (CBUs), which open in mid-air, releasing around 670 tennis ball-sized bomblets. Upon detonation, the bombie propels around 200,000 pieces of shrapnel over an area the size of several football fields. This UXO contamination inhibits long-term development, especially in Xieng Khouang Province (see page 147), making farming in this part a Laos a highly dangerous occupation was simply one of those 'accidents' of war.

**The land war** Within Laos, the war focused on the strategic Plain of Jars in Xieng Khouang Province (see box, page 155) and was co-ordinated from the town of Long Tien (the secret city), tucked into the limestone hills to the southwest of the plain. Known as the most secret spot on earth, it was not marked on maps and was populated by the CIA, the Ravens (the air controllers who flew spotter planes and called in air strikes) and the Hmong.

The Pathet Lao were headquartered in caves in Xam Neua Province, to the north of the plain. Their base was equipped with a hotel cave (for visiting dignitaries), a hospital cave, embassy caves and even a theatre cave.

The Plain of Jars (known as the PDJ, after the French Plaine de Jarres), was the scene of some of the heaviest fighting and changed hands countless times, the Royalist and Hmong forces occupying it during the wet season, the Pathet Lao in the dry. During this period in the conflict Long Tien, known as one of the country's 'alternate' bases to keep nosy journalists away (the word 'alternate' was meant to indicate that it was unimportant), grew to such an extent that it became Laos' second city. James Parker in his book *Codename Mule* claims that the air base was so busy that at its peak it was handling more daily flights than Chicago's O'Hare airport. Others claim that it was the busiest airport in the world. There was also fighting around Luang Prabang and the Bolovan Plateau to the south.

**The end of the war** Although the origins of the war in Laos were distinct from those in Vietnam, the two wars had effectively merged by the early 1970s and it became inevitable that the fate of the Americans to the east would determine the outcome in Laos. By 1970 it was no longer possible for the US administration to shroud the war in secrecy: a flood of refugees had arrived in Vientiane in an effort to escape the conflict.

During the dying days of the US-backed regime in Vientiane, CIA agents and Ravens lived in quarters south of the capital, known as KM-6 – because it was 6 km from town. Another compound in downtown Vientiane was known as 'Silver City' and reputedly also sometimes housed CIA agents. On the departure of the Americans and the arrival of the new regime in 1975, the Communists' secret police made Silver City their new home. Today, Lao people still call military intelligence officers 'Silvers'.

A ceasefire was agreed in February 1973, a month after Washington and Hanoi struck a similar deal in Paris. Power was transferred in April 1974 to yet another coalition government set up under the premiership of Souvanna Phouma.

The neutralist prince once again had a Communist deputy and foreign affairs minister. The Red Prince, Souphanouvong, headed the Joint National Political Council. Foreign troops were given two months to leave. The North Vietnamese were allowed to remain along the Ho Chi Minh Trail, for although US forces had withdrawn from South Vietnam, the war there was not over.

The communists' victories over Saigon (and Phnom Penh) in April 1975 were a catalyst for the Pathet Lao, who advanced on Vientiane. It is widely hailed as the 'bloodless' takeover. Due to the country's mixed loyalties the Pathet Lao government undertook a gradual process of eroding away loyalties to the Royalist government. As the end drew near and the Pathet Lao advanced out of the mountains and towards the more populated Mekong valley – the heartland of the Royalist government – province after province fell with scarcely a shot fired. The mere arrival of a small contingent of Pathet Lao soldiers was sufficient to secure victory – even though these soldiers arrived at Wattay Airport on Chinese transport planes to be greeted by representatives of the Royal Lao government.

Administration of Vientiane by the People's Revolutionary Committee was secured on 18 August. The atmosphere was very different from that which accompanied the Communist's occupation of Saigon in Vietnam the same year. In Vientiane peaceful crowds turned out to hear speeches by Pathet Lao cadres. The King remained unharmed in his palace and while a coffin representing 'dead American imperialism' was burned this was done in a 'carnival' atmosphere. Vientiane was declared 'officially liberated' on 23 August 1975. The coalition government was dismissed and Souvanna Phouma resigned for the last time. All communications with the outside world were cut.

While August 1975 represents a watershed in the history of Laos, scholars are left with something of a problem: explaining why the Pathet Lao prevailed. According to Martin Stuart-Fox, the Lao revolutionary movement "had not mobilized an exploited peasantry with promises of land reform, for most of the country was underpopulated and peasant families generally owned sufficient land for their subsistence needs. The appeal of the Pathet Lao to their lowland Lao compatriots was in terms of nationalism and independence and the preservation of Lao culture from the corrosive American influence; but no urban uprising occurred until the very last minute when effective government had virtually ceased to exist ... The small Lao intelligentsia, though critical of the Royal Lao government, did not desert it entirely and their recruitment to the Pathet Lao was minimal. Neither the monarchy, still less Buddhism, lost legitimacy." Stuart-Fox concludes that it was external factors, and in particular the intervention of outside powers, which led to the victory of the Pathet Lao. Without the Vietnamese and Americans, the Pathet Lao would not have won. For the great mass of Laos' population before 1975, Communism meant nothing. This was not a mass uprising but a victory secured by a small ideologically committed elite and forged in the furnace of the war in Indochina.

As the Pathet Lao seized power, rightist ministers, ranking civil servants, doctors, much of the intelligentsia and around 30,000 Hmong crossed the Mekong and escaped into Thailand, fearing that they would face persecution. Although the initial exodus was large, most refugees fled in the next few years up until 1980 as the Lao government introduced new reforms aimed at wiping out decadence and reforming the economic system.

**The refugee camps** By the late 1980s, a total of 340,000 people – 10% of the population and mostly middle class – had fled the country. At least half of the refugees were Hmong, the US's key allies during the war, who feared reprisals and persecution. From 1988, refugees who had made it across the border began to head back across the Mekong from camps in Thailand and to asylum in the US and France. More than 2000 refugees were also repatriated from Yunnan Province in China. The government offered to return confiscated property so long as they stayed for at least six months and become Lao citizens once again.

Nonetheless, many lived for years in refugee camps, while the better connected secured US, Australian and French passports. For Laos, a large proportion of its human capital drained westwards, creating a vacuum of skilled personnel that would hamper – and still does – reconstruction. But a significant number who had aligned themselves with the Royalists decided to help build a new Laos; they saw themselves as Lao patriots and their duty was to stay.

## Laos under Communism
The People's Democratic Republic of Laos was proclaimed in December 1975 with Prince Souphanouvong as president and Kaysone Phomvihane as secretary-general of the Lao People's Revolutionary Party (a post he had held since its formation in 1955). The king's abdication was accepted and the ancient Lao monarchy was abolished, together with King Samsenthai's 600-year-old system of village autonomy. But instead of executing their vanquished foes, the LPRP installed Souvanna and the ex-king, Savang Vatthana, as 'special advisers' to the politburo. On Souvanna's death in 1984, he was accorded a full state funeral. The king did not fare so well: he later died ignominiously while in detention after his alleged involvement in a counter-revolutionary plot (see below).

Surprisingly, the first actions of the new revolutionary government was not to build a new revolutionary economy and society, but to stamp out unsavoury behaviour. Dress and hairstyles, dancing and singing, even the food served at family celebrations, were all subject to scrutiny by 'Investigation Cadres'. If a person was found not to match up to the Party's standards of good taste they were bundled off to re-education camps.

Relations with Thailand, which in the immediate wake of the revolution remained cordial, deteriorated in late 1976. A military coup in Bangkok led to rumours that the Thai military, backed by the CIA, was supporting Hmong and other right-wing Lao rebels. The regime feared that Thailand would be used as a springboard for a royalist coup attempt. This prompted the arrest of King Savang Vatthana, together with his family and Crown Prince Vongsavang, who were dispatched to a re-education camp in Sam Neua Province, never to be heard from again. In December 1989 Kaysone Phomvihane admitted in Paris that the king had died of malaria in 1984 and that the queen had also died "of natural causes" – no mention was made of Vongsavang.

**Re-education camps** Between 30,000 and 40,000 reactionaries who had been unable to flee the country were interned in remote camps for 're-education'. These camps referred to as Samanaya took their name from the Western word, seminar. The reluctant scholars were forced into slave labour in jungle conditions and subjected to political propaganda for anything from a few months up to 15 years.

By 1978, the re-education policy starting to wind down, although, in 1986, Amnesty International released a report on the forgotten inhabitants of the re-education camps, claiming that 6000-7000 were still being held. By that time incarceration behind barbed wire had ended and internees were 'arbitrarily restricted' rather than imprisoned. They were assigned to road construction and other public works. Nonetheless, conditions for these victims of the war in Indochina suffered from malnutrition, disease and many died prematurely in captivity. It is unclear how many died, but at least 15,000 have been freed. Officials of the old regime, ex-government ministers and former Royalist air force and army officers, together with thousands of others unlucky enough to have been on the wrong side, were released from the camps, largely during the mid- to late 1980s. Most of the surviving political prisoners have now been reintegrated into society. Some work in the tourism industry and one, a former colonel in the Royal Lao Army, jointly owns the **Asian Pavilion Hotel** (formerly the **Vieng Vilai**) on Samsenthai Road in downtown Vientiane.

The Lao, as scores of books like this one keep reminding their readers, are a gentle people and it is hard not to leave the country without that view being reinforced. Even the Lao People's Revolutionary Party seems quaintly inept and it is hard to equate it with its more brutal sister parties in Vietnam, Cambodia, China or the former Soviet Union. Yet five students who meekly called for greater political freedom in 1999 were whisked off by the police and have not been heard of since. So much for soggy ineptness.

**Reflecting on 10 years of 'reconstruction'** Laos' recent political and economic history is covered under Modern Laos (see below). But it is worth ending this account of the country's history by noting the brevity of Laos' experiment with full-blown Communism. Just 10 years after the Pathet Lao took control of Vientiane, the leadership were on the brink of far-reaching economic reforms. By the mid-1980s it was widely acknowledged that Marxism-Leninism had failed the country. The population was still dreadfully poor; the ideology of Communism had failed to entice more than a handful into serious and enthusiastic support for the party and its ways; and graft and nepotism were on the rise.

# Modern Laos

## Politics

President Kaysone Phomvihane died in November 1992, aged 71. His right-hand man, Prince Souphanouvong – the so-called Red Prince – died just over two years later, on 9 January 1995. As one obituary put it, Kaysone was older than he seemed, both historically and ideologically. He had been chairman of the LPRP since the mid-1950s and had been a protégé and comrade of Ho Chi Minh, who led the Vietnamese struggle for independence from the French. After leading the Lao Resistance Government – or Pathet Lao – from caves in Xam Neua Province in the north, Kaysone assumed the premiership on the abolition of the monarchy in 1975. But under his leadership – and following the example of his mentors in Hanoi – Kaysone became the driving force behind the market-orientated reforms. The year before he died, he gave up the post of prime minister for that of president.

His death didn't change much, as other members of the old guard stepped into the breach. Nouhak Phounsavanh – a sprightly 78-year-old former truck driver and hardline Communist – succeeded him as president, but in February 1998 was replaced by 75-year-old General Khamtai Siphandon – the outgoing prime minister and head of the LPRP. Khamtai represents the last of the revolutionary Pathet Lao leaders who fought the Royalists and the Americans. In April 2006, Siphandon, the last of the old guard from the caves in Vieng Xai, was replaced as president by Choummaly Sayasone.

### Recent years

With the introduction of the New Economic Mechanism in 1986 there were hopes that economic liberalization would be matched by political *glasnost*. So far, however, the monolithic Party shows few signs of equating capitalism with democracy. While the Lao brand of Communism has always been seen as relatively tame, it remains a far cry from political pluralism. Laos' first constitution since the Communists came to power in 1975 was approved in 1991. The country's political system is referred to as a popular democracy, yet it has rejected any significant moves towards multi-party reforms.

Take the elections to the 108-seat National Assembly on 24 February 2002. All of the candidates standing for election had been approved by the LPRP's mass organization, the Lao Front for National Construction. While it is not necessary for a candidate to be a member of the LPRP to stand, they are closely vetted and have to demonstrate that they have a 'sufficient level of knowledge of party policy'. As with the previous elections to the National Assembly at the end of 1997, only one of the 108 deputies elected was not a member of the Lao People's Revolutionary Party. This pattern of party cadres maintaining political seats was repeated in the National Assembly elections held in April 2006, where LPRP members won 114 out of 115 parliamentary seats.

On the dreamy streets of Vientiane, the chances of a Tiananmen-style uprising are remote. But the events of the late 1980s and early 1990s in Eastern Europe and Moscow did alarm hardliners – just as they did in Beijing and Hanoi. They can be reasonably confident, however, that in their impoverished nation, most people are more worried about where their next meal is going to come from than they are about the allure of multi-party democracy. Day-to-day politics aren't on the radar of most Lao citizens and many would find it hard to name the president and prime minister.

The greatest concern for the Lao leadership is what effect westernization is having upon the population. The economic reforms, or so the authorities would seem to believe, have brought not only foreign investment and new consumer goods, but also greed, corruption, consumerism and various social ills from drugs to prostitution.

Today, the politburo still largely controlled the country and, for now, sweeping changes unlikely. Most of the country's leaders are well into their 60s and were educated in communist countries like Russia and Vietnam. However, the younger Lao people (particularly those that have studied abroad in Japan, Australia, UK or the US) are starting to embrace new political and economic ideas. The government takes inspiration from Vietnam's success and is more likely to follow the lead of its neighbour rather than adopting any Western model of government.

## Foreign relations

Laos is rapidly becoming a keystone in mainland Southeast Asia and sees its future in linking in with its more powerful and richer neighbours. To this end Laos joined the Association of Southeast Asian Nations (ASEAN) on 23 July 1997, becoming the group's second Communist member (Vietnam joined in July 1995). By joining, Vientiane hoped to be in a better position to trade off the interests of the various powers in the region, thereby giving it greater room for manoeuvre. It was also hoped that Laos would be able to develop on the coat tails of Southeast Asia's economic 'tigers'.

One of Laos' strategies for further integration into the Asian economy is to establish itself as a regional transit point, with new highways dissecting the country at 100 km intervals.

Laos is the only landlocked country in Southeast Asia and Vientiane is keen to pursue a cooperative 'equilibrium policy' with its neighbours. There is a widely held view that Laos – a small, poor, weak and landlocked country – is best served by having multiple friends in international circles. It has often been referred to as a 'buffer' state, which exists to ensure that none of the surrounding countries have to border each other. The leadership in Vientiane is in the tricky situation of having to play off China's military might, Thailand's commercial aggressiveness and Vietnam's population pressures, while keeping everyone happy. The answer, in many people's minds, is to promote a policy of interdependence in mainland Southeast Asia.

**Relations with Thailand** From the 1980s the government took steps to improve its foreign relations – and Thailand has been the main beneficiary. Historically, Thailand has always been the main route for international access to landlocked

Laos. Survival instincts told the Vientiane regime that reopening its front door was of paramount importance. The border disputes with Thailand have now been settled and the bloody clashes of 1987 and 1988, when thousands on both sides lost their lives, are history. Thailand is Laos' largest investor and the success of the market reforms depend more on Thailand than any other country. Economic pragmatism, then, has forced Vientiane to cosy up to Bangkok. This does not mean that relations are warm. Indeed, Vientiane is suspicious of Thai intentions, a suspicion born of a history of conflict.

Thailand is Vientiane's lifeline to the outside world. In 1994 the two old foes agreed to build the Mittaphab – or Friendship – bridge across the Mekong linking Vientiane with Nong Khai in Northeast Thailand. The bridge was built with Australian assistance and opened in 1994 (see box, page 61).

Thais have emerged as one of the main sources of foreign investment in Laos. A number of Thai commercial banks have set up in Laos, along with businesspeople, consultants and loggers. Young Lao, who once attended universities in the old Soviet bloc, are now dispatched to Thai universities. The warming of relations between Bangkok and Vientiane has raised some eyebrows: sceptics say Laos' wealth of unexploited natural resources is a tempting reward for patching things up. Thailand is also the most important player in the Nam Theun II hydropower project. But to its credit, Thailand has prioritised aid to Laos and has signed joint ventures in almost every sector – from science and technology to trade, banking and agriculture. Thai businesspeople have partially taken over the state beer and brewery and the Thai conglomerate Shinawatra (owned by the former disgraced Thai prime minister) has been given telecommunications concessions. Nonetheless, Thai diplomats are only too aware of the poor reputation that their businessmen have in Vientiane. They are regarded as overbearing and superior in their attitude to the Lao and rapacious, predatory and mercenary in their business dealings. The Thai government has even run courses to try and improve business behaviour.

**The sleeping giant awakens: relations with China** In 1988 China and Laos normalized relations and this was followed by a defence co-operation agreement signed in 1993. Recently, Beijing has taken a particular interest in developing Laos' infrastructure, more out of self-interest than altruism. As China continues to develop at a breakneck speed, its interest in Laos' natural resources is expected to escalate, particularly in the areas of timber, iron ore, copper, gold, and gemstones. China is now Laos' second largest trading partner and foreign investor. The Asian Development Bank (ADB) reported that Lao-China trade grew from US$33.1 million in 1990 to US$118.3 million in 2003 and to US$250 million in 2007, for the most part, in China's favour. The economic giant also built numerous roads in Laos pro bono, in exchange for logging the areas around the roads.

Of the US$4313 million in foreign investment approved in 2009, the greatest number of projects were Chinese, at 324.

Chinese companies are investing heavily in Lao's natural resources, including mining, rubber plantations and hydropower (the largest sector), as well as telecommunications, construction materials and hotels and restaurants. Alongside this economic investment, there has been an increase in Chinese migration. The number of Chinese officially living in Laos is 30,000, though the unofficial number is estimated to be 10 times that. Nonetheless, not a bad word is to be whispered about Beijing in the political corridors of Vientiane.

Laos' ever-tightening relationship with China could jeopardize ties with the country's closest ally, Vietnam, which shares a 1300-km-long border with Laos and historically has had poor relations with China.

**Relations with Vietnam** The Lao government has a special relationship with Vietnam, as it was Hanoi that helped the LPRP achieve power. Vietnam is also Laos' biggest trading partner. However, as Laos has turned to the West, Japan and Thailand for economic help, the government has become more critical of its closest Communist ally, Vietnam. Following Vietnam's invasion of Cambodia in December 1978, thousands of Vietnamese moved into northern Laos as permanent colonizers and by 1978 there were an estimated 40,000 Vietnamese regulars in Laos but, in 1987, 50,000 Vietnamese troops withdrew. In 1990 a Vientiane census found 15,000 Vietnamese living illegally in the capital, most of whom were promptly deported. With the death of President Kaysone Phomvihane in November 1992, another historical link with Vietnam was cut. He was half-Vietnamese and most of his cabinet owed their education and their posts to Hanoi's succour during the war years. As the old men of the Lao Communist Party die off, so their replacements are looking elsewhere for investment and political support. They do not have such deep fraternal links with their brothers in Hanoi and are keen to diversify their international relations.

**Relations with the USA** Laos is the only country in Indochina to have maintained relations with the US since 1975, despite the fact that, 30 years since the illegal bombing campaign of Laos subsided, the US has neither offered a substantial sum of money for reparations nor helped to clear the tonnes of unexploded ordnance littering the eastern side of the country. Washington even expected the Lao government to allocate funds to help locate the bodies of US pilots shot down in the war. At a meeting between the Foreign Affairs Minister, General Phoune Sipaseuth, and the US Secretary of State, James Baker, in October 1990, Vientiane pledged to co-operate with the US over the narcotics trade and to step up the search for the 530 American MIAs still listed as missing in the Lao jungle. In 1993, trilateral talks between Laos, Vietnam and the US allowed for greater cooperation in the search for MIAs, many of whom are thought to have been airmen, shot down over the Ho Chi Minh Trail. The MIA charity, based in Vientiane, has since assumed quite a high profile. In 1992, America's diplomatic presence in Laos was upgraded to ambassadorial status from chargé d'affaires and, at the end of 1997, a high-level US mission to Laos promised greater support in the country's bomb-defusing work. However, until 2004, Laos remained one of the few countries to be denied normal trade relations with the US, the others being North Korea, Cuba and Myanmar (Burma).

Under pressure from the US (a dangling carrot perhaps?) Laos has all but eradicated opium, at huge cost to the country socially and economically. Since 1989, the US government has handed over millions for drug control to the Lao government but this hasn't stretched far enough to ensure that former opium producers aren't left starving.

But relations between the two countries have improved. This is driven by the US desire to counterbalance growing Chinese influence in the region. Most mainland Southeast Asian countries are reaping the rewards by simultaneously playing off the two superpowers and securing as much aid and trade as possible from both. In February 2005, a Bilateral Trade Agreement between the US and Laos entered into force.

**Relations with other countries** Fortunately Laos is unwilling to put all its eggs in one basket. Japan is now a major aid donor and Vientiane has also courted other Western countries, particularly Sweden (a long-time ally), France, Germany and Australia, who have donated significant sums of aid. Lao's former lifeline with Moscow is now of scant importance to Laos' economic future.

## Economy

Twenty-five years ago, if the world's financial markets crashed and international trade and commerce collapsed overnight, Laos would have been blissfully immune from the catastrophe. It would be 'farming as usual' the next morning. Since the mid-1980s, though, the government has gradually begun cautiously to tread the free market path, veering off the old command system. Farms have been privatized and the state has to compete for produce with market traders at market prices. Many of the unprofitable state-owned businesses and factories have been leased or sold off.

Centuries of war and 15 years of Communism had little impact on the self-reliant villages of rural Laos. After the 1975 takeover, the Lao government, reliant on aid from Vietnam, decided to assuage this dependency by expanding on their existing economic base – agriculture. To this end, in March 1978 the government launched an agricultural cooperativization scheme – a plan to collectivize agriculture through the development of village-based cooperatives. The government's attempts at cooperativization proved unpopular and unworkable. Just before the cooperativization programme was abruptly suspended in mid-1979 there were 2800 cooperatives accounting for perhaps 25% of farming families. But even these figures overestimate the role of cooperatives at that time, for many were scarcely functioning.

The little work that has been undertaken on agriculture during this period has shown that even when cooperatives were functioning, their members were reluctant participants and there was a good amount of petty obstructionism. The reasons why cooperatives were such a failure are numerous. To begin with and unlike China and Vietnam, there were almost no large landlords, there was little tenancy and there was abundant land. The inequalities that were so obvious in neighbouring countries simply did not exist in Laos. Second, most farmers were subsistence cultivators; capitalism had barely made inroads into the Lao countryside and the forces of commercialization were largely absent. Further and third, the LPRP provided little support either of a technical or financial kind. As a result, farmers – largely uneducated and bound to their traditional methods of production – saw little incentive to change. In some areas it was not so much a lack of interest in cooperatives, but a positive dislike of them. There were reports of farmers slaughtering their cattle, burning their fields and eating their poultry, rather than handing their livestock or crops over to the Party. By mid-1979, when the policy was suspended, the leadership in Vientiane had concluded that their attempts at cooperativization had been a disaster.

After the policy was suspended, the government returned to a free enterprise system in the countryside. Farmers now effectively own their land and, since a new land law was approved by the National Assembly in 1997, they can pass it on to their children and use it as collateral to get a bank loan. They can produce whatever crops they like and can sell these on what has become virtually a free market. Lao farmers, though they may be poor and though technology may be antiquated, are in essence no different in terms of the ways they work than their kinsfolk over the Mekong in Thailand.

Laos made the jump from a sleepy agrarian economy hidden behind a facade of socialism to a reforming economy like China and Vietnam in the 1980s. In English this change is rather blandly named the New Economic Mechanism (NEM). Locally, the more evocative terms *chin thanakan mai* (new thinking) and *kanpatihup setthakit* (reform economy) are used. The origins of the NEM can be traced back to 1982 when the possibility of fundamental reform of the economy was first entertained by a small group within the leadership. The logic for economic reform and the integration of Laos into the regional – and world – economies was pretty compelling. During the decade of command planning from 1975 through to 1985 the economy grew at just 2.9% per year, barely sufficient to meet the needs of a growing population and not enough to fuel the desire for a better standard of living. The government's fear was that, like other communist countries, the failure to bring the Lao people a better standard of living might challenge the supremacy of the Lao People's Revolutionary Party. The decision to opt for reform seemed to be borne out as the economy picked up steam. For the next three or four years the debate continued within this small circle and it was not until 1985 that the NEM was actually pilot-tested in the Vientiane area, making Laos one of the very first countries to embrace 'perestroika'. As late General Secretary Kaysone Phomvihane stated at the Fourth Party Congress in 1986:

"In all economic activities, we must know how to apply objective laws and take into account socio-economic efficiency. At the present time, our country is still at the first stage of the transition period. Hence the system of economic laws now being applied to our country is very complicated. It includes not only the specific laws of socialism but also the laws of commodity production. Reality indicates that if we only apply the specific economic laws of socialism alone and defy the general laws pertaining to commodity production, or vice versa, we will make serious mistakes in our economic undertaking during this transition period" (General Secretary Kaysone Phomvihane, Fourth Party Congress 1986; quoted in Lao PDR 1989).

Under the horrified gaze of Marx and Lenin – their portraits still dominate the plenary hall – it was announced that the state motto had changed from "Peace, Independence, Unity and Socialism" to "Peace, Independence, Democracy, Unity and Prosperity". The last part is largely wishful thinking for one of the poorest countries in Southeast Asia, but it reflected the realization that unless Laos turned off the socialist road fast, it would have had great difficulty digging itself out of the economic quagmire that 15 years' adherence to Marxism had created.

The success of the reforms there led to the NEM being presented at – and adopted by – the critical Fourth Party Congress of 1986. The NEM encompasses a range of reformist policies, much like those adopted in other countries from Russia to Vietnam: a move to a market determination of prices and resource allocation; a shift away from central planning to 'guidance' planning; a decentralization of control to industries and lower levels of government and the encouragement of the private sector; the encouragement of foreign investment and the promulgation of a new investment law allowing more relaxed foreign ownership and 'tax holidays'; a lifting of barriers to internal and external trade.

What Laos was able to achieve by introducing the NEM was a very rapid reorientation of its economy. But the question to be asked is: 'what exactly was being reformed?' The assumption is that Laos, as a so-called transitional economy, was making – is making – the transition from communism to capitalism, from state to market. This, though, misses the point that in 1986 there was remarkably little in Laos to reform. The great majority of the population were poor farmers (and still are) and the country's industrial base was almost non-existent. There were almost no communes to break up and there was no large state industrial sector to dismember. It all meant that the task of the Lao leadership has been comparatively easy when compared with, say, Vietnam. In a sense, Laos was never socialist except in name and so the shift to a market economy involved not a move from socialism to capitalism, but from subsistence to capitalism.

This doesn't mean that reform has been easy, because although Laos may not have had to undo years of socialist reconstruction and development, there was also little that the leadership could build on to promote modernization. There were few skilled workers, low levels of infrastructure, large slices of the country are almost impossible to reach and few entrepreneurs and even fewer people with the money to invest in new ventures. In other words, Laos was short of most of the elements that constitute a modern economy.

To introduce the sweeping reforms former President Kaysone Phomvihane shouldered much of the blame for the miserable state of the economy, admitting that the Party had made mistakes. Laos underwent the political equivalent of an earth tremor in March 1991 at the Fifth Congress of the Lao People's Revolutionary Party (LPRP). Pro-market reforms were embraced and the politburo and central committee got a much-needed transfusion of new blood. At the same time, the hammer and sickle motif was quietly removed from the state emblem and enlightened sub-editors set to work on the national credo, which is emblazoned on all official documents. In August 1991, at the opening of the People's Supreme Assembly, Kaysone Phomvihane, the late President, said: "Socialism is still our objective, but it is a distant one. Very distant." With that statement, Kaysone embraced – somewhat reluctantly, it must be said – the country's market-orientated policy, Chin Thanakan Mai or 'New Thinking'.

At the Congress in 1991 he set the new national agenda: Laos had to step up its exports, encourage more foreign investment, promote tourism and rural development, entice its shifting cultivators into proper jobs and revamp the financial system. In doing so he prioritized the problems but offered no solutions bar the loosening of state control and the promotion of private enterprise.

The first task for the government was to stabilize the value of the local currency, the kip, and introduce market 'discipline' so as to eliminate a booming currency black market. So from 1986, when economic reforms were first introduced, Laos eliminated six of its seven official exchange rates to create a unified market-related rate. By the early 1990s the kip had stabilized at around 700 to the US dollar. The once-booming black market all but disappeared. Although still a non-convertible currency, the kip was as much in demand in Laos as the US dollar and Thai baht. This helped put Laos on a more competitive footing. Unfortunately for supporters of economic reform, the collapse of the Thai baht and the consequent fall in the value of the kip encouraged the Lao government to reintroduce currency controls (see the section below).

During the early years of reform, between 1986 and 1990, the economy grew and from 1991-1995 increased again to 6.5% per year. However economic liberalization also has its risks. The collapse of the Thai baht at the beginning of July 1997 also dragged down the Lao kip while Thailand's fall from economic grace caused Thai investment in Laos to evaporate (Thailand is Laos' largest foreign investor). 1998 saw zero growth and inflation escalated to nearly 100% as the government rather ineptly tried to control events. Since then the economy has stabilized.

## Reform in a period of economic crisis

While Laos might be poor it was not insulated from the effects of Asia's economic crisis. Indeed, it is the reforms of the years since 1986 which has made the country vulnerable to developments beyond its borders. The Lao kip was dragged down by the depreciation of the Thai baht and lost value from US$1 = 978 kip in December 1996 to US$1 = 1780 kip in November 1997. Since then, it has sunk further and when this book went to press, there were 8265 kip to the US dollar. In fact there is no currency in Southeast Asia, with the exception of the Burmese kyat, which has lost more value.

As the currency lost value the government lost its nerve and slapped on currency controls and rounded up the private money changers who have been operating for years in Vientiane. The governor of the Lao central bank blamed "speculative attempts by opportunists" for the Kip's collapse. The trade deficit widened and eight state-owned banks became effectively insolvent. Inflation during 1997 rose and in 1998 continued to escalate to reach 100% by the end of the year. There was also a sharp downturn in investment (remember, Thailand is Laos' largest foreign investor).

The leadership held very different views on how to deal with the crisis. The so-styled conservatives in the politburo wanted the Lao government take a step back from the market and emphasize domestic resources. Reformists wanted further liberalization – à la IMF – and to extricate the country from the economic mess by integrating still more rapidly into the regional and world economies. The outcome of this debate, in typically Lao style, was a bit of both. The leadership took their foot off the pedal of economic reform but did not substantially reverse what was already in place. It also seems that they may have realized the futility of trying to rein back trade with neighbouring Thailand and China given their lack of economic control in many areas.

What was perhaps most surprising about Laos' economic malaise was the absence of any public disturbances. With the economy contracting, inflation running at more than 100%, banks broke, foreign investment evaporating and the government apparently "clueless and helpless as to what to do, one might have expected just a little more public debate and criticism. After all, Thailand and South Korea both saw a change of government, Malaysia the trial and imprisonment of Deputy Prime Minister Anwar Ibrahim and Indonesia the violent dumping of Suharto, president of more than three decades. Laos may be renowned for the relaxed and forgiving ways of its people, but it is hard not to wonder, 'for how much longer?'

## Building up the economy

Laos, as books constantly reiterate, is poor. While it is tempting to mouth those favourite words 'poor but happy', there can be little doubt that the major challenge facing the country is how to promote development. There are few people – whether government ministers or shifting cultivators, businessmen or hawkers – who do not fervently hope that their children will be better off than they. And 'better off' means richer. As Houmpheng Souralay of the Foreign Investment Management Committee said to Singapore's *Sunday Times*, "We want to catch up with our neighbours like Thailand, Cambodia and Vietnam." But, he significantly added, only if those "investments are wholesome and do not erode our cultural identity".

Traditionally, one of Laos' most important sources of foreign exchange was receipts from over-flight rights as the Bolovan Plateau lies on the flight path from Bangkok to Hong Kong and Tokyo. Nearly 100 international flights traverse Lao airspace every day and in the mid-1990s the government was receiving payment for each one. But, today, most of the Laos' foreign exchange is reaped from their natural resources.

The country and its foreign strategists look to four distinct areas for future income. The first concentrates on mining and energy. Mining rights to some of Laos' huge lignite reserves have been sold to Thai investors, while hydropower projects are plentiful. Other untapped mineral resources include reserves of gold, gemstones and iron ore, while foreign companies have undertaken preliminary searches for oil. The second area of interest is agriculture and forestry. Investors are looking at growing feed grains like soya beans and maize for export to Thailand. Raw timber exports are being replaced by processed wood industries. More enlightened analysts also see Laos as a potential large exporter of organic agricultural products – after all, agriculture in the country has never had to rely on biochemical inputs or genetically engineered seeds. The third potential area for ongoing development is tourism, which continues to grow at the rate of knots but the government is wary of Laos going the same way as Thailand. The fourth and final strategy – and the most ambitious – is for Laos to become the service centre between China, Vietnam, Cambodia and Thailand.

The General Council of the World Trade Organisation formally approved the Accession Package of Laos on 26 October 2012. Laos has been a member of WTO since 2 February 2013.

Major development constraints in Laos are the shortage of skilled workers and capital, an undeveloped communication system, poor educational and health resources, rugged terrain and low population density. Add to this a patchwork of cultures and different languages and it is easy to see why the country is difficult to manage. Even with large amounts of public expenditure going into infrastructure, the challenge of linking people to the market and the state remains supremely important. Without roads and transport farmers cannot obtain inputs for agriculture, market any surplus production or increase their incomes.

In an effort to make the business climate more attractive, the state bank now supplies credit to all sectors of the economy. Provincial banks have been told to operate as autonomous commercial banks. State enterprises have been warned that if their bottom line does not show a profit they are out of business. Provinces are free to conclude their own trading agreements with private companies and neighbouring countries – which generally means Thailand.

Tens of thousands of people work for the government in a top-heavy and often corrupt bureaucracy. Working for the Laos government is considered a job for life. Civil servants are paid around half the wage of those working as domestics for expatriate families. No wonder official corruption and profiteering are on the increase. The main financial incentive available to civil servants are the perks offered by NGOs – such as use of a car, per diems for trips away and scholarships to foreign universities. Admirably, most people who work for the civil service in Laos do so for prestige and personal pride; there is little other incentive as the lure of long-term gains, in the form of corruption, usually take years to accrue.

In 2010, and in conjunction with Korea Exchange, Laos opened its own stock market in Vientiane to invigorate the economy in the downturn. In June 2010 Prime Minster Bouasone Bouphavanh told the World Economic Forum on East Asia that Laos is aiming for 'no less than' 8% annual economic growth until 2015. Bouphavanh also told the conference that it wants to elevate its status out of underdevelopment by 2020.

## Hydropower

The country's greatest economic potential lies in its natural resources – timber, gold, precious stones, coal and iron – and hydropower. Laos has been dubbed the 'battery' or 'Kuwait' of Southeast Asia and the government has signed various deals with Thailand, China and Vietnam to sell electricity.

At the beginning of the century, it was estimated that only 1% of the country's hydropower potential of some 18,000 MW had so far been exploited. That proportion grew considerably with the construction of the Nam Theun II (see page 185) dam which has a capacity of 1070 MW. The huge dam was predicted to generate up to US$150 million revenue a year for Laos or approximately US$2 billion over a 25-year period. This is because the project exports the vast majority of the power to Thailand.

A few years ago these grand hydropower plans all seemed eminently sensible: energy-hungry Thailand's economy was rapidly growing and Laos was well placed to meet its needs. But there were two issues that the Lao government and its international advisers failed to take sufficiently into account: the international environmental lobby and an economic slowdown. The Nam Theun II dam, for example, was delayed by the discoveries of rare bats and birds, with financial backing from agencies like the World Bank and the Asian Development Bank held up for years. The World Bank, now all too conscious that its environmental credentials have been tarnished by dam developments in India and elsewhere, went out of its way to ensure that all the required environmental and other studies were undertaken.

But the Nam Theun II dam is not quite the open-and-shut case it might appear, with the international environmental lobby on the side of local people and animals and the dastardly World Bank supporting shadowy businessmen and the interests of international capital. When local people were asked their views of the dam, many welcomed the proposal. Even some environmentalists argued that having the dam might be preferable to having the forests logged. For without the money that can be earned from selling electricity to Thailand one of the few alternatives is selling wood. Plans are underway to further exploit the potential of the Mekong and its tributaries, with many more projects slated for development over the next decade.

### Mining and logging

Mining is also providing large revenue for the country. In the years leading up to 2007, more than 140 mining concessions were allocated, many to Chinese looking for gold, copper, iron, potassium and bauxite. Australia's ORD Rivers Resources in collaboration with China's Nonferrous Metals International Mining Company (CNMIM) plans to develop a 727-sq-km concession on the Bolovan Plateau in southern Laos into one of the world's largest bauxite mines.

The symbol of southern Laos should be the timber truck, gargantuan beasts loaded with decades-old trees dwarfing the small roads. Malaysian, Taiwanese, Chinese and Thai firms have been awarded timber concessions in the country, many of them working in collaboration with the Lao military, which has become an important economic player.

### Agriculture

This remains the mainstay of the Lao economy, accounting for just under half of the country's GDP. Around 80% of Lao citizens are employed in some kind of subsistence agriculture, which they depend on for their survival. Rice is the staple food crop, cultivated by the majority of the population, and nearly three-quarters of Laos' farmers grow enough to sell or barter some of their crop. It is believed that rice accounts for a quarter of the country's GDP. Other primary agricultural products include coffee, corn, sugarcane, vegetables, tobacco, ginger, water buffalo, pigs, cattle, poultry, sweet potatoes, cotton, tea and peanuts.

While Laos may be land rich, this does not mean that everyone necessarily has enough to eat, and the achievement of food security is one of the government's priority. National self-sufficiency does not equate with local food security. Food deficits are common, resulting in many households experiencing both chronic and acute malnutrition. There is also intra-regional variation. For example, Sekong in the south is traditionally a rice deficit province, as is Xieng Khouang in the centre. Further down the scale, from national to regional, provincial, district and village, there are likely to be variations in food security. Even households that are in production surplus may face a consumption deficit due to their having to sell a portion of production to meet demands for cash or to pay off debts.

The growing population poses a challenge to rice farmers. Laos' population is increasing at 2.5% per annum – from 4.25 million in 1990 to 6.8 million in 2009. This means that in the last 20 years Laos has had to feed 50% more people. Luckily, during the same period it increased rice production by 70% (one million tonnes a year). However, the challenge for Lao farmers is whether they will be able to increase the level of rice production as the population demand increases. As Laos' population is expected to grow to 8.8 million by the year 2020, the demand for rice is expected to exceed an additional million tons of rice.

The main agricultural areas are on the Mekong's floodplains, especially around Vientiane and Savannakhet. The government has been successful in expanding the area capable of producing two rice crops a year by developing the country's irrigation infrastructure. Cotton, coffee, maize and tobacco are the other main crops and the production of these and other 'industrial' crops such as soya and mung beans has increased in recent years.

While shifting cultivators continue to pose a 'problem' to the government, their numbers have dropped substantially since 1985 as the land allocation programme has been enthusiastically implemented. This is reflected by the fact that they are now said to cut down 100,000 ha of forest a year, compared with 300,000 in the early 1980s. The situation has improved dramatically since the mid-1970s when Hmong General Vang Pao complained to a National Geographic reporter that "In one year a single family will chop down and burn trees worth US$6000 and grow a rice crop worth US$240."

## Dependency on aid and development aims

Laos depends heavily on imports – everything from agricultural machinery and cars to petrol products, textiles and pharmaceuticals – which are heavily financed by foreign aid. Western bilateral donors are enthusiastically filling the aid gap left by the Socialist bloc. In June 2003, Russia agreed to write off 70% of the loans from the Cold War period.

Countries and private donors are falling over each other to fund projects, particularly anything that involves government reform; NGOs are homing in and development banks are offering soft loans and structural adjustment programmes. As Laos' foreign debt is mostly on highly concessional terms, it is not crippled by repayment schedules, though there is a reasonably hefty bill awaiting them.

## Poverty

As in neighbouring Vietnam, the economic reforms are beginning to widen inequalities. Most of those who are doing well live in towns or at least close to one of the country's main roads. This means that off-road communities, and especially those in remote rural areas, are finding that – at least in relative terms – they are becoming poorer. In addition, because it is mostly minority Lao Soung and Lao Theung who live in these marginal areas, the economic reforms are widening inequalities between ethnic groups. One foreign aid worker was quoted in the Far Eastern Economic Review saying: "When they come down to Vientiane, where the lowland Lao [the Lao Loum] live, it's like Hong Kong to them. Here's money, here's development. In their own villages, there's nothing." As in Vietnam, the need to ensure that the economic reforms bring benefits to all and not just a few, is a key political question. The leadership are acutely aware that widening inequalities could fuel discontent and this is perhaps one reason why the government seems so intent on increasing the number of members of the National Assembly from ethnic minorities

The 2013 Human Development report reported that the average life expectancy at birth was 61.4 in 2000 and 77.8 in 2012. Gross National Income per capita rose from US$1296 in 2000 to US$2435 in 2012. The report stated: "Lao People's Democratic Republic's HDI value for 2012 is 0.543 – in the medium human development category – positioning the country at 138 out of 187 countries and territories. The rank is shared with Cambodia. Between 1985 and 2012, Lao People's Democratic Republic's HDI value increased from 0.346 to 0.543, an increase of 57%."

Maternal mortality remains dangerously high: for every 100,000 live births, 470 women die from pregnancy-related causes.

## The keystone of mainland Southeast Asia

In what sceptics might view as an ultimately futile effort, the leadership in Vientiane have chanced upon an economic future for their country: as the 'keystone' or 'crossroads' of Southeast Asia. Nor is it just Laos' leaders who are drumming up enthusiasm for this notion. The Asian Development Bank (the Asian arm of the World Bank) is at the forefront of developing – and funding – what has become known as the Greater Mekong Sub-region or GMS. This will link southwest China, Thailand, Myanmar (Burma), Cambodia, Vietnam and Laos. And within this scenario, Laos is the crucial pivotal country through which most transport links will have to pass. There is talk of a 'Golden Quadrangle' (as opposed to the infamous Golden Triangle) – even of a Golden Land. This reference draws on ancient Indian texts which talked of 'Suvarnaphum' – a Golden Land – which encompassed modern-day Thailand, Laos, Myanmar and probably Peninsular Malaysia and parts of Indonesia too.

# Footprint Mini Atlas
# Laos

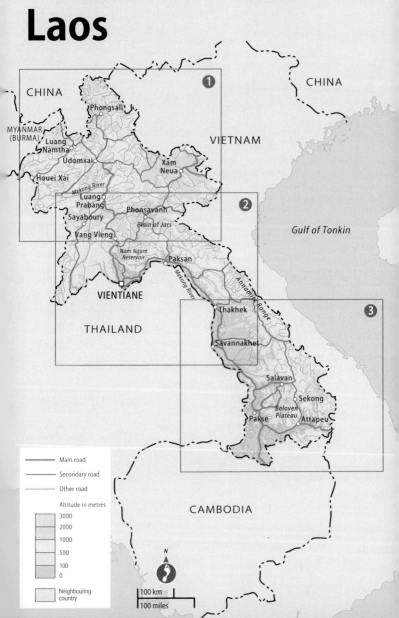

CHINA

MYANMAR
(BURMA)

CHINA

VIETNAM

Phongsali

Luang
Namtha

Udomxai

Xam
Neua

Houei Xai

Mekong River

Luang
Prabang

Phonsavanh

Sayaboury

Plain of Jars

Vang Vieng

Gulf of Tonkin

Nam Ngum
Reservoir

Paksan

VIENTIANE

Mekong River

Annamite Range

Thakhek

THAILAND

Savannakhet

Salavan

Sekong

Pakse

Boloven
Plateau

Attapeu

CAMBODIA

— Main road
— Secondary road
— Other road

Altitude in metres
3000
2000
1000
500
100
0

Neighbouring
country

N

100 km
100 miles

# Map 1

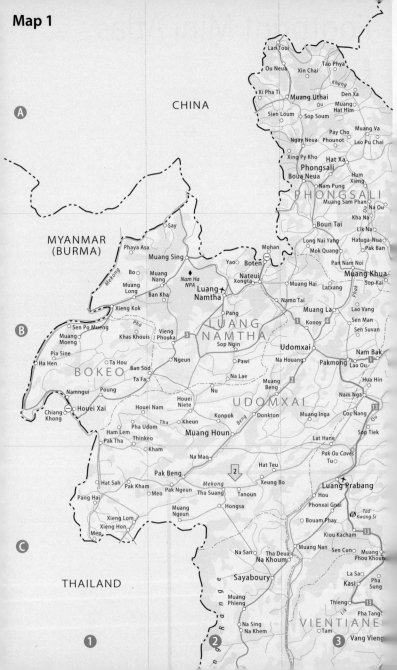

CHINA

MYANMAR
(BURMA)

THAILAND

Lan Toui
Ou Neua
Xin Chai
Tao Phya
Xi Pha Ti
Muang Uthai
Den Xa
Khang
Ou
Muang
Hat Him
Sien Loum
Sop Soum
Pay Cho
Muang Va
Ngay Neua
Phounot
Lao Pu Chai
Xing Py Kho
Hat Xa
Phongsali
Boua Neua
Hum
Xieng
Nam Pung
PHONGSALI
Muang Sam Phan
Na Ou
Kha Na
Say
Boun Tai
Lik Na
Hatuga-Nua
Phaya Asa
Mohan
Long Nai Yang
Pak Ban
Muang Sing
Yao
Boten
Mok Quang
Pan Nam Noi
Bo
Muang
Nang
Nam Ha
NPA
Nateui
Muang Hai
Muang Khua
Sop Kai
Muang
Long
Ban Kha
Luang
Namtha
Xongta
Namo Tai
Latxang
Phat
Xieng Kok
Pha
Pang
Konoy
Muang La
Lao Vang
Sen Man
Sen Suvan
Sen Po Mueng
Khas Khouis
Vieng
Phouka
LUANG
NAMTHA
Sop Ngin
Udomxai
Nam Bak
Lao Ou
Muang
Moeng
Pia Sine
Ta Hou
Ngeun
Pawi
Na Houang
Pakmong
Ha Hen
BOKEO
Ban Sod
Ta Fa
Nu
Na Lae
Muang
Beng
UDOMXAI
Hua Hin
Namngui
Poung
Houei Niete
Konpok
Donkton
Muang Inga
Nam Nga
Chiang
Khong
Houei Xai
Houei Nam
Tha
Kheun
Beng
Coc Nang
Sop Tiek
Ham Lem
Pha Udom
Muang Houn
Lat Hane
Ou
Pak Tha
Thinkeo
Kham
Na Mao
Pak Ou Caves
Tu
Hat Sah
Pak Beng
Hat Teu
Luang Prabang
Pang Hai
Pak Kham
Meo
Pak Ngeun
Tha Suang
Mekong
Xeung Bo
Hou
Tad
Kwang Si
Xieng Lom
Xieng Hon
Muang
Ngeun
Hongsa
Tanoun
Phonxai Gnai
Bouam Phay
Mep
Kiou Kacham
Na San
Tha Deua
Na Khoum
Muang Nan
Sen Cun
Muang
Phou Khoun
Sayaboury
La Sa
Kasi
Pha
Sung
Muang
Phieng
Thieng
Pha Tang
Na Sing
Na Khem
VIENTIANE
Lik
Tam
Vang Vieng

A

B

C

1

2

3

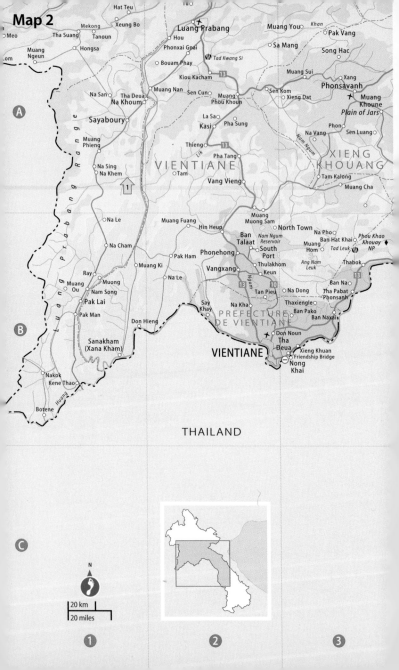

# Map 2

# Map 3

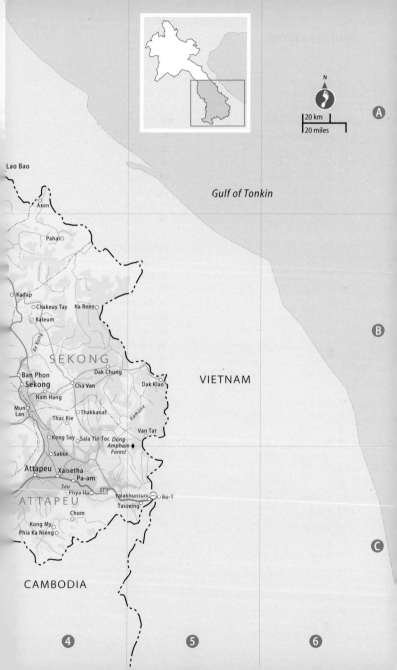

# Map symbols

| | | | |
|---|---|---|---|
| □ | Capital city | ▢ | Building |
| ○ | Other city, town | ▫ | Sight |
| ≈ | International border | ✝ ✝ | Cathedral, church |
| ≈ | Regional border | 🏯 | Chinese temple |
| ⊖ | Customs | 🛕 | Hindu temple |
| ⬭ | Contours (approx) | ⚑ | Meru |
| ▲ | Mountain, volcano | 🕌 | Mosque |
| ⇋ | Mountain pass | ⛩ | Stupa |
| ⊔⊔⊔ | Escarpment | ✡ | Synagogue |
| ⌣ | Glacier | ▤ | Tourist office |
| ⬚ | Salt flat | ⛁ | Museum |
| ⬱ | Rocks | ⊠ | Post office |
| ⩊⩊ | Seasonal marshland | ⒫ | Police |
| ⬚ | Beach, sandbank | ⑤ | Bank |
| ⑄ | Waterfall | @ | Internet |
| ⌐ | Reef | ♪ | Telephone |
| ══ | National highway | ⓜ | Market |
| ── | Paved road | ➕ | Medical services |
| ── | Unpaved or ripio (gravel) road | ⓟ | Parking |
| ---- | Track | ⓒ | Petrol |
| ······ | Footpath | ♌ | Golf |
| ── | Railway | ⁂ | Archaeological site |
| ↦■ | Railway with station | ♦ | National park, |
| ✈ | Airport | | wildlife reserve |
| 🚌 | Bus station | ✲ | Viewing point |
| Ⓜ | Metro station | ▲ | Campsite |
| ---- | Cable car | ⌂ | Refuge, lodge |
| ++++ | Funicular | 🏰 | Castle, fort |
| 🚢 | Ferry | ↘ | Diving |
| ░░░ | Pedestrianized street | 🌲🌴 | Deciduous, coniferous, |
| ) ( | Tunnel | | palm trees |
| → | One way-street | 🌴 | Mangrove |
| ⫼⫼ | Steps | ⌂ | Hide |
| ⨞ | Bridge | ♫ | Vineyard, winery |
| ▬▬ | Fortified wall | ⚗ | Distillery |
| ⬚ | Park, garden, stadium | ⌅ | Shipwreck |
| ● | Where to stay | ✕ | Historic battlefield |
| ❷ | Restaurants | ⇨ | Related map |
| ❶ | Bars & clubs | | |

# Culture

## People

Laos has a population of 6.8 million people, with a growth rate of 1.8% in 2014.

### Ethnic groups

Laos is less a nation state than a collection of different tribes and languages. Its enormous ethnic diversity has long been an impediment to national integration. In total there are more than 60 ethnic groups which are often described as living in isolated, self-sufficient communities. Although communication and intercourse may have been difficult – and remains so – there has always been communication, trade and inter-marriage between the different Lao 'worlds' and today, with even greater interaction, the walls between them are becoming more permeable still.

Laos' ethnically diverse population is usually – and rather simplistically – divided by ecological zone into three groups: the wet rice cultivating, Buddhist Lao Loum of the lowlands, who are politically and numerically dominant, constituting just under half of the total population; the Lao Theung who occupy the mountain slopes and make up about a quarter of the population; and the Lao Soung, or upland Lao, who live in the high mountains and practise shifting cultivation and who represent less than a fifth of Laos' total population. Overall, in Laos the ethnic majority, Lao Loum, are in the minority. The terms were brought into general usage by the Pathet Lao who wished to emphasize that all of Laos' inhabitants were 'Lao' and to avoid the more derogatory terms that had been used in the past – such as the Thai word *kha* (slave), to describe the Mon-Khmer Lao Theung like the Khmu and Lamet. Stereotypical representations of each category are depicted on the 1000 kip note.

Although the words have a geographical connotation, they should be viewed more as contrasting pairs of terms: loum and *theung* mean 'below' and 'above' (rather than hillsides and lowland), while *soung* is paired with *tam*, meaning 'high' and 'low'. These two pairs of oppositions were then brought together by the Pathet Lao into one three-fold division. Thus, the Lao Theung in one area may, in practice, occupy a higher location than Lao Soung in another area. In addition, economic change, greater interaction between the groups and the settlement of

## ON THE ROAD

### Population by ethnic group

| Group | Official category | % of total population |
|---|---|---|
| Tai | Lao Loum | 55 |
| Mon-Khmer | Lao Theung | 35 |
| Tibeto-Burman | Lao Soung | 10 |

## ON THE ROAD

## Lao, Laos and Laotians

Most Lao are not Laotians. And not all Laotians are Lao. Lao tends to be used to describe people of Lao stock. There are, in fact, several times more Lao in northeastern Thailand (Issan) – roughly 20 million – than there are in Laos, with a total population of some 5 million, of whom perhaps a little over a half are ethnic Lao. At the same time not all Laotians – people who are nationals of Laos – are ethnic Lao. There are also significant minority populations including Chinese, Vietnamese, the Mon-Khmer Lao Theung and the many tribal groups comprising the Lao Soung. After a few too many *lao-lao* it is easy to get confused.

lowland peoples in hill areas means that it is possible to find Lao Loum villages in upland areas, where the inhabitants practise swidden, not wet rice, agriculture. So, although it is possible to characterize the hills as inhabited by shifting cultivating Lao Theung of Mon-Khmer descent, in practice the neat delimitation of people into discrete spatial units breaks down and as the years go by is becoming untenable.

### Lao Loum

It has been noted that the Lao who have reaped the rewards of reform are the Lao Loum of T'ai stock – not the Lao Theung who are of Mon-Khmer descent or the ethnic Lao Soung, such as the Hmong but also Akha and Lahu. Ing-Britt Trankell, in her book *On the Road in Laos: an Anthropological Study of Road Construction and Rural Communities* (1993), writes that the Lao Loum's "sense of [cultural and moral] superiority is often manifested in both a patronizing and contemptuous attitude toward the Lao Theung and Lao Sung, who are thought of as backward and less susceptible to socio-economic development because they are still governed by their archaic cultural traditions". This attitude is still prevalent today, where Lao Loum sneer at the cultural practices of other ethnic groups, such as the Akha, as being unmodern. As a result many of these groups are ashamed to wear their traditional clothes in wider society, as there is s a stigma attached.

During the sixth and seventh centuries the Lao Loum arrived from the southern provinces of China. They occupied the valleys along the Mekong and its tributaries and drove the Lao Theung to more mountainous areas. The Lao Loum, who are ethnically almost indistinguishable from the Thais of the Isan region (the Northeast of Thailand), came under the influence of the Khmer and Indonesian cultures and sometime before the emergence of Lane Xang in the 14th century embraced Theravada Buddhism. The majority of Lao are Buddhist but retain many of their animist beliefs. Remote Lao Loum communities still usually have a *mor du* (a doctor who 'sees') or medium. The medium's job description is demanding: he must concoct love potions, heal the sick, devise and design protective charms and read the future.

Today, the Lao Loum are the principal ethnic group, accounting for nearly half the population, and Lao is their mother tongue. As the lowland Lao, they occupy the ricelands of the Mekong and its main tributary valleys. Their houses are made of wood and are built on stilts with thatched roofs – although tin roofs and Thai concrete houses are popular these days. The extended family is spread throughout several houses in one compound.

There are also several tribal sub-groups of this main Thai-Lao group; they are conveniently colour-coded and readily identifiable by their sartorial traits. There are, for example, the Red Tai, the White Tai and the Black Tai – who live in the upland valley areas in Xieng Khouang and Hua Phan provinces. That they live in the hills suggests they are Lao Theung, but ethnically and culturally they are closer to the Lao Loum.

## Lao Theung

The Lao Theung, consisting of 45 different sub-groups, are the descendants of the oldest inhabitants of the country and are of Mon-Khmer descent. They are sometimes called Kha (slave), as they were used as labourers by the Thai and Lao kings and are still poorer than the Lao Loum. Traditionally, the Lao Theung were semi-nomadic and they still live mainly on the mountain slopes of the interior, along the whole length of the Annamite Chain from South China. There are concentrations of Akha, Alak and Ta-Oy on the Bolaven Plateau in the south (see page 232) and Khmu in the north.

The Lao Theung's reliance on slash-and-burn, or shifting, agriculture is slowly being phased out. Traditionally, they would burn a small area of forest, cultivate it for a few years and then, when the soil was exhausted, abandon the land and moved on to a new area until the vegetation had regenerated and replenished the soil. Some groups merely shifted fields in a 10- to 15-year rotation; others not only shifted fields but also their villages, relocating in a fresh area of forest when the land had become depleted of nutrients. To obtain salt, metal implements and other goods that could not be made or obtained in the hills, the tribal peoples would trade resins and animal skins with the settled lowland Lao. Some groups, mainly those living closer to the towns, have converted to Buddhism but many are still animist.

The social and religious beliefs of the Lao Theung and their general outlook on health and happiness are governed by their belief in spirits. The shaman is a key personality in any village. The Alak, from the Bolovan Plateau (see page 232) test the prospects of a marriage by killing a chicken: the manner in which it bleeds will determine whether the marriage will be propitious. Buffalo sacrifices are also common in Lao Theung villages and it is not unusual for a community to slaughter all its livestock to appease the spirits.

Viet Minh guerrillas and American B-52s made life difficult for many of the Lao Theung tribes living in East Laos, who were forced to move away from the Ho Chi Minh Trail. By leaving their birth places the Lao Theung left their protecting spirits, forcing them to find new and unfamiliar ones.

## Lao Soung

The Lao Soung began migrating to Laos from South China, Tibet and Burma, in the early 18th century, settling high in the mountains (some up to 2500 m). The Hmong (formerly known as the Meo) and Yao (also called the Mien) are the principal Lao Soung groups.

## Yao (or Mien)

The Yao mainly live around Nam Tha – deep inside the Golden Triangle, near the borders with Thailand, Myanmar (Burma) and China. They are known as craftspeople – the men make knives, crossbows, rifles and high-quality, elaborately designed silver jewellery, which is worn by the women. Silver is a symbol of wealth among the Yao and Hmong.

The Mien or Yao are unique among the hilltribes in that they have a tradition of writing based on Chinese characters. Mien legend has it that they came from 'across the sea' during the 14th century, although it is generally thought that their roots are in South China where they originated about 2000 years ago.

The Mien village is not enclosed and is usually found on sloping ground. The houses are large, wooden and need to accommodate an extended family of 20 or more. They are built on the ground, not on stilts and have one large living area and four or more bedrooms. As with other tribes, the construction of the house must be undertaken carefully. The house needs to be orientated appropriately, so that the spirits are not disturbed and the ancestral altar installed on an auspicious day.

The Mien combine two religious beliefs: on the one hand they pay their dues to spirits and ancestors (informing them of family developments); and on the other, they follow Taoism as it was practised in China in the 13th and 14th centuries. The Taoist rituals are expensive and the Mien spend a great deal of their lives struggling to save enough money to afford life cycle ceremonies such as weddings and death ceremonies. Their economy is based upon the cultivation of dry rice, maize and small quantities of opium poppy.

**Material culture** The Mien women dress distinctively, with black turbans and red-ruffed tunics, making them easy to distinguish from the other hilltribes. All their clothes are made of black or indigo-dyed homespun cotton, which is then embroidered using distinctive cross-stitching. Their trousers are the most elaborate garments. Unusually, they sew from the back of the cloth and cannot see the pattern they are making. The children wear embroidered caps with red pompoms on the top and by the ears. The men's dress is a simple indigo-dyed jacket and trousers, with little embroidery. They have been dubbed "the most elegantly dressed but worst-housed people in the world".

## Akha (or Kaw)

The Akha, also called as the Ikho, Kho or Kha, have their origins in Yunnan, southern China, and from there spread into Burma (where there are nearly 200,000) and Laos and rather later into Thailand. There are three different Akha groups in northern Laos: the Akha Pouli, the Akha Pen and the Akha Jijaw. Around Muang Sing (see page 136) they constitute 22% of the population. They traditionally speak a Tibeto-Burmese language, which is believed to be represented in nine different written forms.

The Akha are shifting cultivators, growing primarily dry rice on mountainsides but also a wide variety of vegetables. The cultivation of rice is bound up with myths and rituals: the rice plant is regarded as a sentient being and the selection of the swidden, its clearance, the planting of the rice seed, the care of the growing plants and the harvest of the rice, must all be done according to the Akha Way. Any offence to the rice soul must be rectified by ceremonies. The Akha have no word for religion but believe in the 'Akha Way'. They are able to recite the names of all their male ancestors (60 names or more) and they keep an ancestral altar in their homes, at which food is offered up at important festivals and after the rice harvest. The two most important Akha festivals are the four-day Swinging Ceremony, celebrated during August, and New Year, when festivities also extend over four days. When someone dies they are wrapped in cloth, poor people in a white cloth, and rich people in a black cloth. They are kept in a wooden coffin, with a lid similar to a xylophone, for up to a month. A usual ritual *baci* will follow.

Akha villages are identified by their gates, a village swing and high-roofed houses on posts. At the upper and lower ends of the village are gates which are renewed every year. Visitors should walk through them to rid themselves of the spirit of the jungle. The gates are sacred and must not be defiled. Visitors must not touch them and should avoid going through them if they do not intend to enter a house in the village. A pair of wooden male and female carved figures are placed inside the entrance to signify that this is the realm of human beings. The female and male parts of the house are divided and the house has two doorways – one the entrance and the other the exit. C For information on how to behave in an Akha village, see Visiting an Akha village on page 130.

The Akha are relatively sexually liberal. Each village usually has a small courting house, where young men and women can rendezvous privately. Women will generally have a number of partners before settling into marriage and pregnancy prior to marriage is seen as a sign of fecundity. Sexual abstinence is often used as punishment for those who commit offences. Marriage is monogamous; however, the rich and powerful are entitled to additional wives if their first wives can't conceive. Women adopt the husband's lineage upon marriage and move into or close to her partner's family home. Divorce exists but is not common, due to the financial pressures of raising children. A midwife generally delivers babies and men are not allowed in the house when the woman is in labour. Historically, twins born in villages were regarded as a very bad omen and were killed but this practice has now been outlawed and the children are put up for adoption.

Today the Akha are finding it difficult to follow the 'Akha Way'. Their complex rituals set them apart from both the lowland Lao and from the other hilltribes. The conflicts and pressures which the Akha face and their inability to reconcile the old with the new is claimed by some to explain the high incidence of opium addiction.

**Material culture** Akha clothing is made of homespun blue-black cloth (dyed from indigo), which is appliquéd for decoration. The basic clothing of an Akha woman is a headdress, a jacket, a short skirt worn on the hips, with a sash and leggings worn from the ankle to below the knee, though many are starting to wear more mainstream clothing, as they are self-conscious of their traditional dress. They wear their jewellery as an integral part of their clothing, mostly sewn to their head dresses. This is the most characteristic item of Akha clothing and is adorned with jewellery and coins. The coins are made of pure silver and are used as currency (the small coins are worth about 15,000 kip and the large are worth about 50,000 kip). Girls wear similar clothing to the women, except that they sport caps rather than the elaborate headdress of the mature women. The change from girl's clothes to women's clothes occurs through four stages during adolescence. Unmarried girls can be identified by the small gourds tied to their waist and headdress. Men's clothing is much less elaborate. They wear loose-fitting Chinese-style black pants and a black jacket which may be embroidered. Both men and women use cloth shoulder bags.

## Hmong

**Origins** The Hmong are probably the best-known tribe in Laos. In the 19th century, Chinese opium farmers drove many thousands of Hmong off their poppy fields and forced them south into the mountains of Laos. The Hmong did not have a written language before contact with Europeans and Americans and their heritage is mainly preserved through oral tradition. Hmong mythology relates how they flew in from South China on magic carpets. Village storytellers like to propagate the notion that the Hmong are werewolves, who happily devour the livers of their victims. This warrior tribe now mainly inhabits the mountain areas of Luang Prabang, Xieng Khouang and Xam Neua provinces where they practise shifting cultivation.

**Economy and society** Until a few years ago, other Lao and the rest of the world knew the Hmong as the Meo. Unbeknown to anyone except the Hmong, 'Meo' was a Chinese insult meaning 'barbarian' – conferred on them several millennia ago by Chinese who developed an intense disliking for the tribe. Returning from university in France in the mid-1970s, the Hmong's first highly qualified academic decided it was time to educate the world. Due to his prompting, the tribe was rechristened Hmong, their word for 'mankind'. This change has not stopped the Hmong from referring to the Chinese as 'sons of dogs'. Nor has it stopped the Lao Loum from regarding the Hmong as their cultural inferiors. But, again, the feelings are reciprocated: the Hmong have an inherent mistrust of the lowland Lao – exacerbated by many years of war – and Lao Loum guides are relectant to enter Hmong villages.

The Hmong value their independence and tend to live at high altitudes, away from other tribes. This independence in addition to their former association with poppy cultivation and their siding with the US during the war has meant that of all the hilltribes, it is the Hmong who have been most persecuted. They have, in recent history, been perceived as a threat to state security, a group that needs to be controlled and carefully watched.

Hmong villages tend not to be fenced, while their houses are built of wood or bamboo at ground level. Each house has a main living area and two or three sleeping rooms. The extended family is headed by the oldest male; he settles family disputes and has authority over family affairs. Like the Karen, the Hmong too are spirit worshippers and believe in household spirits. Every house has an altar, where protection for the household is sought.

As animists, the Hmong believe everything from mountains and opium poppies to cluster bombs, has a spirit – or *phi* – some bad, some good. Shamans – or witchdoctors – play a central role in village life and decision making. The *phi* need to be placated incessantly to ward off sickness and catastrophe. It is the shaman's job to exorcise the bad *phi* from his patients. Until modern medicine arrived in Laos along with the Americans, opium was the Hmong's only palliative drug. Due to their lack of resistance to pharmaceuticals, the Hmong responded miraculously to the smallest doses of penicillin. Even plasters were revered as they were thought to contain magical powers which drew out bad *phi*.

**Material culture** The Hmong are the only tribe in Laos who make batik; indigo-dyed batik makes up the main panel of their skirts, with appliqué and embroidery added to it. The women traditionally wore black leggings from their knees to their ankles, black jackets (with embroidery) and a black panel or 'apron', held in place with a cummerbund. Even the youngest children wore clothes of intricate design. Traditionally the cloth would have been woven by hand on a foot-treddle/back-strap loom; today it is increasingly purchased from markets and often made of synthetic fabrics. Most Hmong today tend to wear Western-style clothes except for on auspicious occasions, such as Hmong New Year.

The White Hmong tend to wear less elaborate clothing from day to day, saving it for special occasions only. Hmong men wear loose-fitting black trousers, black jackets (sometimes embroidered) and coloured or embroidered sashes.

The Hmong particularly value silver jewellery; it signifies wealth and a good life. Men, women and children wear silver – tiers of neck rings, heavy silver chains with lock-shaped pendants, earrings and pointed rings on every finger. Through their life the Hmong will collect these heavy bands and lock them together with a spirit lock, which holds in their 32 souls. All the family jewellery is brought out at New Year.

**Hmong fighters in the 20th century** In the dying days of the French colonial administration, thousands of Hmong were recruited to help fight the Vietnamese Communists. Vang Pao – known as VP – who would later command 30,000 Hmong mercenaries in the US-backed war against the Pathet Lao, was first picked out by a French colonel in charge of these maquisards (native movements). Later, the Hmong were recruited and paid by the CIA to fight the Pathet Lao. Under General VP, remote mountain villagers with no education were trained to fly T-28 fighter-bombers.

At its peak, VP's army consisted of 250,000 fighters, the majority of whom were Hmong. Around 30,000 Hmong lost their life in the war, over a tenth of the Hmong population at the time. Even after the Pathet Lao's 'liberation' of Vientiane in 1975, Hmong refugees, encamped in hills to the south of the Plain of Jars, were flushed out by Vietnamese troops.

When the war ended in 1975 there was a mass exodus of Hmong from Laos, especially to Thailand. Many ended up in Thai refugee camps, where they lived in terrible conditions, for many years, sometimes decades.

Today more than 100,000 Hmong live in the US – mostly on the west coast and in Minnesota – where they regularly lobby politicians. They are a powerful pressure group but they are increasingly out of touch with the situation in Laos.

Where the US-based Hmong remain important, however, is in the money they remit to their relatives in Laos.

**Hmong insurgency** In Laos, Hmong insurgents have been staging reasonably regular attacks for years. A spate of bombings in Vientiane in 2000 was linked to the Hmong resistance and in 2004-2005 at least 15 civilians were killed by Hmong insurgents in the north of the country. The Hmong claim to be fighting for democracy and freedom but most are living in terrible conditions and starving, so robbery seems a more likely motivation.

The Lao government tends publicly to sidestep the issue, saying there is no official policy towards the Hmong. However, the eradication of opium and the related resettlement programme has had a negative impact on the Hmong and there is evidence of human rights violations against the Hmong by the Lao government. In 2004, video footage was smuggled out of Laos showing the carnage of a military attack on a Hmong rebel group that had taken place; the victims were children. On the other hand, the Lao government has appointed Hmong as governors of Phonsavanh, Xam Neua and Sayaboury provinces.

Between 2004 and 2006 several groups of hundreds of Hmong insurgents surrendered. In December 2006 alone more than 400 members of the Hmong ethnic insurgents and their families came out of the jungle and surrendered to the authorities.

In 2007 American officials in the US arrested Vang Pao, the 77-year-old former CIA-backed general of the Royal Army in Laos, on a conspiracy to stage a coup in Vientiane. The criminal complaint said Vang Pao and the other Hmong defendants formed a committee "to evaluate the feasibility of conducting a military expedition or enterprise to engage in the overthrow of the existing government of Laos by violent means, including murder, assaults on both military and civilian officials of Laos and destruction of buildings and property." This included charges of inspecting shipments of military equipment that were to be shipped to Thailand. That equipment included machine guns, ammunition, rocket-propelled grenade launchers, anti-tank rockets, stinger missiles, mines and C-4 explosives.

In 2009, the US dropped the charges against Vang Pao. He made plans to return to Laos but the government communicated that he would be excecuted if he did. In late 2009 more than 4000 Hmong refugees living in Thailand were forcibly repatriated to Laos.

## Other communities

The largest non-Lao groups in Laos are the Chinese and Vietnamese in the main cities. Many of the Vietnamese were brought in by the French to run the country and stayed. The Chinese have been migrating to Laos for centuries, where they are traders, restaurateurs and shop owners. Chinese immigration has increased in recent years, and with the relaxation in Communist policies there has been an influx of Thais, many in business. In Vientiane there is a small community of Indians running restaurants, jewellery and tailors' shops. Most Europeans are NGO, embassy or mining company staff.

The architecture of Laos reflects its turbulent history and has strong Siamese/Thai, Burmese and Khmer influences. Philip Rawson, in his book *The Art of Southeast Asia*, goes so far as to state that "The art of Laos is a provincial version of the art of Siam." This is unjustified in so far as art and architecture in Laos, though it may show many links with that of Siam/Thailand, also has elements which are unique to it. Unfortunately, little has survived because many of the older structures were built of wood and were ransacked by the Siamese/Thais, Chinese and Vietnamese and then bombed by the Americans. Religious buildings best exhibit the originality of Lao art and architecture.

Like Thailand and Myanmar (Burma), the stupa is the most dominant architectural form in Laos. In its classic Indian form, it is a voluptuous half round – a hemisphere – very like the upturned begging bowl that it is supposed to symbolize. This is surmounted by a shaft representing the Buddha's staff and a stepped pediment symbolizing his folded cloak. In Thailand the stupa has become elongated while in Laos it is also more angular, with four distinct sides. They are referred to as *that* (rather than *chedi*, as in Thailand).

In addition to the *that*, a Lao monastery or *wat* (*vat*) will also have a number of other buildings of which the most important is the *sim* or ordination hall (in Thai, *bot* or *ubosoth*). See box, page 308, for a short rundown on the structures found in an orthodox Lao wat.

### Architectural styles

Lao wats are generally less ornate and grand than those in Thailand, although the temples of Luang Prabang are stunning, with their layered roofs that sweep elegantly towards the ground. There are three main styles of temple architecture in Laos: Luang Prabang, Vientiane and Xieng Khouang. The last of these was almost lost forever because of the destruction wrought on the city of Xieng Khouang during the war.

The Vientiane style is influenced by the central Thai style, with its high, pointed and layered roofs. Most of the main sanctuaries are rectangular and some, such as Wat Phra Kaeo in Vientiane, have a veranda around the entire building – a stylistic feature imported from Bangkok. Most of the larger *sim* have a veranda at the back as well as at the front. Vientiane's wats have higher roofs than those in Luang Prabang, the buildings are taller and the entrances more prominent. The steps leading up to the main entrance are often guarded by *nagas* or *nyaks*, while the doorways themselves are usually flanked by pillars and topped with intricately carved porticoes. That Luang, in Vientiane, historically provided a template for most Lao stupas and its unique shape is found only in Laos and some areas of North and Northeast Thailand. As in other Buddhist countries, many of the stupas contain sacred relics – bones or hairs of the Buddha, or the ashes of kings.

The Luang Prabang architectural style has been influenced by North Thai temples. The roofs of the main sanctuaries almost touch the ground – best exemplified by Wat Xieng Thong in Luang Prabang. The pillars narrow towards

## ON THE ROAD

### The Lao wat

There is no English equivalent of the Lao word wat or vat. It is usually translated as either monastery or temple, although neither is correct. A wat is the focus of a village or town; it serves as places of worship, education, meeting and healing. Without a wat, a village was not, and is not, a 'complete' community.

The wat is a relatively new innovation. Originally, there were no wats, as monks were wandering ascetics. Although the word was in use in the 14th century, it probably referred to shrines. By the late 18th century, the wat had metamorphosed into a monastery. Although wats vary in complexity, most conform to a traditional layout.

Wats are usually separated from the secular world by two walls. Between these walls are the monks' quarters (kutis), perhaps a drum or bell tower (hor kong), used to toll the hours and to warn of danger, and in larger complexes schools and other buildings. Traditionally the kutis were placed on the south side of the wat. It was believed that if the monks slept in front of the main Buddha image they would die young; if they slept to the left they would become ill; and if they slept behind it there would be discord in the community of monks.

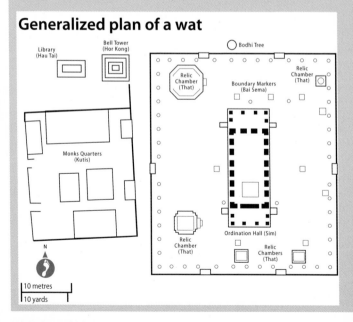

## Generalized plan of a wat

Library (Hau Tai)
Bell Tower (Hor Kong)
Bodhi Tree
Relic Chamber (That)
Relic Chamber (That)
Boundary Markers (Bai Sema)
Monks Quarters (Kutis)
Relic Chamber (That)
Ordination Hall (Sim)
Relic Chambers (That)
N
10 metres
10 yards

The inner wall, which in bigger wats may take the form of a gallery or cloister (*phra rabieng*) lined with Buddha images, represents the division between the worldly and the holy, the sacred and the profane. It is used as a quiet place for meditation. Within the inner courtyard, the holiest building is the ordination hall or *sim*, reserved for monks only. This is built on consecrated ground, and has a ring of eight stone tablets or boundary markers (*bai sema*), sometimes contained in mini-pavilions, arranged around it at the cardinal and subcardinal points and shaped like stylized leaves of the bodhi tree, often carved with representations of Vishnu, Siva, Brahma or Indra, or of *nagas*. Buried in the ground beneath the bai sema are stone spheres – and sometimes gold and jewellery. The *bai sema* mark the limit of earthly power. The ordination hall is a large, rectangular building with high walls and sloping roofs (always odd in number) covered in glazed clay tiles (or wood tiles, in the north). At each end of the roof are *dok sofa*, or 'bunches of flowers', which represent garuda grasping two *nagas* (serpents) in its talons. *Chao faa*, flame-like protrusions are attached to the extreme edge of the downward slope of the roofs. Inside, often through carved and inlaid doors, is the main Buddha image. There may also be subsidiary images. The inside walls of the *sim* may be decorated with murals depicting the Jataka tales or scenes from Buddhist and Hindu cosmology. Like the Buddha, these murals are meant to serve as meditation aids. Many complexes have secondary chapels, or *hor song phra* attached to the main *sim*.

Also in the inner courtyard may be a number of other structures. Among the more common are *that* (chedis), tower-like relic chambers which in Laos and parts of northeastern Thailand take the lotus bud form. These can be massive (such as That Luang in Vientiane, see page 31), and contain holy relics of the Buddha. More often, *thats* are smaller and contain the ashes of royalty, monks or pious lay people.

Another rarer feature is the library or scripture repository (*hau tai*), usually a small, tall-sided building where the Buddhist scriptures can be stored high off the ground. *Salas* are open-sided rest pavilions found anywhere in the wat compound; the *sala long tham* (study hall) is the most impressive of these and is almost like a *sim* or *viharn* without walls. Here the monks say their prayers at noon. In villages wats often consist only of a *sala*, or meeting hall.

It seems that wats are often short-lived. Even great wats, if they lose their patronage, are deserted by their monks and fall into ruin. Unlike churches, they depend on constant support from the laity; the wat owns no land or wealth, and must depend on gifts of food to feed the monks and money for repairs.

the top, as tree trunks were originally used for columns and this form was copied when they started to be made of stuccoed brick. The wats often have a veranda at the back and the front. The most famous wats in Luang Prabang and Vientiane were built with royal patronage. But most wats in Laos were and are built with donations from the local community. Royal wats can be identified by the number of *dok sofa*: more than 10 'flowers' signifies that the wat was built by a king.

The Xieng Khouang style appears to be an amalgam of Vientiane and Luang Prabang influences. The *sim* is raised on a multi-level pediment, as with Vientiane-style *sim*, while the low, sweeping roofs are similar to *sim* in Luang Prabang.

## Arts and crafts

Lao art is well known for its wealth of ornamentation. As in other neighbouring Buddhist countries, the focus has been primarily religious in nature. Temple murals and bas-reliefs usually tell the story of the Buddha's life: the jataka tales. However, there has never been the range of art in Laos that there is in Thailand, as the country has been constantly dominated and influenced by foreign powers. Much of Laos' artistic heritage was destroyed or disappeared over the centuries, as invading neighbours ransacked towns and cities and plundered the finest work. The *Ramayana*, the Hindu epic from India, known in Laos as the *Phra Lak Phra Lam* (see box, page 312) is highly influential and has become part of the Lao cultural heritage. Many of the most elaborate doors and windows of temples are engraved with scenes from this story, depicting the struggle between good and evil. The most outstanding examples of this art form are the huge teak shutters at Wat Xieng Thong in Luang Prabang.

### Sculpture

Sculpture in Laos is more distinctive in style; the best pieces originate from the 16th to 18th centuries. Characteristic of Lao Buddha images is a nose like an eagle's beak, flat, extended earlobes and tightly curled hair. The best examples are in Wat Phra Kaeo and Wat Sisaket in Vientiane.

The 'Calling for Rain' mudra (the Buddha standing with hands pointing towards the ground, arms slightly away from the torso) is distinctively Lao (see page 316). The 'Contemplating the Tree of Enlightenment' mudra is also uniquely Lao – it depicts a standing Buddha with hands crossed in front of the body. There are many examples in the Pak Ou Caves, on the Mekong, 25 km upstream from Luang Prabang (see page 99).

### Textiles

Weaving is a craft almost entirely performed by women. Traditionally, a girl was not considered fit for marriage until she had mastered the art of weaving and the Lao Loum women were expected to weave a corsage for their wedding day. Today these traditions are inevitably less strictly adhered to and there are also a handful of fine male weavers. Even so, a skilled weaver is held in high regard and enjoys a position of respect. Cloth is woven from silk, cotton, hemp and a variety of synthetic materials (mostly polyester) – or in some combination of these.

The finest weaving comes from the north. Around Xam Neua (and especially near Xam Tai), the Lao Neua produce some outstanding pieces. These were handed down through a family as heirlooms, stored in lidded stone jars to protect them from insects, moisture and sunlight and only worn on special occasions. But the recent history of this area forced people to sell their treasured textiles and few remain in situ. Indeed it was feared that the art of traditional weaving had been lost in the area. Only the work of some NGOs and committed supporters has resuscitated high quality weaving in the area (and in Vientiane where some of the best weavers live and work).

Lao Neua textiles are usually woven with a cotton warp and a silk weft and pieces include *pha sinh* (sarong), *pha baeng* (shawl) and blankets. Various methods are employed including *ikat* – where cotton is used (see box, page 52), as the Lao Neua consider that indigo dye does not take well on silk – and supplementary weft techniques. Pieces show bold bands of design and colour and the *pha sinh* is usually finished with a separate handwoven border. Among the designs are swastika motifs, *hong* (geese), diamond shapes, *nyak* (snake) heads, lions and elephants.

The Lao Loum of the Luang Prabang area also have a fine weaving tradition. *Pha sinh* produced here tend to have narrow vertical stripes, often alternating between dark and light. Silk tends to be used throughout on the finer pieces, although the yarn may be imported rather than locally produced and it is coloured using chemical dyes. Motifs include zigzags, flowers and some designs that are French in inspiration.

Around Pakse in the south and also in central Laos around Savannakhet and Thakhek designs are influenced by the Khmer and closest to those produced in the Isan region of northeast Thailand. *Matmii* ikat-woven cotton cloth is most characteristic. Designs, handed down by mothers to their daughters, are invariably geometric and encompass a broad range from simple *sai fon* (falling rain) designs where random sections of weft are tied, to the more complex *mee gung* and *poom som*. The less common *pha kit* is a supplementary weft *ikat*, although designs are similar to those in *matmii*. *Pha fai* is a cotton cloth, in blue or white and sometimes simply decorated, for everyday use and also used as part of the burial ceremony, when a white length of *pha fai* is draped over the coffin.

## ON THE ROAD

## The Lao Ramayana: the Phra Lak Phra Lam

The *Phra Lak Phra Lam* is an adaptation of the Indian Hindu classic, the *Ramayana*, written by the poet Valmiki about 2000 years ago. This 48,000 line epic odyssey, likened to the works of Homer, was introduced into mainland Southeast Asia in the early centuries of the first millennium. The heroes were transposed to a mythical Southeast Asian landscape.

The Lao, and Thai, versions of the *Ramayana* follow that of the original Indian story. They tell of the life of Ram (Rama), the King of Ayodhia. In the first part of the story, Ram renounces his throne following a long and convoluted court intrigue and flees into exile. With his wife Seeda (Sita) and trusted companion Hanuman (the monkey god), they undertake a long and arduous journey. In the second part, his wife Seeda is abducted by the evil king Ravana, forcing Ram to wage battle against the demons of Langka Island (Sri Lanka). He defeats the demons with the help of Hanuman and his monkey army and recovers his wife. In the third and final part of the story – and here it diverges sharply from the Indian original – Seeda and Ram are reunited and reconciled with the help of the gods (in the Indian version there is no such reconciliation). There are also numerous sub-plots which are original to the *Phra Lak Phra Lam*, many building upon local myth. In tone and issues of morality, the Lao and Thai versions are less puritanical than the Indian original. There are also, of course, differences in dress, ecology, location and custom.

## Literature

Lao literature is similar to Thai and is likewise also influenced by the Indian epic the *Ramayana*, which in Laos is known as the *Phra Lak Phra Lam* (see box, above). Scenes from the *Phra Lak Phram Lam* can often be seen depicted in temple murals. The first 10 jataka tales, recounting the last 10 lives of the Gautama Buddha (the historic Buddha), have also been a major inspiration for Lao literature. The versions that are in use in Laos are thought to have been introduced from Lanna Thai (northern Thailand, Chiang Mai) in the 16th century, or perhaps from the Mon area of present day Myanmar and Thailand. In these 10 tales, known as the *Vesantara Jataka*, the Buddha renounces all his earthly possessions, even his wife and children. Although the jataka tales in Laos are linked with Buddhism and therefore with India, the stories have little in common with the Indian originals. They draw heavily on local legends and folklore, animist tales provided with a Buddhist gloss.

Traditionally texts were recorded on palm leaves, the letters were inscribed with a stylus and the grooves darkened with oil. A palm leaf manuscript kept under good conditions in a well-maintained *hau tai* or library can last 100 years or more.

With the incorporation of Laos into French Indochina in the late 19th century, the Lao elite renounced traditional Lao literature in favour of the French language and artistic traditions. Many of the Lao elite received a French-style education. Lao literature came to be looked down upon as simplistic and most scholars wrote instead in French.

In 1778 the Thais plundered Laos and along with the two most sacred Buddha images – the Phra Bang and the Phra Kaeo (Emerald Buddha) – they pillaged Lao religious literature and historical documents. Most Lao manuscripts – or *kampi* – are 40-50 cm long, pierced with two holes and threaded together with cord. A bundle of 20 leaves forms a *phuk* and these are grouped together into *mat*, which is then wrapped in a piece of cloth.

## Language

The official language is Lao, the language of the ethnic majority. Lao is basically a monosyllabic, tonal language. It contains many polysyllabic words borrowed from Pali and Sanskrit (ancient Indian dialects) as well as words borrowed from Khmer. It has six tones, 33 consonants and 28 vowels. It is also spoken in Northeast Thailand and North Cambodia, which was originally part of the kingdom of Lane Xang. Lao and Thai, particularly the Northeast dialect, are mutually intelligible. French is still spoken in towns – particularly by the older generation – and is often used in government, but English is on the increase.

Lao script is similar to Thai. One of the kings of the Sukhothai Dynasty, Ramkhamhaeng, devised the Thai alphabet in 1283 and introduced the Thai system of writing. Modelled on this early Thai script, Lao is written from left to right with no spacing between the words.

The leadership in the Lao PDR has attempted to make Lao the national language, in fact as well as in rhetoric. Because it is so similar to Thai, there has also been an attempt to maintain a difference between the two countries' languages. To do this it was necessary to establish an national version of spoken Lao which could be taught in schools, promoted in the media, and used in government. This effort at language engineering can be dated from the 1930s, and saw further refinements in the 1940s-1950s, 1970s and 1990s. While this has been successful in that Lao remains significantly different from Thai, the major influence on the Lao language today remains that of Thai. ▶▶ *See also Language, page 338.*

## Dance, drama and music

Lao music, songs and dances have much in common with those of Thailand. Instruments include bamboo flutes, drums, gongs, cymbals and pinched or bowed string instruments shaped like banjos. The national instrument is the *kaen*, a hand-held pipe organ made from bamboo, similar to the South American pan pipes. Percussion is an important part of a Lao orchestra and two of the most common instruments are the *nang nat*, a xylophone and the *knong vony*, a series of bronze cymbals suspended from a wooden frame. The *seb noi* orchestra – a consortium of these instruments – is used to introduce or conclude vocal recitals. The *seb gnai* orchestra includes two big drums and a Lao-style clarinet.

Despite the lack of written notation, many epic poems and legends have survived to the present day as songs, passed, with the composition itself, from generation to generation. Early minstrels took their inspiration from folklore, enriched by Indian myths. Traditional Lao music can now only be heard during performances of the *Phra Lak Phra Lam* (see box, page 312), the Lao version of the Indian epic the Ramayana. Many monasteries have experts on percussion who play every Buddhist sabbath. There is also a strong tradition of Lao folk music, which differs between tribal groups.

Secular songs, drawing on Lao literature for inspiration, are known as *mau lam* and can be heard at festivals not just in Laos but also in Northeast Thailand (where they are known as *mor lam*), which is also, culturally, 'Lao'. Indeed, some of the best performers are based there, and it is also a good place to pick up music of famous *mor lam/mau lam* singers.

In Vientiane and the provincial capitals, younger Lao tend to opt for Western-style pop although their is a distinctively Lao/Thai sound to a lot of the music played in the beer gardens and pubs.

Classical Lao theatre and dance have Indian origins, probably imported from the Cambodian royal courts in the 14th century. Thai influence has also crept in over the years.

# Religion

## Theravada Buddhism

Theravada Buddhism, from the Pali word *thera* (elders), means the 'way of the elders' and is distinct from the dominant Buddhism practised in India, Mahayana Buddhism or the 'Greater Vehicle'. The sacred language of Theravada Buddhism is Pali rather than Sanskrit, Bodhisattvas (future Buddhas) are not given much attention and emphasis is placed upon a precise and 'fundamental' interpretation of the Buddha's teachings, as they were originally recorded. By the 15th century, Theravada Buddhism was the dominant religion in Laos – as it was in neighbouring Siam (Thailand), Myanmar and Cambodia. Buddhism shares the belief, in common with Hinduism, in rebirth. A person goes through countless lives and the experience of one life is conditioned by the acts in a previous one. This is the Law of Karma (act or deed, from Pali *kamma*), the law of cause and effect. But, it is not, as commonly thought in the West, equivalent to fate.

For most people, nirvana is a distant goal and they merely aim to accumulate merit by living good lives and performing good deeds such as giving alms to monks. In this way the layman embarks on the Path to Heaven. It is also common for a layman to become ordained, at some point in his life (usually as a young man), for a three month period during the Buddhist Rains Retreat. An equally important reason for a man to become ordained is so that he can accumulate merit for his family, particularly for his mother, who as a woman cannot become ordained

Monks should endeavour to lead stringently ascetic lives. They must refrain from murder, theft, sexual intercourse, untruths, eating after noon, alcohol, entertainment, ornament, comfortable beds and wealth. They are allowed to own only a begging bowl, three pieces of clothing, a razor, needle, belt and water filter. They can only eat food that they have received through begging. Anyone who is male, over 20 and not a criminal can become a monk. The 'Way of the Elders', is believed to be closest to Buddhist as it developed in India. It is often referred to by the term 'Hinayana' (Lesser Vehicle), a disparaging name foisted onto Theravadans by Mahayanists. This form of Buddhism is the dominant religion in the mainland Southeast Asian countries of Laos, Thailand, Cambodia and Myanmar (Burma).

In Theravadan Buddhism, the historic Buddha, Sakyamuni, is revered above all else and most images of the Buddha are of Sakyamuni. Importantly and unlike Mahayana Buddhism, the Buddha image is only meant to serve as a meditation aid; it does not embody supernatural powers and is not supposed to be worshipped. However, the popular need for objects of veneration has meant that most images are worshipped. Pilgrims bring flowers and incense and prostrate themselves in front of the image. This is a Mahayanist influence which has been embraced by Theravadans.

## ON THE ROAD

## Mudras and the Buddha image

Artists producing images of the Buddha are trying to be faithful to a tradition which can be traced back over centuries, creating not merely a work of art but an object of and for worship. The Pali texts of Theravada Buddhism add the 108 auspicious signs, long toes and fingers of equal length, body like a banyan tree and eyelashes like a cow's. The Buddha can be represented either sitting, lying (indicating paranirvana), or standing, and (in Thailand) occasionally walking. He is often represented standing on an open lotus flower: the Buddha was born into an impure world, and likewise the lotus germinates in mud but rises above the filth to flower. Each image is represented in a particular mudra or 'attitude', of which there are 40. The most common are:

**Abhayamudra** – dispelling fear or giving protection; right hand (sometimes both hands) raised, palm outwards, usually with the Buddha in a standing position.
**Varamudra** – giving blessing or charity; the right hand pointing downwards, the palm facing outwards, with the Buddha either seated or standing.
**Vitarkamudra** – preaching mudra; the ends of the thumb and index finger of the right hand touch to form a circle, symbolizing the Wheel of Law. The Buddha can either be seated or standing.
**Dharmacakramudra** – 'spinning the Wheel of Law'; a preaching mudra symbolizing the teaching of the first sermon. The hands are held in front of the chest, thumbs and index fingers of both joined, one facing inwards and one outwards.
**Bhumisparcamudra** – 'calling the earth goddess to witness' or 'touching the earth'; the right hand rests on the right knee with the tips of the fingers 'touching ground', thus calling the earth goddess Dharani/Thoranee to witness his enlightenment and victory over Mara, the king of demons. The Buddha is always seated.
**Dhyanamudra** – meditation; both hands resting open, palms upwards, in the lap, right over left.

Other points of note:
**Vajrasana** – yogic posture of meditation; cross-legged, both soles of the feet visible.
**Virasana** – yogic posture of meditation; cross-legged, but with the right leg on top of the left, covering the left foot (also known as paryankasana).
**Buddha under Naga** – the Buddha is shown in an attitude of meditation with a cobra rearing up over his head. This refers to an episode in the Buddha's life when he was meditating; a rain storm broke and Nagaraja, the king of the *nagas* (snakes), curled up under the Buddha (seven coils) and then used his seven-headed hood to protect the Holy One from the falling rain.
**Buddha calling for rain** – the Buddha is depicted standing, both arms held stiffly at the side of the body, fingers pointing downwards.

**Bhumisparcamudra** – calling the earth goddess to witness. Sukhothai period, 13th-14th century.

**Dhyanamudra** – meditation. Sukhothai period, 13th-14th century.

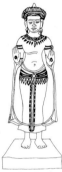

**Abhayamudra** – dispelling fear or giving protection. Lopburi Buddha, Khmer style 12th century.

**Vitarkamudra** – preaching, "spinning the Wheel of Law". Dvaravati Buddha, 7th-8th century, seated in the "European" manner.

**Abhayamudra** – dispelling fear or giving protection; subduing Mara position. Lopburi Buddha, Khmer style 13th century.

**The Buddha** 'Calling for rain'.

## Buddhism in Laos

The Lao often maintain that the Vientiane area converted to Buddhism at the time of the Moghul emperor Asoka. This seems suspiciously early and is probably untrue. The original stupa at That Luang, so it is claimed, was built to encase a piece of the Buddha's breastbone provided by Asoka. Buddhism was undoubtedly practised before Fa Ngum united Lane Xang and created a Buddhist Kingdom in the mid-14th century. He was known as the Great Protector of the Faith and brought the Phra Bang, the famous golden statue – the symbol of Buddhism in Laos – from Angkor in Cambodia to Laos.

Buddhism was gradually accepted among the lowland Lao but many of the highland tribes remain animist. Even where Buddhism has been practised for centuries, it is usually interwoven with the superstitions and rituals of animist beliefs. Appeasing the spirits and gaining merit are integral features of life. Most highlanders are animists and the worship of *phi* or spirits was central to village life throughout the revolutionary years, despite being officially banned by the government. Similarly, the baci ceremony – when strings representing guardian spirits are tied around the wrists of guests – is still practised in Laos.

In the late 1500s, King Setthathirat promoted Buddhism and built many monasteries or wats. Buddhism was first taught in schools in the 17th century and prospered until the Thai and Ho invasions of the 18th and 19th centuries when many wats were destroyed. With the introduction of socialism in 1975 Buddhism was banned from primary schools and the giving alms to monks was prohibited. With the increasing religious tolerance of the regime Buddhism is undergoing a revival and wats are being restored.

In line with Buddhist tradition, materialism and the accumulation of personal wealth is generally frowned on in Laos. Poverty is admired as a form of spirituality. This belief proved rather convenient for the Communist regime, when it was taken to extremes.

It is important to draw a distinction between 'academic' Buddhism, as it tends to be understood in the West and 'popular' Buddhism, as it is practised in Laos. In Laos, Buddhism is a syncretic religion: it incorporates elements of Brahmanism, Animism and ancestor worship. Amulets are worn to protect against harm and are often sold in temple compounds. In the countryside, farmers have what they consider a regard for the spirits (*phi*) and demons that inhabit the rivers, trees and forests. Astrologers are widely consulted by urban and rural dwellers alike. These aspects of Lao Buddhism are perceived to be complementary, not in contradiction, with Buddhist teachings.

## Buddhism under Communism

Buddhism's relationship with Communism has been complex and usually ambivalent. As the Pathet Lao began their revolutionary mission they saw in the country's monks a useful means by which to spread their message. Many monks were conscious of the inequalities in society and the impoverished conditions in which many people lived. Indeed most of them came from poor rural backgrounds. In addition many saw themselves as the guardians of Lao culture and as the US became more closely involved in the country so they increasingly felt that it was their job to protect the people against the spread of an alien culture. Therefore, right from the start, monks had a natural sympathy with the ideals of the Pathet Lao. Indeed, significant numbers renounced their vows and joined the revolution.

The Pathet Lao, for their part, saw the monks as a legitimizing force which would assist in their revolutionary efforts. Monks were often the most respected individuals in society and if the Pathet Lao could somehow piggy-back on this respect then they too, it was reasoned, would gain in credibility and respect. The Rightist government also tried to do the same, but with notably less success.

With the victory of the Pathet Lao in 1975, their view of the *sangha* (monkhood) changed. No longer were monks a useful vehicle in building revolution; overnight they became a potential threat. Monks were forced to attend re-education seminars where they were instructed that they could no longer teach about merit or *karma*, two central pillars of Buddhism. Their sermons were taped by Pathet Lao cadres to be scrutinized for subversive propaganda and a stream of disillusioned monks began to flee to Thailand. So the *sangha* was emasculated as an independent force. Monks were forced to follow the directives of the Lao People's Revolutionary Party and the *sangha* came under strict Party control. Monasteries were expected to become mini-cooperatives so that they did not have to depend on the laity for alms, and they were paid a small salary by the state for undertaking teaching and health work.

The success of the Pathet Lao's policy of marginalization can be seen in the number of monks in the country. In 1975 there were 20,000 monks. By 1979 this had shrunk to 1700.

However, before the *sangha* could sink into obscurity and irrelevance, the government eased its policy in 1979 and began to allow monks and the *sangha* greater latitude. In addition and perhaps more importantly, the leadership embraced certain aspects of Lao culture, one of which was Theravada Buddhism. The memorial to the revolutionary struggle in Vientiane, for example, was designed as a Buddhist *that* (stupa) and government ministers enthusiastically join in the celebration of Buddhist festivals.

## Animism

While the majority of the population (about 60-65%) follow Theravada Buddhism, Animism is practised by about 30% of the population. The term Animism derives from the Latin word 'anima', meaning mind or soul. At a very basic level, Animism refers to a belief in spirits. Animism is particularly common among Lao Theung and Lao Soung groups minority groups but elements of Animism have also infiltrated or been grafted onto Buddhism and Lao culture at a broader level. Most people believe in *phi*, spirits, which are seen as fundamental to their relationship with nature and the community. The word *phi* has even been adopted into Lao language to mean ghost, while *phi-baa* means crazy. Many Lao people believe that spiritual forces need to be placated, usually through a *baci* ceremony (see page 16), as they can cause illness, disease or bad luck. Inexplicable events –

including strange behaviour by foreign visitors – are often attributed to 'ghosts'. Buddhist monks are often called upon to exorcize bad spirits and most wats have a small spirit house in the grounds. Animists generally suffer little discrimination from the government; however, some practises are discouraged for health and security reasons.

## Christianity in post-1975 Laos

The smallest religious group in Laos are Christians, including Roman Catholics, who account for around 2% of the population. There are 30,000 to 40,000 Catholics in the country, many of them ethnic Vietnamese, concentrated in urban centres along the Mekong River.

Following the revolution, many churches were turned into community centres. Vientiane's Evangelical Church has held a Sunday service ever since 1979 but it is only in recent years that Christians have felt free to worship openly. In 1989 the first consultation between the country's Christian leaders (Protestant and Roman Catholic) was authorized by the government; it was the first such meeting since 'liberation' and was also attended by government representatives and two Hmong leaders of the Buddhist Federation.

It's illegal for foreigners to proselytize in Laos; persons found guilty can be subject to arrest and deportation. Foreign missionaries were ejected from Laos in 1975 and, today, foreign NGOs affiliated with religious organizations are only allowed to work in the country on the condition that they don't try to spread their religion. Not many Buddhists have converted to Christianity but it seems to be growing among the animist hilltribes. The US Bible Society has published a modern translation of the Bible into Lao but tribal-language editions do not yet exist.

# Land &
# environment

## Geography

Laos stretches about 1000 km from north to south, while distances from east to west range from 140 to 500 km. The country covers 236,800 sq km – less than half the size of France and just a third of the size of Texas. Only 24% of the population lives in towns. The country has the lowest population density in Asia, with 22 people per sq km.

Rugged mountains cover more than three-quarters of the country and with few all-weather roads (there are just 4000 km of sealed roads), rivers remain important communication routes. Historically, the Mekong River was the country's economic artery. On its banks nestle Laos' most important cities: in the north the small, colourful former royal capital of Luang Prabang, further south the administrative and political capital of Vientiane and farther south still the regional centres of Thakhek, Savannakhet and Pakse.

The lowlands of the Mekong valley form the principal agricultural areas, especially around Vientiane and Savannakhet and these are home to the lowland Lao. The Mekong has three main tributaries: the Nam Ou and Nam Tha from the north and the Nam Ngum, which flows into Vientiane Province.

Much of the northern half of Laos is 1500 m or more above sea level and its karst limestone outcrops are dissected by steep-sided river valleys. Further south, the Annamite chain has an average height of 1200 m. Heavily forested, rugged mountains form a natural barrier between Laos and Vietnam. Most of the country is a mixture of mountains and high plateau. There are four main plateau: the Xieng Khouang plateau, better known as the Plain of Jars, in the north, the Nakai and the limestone Khammuoane plateau in the centre and the 10,000 sq km Bolovan Plateau to the south. The highest peak is the 2800 m Bia Mountain, which rises above the Xieng Khouang plateau to the northeast.

## Vegetation

Much of Laos is forested. The vegetation is rich and diverse: a mix of tropical and subtropical species. Grassy savannah predominates on plateau areas such as the Plain of Jars. In the forests, some hardwoods tower to over 30 m, while tropical palms and mango are found in the lowlands and large stands of pine in the remote northern hills.

Rural people rely heavily on the Mekong River and its watershed for everything from transport to rice production and fishing. It is estimated that 80% of the country is located near the Mekong, its tributaries or in the watershed. Over half of all protein consumed in rural areas comes from fish, frogs and other river creatures. Agriculture is of utmost importance, with about 80% of the population engaged in subsistence farming.

In the mid-20th century over 70% of the country was covered with forest. Today, this has been reduced to around 40% and of this only 17% remains old growth tropical forest. The rattan, cardamom, mushrooms, orchids and wild meat gathered from these forests are essential to rural livelihoods. The Lao government has established 20 National Protected Areas or NPAs, plus two corridor areas, covering 14.3% of the country. Although this is a step forward, illegal hunting and logging is still rife in most areas.

Logging provides a large slice of Laos' export earnings. Officially, around 450,000 cu m of forest are felled each year for commercial purposes but this is probably an underestimate owing to the activities of illegal loggers, many of whom are Chinese, Vietnamese and Thai. In addition, shifting cultivators clear around 100,000 ha of forest a year.

## Wildlife

Mammals include everything from wildcats, leopards and tigers to bears, wild cattle and small barking deer. Laos is also home to the large Asian elk, rhinoceros, elephants, monkeys, gibbons and ubiquitous rabbits and squirrels. There is an abundant reptilian population, including cobras, kraits, crocodiles and lizards. The lower reaches of the Mekong River, marking the border between Cambodia and Laos, is the last place in Indochina where the rare Irrawaddy dolphin is to be found. However, dynamite fishing is decimating the population and today there are probably under 20 left.

Another rare denizen of the Mekong is the *pa buk* (*Pangasianodon gigas*) which weighs up to 340 kg. This riverbed-dwelling fish is a delicacy and has been for many years – its roe was paid as tribute to China in the late 19th century. By the 1980s the numbers of *pa buk* had become severely depleted. However, a breeding programme is having some success and pa buk fingerlings are now being released into the Mekong.

In 2004, the Lao government joined CITES, the world's foremost conservation treaty regulating the global trade in endangered species. In spite of this, there is an enormous problem of smuggling rare animals out of Laos, mainly to South Korea and China. Poachers peddle animals across the country's borders; and the authors of 'Wildlife Trade in Laos: the End of the Game', published in 2001, suspected that trade in wildlife was the second-largest source of income (after fishing) in Lao villages, worth around US$35 million per year. A damning report in the *Guardian* in 2010 suggested that little has changed.

Regardless, Laos is still home to a diverse range of wildlife with some 800 bird and 100 mammal species. New species are popping up on an almost annual basis. The degree to which Laos' flora and fauna are under-researched was illustrated in 1999 when it was announced that an unknown species of striped rabbit had been discovered nibbling the grass in the mountains dividing Laos from Vietnam. This area of Indochina has proved a cornucopia of unknown animals. During the 1990s scientists discovered one antelope, several species of deer, an ox and even a remnant herd of Javan rhinoceros, a species previously thought to be confined to a small corner of West Java.

## Birds

Laos is nowhere near as popular a destination for birdwatchers as neighbouring Vietnam and Cambodia but there has been a flurry of interest in the birding community since the discovery of a bizarre-looking bald-headed bird in 2009. The bare-faced bulbul is the first new species of Asian bulbul to be discovered in more than 100 years. It inhabits a remote area of rugged limestone karsts in Kammouane Province, 250 km south of Vientiane. Two other scarce inhabitants of limestone karst forest in the region, the sooty babbler and red-collared woodpecker, are also found here. See www.vietnambirding.com for information.

# Books

## Art and culture

**Dakin, Brett**  *Another Quiet American*, Asia Books (2003). Dakin's experiences of working in Laos, with some interesting cultural insights.

**Evans, Grant**  *Laos: Culture and Society*, Chiang Mai, Thailand: Silkworm Books (1999). Edited volume written by assorted scholars of Laos. Highly informed; for those who really want to know about the country.

**Fay, Kim**  *To Asia with Love: A Connoisseur's Guide to Cambodia, Laos, Thailand Vietnam*, Global Directions Inc/Things Asian Press (2005). Great anthology of ideas, inspirations and experiences of Southeast Asia from the people who live there.

**Phia Sing**  *Traditional Recipes of Laos*, Totnes, Devon, UK: Prospect Books (1995). The best Lao cookbook available. The recipes were collected by the chief chef at the Royal Palace in Luang Prabang, Phia Sing, in the 1960s. They have been translated into English and made more user-friendly by replacing some of the more esoteric ingredients with ones available in the West.

## Economics, politics, development

**Dommen, Arthur J**  *Laos: Keystone of Indochina*, Boulder: Westview Press (1985). Out of date but a reasonable overview.

**Evans, Grant**  *Lao Peasants under Socialism*, New Haven: Yale University Press (1990). The definitive account of farmers in modern Laos. A new edition published by Silkworm Books in Chiang Mai (Thailand) takes into account economic changes brought about by the New Economic Mechanism.

**Stuart-Fox, Martin**  *Contemporary Laos*, St Lucia: Queensland University Press (1982). A useful overview of Laos up to 1980.

**Stuart-Fox, Martin**  *Laos – Politics, Economics and Society*, London: Francis Pinter (1986). Out of date but a good single volume summary of the country providing historical and cultural background.

**Stuart-Fox, Martin**  *Buddhist Kingdom, Marxist State: the Making of Modern Laos*, Bangkok: White Lotus (1996). A collection of Stuart-Fox's various papers published over the years and brought up to date. Especially good on recent history.

**Zasloff, J J and Unger, L** (eds) *Laos: Beyond the Revolution*, Macmillan, Basingstoke (1991). Edited volume with a mixed collection of papers; the chapters on the country's economics and politics are already rather dated.

## History

**Kremmer, Christopher**  *Bamboo Palace*, HarperCollins Australia. Traces Kremmer's attempts to unravel the mystery surrounding the Lao royal family.

**Stuart-Fox, Martin and Kooyman, Mary**  *Historical Dictionary of Laos*, New York: the Scarecrow Press (1992). Takes a dictionary approach to Laos' history which is fine if you are looking up a fact or two, but doesn't really lend itself to telling a narrative.

**Stuart-Fox, Martin**  *A History of Laos*, CUP: Cambridge (1997). Concentrates on the modern period.

## Language

**Higbie, James** *Lao-English/English-Lao Dictionary and Phrasebook*, Hippocrene Books, Inc.

**Marcus, Russell** *Lao-English/English-Lao Dictionary*, Charles E Tuttle Co, USA (1983). Perhaps the best dictionary available; US$16.95 from www.world language.com.

**Phone Bouaravong** *Learning Lao for Everyone*. Locally produced, with tapes.

**Werner, Klaus** *Learning and Speaking Lao*. Useful and cheaper guide to the Lao language than Marcus Russell's.

## Laos and the Indochina War

**Castle, Timothy** *A War in the Shadow of Vietnam: US Military Aid to the Royal Lao Government 1955-1975*, New York: Columbia University Press (1993).

**Evans, Grant and Rowley, Kelvin** *Red Brotherhood at War, Vietnam Cambodia & Laos since 1975*, Verso (1990).

**Evans, Grant** *Yellow Rainmakers: Are Chemical Weapons Being Used in Southeast Asia*, Verso (1983).

**McCoy, Alfred W** *The Politics of Heroin: CIA Complicity in the Global Drugs Trade*, Lawrence Hill/Chicago Review Press (1991). Originally published at the beginning of the 1970s, the classic study of the politics of drugs in mainland Southeast Asia.

**Parker, James** *Codename Mule: Fighting the Secret War in Laos for the CIA*, Annapolis, Maryland: Naval Institute Press (1995). Personal story of Americans fighting in Laos. Much of it deals with fighting on the Plain of Jars.

**Pyle and Faas** *Lost Over Laos*, De Capo Press (2003). The story of 4 photographers who died in Laos in 1971 and the search, years later, to recover the crash site.

**Ratnam, P** *Laos and the Superpowers*, Tulsi Publishing, India (1980).

**Robbins, Christopher** *Air America: the Story of the CIS's Secret Airlines*, New York: Putnam Books (1979). The earlier of Robbins' 2 books on the secret war. Made into a film of the same name starring Mel Gibson.

**Robbins, Christopher** *The Ravens: Pilots of the Secret War of Laos*, New York: Bantam Press (1989). The best known of all the books on America's secret war in Laos. The story it tells seems almost too incredible to be true.

**Warner, Roger** *Back Fire: the CIA's Secret War in Laos and its Link to the War in Vietnam*, New York: Simon and Schuster (1995). The best of the more recent books recounting the experiences of US servicemen in Laos. Excellent, engaging read. Also published as Shooting at the Moon.

## Travel and geography

**De Carne, Louis** *Travels in Indochina and the Chinese Empire*, London: Chapman Hall (1872). Recounts De Carne's experiences in Laos in 1872, some years before the country was colonized by the French.

**Dooley, Tom** *The Edge of Tomorrow*, Farrar, Strauss & Cudahy (1958).

**Du Pont De Bie, Natacha** *Ant Egg Soup: The Adventures of a Food Tourist in Laos*, Sceptre (2004). A wonderful portrait of Lao culture and food through the eyes of a food tourist.

**Garstin, Crosbie** *The Voyage from London to Indochina*, Heinemann (1928). Hilarious, irreverent journey through Indochina.

**Hoskins, John** *The Mekong*, Bangkok: Post Publishing (1991). This is a large format coffee table book with excellent glossy photographs and a modest text. Widely available in Bangkok.

**Lewis, Norman** *A Dragon Apparent: Travels in Cambodia, Laos and Vietnam (1951).* One of the finest travel books; reprinted by Eland Books but also available second-hand from many bookshops.

**Maugham, Somerset** *The Gentlemen in the Parlour: a Record of a Journey from Rangoon to Haiphong, Heinemann: London (1930).* An account of Maugham's journey through Southeast Asia, in classic limpid prose.

**McCarthy, James** *Surveying and Exploring in Siam with Descriptions of Laos Dependencies and of Battles against the Chinese Haws, White Lotus: Bangkok (1994).* First published in 1900. An interesting account by Englishman James McCarthy, who was employed by the government of Siam as a surveyor and adviser.

**Mouhot, Henri** *Travels in Indochina, Bangkok: White Lotus (1986).* An account of Laos by France's most famous explorer of Southeast Asia. He tried to discover a 'back door' into China by travelling up the Mekong, but died of Malaria in Luang Prabang in 1860. The book has been republished by White Lotus and is easily available in Bangkok; there is also a more expensive reprint available from OUP (Kuala Lumpur).

**Murphy, Dervla** *One Foot in Laos, John Murphy Publisher (1999).* This is an interesting, off-the-beaten-track travelogue of adventures and mishaps during a journey through Laos.

**Stewart, Lucretia** *Tiger Balm: Travels in Laos, Cambodia and Vietnam, London: Chatto and Windus (1998).*

## Books on Southeast Asia

**White Lotus,** www.thailine.com/lotus, is a Bangkok-based publisher specializing in English-language books (with many reprints of old books) on the region.

**Dingwall, Alastair** *Traveller's Literary Companion to Southeast Asia, In Print: Brighton (1994).* Extracts from books by Western and regional writers on Southeast Asia. A good overview of what is available.

**Dumareay, Jacques** *The Palaces of South-East Asia: Architecture and Customs, OUP: Singapore (1991).* A broad summary of palace art and architecture in Southeast Asia.

**Fraser-Lu, Sylvia** *Handwoven Textiles of South-East Asia, OUP: Singapore (1988).* Large well-illustrated book with informative text.

**Higham, Charles** *The Archaeology of Mainland Southeast Asia from 10,000 BC to the Fall of Angkor, CUP: Cambridge (1989).* Best summary of changing views of the archaeology of the mainland.

**Reid, Anthony** *Southeast Asia in the Age of Commerce 1450-1680: the Lands below the Winds, Yale University Press: New Haven (1988).* Perhaps the best history of everyday life in Southeast Asia, looking at such themes as physical wellbeing, material culture and social organization. Also Volume 2 (1993) Southeast Asia in the Age of Commerce 1450-1680: Expansion and Crisis, Yale University Press: New Haven.

**Rigg, Jonathan** *Southeast Asia: the Human Landscape of Modernization and Development, London: Routledge (1997).* Focuses on how people have responded to the challenges and tensions of modernization.

**SarDesai, DR** *Southeast Asia: Past and Present*, Macmillan: London (1989). Skillful but at times frustratingly thin history of the region from the 1st century to the withdrawal of US forces from Vietnam.

**Steinberg, DJ et al** *In Search of Southeast Asia: a Modern History,* University of Hawaii Press: Honolulu (1987). The best standard history of the region.

**Tarling, Nicholars** *(edit) Cambridge History of Southeast Asia,* CUP: Cambridge (1992). 2-volume edited study by theme and region, with contributions from most of the leading historians of the region. The history is fairly conventional.

# Practicalities
# Laos

# **Getting** there

Air

The easiest and cheapest way to access the region is via **Bangkok**, **Hong Kong** or **Kuala Lumpur**. Most major airlines have direct flights from Europe, North America and Australasia to these hubs. Laos is only accessible from within Asia.

There are international flights to **Vientiane** from the following countries: **Cambodia** (Phnom Penh and Siem Reap), **China** (including Kunming and Nanning), **Thailand** (including Bangkok and Chiang Mai) and **Vietnam** (Hanoi and Ho Chi

---

**TRAVEL TIP**

## Packing for Laos

It is possible to buy most toiletries, as well as things like medicines and peanut butter, in Vientiane. Luang Prabang, Savannakhet and Pakse also stock most basic items. Outside these cities little is available beyond such items as soap, washing powder, batteries, shampoo, and the like. Suitcases are not ideal if you are intending to travel overland by bus. A backpack, or even better a travel pack (where the straps can be zipped out of sight), is recommended.

In terms of clothing, most people in Laos dress tidily and modestly. Strappy T-shirts and tiny shorts are not appropriate; they are considered disrespectful. Laos is relatively casual and suits are not necessary. Don't pack too many clothes; laundry services are cheap, and the turnaround is rapid.

You may want to pack antacid tablets for indigestion; antibiotics for travellers' diarrhoea; antiseptic ointment; anti-malarials (see page 337); mosquito repellents; travel sickness tablets; painkillers; condoms/contraceptives; tampons/sanitary towels; high-factor sun screen and a sun hat, and a blow-up pillow.

For longer trips involving jungle treks take a clean needle pack, clean dental pack and water filtration devices. However, be wary of carrying disposable needles as customs officials may find them suspicious. If you are a popular target for insect bites or develop lumps quite soon after being bitten, carry an Aspivenin kit. This syringe suction device is available from many chemists and draws out some of the allergic materials and provides quick relief.

Make sure your passport is valid for at least six months and take photocopies of essential documents, passport ID and visa pages and student ID card. Spare passport photos are needed for each entry into Laos and useful in case of loss or theft.

Other useful items include spare digital camera memory cards; bumbag/money belt; cotton or silk sheet sleeping bag; earplugs; mosquito net; padlock; sun glasses; Swiss Army knife; torch; travel wash; umbrella; wet wipes; plastic bags; and bandana for dusty *songthaew* rides.

Minh City) and **Malaysia** (Kuala Lumpur). Most people visiting Laos from outside Southeast Asia travel via Bangkok.

There are also flights from Hanoi, Bangkok and Chiang Mai to **Luang Prabang**. A cheaper option for getting to Laos from Bangkok is to fly to Udon Thani in Thailand, about 50 km south of the border, and travel overland from there, crossing at the Friendship Bridge (see page 61).

An alternative route is to fly from Bangkok to Chiang Rai in Thailand, before overlanding to Chiang Khong and crossing into northern Laos at **Houei Xai**. From Houei Xai there are flights to Vientiane and boats to Luang Prabang via Pakbeng.

## Road and river

Laos is a landlocked country. There are more than a handful of border crossings between Laos and its neighbours, making cross-regional travel easy. Laos 30-day visas are available on arrival at nearly all of these border crossings. For much of its length, the Lao–Thai border is defined by the Mekong, with bridges and ferries linking the two countries. To the east, the Annamite mountain range forms a spine separating Laos from Vietnam, with a few cross-border buses running from Vientiane and Savannakhet. However, borders with Vietnam have opened up across the length of the country in recent years. There is only one official border crossing between Laos and Cambodia in the south, and between Laos and China in the north. For details of border crossings, see box, page 332.

# Getting around

## Air

**Lao Airlines** runs domestic flights from Vientiane to Luang Prabang, Phonsavanh (Xieng Khouang), Pakse, Houei Xai, Udomxai, Luang Namtha and Savannakhet.

## Road

Roads have greatly improved in recent years, making journeys much faster. Quite a few bus, truck, tuk-tuk, *songthaew* (see below) and taxi drivers understand basic English, French or Thai, although it is helpful to have the name of the place you are trying to get to written out in Lao. Many people will not know road names, but will know all the sights of interest.

### Bus/truck/minivan

It is possible to travel to most areas by bus, truck or *songthaew* (converted pickup truck) in the dry season, although road travel in the rainy season can be tricky if not impossible in some areas. VIP buses are comfortable night buses, usually allowing you to sleep – but watch out for karaoke on board (earplugs may be useful). In the south, an overnight bus plies the route from Pakse to Vientiane. Book a double bed if you don't want to sleep next to a stranger. Robberies have been reported on the night buses so keep your valuables secure.

A decent network of minivans transport foreigners from one main tourist destination to another; for example, Luang Prabang to Vang Vieng. Pick-ups from guesthouses are usually part of the service.

### Car hire

Car hire is possible both with and without a driver. Insurance is generally included (you will need an international driver's permit). Check **Avis** ⓘ *www.avis.la*, for current rates.

## TRAVEL TIP
### Official border crossings

**Cambodia–Laos**
Don Kralor–Voen Kham (Laos visas now available at the border), page 263.

**China–Laos**
Mohan-Boten, page 132.

**Myanmar (Burma)–Laos**
Foreigners are not permitted to enter or leave Laos through Myanmar (Burma).

**Thailand–Laos**
Friendship Bridge, Nong Khai–Vientiane, page 61.
Chiang Khong–Houei Xai, page 140.
Beung Kan–Paksan, page 181 (Lao visa required in advance).
Nakhon Phanom–Thakhek, pages 191.
Mukdahan–Savannakhet, page 207.
Chongmek–Vang Tao (near Pakse), page 215.

**Vietnam–Laos**
Tay Trang–Sop Hun, page 121.
Nam Xoi–Na Maew, page 165 (Lao visa required in advance).
Nam Khan–Nong Het, page 160.
Cau Treo–Nam Phao, page 184.
Lao Bao–Dansavanh, page 204.
Bo Y–Yalakhuntum, page 246.

### Motorbike and bicycle hire
There are an increasing number of motorcycles available to hire from guesthouses and shops in major towns. 110cc bikes cost around US$10 per day. Bicycles are a cheap way to see the sights. Many guesthouses have bikes for rent at around US$2 per day. Mountain bikes can be rented from specialist outlets.

### Tuk-tuk
The motorized three-wheelers known as 'jumbos' or tuk-tuks are large motorbike taxis with two bench seats in the back. You'll find them in most cities and metropolitan areas. They can be hired by the hour or the day to reach destinations out of town.

In city centres make sure you have the correct money for your tuk-tuk as drivers are often conveniently short of change.

## River

It is possible to take river boats up and down the Mekong and its main tributaries. Boats stop at Luang Prabang, Pakbeng and Houei Xai in the northwest; Nong Khiaw and Phongsali on the Nam Ou River in the north; and around Don Deth and Don Khong in the south. Luxury services operate between Houei Xai and Luang Prabang and between Pakse and Wat Phou in Champasak Province. Aside from the route down from Houei Xai to Luang Prabang, often there are no scheduled services, and departures may be limited in the dry season. Take food and drink and expect crowded conditions on the Houei Xai–Luang Prabang route. Speedboats cover some routes, but are dangerous and uncomfortable.

## Maps

The *GT Rider Lao* map (www.gt-rider.com) found in bookstores and other shops in Vientiane is probably the most accurate map of the country. The National Tourism Authority has also put together pretty good provincial maps of Laos, using the *GT Rider* map as a base. These are available at provincial tourism offices. *Hobo Maps* (www.hobomaps.com) produces some highly detailed and recommended maps of certain towns and areas. The best selection of maps in the UK is available from **Stanfords** ⓘ *12-14 Long Acre, London WC2E 9LP, T020-7836 1321, www.stanfords.co.uk.*

# Local customs and conduct

### Bargaining/haggling

While bargaining is common in Laos – in the market or in negotiating a trip on a tuk-tuk, for example – it is not heavy-duty haggling. The Lao are extremely laid-back and it is rare to be fleeced; don't bargain hard with them, it may force them to lose face and reduce prices well below their profit margin. For most things, you won't even really need to bargain. Having said that, beware of tuk-tuk drivers (where possible, try to flag down tuk-tuks rather than taking those waiting on street corners) and find out in advance from your hotel or guesthouse how much a journey should cost. Approach bargaining with a sense of fun; a smile or joke always helps.

### Clothing

Informal, lightweight clothing is all that is needed, although a sweater and a few warm layers are vital for the highlands in the winter months (November to March). An umbrella is useful during the rainy season (June and July) or during the intense heat as a parasol. Sleeveless shirts and singlets, very short shorts and skirts are considered disrespectful. Please respect this even though many tourists do not. When visiting monasteries (wats) women should keep their shoulders covered and take their shoes off. One of the main reasons for the tight controls on tourism in Laos is because of the perceived corrosive effects that badly dressed tourists were having on Lao culture. The assumption was that scruffy dress was a reflection of character. If you are bathing in public, particularly in rural areas, wear a sarong. It is expected that people will take their shoes off before entering a Lao home.

### Conduct

**Wats** Monks are revered, don't touch their robes. If talking to a monk your head should be lower than his. Avoid visiting a wat around 1100 as this is when the monks have their morning meal. It is considerate to ask the abbot's permission to enter the *sim* and shoes should be removed before entry. When sitting down, feet should point away from the altar and main image. Arms and legs should be fully covered when visiting wats. A small donation is often appropriate (kneel when putting it into the box).

**Forms of address** Lao people are addressed by their first name, not their family name, even when a title is used.

**Greeting** The nop or wai – with palms together below your chin and head bowed, as if in prayer – remains the traditional form of greeting. Shaking hands, though, is very widespread – more so than in Thailand. This can be put down to the influence of the French during the colonial period. Sabaidee (hello) is also a good way to greet. Avoid hugging and kissing to greet Lao people, as they tend to get embarrassed.

**In private homes** Remove your shoes. When seated on the floor you should tuck your feet behind you.

**Eating** At a meal, a guest should not begin eating until the host has invited him or her to do so. Nor should the guest continue eating after everyone else has finished. It is also customary for guests to leave a small amount of food on their plate; to do otherwise would imply that the guest was still hungry and that the host had not provided sufficient food. Sharing is an important part of meal times; plates of food are ordered and shared amongst everyone. Lao people often invite tourists to eat with them or share on buses, and it is a nice gesture if this is reciprocated (though Lao people tend to be shy so don't take any refusal as a rejection). Most Lao are tolerant of other cultures and don't expect things such as eating etiquette to be strictly adhered to.

**General** Pointing with the index finger is considered rude. If you want to call someone over, gesture with your palm facing the ground and fingers waving towards you (as opposed to the other direction). In Laos your head is considered 'high' and feet are considered 'low'. So try to keep your feet low, don't point them at people or touch people with your feet. Don't pat children on the head (or touch people's heads in general), as it is the considered the most sacred part of the body.

Lao people have a passive nature. Yelling or boisterous people tend to send them into panic mode. If a dispute arises, a smile and a joke will do the trick. Likewise when bargaining, keep a sense of humour – the funnier you are, the more successful you will be.

The Lao are proud people and begging is just not the done thing, so don't hand out money (or medicine) to local villagers. If you want to give a gift or a donation to someone, it is best to channel it through the village elder.

# Essentials A-Z

## Accident and emergency

Contact the relevant emergency service and your embassy. Make sure you obtain police/medical records in order to file insurance claims. If you need to report a crime, visit the local police station and take a local with you who speaks English. **Ambulance** T195, **Fire** T190, **Police** T191.

## Children

Lao people love small children and it is not uncommon for waiters and waitresses to spend the whole evening looking after and entertaining your offspring.

**Food and drink**
Fruit can be bought cheaply: papaya and banana are excellent sources of nutrition, and can be self-peeled, ensuring cleanliness. Powdered milk is available in provincial centres, although most brands have added sugar. Avoid letting your child drink tap water as it may carry parasites. Bottled water is sold widely.

**Disposable nappies**
These can be bought in Vientiane and other larger provincial capitals, but are expensive.

**Transport**
Public transport may be a problem; long bus journeys are restrictive and uncomfortable. Chartering a car is undoubtedly the most convenient way to travel overland if you have children.

## Customs and duty free

The duty free allowance is 500 cigarettes, 2 bottles of wine and a bottle of liquor. Laos has a strictly enforced ban on the export of antiquities and all Buddha images.

## Disabled travellers

Considering the proportion of the region's population that are seriously disabled, foreigners might expect better facilities and allowances for the immobile. But in Laos, pavements are often uneven, there are potholes and missing drain covers galore, pedestrian crossings are ignored, ramps are unheard of, lifts are few and far between and escalators are seen only in magazines and high-end hotels and a sprinkling of shopping complexes. For further information contact **Disability Rights UK**, www.disabilityrightsuk.org.

## Drugs

Drug use is illegal and there are harsh penalties ranging from fines through to imprisonment or worse. Police have been known to levy heavy fines on people in Vang Vieng for eating so-called 'happy' foods, or for being caught in possession of drugs. Though opium has in theory been eradicated, it is still for sale in northern areas and people have died from overdosing. *Yaa baa* (a methamphetamine and caffeine tablet) is also available here and should be avoided at all costs.

## Electricity

Voltage 220, 50 cycles in the main towns. 110 volts in the country; 2-pin sockets are common. Blackouts used to be frequent outside Vientiane as many smaller towns are not connected to the national grid and only have power during the evening. Nowadays even remote areas are being wired up.

## Embassies and consulates

For a list of embassies and consulates in Laos see http://embassy.goabroad.com/embassies-in/laos.

## GLBT

Gay and lesbian travellers should have no problems in Laos. Openly sexual behaviour, whether straight or gay, is contrary to local culture and custom. Officially, it is illegal for any foreigner to have a sexual relationship with a Lao person they aren't married to.

## Health

See your GP or travel clinic at least 6 weeks before departure for general advice on travel risks and vaccinations. Try phoning a specialist travel clinic if your own doctor is unfamiliar with health conditions in Laos. Make sure you have sufficient medical travel insurance, get a dental check, know your own blood group and, if you suffer a long-term condition such as diabetes or epilepsy, obtain a **Medic Alert** bracelet/necklace (www.medicalert.co.uk). If you wear glasses, take a copy of your prescription.

It is risky to buy medicine, and in particular antimalarials, in developing countries, as they may be substandard or part of a trade in counterfeit drugs.

## Vaccinations

It is advisable to vaccinate against polio, tetanus, typhoid, hepatitis A, and rabies if going to more remote areas. Japanese encephalitis may be advised for some areas, depending on the duration of the trip and proximity to rice-growing and pig-farming areas. Yellow fever does not exist in Laos. However, the authorities may wish to see a certificate if you have recently arrived from an endemic area in Africa or South America.

## Health risks

Malaria is prevalent in Laos and remains a serious disease; about a third of the population contracts malaria at some stage during their lives. It is transmitted through mosquitos, which bite at night. Most people will need to consider a malaria prophylaxis other than chloroquine, since there is such a high level of resistance to it. Always check with your doctor or travel clinic for the most up-to-date advice before going to Laos.

The most serious viral disease is **dengue fever**, which is hard to protect against as the mosquitos bite throughout the day as well as at night.

Bacterial diseases include **tuberculosis** (TB) and some causes of the more common traveller's **diarrhoea**. Each year there is the possibility that **avian flu** or **SARS** might rear their ugly heads. Check news reports. just before you go to Laos. If there is a problem in an area you are due to visit you may be advised to have an ordinary flu shot or to seek expert advice. There are high rates of **HIV** in the region, especially among sex workers. **Rabies** and **schistosomiasis** (bilharzia, a water-borne parasite) may be a problem in some parts of Laos.

## Medical services

Hospitals are few and far between and medical facilities are poor in Laos. Emergency treatment is available at the **Mahosot Hospital** and **Clinique Setthathirath** in Vientiane. The Australian embassy also has a clinic for Commonwealth citizens with minor ailments. There are also hospitals in Pakse, Phonsavanh and Savannakhet. Better facilities are available in Thailand and emergency evacuation to Nong Khai or Udon Thani (Thailand) can usually be arranged at short notice. In cases of emergency where a medical evacuation is required, contact **Lao West Coast Helicopter**, Hangar 703, Wattay International Airport, T021-512023, www.laowestcoast.com. Contact your embassy or consulate for a list of doctors and dentists who speak your language, or at least some English. Healthcare can be expensive, especially hospitalization. Make sure you have adequate insurance (see below).

### Thailand

**Aek Udon Hospital**, Udon Thani, Thailand, T+66 42-342555, www.aek udon.com. A 2½-hr trip from Vientiane.
**Bumrungrad Hospital**, 33 Sukhumvit 3, Bangkok, T+66 2-667 1000, www. bumrungrad.com. The best option: a world-class hospital with excellent medical facilities.
**Wattana Hospital Group**, at Udon Thani T+66 42-325999, and Nong Khai, T+66 42-465201, www.wattanahospital.net. The latter in particular is a better alternative to the hospitals in Vientiane and only a 40-min trip from the capital.

## Useful websites

**www.btha.org** British Travel Health Association.
**www.cdc.gov** US government site that provides excellent advice on travel health and details of disease outbreaks.
**www.fco.gov.uk** British Foreign and Commonwealth Office travel site has useful information on each country, people, climate and a list of UK embassies/consulates.

## Insurance

Always take out travel insurance before you set off and read the small print carefully. Check that the policy covers the activities you intend or may end up doing. Also check exactly what your medical cover includes, ie ambulance, helicopter rescue or emergency flights back home. Also check the payment protocol. You may have to cough up first before the insurance company reimburses you. It is always best to dig out all the receipts for expensive personal effects such as jewellery or cameras. Take photos of these items and note down all serial numbers.

## Internet

Wi-Fi can now be found in cafés, hotel and bars in all major tourist centres. These places will also have some dedicated internet/gaming cafés.

## Language

Lao is the national language but there are many local dialects, not to mention the languages of the minority groups. Lao is closely related to Thai and, in a sense, is becoming more so as the years pass. Though there are important differences between the languages, they are mutually intelligible – just about. French is spoken, though only by government officials, hotel staff and educated people over 40. However, most government officials and many shopkeepers have some command of English. See also Useful words and phrases, page 345, and Glossary, page 347.

## Media

The *Vientiane Times*, www.vientiane times.org.la, is published 5 days a week and provides quirky pieces of information and some interesting cultural and tourist-based features, as well as eye-catching stories translated from the local press and wire service. The national TV station broadcasts in Lao. In Vientiane **CNN**, **BBC**, **ABC** and a range of other channels are broadcast. Thailand's **Channel 5** gives English subtitles to news. The **Lao National Radio** broadcasts news in English. The **BBC World Service** can be picked up on shortwave.

## Money

*Exchange rate: US$1 = 8095 kip; €1 = 9407; £1 = 12,274 kip (Feb 2015).*

The kip is the official currency. The lowest commonly used note is the 500 kip. US dollars and sometimes Thai baht (฿) can be used as cash in some tourist shops, restaurants and hotels, and the Chinese Yuan (¥) is starting to be more widely accepted in northern parts of Laos, close to the Chinese border. A certain amount of cash (in US$ or Thai baht) can also be useful in an emergency.

Banks include the **Lao Development Bank** and **Le Banque pour Commerce Exterieur Lao** (BCEL). ATMs are now widely available in all but the smallest of towns.

Payment by credit card is becoming steadily easier – although beyond the more upmarket hotels and restaurants in Vientiane and Luang Prabang, you should not expect to be able to get by on plastic in Laos.

## Cost of travelling

An increase in domestic flights means that the bruised bottoms, dust-soaked clothes and stiff limbs that go hand-in-hand with some of the longer bus/boat rides can often be avoided. However, as roads gradually improve and journey times diminish, buses and minivans have emerged above both planes and boats as the preferred (not to mention most reasonably priced) transportation option.

Long overnight bus journeys cost from around 200,000 kip. Budget accommodation costs US$3-10; a mid-range hotel costs US$20-30. Local food is very cheap and it is possible to eat well for under US$2 a meal. It's possible to splurge in upmarket restaurants in Luang Prabang and Vientiane.

## Opening hours

**Banks** Mon-Fri 0830-1600 (some close at 1500).

**Bars/restaurants** Usually close around 2200-2300 depending on how strictly the curfew is being reinforced. In smaller towns, most restaurants and bars close by 2200.

**Businesses** Mon-Fri 0900-1700; those that deal with tourists open a bit later and also over the weekend. Government offices close at 1600 and take a 1- to 2-hr lunch break.

**Post offices** In general, post offices open 0800-1200 and 1300-1600.

**Shops** Most keep regular business hours but those catering to tourists stay open longer into the evening.

## Photography

Sensitivity pays when taking photographs. Be very wary in areas that have (or could have) military importance, such as airports, where photography is prohibited. Also exercise caution when photographing official functions and parades. Always ask permission before taking photographs in a monastery and before photographing groups of people or individuals.

## Police

If you are robbed, your insurer will need you to obtain a police report. You may find the police will try to solicit a bribe for this service. Although not ideal, you will probably have to pay this fee to obtain your report. Laws aren't strictly enforced but when the authorities do prosecute people the penalties can be harsh, ranging from deportation through to prison sentences. If you are arrested, seek embassy and consular support as soon as possible. If you are arrested or encounter police, try to remain calm and friendly. Although drugs are available throughout the country, the police levy hefty fines and punishments if caught.

## Post

The postal service is inexpensive and reliable but delays are common. As the National Tourism Authority assures: in Laos the stamps will stay on the envelope. Contents of outgoing parcels must be examined by an official before being sealed. Incoming mail should use the official title, Lao PDR. There is no mail to home addresses or guesthouses, so mail must be addressed to a PO Box. The post office in Vientiane has a Poste restante service. EMS (Express Mail Service) is available from main post offices in larger towns. In general, post offices open 0800-1200 and 1300-1600. In provincial areas, **Lao Telecom** is usually attached to the post office. **DHL, Fedex** and **TNT** have offices in Vientiane.

## Public holidays

1 Jan  **New Year's Day.**
6 Jan  **Pathet Lao Day.**
20 Jan  **Army Day.**
8 Mar  **Women's Day.**
22 Mar  **People's Party Day.**
14-16 Apr  **Lao New Year.**
1 May  **Labour Day.**
1 Jun  **Children's Day.**
2 Dec  **Independence Day.**

## Safety

The US State Department's travel advisories: **Travel Warnings & Consular Information Sheets**, www.travel.state.gov.

The **UK Foreign and Commonwealth Office**'s travel warning section, www.fco.gov.uk/en/travel-and-living-abroad.

Crime rates are very low but it is advisable to take the usual precautions. Most areas of the country are now safe – a very different state of affairs from just over a decade ago when foreign embassies advised tourists not to travel along certain roads and in certain areas (in particular Route 13 between Vientiane and Luang Prabang; and Route 7 between Phonsavanh and Route 13). Today these risks have effectively disappeared.

If riding on a motorbike or bicycle, don't carry your bag strap over your shoulder – if someone goes to snatch your bag you could get pulled off the bike and end up seriously hurt. In the Siphandon and Vang Vieng areas, theft seems to be more common. It's advisable to use a hotel security box if available.

Road accidents are on the increase. The hiring of motorbikes is becoming more popular and consequently there are more tourist injuries. Wear a helmet.

Be careful around waterways, as drowning is one of the primary causes of tourist deaths. Be particularly careful during the rainy season (May-Sep) as rivers have a tendency to flood and can have extremely strong currents. Make sure if you are kayaking, tubing, canoeing, travelling by fast-boat, etc, that proper safety gear, such as life jackets, is provided. 'Fast-boat' river travel can be dangerous due to excessive speed and the risk of hitting something in the river and capsizing.

Xieng Khouang Province, the Bolaven Plateau, Xam Neua and areas along the Ho Chi Minh Trail are littered with bombies (small anti-personnel mines and bomblets from cluster bomb units). There are also numerous, large, unexploded bombs; in many villages they have been left lying around. Only walk on clearly marked or newly trodden paths. Consult the **Mines Advisory Group** (www.maginternational.org), which works in Laos.

### Travel advisories
**www.travel.state.gov** US State Department's travel advisory issues *Travel Warnings & Consular Information Sheets*. **www.fco.gov.uk/en/travel-and-living-abroad** The UK Foreign and Commonwealth Office's travel warning section.

### Student travellers
There are few specific student discounts in Laos. Anyone in full-time education is entitled to an **International Student Identity Card** (www.isic.org). These are issued by student travel offices and travel agencies and offer special rates on all forms of transport and other concessions and services. They sometimes permit free admission to museums and sights, at other times a discount on the admission.

## Telephone

The country code for Laos is +856. The IDD code (for dialing out of Laos) is 00. International operator: T170. Directory enquiries: T16 (national); T171 (international).

Public phones are available in Vientiane and other major cities. You can also go to **Lao Telecom** offices to call overseas. Phone cards are widely available in most convenience stores. Mobile telephone coverage is now good across the country. Pay-as-you-go SIM cards are available cheaply and 3G service is good.

## Time

Laos is 7 hrs ahead of GMT.

## Tipping

Tipping is rare, even in hotels. However, it is a more usual and expected to tip guides. In some of the more expensive restaurants a 10% tip is appreciated if service charge is not included on the bill. If someone offers you a lift, it is a courtesy to give them some money to help cover the cost of fuel.

## Tourist information

Contact details for tourist offices and other information resources are given at the start of listings in the relevant town. Many provincial tourist offices now have an Eco Guide Unit attached or operating from a separate office. The best in the country is the one in Savannakhet.

The **Laos National Tourism Authority**, Lane Xang, Vientiane, T021-212248, www.tourismlaos.org, provides a range of maps and brochures.

Some provincial tourist offices are excellent and staffed with helpful, knowledgeable and willing people. There are particularly good tourism offices in Thakhek, Vieng Xai, Xam Neua, Udomxai and Phongsali. The tourism authority has teamed up with local tour operators to provide a number of ecotourism opportunities, such as trekking and village homestays.

### Useful websites

www.asean-tourism.com
www.ecotourismlaos.com
www.visit-mekong.com
www.mekongtourism.org
www.stdplaos.com
www.travelfish.org
www.visit-mekong.com/laos/

## Tour operators

Numerous tour operators offer organized trips to this region of Southeast Asia, ranging from a whistle-stop tour of the highlights to specialist trips that focus on a specific destination or activity.

## UK

**Audley Travel**, New Mill, New Mill Lane, Witney, Oxfordshire OX29 9SX, T01993-838000, www.audleytravel.com.
**Buffalo Tours UK**, The Old Church, 89B Quicks Rd, Wimbledon, London, SW19 1EX, T020-8545 2830, www.buffalotours.com.
**See Asia Differently**, T020-8150 5150. www.seeasiadifferently.com. A UK/Asian-based tour company specializing in customized Southeast Asian tours.

## Australia and New Zealand

**Buffalo Tours**, L9/69 Reservoir St, Surry Hills, Sydney, Australia 2010, T61-2-8218 2198, www.buffalotours.com.
**Intrepid Travel**, 360 Bourke St, Melbourne, Victoria 3000, T03-8602 0500, www.intrepidtravel.com.

## North America

**Adventure Center**, 1311 63rd St, Suite 200, Emeryville, CA, T1-800 2278747, www.adventurecenter.com.

## Southeast Asia

**Buffalo Tours**, No 102/5 Kaysone Phomvihane Rd, Luang Prabang, Laos, T071-254395, www.buffalotours.com.
**Exotissimo**, 4666 - 06/044 Pangkham St, Vientiane, Laos, T021-241861, 44/3 Ban Vat Nong, Khemkong Rd, Luang Prabang, Laos, T071-252879, www.exotissimo.com.
**Luxury Travel Company**, 5 Nguyen Truong To St, Ba Dinh District, Hanoi, Vietnam, T+84 4 3817, www.luxurytravelvietnam.com.

## Visas

A 30-day **tourist visa** can be obtained at most (but not all) borders. See Official border crossings, page 332. Visa prices are based on reciprocity with countries.

'Overtime fees' are often charged if you enter after 1600 or on a weekend. To get a visa you need a passport photograph and the name of a hotel you plan on staying in.

The Lao government also issues **business visas** that are available for 30 days with the possibility of extending. This is a more complicated process and usually requires a note from an employer or hefty fees from a visa broker. These visas are best organized from your home country and can take a long time to process.

Tourist visa extensions can be obtained from the **Lao Immigration Office** in the **Ministry of the Interior** opposite the Morning Market in Vientiane, on Phai Nam Rd, T021-212529. Travel agencies in Vientiane and other major centres can also handle this service for you for a fee.

## Women travellers

While women travelling alone can face more problems than men or couples, these are far less pronounced in Laos than in most countries, and it is rare for women to be harassed. Nonetheless, women should take the usual precautions. It is illegal for a foreigner to be in a sexual relationship with a local, unless married. You may often get asked if you are married; just a friendly conversation starter.

Displays of public affection are frowned upon, especially in rural areas. What may be considered in the West as friendly affection, such as putting your arm around someone, could be misconstrued as romantic love in Laos.

If you are bathing in a waterfall or river, wear a sarong, as the locals are embarrassed by the sight of bare flesh. Tampons and sanitary towels can be purchased in major towns but are in short supply elsewhere.

## Working in Laos

Work is not easily available in Laos and is in great demand. Laos has one of the highest retention rates of foreign workers in the region, as once they get there they don't want to leave. There is a vibrant expat community, mostly of aid workers as well as the usual diplomatic corps. But, unlike in Thailand, there is little scope for foreigners to teach English. Jobs are advertised in the *Vientiane Times*.

### Voluntary work

This can take the shape of long-term professional posts for humanitarian specialists and aid workers or short-, medium- and long-term positions, lasting from 2 weeks up to 9 months, for those taking sabbaticals and gap years, or young people looking for hands-on practical field experience. All these can be undertaken at a grassroots level. As a general rule, social work and environmental work are the largest sectors in the programmes offered by local NGOs in Laos.

There are several umbrella groups offering useful information and links to vetted organizations. **Working Abroad** (www.workingabroad.com) offers information on opportunities (paid and voluntary) in over 150 countries worldwide, including Laos. A good one-stop shop is **www.yearoutgroup. org**, a not-for-profit group representing, among others, **SWP, i-to-i, Outreach International, Bunac, Greenforce** and **Raleigh International**. Also worth checking out is **World Wide Volunteering** (www.wwv.org.uk), which organizes projects in more than 200 countries.

Other worthwhile organizations include **VSO** (www.vso.org.uk) in the UK; the **Youth Ambassador Program** (www.ausaid.gov.au/youtham) in Australia; **CUSO** (www.cuso-vso.org) in Canada, and the **United Nations Volunteers** website, www.unv.org.

# Useful words & phrases

## Greetings

**yes/no** men/baw
**thank you** kop jai
**no thank you** baw, kop jai
**hello/goodbye** suh-bye-dee/lah-gohn
**What is your name?** Chow seu yang?
**My name is...** Koi seu....
**Excuse me, sorry** Ko toat
**Can/do you speak** Koy pahk pah-sah
**English?** Anhg-geet?
**A little, a bit** Noi, hoi
**Where?** You-sigh?
**How much is...?** Tow-dai?
**It doesn't matter** Baw penh yang
**Pardon?** Kow toat?
**I don't understand** Kow baw cow-chi
**How are you?** Chao suh-bye-dee-baw?
**not very well** baw suh-bye

## Getting around

**Where is the** Sa ta ni lot
**train/bus station?** phai/mee yu sai?
**How much to go to...?** Khit la ka taw dai...?
**That's expensive** Pheng-lie
**Will you go for...kip?** Chow ja pai...kip?
**What time does the bus/train leave for...?** Lot mea oak jay mong...?
**Is it far?** Kai baw?
**Turn left/turn right** Leo sai/leo qua
**Go straight on** Pai leuy
**River** xe/se, houei/houai
**Town** muang/mouang
**Mountain** phou

## Sleeping

**What is the charge** Kit laka van nuang
**each night?** taw dai?
**Is the room air conditioned?** Hong me ai yen baw
**Can I see the room first, please?** Koi ko beunghong dea?
**Does the room have hot water?** Hong me nam hawn baw?
**Does the room have a bathroom?** Me hang ap nam baw?
**Can I have the bill, please?** Koi ton han bai hap

## Eating

**Can I see a menu?** Kho beung lay kan arhan?
**Can I have...?** Khoy tong kan...?
**I am hungry** Koy heo kao
**I am thirsty** Koy heo nahm
**I want to eat** Koh yahk kin kao
**Where is a restaurant?** Lahn ah hai you-sigh?
**breakfast** arhan sao
**lunch** arhan athieng
**It costs....kip** Lah-kah ahn-nee...kip

## Time

**in the morning** muh-sao
**in the afternoon** thon-by
**in the evening** muh-leng
**today** muh-nee
**tomorrow** muh-ouhn
**yesterday** muh van-nee

**Monday** Van Chanh
**Tuesday** Van Ang Khan
**Wednesday** Van Pud
**Thursday** Van Pa Had
**Friday** Van Sook
**Saturday** Van Sao
**Sunday** Van Arthid

## Numbers

**1** nung
**2** song
**3** sahm
**4** see
**5** hah
**6** hoke
**7** chet
**8** pet
**9** cow
**10** sip
**11** sip-et
**12** sip-song
**20** sao
**21** sao-et
**22** sao-song
**30** sahn-sip
**100** hoy
**101** hoy-nung
**150** hoy-hah-sip
**200** song-hoy
**1000** phan
**10,000** sip-phan
**100,000** muun
**1,000,000** laan

## Basic vocabulary

**airport** deune yonh
**bank** had xay
**bathroom** hong nam
**beach** heva
**beautiful** ngam
**bicycle** loht teep
**big** nyai
**boat** quoi loth bath
**bus** loht-buht

**bus station** hon kay ya
**buy** sue
**chemist** han kay ya
**clean** sa ard
**closed** arte
**cold** jenh
**day** vanh (or) mua
**delicious** sehb
**dirty** soka pox
**doctor** than mah
**eat** kinh
**embassy** Satan Tood
**excellent** dee leuth
**expensive** pheng
**food** ah-han
**fruit** mak-mai
**hospital** hong moh
**hot (temperature)** hawn
**hotel** hong
**island** koh (or) hath
**market** ta lath
**medicine** ya pua payad
**open** peud
**petrol** nahm-mahn-eh-sahng
**police** lam louad
**police station** poam lam louad
**post office** hong kana pai sa nee
**restaurant** han arhane
**road** tha nonh
**room** hong
**shop** hanh
**sick (ill)** bo sabay
**silk** mai
**small** noy
**stop** yoot
**taxi** loht doy-sanh
**that** nahn
**this** nee, ahn-nee
**ticket (air)** pee yonh
**ticket (bus)** pee lot mea
**toilet** hong nam
**town** nai mouang
**very** lai-lai
**water** nam (or) nah
**what** men-nyung

# Glossary

**Amitabha** the Buddha of the Past

**Amulet** protective medallion

**Arhat** one who has perfected himself

**Avadana** Buddhist narrative, telling of the deeds of saintly souls

**Avalokitsvara** also known as Amitabha and Lokeshvara, the name means 'World Lord'; he is the compassionate male Bodhisattva, saviour of Mahayana Buddhism. Represents the central force of creation in the universe

**Bai sema** boundary stones marking consecrated ground around a bot

**Ban** village; shortened from muban

**Bhikku** Buddhist monk

**Bodhi** the tree under which the Buddha achieved enlightenment (*Ficus religiosa*)

**Bodhisattva** a future Buddha. In Mahayana Buddhism, someone who has attained enlightenment, but postpones nirvana to help others reach it

**Boun** Lao festival

**Brahma** the Creator, one of the gods of the Hindu trinity, usually represented with four faces, and often mounted on a hamsa

**Brahmin** a Hindu priest

**Bun** to make merit

**Caryatid** elephants, often used as buttressing decorations

**Champa** rival empire of the Khmers, of Hindu culture, based in present day Vietnam

**Chao** title for Lao kings

**Charn** animist priest who conducts the *basi* ceremony in Laos

**Chat** honorific umbrella or royal parasol

**Chedi** religious monument containing relics of the Buddha or other holy remains

**Chenla** Chinese name for Cambodia before the Khmer era

**Deva** a Hindu-derived male god

**Devata** a Hindu-derived goddess

**Dharma** the Buddhist law

**Dok sofa** frond-like construction surmounting temple roofs in Laos. Over 10 flowers means the wat was built by a king

**Dtin sin** decorative border on a skirt

**Funan** the oldest Indianised state of Indochina and precursor to Chenla

**Ganesh** elephant-headed son of Siva

**Garuda** divine bird, with predatory beak and claws, and human body; the king of birds, enemy of naga and mount of Vishnu

**Gautama** the historic Buddha

**Geomancy** divination by lines and figures

**Gopura** crowned or covered gate, entrance to a religious area

**Hamsa** sacred goose, Brahma's mount; in Buddhism it represents the flight of doctrine

**Hinayana** 'Lesser Vehicle', major Buddhist sect, usually termed Theravada Buddhism

**Hor kong** a pavilion built on stilts where the temple drum is kept

**Hor song phra** secondary chapel

**Hor takang** bell tower

**Hor tray/trai** library where manuscripts are stored in a Lao or Thai temple

**Hor vay** offering temple

**Indra** the Vedic god of the heavens, weather and war

**Jataka(s)** the birth stories of the Buddha; they normally number 547; the last 10 are the most important

**Kala (makara)** a demon ordered to consume itself; often sculpted with grinning face and bulging eyes over entrances

**Kathin/krathin** a month period during the 8th lunar month when lay people present robes and gifts to monks

**Ketumula** flame-like motif above the Buddha head

**Kinaree** half-human, half-bird, usually depicted as a heavenly musician

**Kirtamukha** see kala

**Krishna** incarnation of Vishnu

**Kuti** living quarters of monks in a temple

**Laterite** bright red tropical soil/stone commonly used in Khmer monuments

**Linga** phallic symbol and one of the forms of Siva. Embedded in a pedestal shaped to allow drainage of lustral water poured over it. Typically has a succession of cross sections: from square at the base through octagonal to round. These symbolize, in order, the trinity of Brahma, Vishnu and Siva

**Lokeshvara** see Avalokitsvara

**Mahabharata** a Hindu epic text

**Mahayana** 'Greater Vehicle', major Buddhist sect

**Maitreya** the future Buddha

**Makara** mythological aquatic reptile often found with the kala framing doorways

**Mandala** a focus for meditation; a representation of the cosmos

**Mara** personification of evil and tempter of the Buddha

**Meru** sacred mountain at the centre of the world in Hindu-Buddhist cosmology

**Mondop** Cube-shaped building, often topped with a conical structure. Contains an object of worship like a footprint of the Buddha

**Muang** administrative unit

**Mudra** gesture of the hands of the Buddha

**Nak Lao** river dragon, a mythical guardian creature (see naga)

**Naga** benevolent mythical water serpent, enemy of Garuda

**Naga makara** fusion of naga and makara

**Nalagiri** the elephant let loose to attack the Buddha, who calmed him

**Nandi/nandin** bull, mount of Siva

**Nirvana** release from the cycle of suffering in Buddhist belief; 'enlightenment'

**Nyak** mythical water serpent (see naga)

**Pa kama** Lao men's all-purpose cloth

**paddy/padi** unhulled rice

**Pali** sacred language of Theravada Buddhism

**Parvati** consort of Siva

**Pathet Lao** Communist party based in the northeastern provinces of Laos until they came to power in 1975

**Pha biang** shawl worn by women in Laos

**Pha sin** piece of cloth, similar to sarong

**Phi** spirit

**Phra sinh** see *pha sin*

**Pra Lam** Lao version of the Ramayana

**Pradaksina** pilgrims' clockwise circumambulation of holy structure

**Prah** sacred

**Prang** form of stupa built in Khmer style, shaped like a corn cob

**Prasada** stepped pyramid (see prasat)

**Prasat** residence of a king or of the gods (sanctuary tower), from the Indian *prasada*

**Rama** incarnation of Vishnu, hero of the Indian epic, the Ramayana

**Ramakien** Lao version of the Ramayana

**Ramayana** Hindu romantic epic

**Sakyamuni** the historic Buddha

**Sal** the Indian sal tree (*Shorea robusta*), under which the historic Buddha was born

**Sangha** the Buddhist order of monks

**Sim/sima** main sanctuary and ordination hall in a Lao temple complex

**Singha** mythical guardian lion

**Siva** the Destroyer, one of the 3 gods of the Hindu trinity; the sacred linga was worshipped as a symbol of Siva

**Sofa** see *dok sofa*

**Sravasti** the miracle at Sravasti when the Buddha subdues the heretics

**Stupa** chedi

**Tavatimsa** heaven of the 33 gods at the summit of Mount Meru

**Thanon** street

**That** shrine housing Buddhist relics, a spire or dome-like edifice commemorating the Buddha's life or a funerary temple for royalty

**Theravada** 'Way of the Elders'; major Buddhist sect also known as Hinayana Buddhism ('Lesser Vehicle')

**Traiphum** the 3 worlds of Buddhist cosmology – heaven, hell and earth

**Trimurti** the Hindu trinity of gods: Brahma, the Creator, Vishnu the Preserver and Siva the Destroyer

**Tripitaka** Theravada Buddhism's Pali canon

**Ubosoth** see bot

**Urna** dot or curl on the Buddha's forehead

**Usnisa** the Buddha's top knot or 'wisdom bump'

**Vahana** 'vehicle', a beast, upon which a *deva* or god rides

**Viharn** assembly hall in a monastery

**Vishnu** the Protector, one of the gods of the Hindu trinity

# Index → *Entries in bold refer to maps*

# Advertisers' index

## FOOTPRINT

### Features

# Credits

**Footprint credits**

**Editor**: Nicola Gibbs
**Production and layout**: Emma Bryers
**Maps**: Kevin Feeney
**Colour section**: Angus Dawson

**Publisher**: Patrick Dawson
**Managing Editor**: Felicity Laughton
**Administration**: Elizabeth Taylor
**Advertising sales and marketing**:
John Sadler, Kirsty Holmes

**Photography credits**
**Front cover**: Handmade umbrellas
Copyright: livertoon/shutterstock.com
**Back cover top**: Night Market at
Luang Prabang
Copyright: PlusONEshutterstock
**Back cover bottom**: Naga at the
Wat Xieng Thong, Luang Prabang
Copyright: Luciano Mortula/
Dreamstime.com

**Colour section**
**Inside front cover**: Superstock: Hemis.fr/
Hemis.fr; David W Lloyd. **Page 1**: Superstock:
DELOCHE /BSIP. **Page 2**: Superstock: Robert
Harding Picture Library/Robert Harding Picture
Library. **Page 4**: Superstock: age fotostock/
age fotostock, Dave Stamboulis/age fotostock;
David W Lloyd. **Page 5**: dreamstime: Dave
Stamboulis/age fotostock, Frans Lemmens/
Frans Lemmens; Superstock: Animals Animals/
Animals Animals. **Page 6**: Superstock: Robert
Harding Picture Library/Robert Harding
Picture Library, Animals Animals/Animals
Animals, imageBROKER/imageBROKER.
**Page 7**: Superstock: Olaf Schubert/imagebr/
imageBROKER, imageBROKER/imageBROKER,
Travel Library Limited/Travel Library Limited.
**Page 10**: Superstock: Tips Images/Tips Images

Printed in India by Thomson Press Ltd,
Faridabad, Haryana, India

**Publishing information**
Footprint Handbooks Laos
7th edition
© Footprint Handbooks Ltd
March 2015

ISBN: 978 1 910120 29 3
CIP DATA: A catalogue record for this
book is available from the British Library

® Footprint Handbooks and the
Footprint mark are a registered
trademark of Footprint Handbooks Ltd

Published by Footprint
6 Riverside Court
Lower Bristol Road
Bath BA2 3DZ, UK
T +44 (0)1225 469141
footprinttravelguides.com

Distributed in the USA by
National Book Network, Inc.

Every effort has been made to ensure that
the facts in this guidebook are accurate.
However, travellers should still obtain
advice from consulates, airlines, etc about
travel and visa requirements before
travelling. The authors and publishers
cannot accept responsibility for any loss,
injury or inconvenience however caused.

# Join us online...